Study Guide

for use with

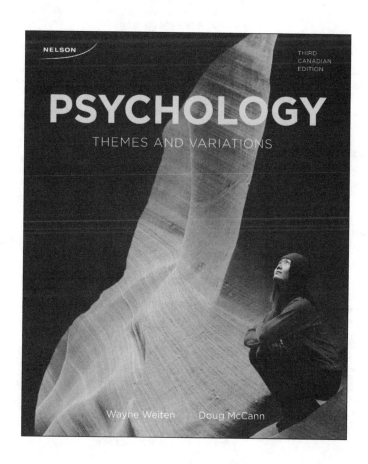

NELSON

THIRD
CANADIAN
EDITION

PSYCHOLOGY
THEMES AND VARIATIONS

Wayne Weiten   Doug McCann

RICHARD B. STALLING
BRADLEY UNIVERSITY

RONALD E. WASDEN
BRADLEY UNIVERSITY

ANDREW J. HOWELL
GRANT MacEWAN UNIVERSITY

NELSON   EDUCATION

NELSON / EDUCATION

Study Guide
by Richard B. Stalling, Ronald E. Wasden, and Andrew J. Howell

for use with *Psychology: Themes and Variations*, **Third Canadian Edition**
by Wayne Weiten and Doug McCann

Vice President, Editorial Higher Education:
Anne Williams

Senior Acquisitions Editor:
Lenore Taylor-Atkins

Marketing Manager:
Ann Byford

Managing Developmental Editor:
Sandy Matos

Content Production Manager:
Claire Horsnell

Copy Editor:
Heather Sangster at Strong Finish

Manufacturing Manager:
Joanne McNeil

Design Director:
Ken Phipps

Managing Designer:
Franca Amore

Cover Design:
Martyn Schmoll

Cover Image:
© Corbis

Printer:
RR Donnelley

ISBN-13: 978-0-17-663330-1
ISBN-10: 0-17-663330-8

To the Student

In Weiten and McCann's *Psychology: Themes and Variations, Third Canadian Edition,* you will encounter a truly remarkable book. The authors have an extraordinary ability to create vivid, self-relevant examples that weave the diverse fields of psychology into a fabric. We are amazed at the breadth and the beauty of this text.

So, what is there left for us to do? It turns out that the concepts in an introductory course are complex. It is also the case that understanding and memory are not automatic. How does one process information and put things into memory? We remember more easily if we can relate concepts to our selves, the self-reference effect. And we also remember through the process of elaboration, thinking of examples and links to information already in memory (described in Chapter 7: Human Memory). So that is what we've tried to do in this study guide, to provide examples and practice, with the goal in mind of helping the student remember, both for practical reasons now (e.g., tests) and for use in the future after the course is over.

What's the best way to work with this study guide? There are four parts for each chapter: the *Review of Key Ideas* (comprising most of each Study Guide chapter), the *Review of Key Terms* (a matching exercise involving important concepts), the *Review of Key People* (matching confined to major researchers in each area), and a *Self-Quiz*. We suggest that you try this: Work on each learning objective one at a time. Read each objective, read the part of the textbook that relates to it, and then complete the exercises and check your answers. Finally, do the matching exercises and take the Self-Quiz.

You may find it more useful to select only certain parts of the study guide that provide practice with particular concepts. (For example, if you are having difficulty understanding the Freudian defence mechanisms or the difference between operant and classical conditioning, do the practice exercises relating to these specific topics.) Whatever method you use, the learning objectives will serve as an excellent review. At the end of your study of a particular chapter, you can quiz yourself by reading over the learning objectives, reciting answers aloud, and checking your answers. This procedure roughly parallels the SQ3R study technique introduced in the Personal Application section of Chapter 1.

We hope you will find this study guide to be a useful tool for mastering the textbook material, and we hope that you become as enthralled about psychology as are each of us.

Rick Stalling
Ron Wasden
Andrew Howell

Table of Contents

CHAPTER ONE
THE EVOLUTION OF PSYCHOLOGY

REVIEW OF KEY IDEAS

1. **Identify early influences in the development of psychology.**

    1-1. Ancient Greek philosophers such as _____ and _____ debated issues relevant to psychology.

    1-2. The distinction between mind and body was emphasized by _____. He viewed mental processes such as memory and perception as properties of the (mind/body); as part of nature, they were seen as open to study.

    1-3. _____ was a second early influence in the course of psychology.

    Answers: 1-1. Socrates, Aristotle **1-2.** Descartes, body **1-3.** Physiology

FROM SPECULATION TO SCIENCE: HOW PSYCHOLOGY DEVELOPED
2. **Summarize Wundt's accomplishments and contributions to psychology.**

    2-1. If you ask most college graduates to name the founder of psychology, they might mention the name of a famous psychologist (for example, maybe Sigmund Freud), but they almost certainly would *not* say Wilhelm Wundt. Yet among psychologists Wundt is generally acknowledged to be the "_____" of our field.

    2-2. Wundt established the first experimental psychology _____, in Leipzig, Germany, in 1879. He also established the first _____ devoted to publishing psychological research.

    2-3. The subject matter of Wundt's psychology was (consciousness/behaviour).

    2-4. Wundt's major contributions to the evolution of psychology may be summarized as follows: He is the _____ of psychology as an independent academic field, and he insisted that psychology can and must use the _____ method.

    Answers: 2-1. founder **2-2.** laboratory, journal **2-3.** consciousness **2-4.** founder, scientific (experimental). (Personal note from RS: I visited Leipzig in the former East Germany recently and looked for the famous founding laboratory. It wasn't there! I found Wundt Street, but no lab. An English–U.S. bombing raid destroyed the laboratory in 1943.)

3. Summarize Hall's accomplishments and contributions to psychology.

3-1. Wundt had many important students; among them was G. Stanley Hall, an American. In 1883, just four years after Wundt created his laboratory in Leipzig, Hall established the first American psychological _____ at Johns Hopkins. Hall also founded America's first _____ devoted to publishing material in the field of psychology.

3-2. In 1892, with 26 of his colleagues, Hall began the American Psychological Association, known by the initials _____. Hall also became the first _____ of the association. The APA now includes more than 155 000 members.

Answers: 3-1. laboratory, journal **3-2.** APA, president.

4. Describe structuralism and its impact on the subsequent development of psychology.

4-1. Another of Wundt's students, Edward Titchener, developed the school of psychology known as _____. The major tenet of this viewpoint was that psychology should study the structure of _____ by breaking it down into its basic components or _____.

4-2. These basic elements of consciousness were thought to be the sensations (or images or feelings) that people reported when they observed some object. Subjects were trained to first observe (or listen to) something and to then, after careful introspection, report on their conscious experience. Thus, the subject matter of structuralism was _____, and its method involved training observers in the technique of _____.

Answers: 4-1. structuralism, consciousness, elements **4-2.** consciousness, introspection.

5. Describe functionalism and its impact on the subsequent development of psychology.

5-1. Rather than breaking down consciousness into basic elements, the _____ school emphasized determining the _____ or purpose of consciousness.

5-2. The origins of functionalism are associated with William James. Influenced by Darwin's concept of natural selection, James concluded that psychology should study the basic (elements/purpose) of consciousness.

5-3. Which "school" is characterized by each of the following descriptions? Place an "S" for structuralism or "F" for functionalism in the appropriate blanks.

_____ Concerned with the purpose (or function) of consciousness.

_____ Trained observers to introspect about consciousness.

_____ Assumed that consciousness could be broken down into basic elements (in the same way that physical matter is comprised of atoms).

_____ Interested in the flow of consciousness.

_____ Focused on the <u>adaptive</u> (evolutionary) value of consciousness.

_____ Emphasized <u>sensation</u> and <u>perception</u> in vision, hearing, and touch.

5-4. The focus of functionalism may have attracted women into the field of psychology, including Mary Washburn, whose book *The Animal Mind* served as a precursor to _____; Leta Hollingworth, who did work on children's intelligence; and Mary Whiton Calkins, who served as the first female president of the _____

_____ _____.

5-5. While neither structuralism nor functionalism survived as viable theories of psychology, functionalism had a more lasting impact. The emphasis of functionalism on the practical (or the adaptive or purposeful) led to the development of these two areas of modern psychology: _____ and _____ psychology.

Answers: **5-1.** functionalist, function **5-2.** purpose **5-3.** F, S, S, F, F, S **5-4.** behaviourism, American Psychological Association **5-5.** behaviourism, applied.

6. Summarize Watson's views on the appropriate subject matter of psychology, nature versus nurture, and animal research.

6-1. A literal translation of the root words of psychology (*psyche* and *logos*) suggests that psychology is the study of the _____. For both Wundt and James, this was the case: they studied human _____. For Watson, however, the subject matter of psychology was _____.

6-2. Watson believed that psychology could not be a science unless it, like the other sciences, concentrated on _____ rather than unobservable events.

6-3. Which of the following are observable behaviours? Place an "O" in the blank if the event is observable and an "N" if it is not.

_____ writing a letter

_____ feeling angry

_____ saying "Please pass the salt"

_____ passing the salt

_____ perceiving a round object

_____ experiencing hunger

_____ walking rapidly

6-4. Watson largely discounted the importance of genetic inheritance. For Watson, behaviour was governed by the _____.

6-5. Watson also made a shift away from human introspection by using _____ as the subjects for research. Why the change in orientation? First, animal behaviour is observable; human consciousness is not. Second, the environment of laboratory animals, in contrast to that of humans, is subject to much more _____.

6-6. Let's briefly review structuralism and behaviourism.

    (a) As defined by the structuralists, what was the subject matter of psychology?

    (b) For behaviourists, what was the subject matter of psychology?

    (c) While structuralists and behaviourists differed in their views of the subject matter of psychology, their approach to the new field was similar in one major respect. In what way were the two systems similar?

Answers: 6-1. soul (or mind), consciousness, behaviour **6-2.** observable (behaviour) **6-3.** O, N (you can't see or hear your own or another person's feelings of anger; you may see the results of anger), O, O, N (you can't see or hear perception), N (you can't see or hear hunger), O **6-4.** environment **6-5.** animals, control (or manipulation) **6-6.** (a) conscious experience (consciousness), (b) animal or human behaviour, (c) They studied "parts" rather than "wholes." Both systems believed that the task of psychology was to break down psychological phenomena into their smallest elements. (For the structuralists, the smaller elements were the sensations or images that made up consciousness; for the behaviourists, the elements were the stimulus–response bonds thought to make up behaviour.)

7. Summarize Freud's principal ideas and why they inspired controversy.

7-1. For Wundt, the subject matter of psychology was human consciousness. For Freud, a major subject of study was what he termed the _____. With this concept, Freud asserted that human beings are (aware/unaware) of most of the factors that influence their thoughts and behaviour.

7-2. There is a word beginning with *s* that means the same thing as feces. This word, however, may be more likely to cause laughter, embarrassment, or anger than the word *feces*. Why do two words that mean the same thing produce such differing reactions? Freud would assert that our more emotional response to one of the words would be caused by the

_____.

7-3. Although generally not accessible to us, the unconscious is revealed in several ways, according to Freud. Freud thought, for example, that the unconscious is revealed in mistakes, such as "_____ of the tongue," or the symbolism in nighttime

_____.

7-4. Freud's ideas were (and still are) considered quite controversial. The general public tended to find Freud's ideas unacceptable because of his emphasis on _____. And scientific psychologists, with their increasing emphasis on observable behaviour, rejected Freud's notion that we are controlled by _____ forces. Nonetheless, Freud's theory gradually gained prominence and survives today as an influential theoretical perspective.

Answers: 7-1. unconscious, unaware **7-2.** unconscious **7-3.** slips, dreams **7-4.** sex (or sexuality, sexual instincts), unconscious.

8. Summarize Skinner's work, views, and influence.

8-1. While he did not deny their existence, Skinner said that (mental/environmental) events are not observable and cannot be studied scientifically.

8-2. The fundamental principle of behaviour, according to Skinner, is that organisms will tend to _____ behaviours that lead to positive outcome (and tend not to repeat responses that lead to neutral or negative outcomes).

8-3. Skinner asserted that because behaviour is under the lawful control of the environment, our feeling of _____ is an illusion.

8-4. According to Skinner, to adequately account for and predict behaviour psychologists must understand:

    a. the relationship between thinking and behaviour

    b. the physiological basis of action

    c. the way environmental factors affect behaviour

    d. all of the above

8-5. Skinner's influence went beyond academia due in part to his 1948 book, _____, in which he presented a fictional account of a utopian society based on behavioural principles, and his 1971 book, *Beyond Freedom and Dignity*. Within the discipline of psychology, Skinner's influence was reflected in a 1990 survey of psychologists' opinions concerning the field's most important contributors, in which he ranked number _____.

Answers: 8-1. mental **8-2.** repeat **8-3.** free will **8-4.** c. (NOT d. Although Skinner acknowledged that thinking exists and that physiology is the basis of behaviour, he thought that explanations in terms of these factors did not contribute to a science of behaviour.) **8-5.** *Walden Two*, one.

9. Summarize Rogers's and Maslow's ideas and the contributions of humanistic psychology.

9-1. Both Rogers and Maslow, like other _____ psychologists, emphasized the (<u>similarities/differences</u>) between human beings and other animals.

9-2. While Freud and Skinner stressed the way in which behaviour is *controlled* (by unconscious forces or by the environment), Rogers and Maslow emphasized human beings' _____ to determine their own actions.

9-3. Rogers and Maslow also asserted that human beings have a drive to express their inner potential, a drive toward personal _____.

9-4. Perhaps the greatest contribution of the humanistic movement has been in producing (<u>scientific findings/new approaches</u>) in psychotherapy.

Answers: 9-1. humanistic, differences **9-2.** freedom **9-3.** growth (or expression) **9-4.** new approaches.

10. Describe important contributions to the emergence of experimental psychology in Canada.

10-1. The first experimental psychology laboratory in Canada was established in the year _____ by _____ _____ _____ at the University of _____.

10-2. Early psychology courses were often taught through the department of philosophy. The first department of psychology was established in the year _____ at _____ University, followed by departments established at the universities of _____, _____ _____, and _____.

10-3. The Canadian Psychological Association was formed in the year _____ to advance psychology as a science, and currently has more than _____ thousand members.

10-4. Women currently make up about _____% of Canadian full-time psychology professors, and women outnumber men in psychology graduate programs. Women who have made particularly significant contributions to Canadian psychology include Brenda Milner, one of the founders of _____ in Canada. Mary Salter Ainsworth made important contributions to _____ theory and developmental psychology. Mary Wright has the distinction of being the first female president of the Canadian Psychological Association. Doreen Kimura has contributed importantly to our understanding of the neuromotor mechanisms in human communication and of _____ _____ in cognition.

Answers: 10-1. 1891, James Mark Baldwin, Toronto **10-2.** 1924, McGill, Toronto, Western Ontario, Manitoba **10-3.** 1939, five **10-4.** 30, neuropsychology, attachment, sex differences.

11. Use the Featured Study to discuss the strengths and weaknesses of some research methods.

11-1. Prior to this study by Craig and Pepler of York University, research on bullying made use of _____ methodologies rather than directly observing bullying behaviour.

11-2. In this research, observers rated the behaviour of both _____ and socially competent children as reflected in videotaped recordings of lunch and recess activities.

11-3. Results showed that about ____% of bullying episodes involved verbal aggression, _____% involved physical aggression, and 21% involved a mixed of both types of aggression. Boys engaged in about _____ as much bullying as girls. Aggressive children (did/did not) engage in more bullying than socially competent children.

11-4. Naturalistic observation research such as the Featured Study has the advantage of documenting behaviour outside of the _____, but does not allow clear statements concerning the _____ of behaviour. Naturalistic observation research also raises the possibility that the process of being observed alters participants' behaviour.

Answers: 11-1. questionnaire **11-2.** aggressive **11-3.** 50, 29, twice, did not **11-4.** laboratory, causes.

12. Describe the typical areas of expertise of various types of applied or professional psychologists.

12-1. Applied psychology is the part of psychology that is concerned with (research issues/practical problems). Prominent among the applied areas of psychology is the field of _____ psychology, which deals with the treatment of psychological disorders.

12-2. Other applied areas followed later, including the fields of industrial and _____ psychology, counselling psychology, and school psychology.

Answers: 12-1. practical problems, clinical **12-2.** organizational.

13. Explain how historical events have contributed to the emergence of psychology as a profession.

13-1. Clinical psychologists were relatively rare in a field devoted primarily to research. One of the historical events that changed this picture was the advent of _____. With the increased need for screening recruits and treating emotional casualties, the Veterans Administration began funding many new training programs in the field of _____ psychology.

13-2. In the United States, some psychologists became concerned with an increasing emphasis on applied psychology within the American Psychological Association. They formed their own association, the _____ _____ _____. Similarly, the Canadian Society for _____, _____ and _____ _____ was established.

13-3. In contrast to its founding in the 19th century as a research or academic endeavour, psychology in the 20th century has developed a prominent _____ branch directed toward solving practical problems.

Answers: 13-1. World War II, clinical. **13-2.** American Psychological Society, Brain, Behaviour, Cognitive Science **13-3.** applied (or professional).

14. Describe two recent trends in research in psychology that reflect a return to psychology's intellectual roots.

14-1. Two recent trends in research in psychology involve the re-emergence of areas largely discarded or ignored by the behaviourists. What are these two areas?

14-2. Think about sucking on a lemon. When you do, the amount of saliva in your mouth will increase measurably. While it would be enough to describe your observable response as a function of my observable instruction, it is also obvious that thinking, or cognition, is involved: My instruction changed your _____ image, which was accompanied by a change in salivation.

14-3. The study of mental imagery, problem solving, and decision making involves _____ processes. The second, more recent trend also concerns "internal" processes: Research on electrical stimulation of the brain, brain specialization, and visual signals involves _____ processes.

14-4. A Canadian psychologist who was an early pioneer in studying physiological processes was
_____ _____. Hebb completed his Ph.D. at Harvard with Lashley, and
joined the faculty of _____ University in Montreal. Hebb argued that the basis of
behaviour could be found in the _____. He introduced the concept of the
_____, which provided an early model for how neural networks might operate.
The Canadian Psychological Association named one of its most prestigious awards after
Hebb.

Answers: 14-1. cognition (consciousness or thinking) and physiological (or biological) processes
14-2. mental **14-3.** cognitive, physiological (or biological) **14-4.** Donald Hebb, McGill, brain, cell-assembly.

15. Explain why Western psychology traditionally had scant interest in other cultures and why this situation has begun to change.

15-1. Several factors contributed to the narrow focus of Western, and especially North American, psychology:

(a) First, studying other cultures is expensive and time consuming. It's much
_____ for researchers to study people in their own country (and
especially middle-class students at their own schools).

(b) Second, some psychologists worry that study of diverse groups may inadvertently
foster _____, especially with regards to groups that have historically
been the objects of prejudice.

(c) Third, there may be a tendency among Western psychologists to view their own group
as superior, the group tendency referred to as _____.

15-2. The situation has begun to change in recent years for two primary reasons: (1) increased
communication and trade worldwide, the so-called _____ economy or
global interdependence; and (2) increased diversity of ethnic groups within the countries of
the Western World, including the _____ mosaic characteristic of the
Western World.

Answers: 15-1. (a) cheaper (easier), (b) stereotypes, (c) ethnocentrism **15-2.** global, multicultural.

16. Summarize the basic tenets of evolutionary psychology.

16-1. According to evolutionary psychologists, all aspects of human behaviour—including not
only aggression and mate selection but also perception, language, personality, and
cognition—are strongly influenced by the _____ value that these factors
have had for the human species.

16-2. While Darwin's influence is clear in other psychological theories (e.g., James's, Freud's,
and Skinner's), the new emphasis on natural selection is (<u>less/more</u>) comprehensive and
widely researched than the earlier versions.

16-3. The viewpoint has its critics. Some charge that human behaviour is the result of _____ and socialization, that evolutionary conceptions are simply posthoc accounts rather than explanations, and that the theory is not subject to scientific _____. Nonetheless, the viewpoint has gained a high degree of acceptance and is clearly a major new perspective in contemporary psychology.

Answers: 16-1. survival (or adaptive) **16-2.** more **16-3.** learning, testing.

17. Summarize the focus taken within the movement called positive psychology.

17-1. Martin Seligman is a major contributor to a new movement in psychology called _____ psychology, which uses theory and research to better understand the positive, adaptive, creative, and fulfilling aspects of human existence.

17-2. The first area of interest within positive psychology is positive _____ _____ (positive emotions), the second is positive _____ _____ (strengths and virtues), and the third is positive _____ and _____.

Answers: 17-1. positive **17-2.** subjective experiences, individual traits, institutions, communities.

PSYCHOLOGY TODAY: VIGOROUS AND DIVERSIFIED

18. Discuss the growth of psychology and the most common work settings for contemporary psychologists.

18-1. Psychology can be defined as the _____ that studies behaviour and the _____ and _____ processes that underlie it, and it is the _____ that applies the accumulated knowledge of this science to practical problems.

18-2. Psychology was founded in a university, and earlier in this century almost all psychologists were employed as academics. Today, however, more than two-thirds of psychologists are employed in (university/nonacademic) settings that include hospitals, business and industry, schools, and government agencies.

Answers: 18-1. science, physiological, cognitive, profession **18-2.** nonacademic.

19. List and describe seven major research areas in psychology.

19-1. Read over the descriptions of the research areas in Figure 1.6. Then match the names of the areas with the sampled research topics by placing the appropriate letters in the blanks. (Note that the separation between these areas is not always perfect. For example, a personality theorist might also be a psychometrician who has a physiological focus in explaining behaviour. Nonetheless, the following topics have been chosen so that one answer is correct for each.)

A. Experimental ____ attitude change, group behaviour

B. Physiological ____ personality and intelligence assessment, test design, new statistical procedures

C. Cognitive _____ personality assessment, personality description

D. Developmental _____ "core" topics (e.g., perception, conditioning, motivation)

E. Psychometrics _____ influence of the brain, bodily chemicals, genetics

F. Personality _____ child, adolescent, and adult development

G. Social _____ memory, decision making, thinking

19-2. Here's a mnemonic device to remember the list of seven research areas: Peter Piper Picked Some Exceptionally Costly Dills. List the seven research areas by matching them with the first letter of each word.

Answers: **19-1.** G, E, F, A, B, D, C **19-2.** physiological, psychometrics, personality, social, experimental, cognitive, developmental.

20. List and describe the four professional specialties in psychology.

20-1. Review Figure 1.7. Then match the following specialties with the descriptions by placing the appropriate letter in the blanks.

A. Clinical _____ Treatment of less severe problems and problems involving family, marital, and career difficulties.

B. Counselling _____ Treatment of psychological disorders, behavioural and emotional problems.

C. Educational and school _____ Involves work on curriculum design and achievement testing in school settings.

D. Industrial and organizational _____ Psychology applied to business settings; deals with personnel, job satisfaction, etc.

20-2. What is the difference between psychology and psychiatry? The major difference is a matter of degree (this is a pun, folks). Psychiatrists have _____ degrees. Clinical psychologists generally have _____ degrees (although some clinical psychologists have Ed.D. or Psy.D. degrees).

20-3. The major portion of psychiatrists' training occurs in _____ schools and in the residency programs in psychiatry that follow medical school. Clinical psychologists' training occurs in _____ schools.

20-4. While clinical psychologists and psychiatrists frequently use the same psychotherapeutic treatment procedures, only _____, as physicians, are licensed to prescribe drugs and engage in other medical treatment.

Answers: **20-1.** B, A, C, D **20-2.** medical (M.D.), Ph.D. **20-3.** medical, graduate **20-4.** psychiatrists.

21. Summarize the text's three unifying themes relating to psychology as a field of study.

21-1. When my (R.S.'s) older daughter, Samantha, was about three years old, she pulled a sugar bowl off of a shelf and broke it while I was not present. Later, when I surveyed the damage, I said, "I see you've broken something." She said, "How do yer know, did yer see me do it?" I was amused, because while it was obvious who had broken it, her comment reflected psychology's foundation in direct observation. **Theme 1** is that psychology is _____. Empiricism is the point of view that knowledge should be acquired through _____.

21-2. My daughter's comment caused me to think about one other aspect of empiricism: she expressed *doubt* (albeit somewhat self-servingly with regard to the sugar bowl). One can describe belief systems along a continuum from *credulity*, which means ready to believe, to *scepticism*, which means disposed toward doubt. Psychology, and the empirical approach, is more disposed toward the _____ end of the continuum.

21-3. We would ordinarily think that if one theory is correct, any other theory used to explain the same data must be wrong. While scientists do pit theories against each other, it is also the case that apparently contradictory theories may both be correct—as with the explanation of light in terms of both wave and particle theories. Thus, **Theme 2** indicates that psychology is theoretically _____.

21-4. Psychology tolerates (and in fact encourages) different theoretical explanations because:

21-5. As is the case with science in general, psychology does not evolve in a vacuum. It is influenced by and influences our society. For example, the current interest in cultural diversity has prompted increased interest in cross-cultural research, which in turn affects the viewpoints in our society. As stated in **Theme 3**, psychology evolves in a _____ context.

Answers: 21-1. empirical, observation **21-2.** scepticism **21-3.** diverse **21-4.** more than one theory may be correct; or, one theory may not adequately explain all of the observations **21-5.** sociohistorical.

22. Summarize the text's four unifying themes relating to psychology's subject matter.

22-1. When looking for an explanation of a particular behaviour, someone might ask, "Well, why did he do it? Was it greed or ignorance?" The question implies the very human tendency to reason in terms of (one cause/multiple causes) for each event.

22-2. What influences the course of a ball rolled down an inclined plane? Gravity. And also friction. And the presence of other objects, and a number of other factors. That is the point of **Theme 4**: even more than is the case for physical events, behaviour is determined by _____ _____.

22-3. Among the multiple causes of human behaviour is the category of causes referred to as *culture*. Cultural factors include the customs, beliefs, and values that we transmit across generations—what we eat, how we walk, what we wear, what we say, what we think, and so on. **Theme 5** indicates that our behaviour is shaped by our _____ heritage.

22-4. For example, North Americans may believe that "the squeaky wheel gets the grease," whereas Asians may believe that "the nail that stands out gets pounded down." While we are shaped by our _____ _____, we are often (aware/unaware) of the precise rules and customs that affect us.

22-5. **Theme 6** relates to the influence of heredity and environment. What is the consensus among psychologists about the effect of heredity and environment on behaviour?

22-6. The scientific method relies on observation, but observation by itself isn't sufficient. Why isn't it?

22-7. **Theme 7** indicates that our experience is subjective. What does this mean?

Answers: **22-1.** one cause **22-2.** multiple causes **22-3.** cultural **22-4.** cultural heritage, aware
22-5. Theme 6 states that heredity and environment *jointly* affect behaviour. While the relative influence of each is still debated, theorists no longer assert that behaviour is entirely a function of one or the other.
22-6. Because (Theme 7) people's experience of the world is highly subjective. **22-7.** Different people experience different things; even if we observe the same event at the same time, we do not "see" the same things; we selectively focus on some events and ignore others.

PERSONAL APPLICATION * IMPROVING ACADEMIC PERFORMANCE

23. **Discuss three important considerations in designing a program to promote adequate studying.**

    23-1. Three features of successful studying are listed below. Elaborate on them by providing some of the details asked for.

        (a) A schedule: When should you plan your study schedule? Should you write it down? Should you do the simpler tasks first or begin with the major assignments? What is a major difference between successful and unsuccessful students regarding time management?

(b) A place: What are the major characteristics of a good study place?

(c) A reward: When should you reward yourself? What kinds of rewards are suggested?

Answers: 23-1. (a) Set up a general schedule for a particular semester and then, at the beginning of each week, plan the specific assignments for each study session. Put your plans in writing. It may be best to tackle the major assignments first, breaking them into smaller components. Successful students regulate their time more effectively than unsuccessful students. (b) Find one or two places to study with minimal distractions: little noise, few interruptions. (c) Reward yourself shortly after you've finished a particular amount of studying; snacking, watching TV, or calling a friend are suggested. **Suggestion:** You are studying now. Is this a good time for you? If it is, why not write out your weekly schedule now. Include schedule preparation as part of your study time.

24. Describe the SQ3R method and explain what makes it effective.

24-1. Below are descriptions of an individual applying the five steps of the SQ3R method to Chapter 1 of your text. The steps are not in the correct order. Label each of the steps and place a number in the parentheses which indicates the correct order.

( ) _____ Vanessa looks at the title of the first subsection of the chapter. After wondering briefly what it means for psychology to have "parents," she formulates this question: How was the field of psychology influenced by philosophy and physiology?

( ) _____ Vanessa turns to the back of Chapter 1 and notes that there is a chapter review. She turns back to the first page of the chapter, sees that the outline on that page matches the review at the end, and browses through some of the other parts of the chapter. She has a rough idea that the chapter is going to define the field and discuss its history.

( ) _____ Keeping in mind the question she has posed, Vanessa reads the section about the meeting of psychology's "parents" and formulates a tentative answer to her question. (She also formulates some additional questions: "Who was Descartes?" and "What method did philosophers use?")

( ) _____ Vanessa answers her first question as follows: "Philosophy (one of the parents) posed questions about the mind that made the study of human thinking and actions acceptable; physiology (the other parent) contributed the scientific method." She decides to note down her answer for later review.

( ) _____When she has finished step 4 for all sections, Vanessa looks over the entire chapter, section by section. She repeats the questions for each section and attempts to answer each one.

24-2. What makes the SQ3R technique so effective?

Answers: 24-1. (2) Question, (1) Survey, (3) Read, (4) Recite, (5) Review **24-2.** It requires active processing and identifying key ideas.

25. Summarize advice provided on how to get more out of lectures.

25-1. Indicate T (for true) or F (for false) for the following statements:

_____ Poor class attendance is associated with poor grades.

_____ Research has shown that the average student records less than 40% of the crucial ideas in lectures.

25-2. Using a few words for each point, summarize the four points on getting more out of lectures.

Answers: 25-1. T, T **25-2.** Listen actively; focus full attention on the speaker and try to anticipate what's coming. For complex material, read ahead. Take notes in your own words, and attend to clues about what is most important. Consider asking questions during lectures (to keep involved and to clarify points presented).

26. Summarize advice provided on improving test-taking strategies.

26-1. Is it better to change answers on multiple-choice tests or to go with one's first hunch?

26-2. Following are situations you may encounter while taking a test. Reread the section on general test-taking tips and then indicate what you would do in each situation.

(a) You run into a particularly difficult item:

(b) The answer seems to be simple, but you think you may be missing something:

(c) The test is a timed test:

(d) You have some time left at the end of the test:

26-3. Following are samples of the situations mentioned under the discussion of tips for multiple-choice and essay exam questions. Based on the suggestions, what would you do?

(a) In a multiple-choice test, item *c* seems to be correct, but you have not yet read items *d* and *e*: What would you do next?

(b) You know that items *a* and *b* are correct, you are unsure of items *c* and *d*, and item *e* is an "all of the above" option. Which alternative (a, b, c, d, or e) would you choose?

(c) You have no idea which multiple-choice alternative is correct. You note that option *a* has the word "always" in it, items *b* and *c* use the word "never," and item *d* says "frequently."

(d) You have read the stem of a multiple-choice item but you have not yet looked at the options.

(e) Faced with an essay, you wonder whether to simply begin writing and let the ideas flow or to spend a few minutes in organization.

Answers: 26-1. In general, changing answers seems to be better. Available research indicates that people are more than twice as likely to go from a wrong answer to a right one as from a right answer to a wrong one. **26-2.** (a) Skip it and come back to it, if time permits. (b) Maybe the answer is simple! Don't make the question more complex than it was intended to be. (c) Budget your time, checking the proportion of the test completed against the time available. (d) Review, reconsider, check over your answers. **26-3.** (a) Read all options. (b) Answer *e*. (c) Answer *d*. (Still good advice and generally the best procedure to follow. But note that some professors, aware of the strategy, may throw in an item in which "always" is part of a correct answer! It's sort of like radar detectors: someone builds a better detector and someone else tries to build radar that can't be detected.) (d) Try to anticipate the correct answer *before* reading the options. (e) Spend a few minutes looking over the questions and allocating time, planning, organizing, and possibly even outlining. Many examiners will appreciate your use of headings or numbers to identify points made.

CRITICAL THINKING APPLICATION * DEVELOPING CRITICAL THINKING SKILLS: AN INTRODUCTION

27. Explain the nature of critical thinking skills and why they need to be taught.

27-1.   The previous section on test-taking strategies asked whether it is better to change answers or go with one's first hunch. Actually, that is a critical thinking question. While our hunches are often pretty good, sometimes they don't lead to the desired outcome. When we use critical thinking, we use the same principles that we would use in a _____ investigation. We also use formal and informal rules of _____ and carefully evaluate the quality of _____.

27-2.   Critical thinking is not something that we come by naturally. And, critical thinking (<u>is also/is not</u>) a normal part of instruction in most subject areas. So, for people to develop the skill of critical thinking, it has to be deliberately and consciously _____.

Answers: 27-1. scientific, logic, information **27-2.** is not, taught.

28. **Discuss some weaknesses in evolutionary explanations for gender differences in spatial abilities.**

28-1. Some evidence suggests that males tend to have slightly better visual-spatial perception than females, and that females have a better memory for locations. The reason for these gender differences, according to evolutionary psychologists, is that in our evolutionary past natural selection favoured a division of labour in which men were _____ and women were _____. Hunting (aiming a spear, travelling long distances) required _____ perception, while gathering required _____ for locations of food.

28-2. As previously discussed, evolutionary psychology is a major new theoretical perspective in psychology. While the interpretation of the evolutionary psychologists is certainly plausible, critical thinking urges us to consider the following two questions when assessing a truth claim: (1) Are there _____ explanations for these results? And, (2) are data available that _____ the evidence provided?

28-3. It turns out that the answer to both of these questions is a qualified "yes." For example, it may be that most cultures encourage male children to engage in visual-spatial activities (e.g., playing with blocks) that would provide an _____ interpretation to one based on evolutionary principles. In addition, some scholars have suggested that women in early hunter-gatherer societies often did, in fact, travel long distances to obtain food and were also involved in hunting. While certainly not "disproving" evolutionary theory, this type of evidence would _____ some of the data presented by evolutionary psychologists.

Answers: **28-1.** hunters, gatherers, visual-spatial, memory **28-2.** alternative, contradicts
28-3. alternative, contradict (or challenge, dispute, weaken).

✳ *REVIEW OF KEY TERMS*

Applied psychology	Ethnocentrism	Psychoanalytic theory
Behaviour	Evolutionary psychology	Psychology
Behaviourism	Functionalism	SQ3R
Clinical psychology	Humanism	Stimulus
Cognition	Introspection	Structuralism
Critical thinking	Natural selection	Testwiseness
Culture	Positive Psychology	Theory
Empiricism	Psychiatry	Unconscious

_____   **1.** Any detectable input from the environment.

_____   **2.** The branch of psychology concerned with practical problems.

_____   **3.** School of thought based on notion that the task of psychology is to analyze consciousness into its basic elements.

_____   **4.** Observation of one's own conscious experience.

_____   **5.** School of thought asserting that psychology's major purpose was to investigate the function or purpose of consciousness.

_____   **6.** The theoretical orientation asserting that scientific psychology should study only observable behaviour.

	7.	An observable activity or response by an organism.
_____	8.	Examines behavioural processes in terms of their adaptive or survival value for a species.
_____	9.	The use of cognitive skills and strategies to increase the probability of a desirable outcome.
_____	10.	Freudian theory that explains personality and abnormal behaviour in terms of unconscious processes.
_____	11.	According to psychoanalytic theory, that portion of the mind containing thoughts, memories, and wishes not in awareness but nonetheless exerting a strong effect on human behaviour.
_____	12.	The psychological theory asserting that human beings are unique and fundamentally different from other animals.
_____	13.	The tendency to view one's own group as superior to other groups.
_____	14.	Widely shared customs, beliefs, values, norms, and institutions that are transmitted socially across generations.
_____	15.	The branch of psychology concerned with the diagnosis and treatment of psychological disorders.
_____	16.	Mental processes or thinking.
_____	17.	The science that studies behaviour and the physiological and cognitive processes that underlie it, and the profession that applies this knowledge to solving various practical problems.
_____	18.	The branch of medicine concerned with the diagnosis and treatment of psychological problems and disorders.
_____	19.	The point of view that knowledge should be based on observation.
_____	20.	A system of ideas used to link together or explain a set of observations.
_____	21.	A five-step procedure designed to improve study skills.
_____	22.	Ability to use the characteristics and formats of a test to maximize one's score.
_____	23.	The Darwinian principle that characteristics that have a survival advantage for a species are more likely to be passed on to subsequent generations.
_____	24.	Uses theory and research to better understand adaptive, creative, and fulfilling aspects of human existence.

Answers: 1. stimulus **2.** applied psychology **3.** structuralism **4.** introspection **5.** functionalism
6. behaviourism **7.** behaviour **8.** evolutionary psychology **9.** critical thinking **10.** psychoanalytic theory
11. unconscious **12.** humanism **13.** ethnocentrism **14.** culture **15.** clinical psychology **16.** cognition
17. psychology **18.** psychiatry **19.** empiricism **20.** theory **21.** SQ3R **22.** testwiseness **23.** natural selection
24. positive psychology.

REVIEW OF KEY PEOPLE

Sigmund Freud
G. Stanley Hall
Donald Hebb
William James

Brenda Milner
Carl Rogers
Martin Seligman

B.F. Skinner
John B. Watson
Wilhelm Wundt

_____ 1. Founded experimental psychology and the first experimental psychology laboratory.

_____ 2. Established the first American research laboratory, launched America's first psychological journal, and was first the president of the APA.

_____ 3. Chief architect of functionalism; described a "stream of consciousness."

_____ 4. Founded behaviourism.

_____ 5. Devised the theory and technique known as psychoanalysis.

_____ 6. Identified operant conditioning.

_____ 7. A major proponent of "humanistic" psychology.

_____ 8. A Canadian psychologist who described the concept of the cell-assembly.

_____ 9. A founder of positive psychology.

_____ 10. A founder of neuropsychology in Canada.

Answers: 1. Wundt **2.** Hall **3.** James **4.** Watson **5.** Freud **6.** Skinner **7.** Rogers. **8.** Hebb. **9.** Seligman **10.** Milner.

SELF-QUIZ

1. According to the historical school of psychology known as structuralism, what is the purpose of psychology?
   a. to study behaviour
   b. to discover the smaller elements that comprise consciousness
   c. to explore the unconscious
   d. to examine the purposes of conscious processes

2. What disciplines are considered the two parents of psychology?
   a. anthropology and chemistry
   b. medicine and physics
   c. physiology and philosophy
   d. biology and sociology

3. Who is Wilhelm Wundt?
   a. He founded the first experimental laboratory.
   b. He founded the American Psychological Association.
   c. He discovered the classically conditioned salivary reflex.
   d. He founded behaviourism.

4. For John B. Watson, what was the appropriate subject matter of psychology?
   a. animal behaviour
   b. the unconscious
   c. consciousness
   d. human physiology

5. Which of the following represents a major breakthrough in the development of applied psychology?
   a. the use of the method of introspection
   b. the functionalist school of thought
   c. the establishment of the first animal laboratory
   d. Wundt's founding of experimental psychology

6. Within the field of psychology, why did Freud's ideas encounter resistance?
   a. because he emphasized human consciousness
   b. because he emphasized human behaviour
   c. because he emphasized introspection
   d. because he emphasized the unconscious

7. Which of the following statements describe the major principle of operant conditioning?
   a. Human behaviour derives in part from free will, and animal behaviour is determined by the environment.
   b. Humans and other animals tend to repeat responses that are followed by positive outcomes.
   c. Most human behaviour is based on thoughts, feelings, and wishes that we are unaware of.
   d. Human beings are fundamentally different from other animals.

8. In their explanations for human behaviour, which of the following theorists tends to emphasize concepts of freedom and potential for personal growth?
   a. Carl Rogers
   b. Sigmund Freud
   c. B.F. Skinner
   d. John Watson

9. Recent research trends in psychology involve two areas largely ignored by early behaviourists. What are these two areas?
   a. observable and measurable responses
   b. cognition (thinking) and physiological processes
   c. classical and operant conditioning
   d. the effect of environmental events and the behaviour of lower animals

10. What core area of psychological research is primarily devoted to the study of such topics as memory, problem solving, and thinking?
    a. physiological
    b. social
    c. cognitive
    d. personality

11. Which of the following does NOT refer to an aspect of critical thinking?
    a. analysis of problems in terms of scientific principles
    b. making decisions based on formal and informal logic
    c. thinking that includes consideration of probabilities
    d. thinking that reflects one's preconceived expectations

12. Considering the assertion that "psychology is empirical," what is psychology based on?
    a. introspection
    b. logic
    c. observation
    d. mathematics

13. In looking for the causes of a particular behaviour, what do psychologists assume?
    a. one cause or factor
    b. multifactorial causation
    c. free will
    d. infinite causation

14. What do contemporary psychologists generally assume that human behaviour is determined by?
    a. heredity
    b. environment
    c. heredity and environment acting together
    d. heredity, environment, and free will

15. What does SQ3R stand for?
    a. search, question, research, recommend, reconstitute
    b. silence, quietude, reading, writing, arithmetic
    c. summarize, quickly, read, research, reread
    d. survey, question, read, recite, review

16. What type of research methodology was used in the Featured Study on bullying?
    a. questionnaires
    b. case study
    c. review of archival records
    d. naturalistic observation

17. Who is a founder of positive psychology?
    a. Watson
    b. Skinner
    c. Freud
    d. Seligman

18. Which of the following has been offered as a criticism of evolutionary psychology?
    a. Humans share many features with other animals.
    b. Human behaviour chiefly reflects learning and socialization.
    c. Evolutionary psychologists place too much emphasis on laboratory research.
    d. Adaptive aspects of human behaviour provide survival or reproductive advantages.

Answers: 1. b **2.** c **3.** a **4.** a **5.** b **6.** d **7.** b **8.** a **9.** b **10.** c **11.** d **12.** c **13.** b **14.** c **15.** d. **16.** d **17.** d **18.** b.

Chapter Two

The Research Enterprise in Psychology

REVIEW OF KEY IDEAS

THE SCIENTIFIC APPROACH TO BEHAVIOUR

1. **Describe the goals of the scientific enterprise in psychology.**

   1-1.   The three interrelated goals of psychology and the other sciences are: (a) measurement and description, (b) understanding and prediction, and (c) application and control. Match each of the following descriptions with the goal it represents by placing the appropriate letters in the blanks. (There is considerable overlap among these goals; pick the closest match.)

   _____ Muscle relaxation techniques are found to be useful in reducing anxiety and improving concentration and memory.

   _____ A psychologist develops a test or procedure that measures anxiety.

   _____ Researchers find that participants in an experiment conform more to the judgments of someone similar to themselves than to those of someone who is dissimilar.

   Answers: 1-1. c, a, b.

2. **Explain the relations between theory, hypothesis, and research.**

   2-1.   What's a theory? Your text defines a theory as a system of ideas that is used to explain a set of observations. So, a theory is a *system*, which means that it integrates (or organizes or classifies) a series of observations; and it helps _____ those observations. And, it does one thing more: it suggests ideas, or predictions, or _____, to be tested in research.

   2-2.   Researchers can't test a theory all at once, but they can test one or two hypotheses derived from the theory. This is the relationship between theory, hypothesis, and research: theories suggest _____ (questions or predictions), which are then tested in _____. If the hypotheses are supported, confidence in the concepts of the _____ is strengthened.

   Answers: 2-1. explain, hypotheses (or questions) **2-2.** hypotheses, research, theory.

3. Outline the steps in a scientific investigation.

3-1. Following are the five steps generally used in performing a scientific investigation. Fill in the missing key words.

a. Formulate a testable _____.

b. Select the research _____ and design the study.

c. _____ the data.

d. _____ the data and draw conclusions.

e. _____ the findings.

3-2. Following are descriptions of various phases in the study by Dutton and Aron (1974). Indicate which step of this study is being described by placing a letter from the previous question (a, b, c, d, or e) in the appropriate blank.

_____ The authors prepared a report of their findings that was accepted for publication in *Journal of Personality and Social Psychology*.

_____ The researchers used statistics to determine whether their hypotheses were supported.

_____ Dutton and Aron thought that arousal would heighten sexual attraction. Before they began, they made precise operational definitions of both arousal and sexual attraction.

_____ The researchers decided to compare males crossing a high bridge with those crossing a low bridge in terms of their sexual attraction toward an experimental confederate they met after crossing the bridge.

_____ The researchers recorded the number of calls to the experimental confederate after participants crossed one of the bridges.

Answers: 3-1. (a) hypothesis, (b) method, (c) collect, (d) analyze, (e) report (publish, write up) **3-2.** e, d, a, b, c.

4. Discuss the advantages of the scientific approach.

4-1. We may agree with the commonsense adage "haste makes waste." Although we agree, it's not absolutely clear what the proverb means. What are the two major advantages of the scientific approach over the commonsense approach?

Answers: 4-1. First, scientific descriptions generally have a clarity and precision lacking in commonsense proverbs. (While we have a general idea about the meaning of haste, for example, we don't know precisely when, in what way, or how much haste we should avoid.) Second, science is relatively intolerant of error (before accepting a conclusion, scientists will demand objective evidence from empirical studies that support the idea).

5. **Describe the experimental method, explaining independent and dependent variables, experimental and control groups, and extraneous variables.**

5-1.   Dutton and Aron proposed that *sexual attraction* is caused (in part) by level of *arousal*. What was their independent variable? _____ Dependent variable? _____

5-2.   The variable that is manipulated or varied by the experimenter is termed the _____ variable. The variable that is affected by, or is dependent on, the manipulation is termed the _____ variable.

5-3.   What is the name of the variable that *results from* the manipulation? _____ What is the name of the variable that *produces* the effect? _____

5-4.   The group of subjects that receives the experimental treatment is known as the _____ group; the group that does not is known as the _____ group.

5-5.   Control and experimental groups are quite similar in most respects. They differ in that the experimental group receives the experimental _____, and the control group does not. Thus, any differences found in the measure of the _____ variable are assumed to be due to differences in manipulation of the _____ variable.

5-6.   In Dutton and Aron's study, the experimental group experienced a high level of _____. Results were that the experimental group, the high arousal group, had a greater tendency to _____ _____ _____ _____ an opposite-sex other than did the control group.

5-7   In the research described by Wolfe and colleagues (2003), the type of treatment that teens received is the _____ variable, and the experience of abuse in relationships is the _____ variable.

5-8.   An extraneous variable is any variable other than the _____ variable that seems likely to cause a difference between groups as measured by the _____ variable. In the Dutton and Aron study, a possible confounding variable was differences in _____.

5-9.   To review the parts of an experiment: Suppose a researcher is interested in the effect of a drug on the running speed of rats. The _____ group is injected with the drug, and the _____ group is not. Whether or not the rats received the drug would be the _____ variable, and running speed would be the _____ variable.

5-10. Suppose also that the average age of the experimental rats is two years, while the average age of the control rats is three months. What is the extraneous variable in this experiment? _____ Why does this variable present a problem?

5-11. Researchers generally control for extraneous variables through random _____ of subjects to groups. Write a definition of this procedure.

5-12. A _____-_____ design involves subjects serving as their own control group. This is in contrast to a _____-_____ design, in which comparisons are made between two groups of participants.

Answers: 5-1. arousal, attraction (note that a second independent variable in the study was sex of the experimental confederate) **5-2.** independent, dependent **5-3.** dependent, independent **5-4.** experimental, control **5-5.** treatment, dependent, independent **5-6.** arousal, become sexually attracted toward **5-7.** independent, dependent **5-8** independent, dependent, personality **5-9.** experimental, control, independent, dependent **5-10.** age. Any difference between groups could be due to age rather than the independent variable **5-11.** assignment. All subjects have an equal chance of being assigned to any group or condition. **5-12.** within-subjects, between-subjects.

6. Describe the Featured Study on the effects of fear on sexual attraction.

6-1. The purpose of the study was to examine whether strong emotional arousal experienced by men would enhance their _____ toward an attractive female.

6-2. This question arose from Schacter's (1964) theory of emotion, which suggests that _____ cues may at times be used to re-label emotional experiences.

6-3. Participants were men who crossed either a high, unstable bridge or a low, solid bridge. They were then met by a male or female experimental confederate. They then completed the _____ _____ _____ (TAT) to measure their sexual imagery and were given the confederate's phone number.

6-4. Thus, the study manipulated two _____ variables. One was the type of bridge crossed by the participant, which generated either _____ or _____ fear/arousal. The second was the sex of the experimental confederate.

6-5. The _____ variables included amount of _____ _____ on responses to the TAT and the number of _____ _____ made to the experimental confederate.

6-6. Results were as follows: Compared with men who crossed the low, stable bridge, men who crossed the high, unstable bridge revealed _____ sexual imagery in their TAT stories and were _____ likely to call the female experimental confederate.

Answers: 6-1. attraction **6-2.** environmental **6-3.** Thematic Apperception Test **6-4.** independent, high, low **6-5.** dependent, sexual imagery, telephone calls **6-6.** more, more.

7. Explain the major advantages and disadvantages of the experimental method.

7-1.   What is the major advantage of the experimental method?

7-2.   What are the two major disadvantages of the experimental method?

7-3.   Suppose a researcher is interested in the effect of drinking large amounts of coffee on health (e.g., 30 cups per day over an extended period of time). What would be a major *disadvantage* of using the experimental method to examine this particular question?

7-4.   What is a way in which a researcher can overcome the limitation of an experiment being artificial?

Answers: 7-1. The major advantage is that it permits researchers to make cause–effect conclusions. **7-2.** The major disadvantages are that (a) precise experimental control may make the situation so artificial that it does not apply to the real world, and (b) ethical or practical considerations may prevent one from manipulating independent variables of interest. **7-3.** To the extent that excessive coffee drinking is a suspected factor in health problems, it would be unethical, and perhaps impossible, to require an experimental group to drink that much per day. **7-4.** A field experiment could be conducted that occurs in a real-life setting.

LOOKING FOR LINKS: DESCRIPTIVE RESEARCH

8. Discuss three descriptive/correlational methods: naturalistic observation, case studies, and surveys.

8-1.   Naturalistic observation involves study of human beings or animals in their natural environments conducted without direct intervention from the observer. What is a strength and what is a limitation of naturalistic observational research?

8-2.   A case study is an in-depth and generally highly subjective or impressionistic report on (<u>a group of people/a single individual</u>) that may be based on interviews, psychological testing, and so on.

8-3.   The third descriptive procedure is the survey technique. Surveys use _____ to find out about specific aspects of human attitudes or opinions.

8-4.   List the three descriptive/correlational methods in the space below.

Answers: 8-1. Strengths include less artificiality, usefulness when studying a new area of behaviour, and ability to study animals; weaknesses include reactivity and ability to statistically analyze observations. **8-2.** a single individual **8-3.** questionnaires (or interviews) **8-4.** naturalistic observation, case studies, surveys.

9. **Explain the major advantages and disadvantages of descriptive/correlational research.**

9-1.   While descriptive/correlational methods extend the scope of psychological research, they do not permit scientists to _____ variables. Nor do they permit one to demonstrate _____ relationships among variables.

9-2.   For example, suppose you have data indicating that people who happen to drink a lot of coffee tend to have cardiovascular problems. Is this experimental or descriptive/correlational research? _____ Would it be correct to conclude (from these data) that coffee drinking causes cardiovascular problems?

_____

9-3.   An advantage of descriptive/correlational methods is that they allow researchers to study phenomena that they could not study with experimental methods. Thus, the descriptive/correlational methods (<u>narrow/broaden</u>) the scope of phenomena studied.

Answers: 9-1. manipulate (or control), cause–effect (or causal) **9-2.** descriptive/correlational (because the variables are not manipulated by the experimenter), no **9-3.** broaden.

LOOKING FOR CONCLUSIONS: STATISTICS AND RESEARCH

10. **Describe three measures of central tendency, two measures of variability, and the normal distribution.**

10-1.   To review the meaning of the three measures of central tendency, determine the mean, median, and mode of the following scores: 3, 5, 5, 5, 6, 6, 7, 9, 80.

Mean: _____

Median: _____

Mode: _____

10-2.   One can describe a group of data with a single number by using one of the measures of central tendency. In the blanks below, indicate which measure of central tendency is being described.

_____ The score that occurs most frequently.

_____ The sum of all scores divided by the total number of scores.

_____ Half the scores fall above this measure and half below.

_____ Very sensitive to extreme scores.

_____ Usually the most useful, because it may be used in further statistical manipulations.

_____ The middle score.

10-3. What is the median of data set A, below? _____ Of set B? _____ Which of these sets is more variable, A or B? _____

A. 30, 40, 50, 60, 70 B. 10, 30, 50, 70, 90

10-4. Data from a frequency distribution can be presented in a line figure called a _____ polygon. An asymmetric frequency polygon in which scores pile up at the high end of the scale is called a _____ _____ distribution.

10-5. What are the names of two statistics used to measure variability? _____ and _____ _____.

10-6. The standard deviation is useful in understanding a symmetrical distribution that represents how many human characteristics are distributed in a population. This distribution is called the _____ _____. Scores under a normal curve are dispersed in a fixed pattern based on the _____ _____. Scores from a normal distribution can also be readily converted into _____ scores.

Answers: **10-1.** 14, 6, 5 **10-2.** mode, mean, median, mean, mean, median **10-3.** 50, 50, B **10-4.** frequency, negatively skewed **10-5.** range, standard deviation **10-6.** normal curve (or distribution), standard deviation, percentile.

11. Distinguish between positive and negative correlations.

11-1. Which of the following relationships are positive and which are negative? (Indicate with a + or - sign.)

_____ The better students' grades are in high school, the better their grades tend to be in college.

_____ The more alcohol a person has drunk, the slower his or her reaction time.

_____ The higher the anxiety, the poorer the test performance.

_____ The greater the arousal, the greater the sexual attraction.

11-2. Which of the following indicates the *strongest correlational relationship*?
a. 1.12
b. -0.92
c. .58
d. .87

Answers: **11-1.** +, -, -, + **11-2.** b (not *a*, because correlations cannot exceed +1.00 or -1.00).

12. Discuss correlation in relation to prediction and causation.

12-1. Suppose you have data indicating that the more money people make, the less depressed they report being on a mood survey. Thus, if you know the incomes of people in a comparable group, you should be able to _____, with some degree of accuracy, their self-reported depressed mood.

12-2. The accuracy of your prediction will depend on the size of the correlation coefficient.

Which of the following correlation coefficients would allow you to predict with the greatest accuracy?

a. +.41

b. +.54

c. -.65

12-3. What kind of conclusion is justified on the basis of the previous relationship, a conclusion involving prediction or one involving a statement about causation? _____

12-4. Consider the relationship described in an earlier question: You discover that the more money people make, the greater their happiness. Which of the following conclusions is justified? Explain why.

a. Money makes people happy.

b. Happiness causes people to earn more money.

c. Both happiness and money result from some unknown third factor.

d. Any of the above

12-5. Again consider the relationship between money and happiness. Assume that money does not cause happiness, and happiness does not cause money. What possible *third factor* can you think of that could cause both? (I'm asking you to make a wild speculation here just to get the idea of how third variables may operate.)

12-6. We aren't justified in making causal conclusions from a correlation, but we can predict. Let's examine what prediction means in the case of our hypothetical example. If the relationship really exists, what prediction would you make about people who are rich? What prediction would you make concerning people who are unhappy?

Answers: 12-1. predict **12-2.** c **12-3.** prediction (Generally, one can't make causal conclusions from a correlation.) **12-4.** d. Any of the statements is a possible *causal* explanation of the relationship, but we don't know which one(s) may be correct because the data are correlational. Therefore, *no causal conclusions* are justified. **12-5.** For example, poor health might cause one to be both unhappy *and* poverty stricken (while good health would cause one to be both happy and wealthy). Intelligence, aggressiveness, stubbornness, or a number of other physiological or behavioural factors could be causally related *both* to income and to happiness without those two factors being causes of one another. **12-6.** You would predict that a group that was rich would also be happy, and that a group that was unhappy would be poor. No causation is implied in these statements.

13. Explain the meaning of statistical significance.

13-1. In the hypothetical experiment described in your text, there are two groups, largely equivalent except that the _____ group receives the computerized tutoring sessions and the _____ group does not. What is the hypothesis of this experiment?

13-2. Researchers statistically evaluate the hypothesis by comparing means and determining the likelihood or probability that a difference between means of the size obtained (or larger) would occur by _____. If the probability that such a difference would occur by chance is very low, say fewer than 5 times in 100, the researchers would conclude that the difference (is/is not) due to chance. They would declare the difference statistically _____ at the _____ level of significance.

13-3. Statistically significant does not mean important or significant in the usual sense of that word. What does statistically significant mean?

13-4. How do we reach a conclusion when the results of different studies often produce contradictory results? One method for doing so is the relatively new technique known as _____, a (statistical/journalistic) technique for combining results from many different studies.

Answers: 13-1. experimental, control. The hypothesis is that special tutoring would increase reading scores. **13-2.** chance, is not, significant, .05 **13-3.** It means that a difference that large would be rare on a chance basis, so it is assumed *not* to be due to chance; or, more simply, it is assumed that the difference between means is due to treatment. **13-4.** meta-analysis, statistical.

LOOKING FOR FLAWS: EVALUATING RESEARCH

14. Explain the role of replication in science, identify what makes a sample representative, and discuss the problem of sampling bias.

14-1. Identifying erroneous findings occurs through the process of _____. Research studies conducted on the same topic can be analyzed together through the process of _____-_____, which can indicate the strength and generalizability of a variable's effects.

14-2. Sampling bias exists when the sample is not representative of the _____ from which it was drawn.

14-3. Suppose that Professor Brutalbaum distributes a questionnaire in an attempt to find out how the students react to his teaching. The day that he chooses for the evaluation, the day before a scheduled vacation, about half the students are absent. Is the sample that attended class that day a representative sample of the class? _____ What is a representative sample?

14-4. Psychological research has relied heavily on so-called WEIRD samples, which likely distorts findings in many research areas. What does WEIRD stand for?

Answers: 14-1. replication, meta-analysis **14-2.** population **14-3.** No. A representative sample is one that is similar in composition to the population from which it is drawn. In this case, it seems likely that students who attend are different from those who do not (e.g., perhaps more enthusiastic, harder

working, more fearful). Since the sample is not representative, the flaw illustrated is *sampling bias*.
14-4. Western, educated, industrialized, rich, and democratic.

15. Explain when placebo effects are likely to be a problem.

15-1. A student in Professor Brutalbaum's class orders some audio tapes that promise to produce sleep learning. (Brutalbaum is dubious, because from his observations students sleep a lot in class but still don't seem to learn very much.) The student runs the experiment in Brutalbaum's class. She describes the anticipated sleep-learning benefits to the class and then *gives the sleep tapes to a random half of the students and nothing to the other half.* After the next test, she analyzes the results. The mean test score of the experimental group is statistically significantly higher than that of the control group. What is the flaw in this experiment?

a. sampling bias

b. possible placebo effects

c. time of day

d. none of the above

15-2. What are placebo effects?

Answers: 15-1. b **15-2.** Placebo effects: the tendency for people's behaviour to change because of their expectation that the treatment will have an effect.

16. Describe the typical kinds of distortions that occur in self-report data.

16-1. Professor Brutalbaum is now concerned about class attendance and decides to find out what proportion of students miss class regularly. He distributes a questionnaire asking students to indicate how many classes they have missed. Which of the four common flaws is he likely to encounter? _____

16-2. For a number of reasons, people may not answer questions correctly, including the fact that they may not understand the question or may not remember accurately. Respondents also frequently want to create a favourable impression, the response tendency known as the social _____ bias. Some measures are less susceptible to socially desirable responding, including _____ measures, such as the Implicit Association Test. People may also be predisposed to respond in particular ways regardless of the question, for example, to agree or disagree regardless of content. This type of response tendency is known as a response _____. Another concern is the _____ effect, which occurs when an overall evaluation of a person or thing spills over to more specific ratings.

Answers: 16-1. distortions in self-report **16-2.** desirability, implicit, set, halo.

17. Describe Rosenthal's research on experimenter bias.

17-1. When we ask a question, we frequently expect a particular answer. When scientists form a hypothesis, they also may expect a particular answer, and in some cases the scientist's hypotheses or expectations may influence the answers that they obtain. When a researcher's expectations about the outcome of a study influence the results, then the flaw in procedure known as _____ has occurred.

17-2. Experimenter bias or influence may occur in subtle ways. Rosenthal has repeatedly demonstrated that when the experimenter merely knows which treatment condition a subject is in, the fact of that knowledge or expectation alone may influence the subject's behaviour. For this reason it is extremely important in research to maintain the _____ procedure, in which neither participants nor experimenters know which treatment condition the subject is in.

Answers: 17-1. experimenter bias **17-2.** double-blind.

LOOKING INTO THE FUTURE: THE INTERNET AND PSYCHOLOGICAL RESEARCH

18. Discuss the pros and cons of Internet-mediated research.

18-1. In the space below, identity advantages of Internet-based research.

18-2. In the space below, identity disadvantages of Internet-based research.

Answers: 18-1. Advantages include larger and more diverse samples, and more efficient collection of data. **18-2.** Disadvantages include sample bias due to self-selection, higher dropout rates, and less control over data collection.

LOOKING AT ETHICS: DO THE ENDS JUSTIFY THE MEANS?

19. Discuss the pros and cons of deception in research with human subjects.

19-1. In the space below, present arguments against the use of deception in research. What is the major argument in defence of the use of deception in research?

Answers: 19-1. Deception is, after all, lying; it may undermine people's trust in others; it may cause distress. Many research issues could not be investigated without deception.

20. **Identify the four key principles of psychological research as set forth by the Canadian Psychological Association.**

    20-1. Fill in the spaces below to describe each of the four key principles:

        Principle I: Respect for the _____ of Persons.

        Principle II: Responsible _____.

        Principle III: Integrity in _____.

        Principle IV: Responsibility to _____.

    20-2. Treating all individuals respectfully and fairly (for example, regardless of their culture or nationality) would fall under principle number _____.

    20-3. The ethical conduct of research with animals is also governed by guidelines developed by the Canadian Council on the _____ ____ _____.

Answers: 20-1. Dignity, Caring, Relationships, Society **20-2.** I **20-3.** Care of Animals.

PUTTING IT IN PERSPECTIVE

21. **Explain how this chapter highlighted two of the text's unifying themes.**

    21-1. One of the text's unifying themes is that psychology is _____ , which means that its conclusions are based on systematic _____ , and that it tends to be (skeptical/credulous).

    21-2. In what way did the discussion of methodology suggest that psychology tends to be skeptical of its results?

    21-3. People's experience of the world is highly subjective. Which of the methodological problems discussed point out psychology's awareness of the subjective nature of our experience?

Answers: 21-1. empirical, observation (research), sceptical **21-2.** Researchers constantly look for methodological flaws and subject their results to critical scrutiny by other scientists. **21-3.** Behavioural scientists try to guard against subjective reactions by building in appropriate experimental controls for *placebo effects* and *experimenter bias*.

22. Describe the nature of technical journals.

22-1. A journal publishes technical material in a field, generally the results of research or other scholarly activity. Since journal articles are written primarily for (the layperson/other professionals), they frequently contain technical language that makes it difficult for people outside the field to understand.

22-2. In psychology, most journal articles are reports of research or other empirical studies. Some journals also publish articles that summarize findings from a large number of studies; these articles are known as _____ articles. Some review articles employ the statistical technique of _____ - _____, a procedure that combines the results of many different studies.

Answers: 22-1. other professionals **22-2.** review, meta-analysis.

23. Explain how to use PsycINFO, and discuss the advantages of computerized literature searches.

23-1. PsycINFO is a computerized database that contains abstracts or concise _____ of articles published in psychological journals.

23-2. To find information about a particular journal article referred to in the popular press, for example, you could begin your search by entering the name of the _____. If you have an idea of when the article was published, you could further narrow your search by entering the approximate _____ in which the article may have been published.

23-3. You can also search under topic. To further reduce your search, enter _____ topics (e.g., insomnia and mood). By pairing two topics you are more likely to find articles relevant to your particular question.

23-4. The advantages of computerized over manual searches (in the print journal *Psychological Abstracts*) include:

a. speed or power

b. decreased likelihood of missing relevant articles

c. the option of pairing topics in a search

d. all of the above

Answers: 23-1. summaries **23-2.** author, years (dates, time period) **23-3.** two **23-4.** d.

24. Describe the standard organization of journal articles reporting on empirical research.

24-1. In the blanks below, list the six parts of the standard journal article in the order in which they occur. (The initial letters of each section are listed on the left.)

A _____

I _____

M _____

R _____

D _____

R _____

(Hint: A way to remember the first letter of these parts of a journal, in order, is with the acrostic "Andrew Is Most Relaxed During a Run").

24-2. In the blanks below, match the name of the sections of the standard journal article with the descriptions.

_____ States the hypothesis and reviews the literature relevant to the hypothesis.

_____ A list of all the sources referred to in the paper.

_____ A summary.

_____ Presents the data; may include statistical analyses, graphs, and tables.

_____ Describes what the researchers did in the study; includes participants, procedures, and data collection techniques.

_____ Interprets or evaluates the data and presents conclusions.

Answers: 24-1. abstract, introduction, method, results, discussion, references **24-2.** introduction, references, abstract, results, method, discussion.

CRITICAL THINKING APPLICATION * THE PERILS OF ANECDOTAL EVIDENCE: "I HAVE A FRIEND WHO …"

25. Explain why anecdotal evidence is flawed and unreliable.

25-1. Anecdotal evidence consists of personal stories that support a particular point of view. Anecdotes are frequently persuasive because they are concrete and vivid and, therefore, easy to _____.

25-2. What's wrong with anecdotal evidence? First, one cannot generalize from a single case. Although a political candidate's story about a coal miner named Bob (or a physician named Alice, etc.) may be memorable, Bob's experiences cannot be _____ to other people or situations.

25-3. Second, people tend to represent themselves in the most favourable light. To the extent that Bob is the source of the anecdote, Bob's self-report data may reflect the social _____ bias.

25-4. In addition, stories change with the telling, so that later versions may bear little resemblance to the original event. Stories one has heard second- or third-hand, so-called ___ evidence, are likely to be particularly unreliable.

25-5. Nor is it likely that Bob, or the story about Bob, was picked randomly. The candidate selects an anecdote to make a particular point, a process similar to _____ bias in a research setting. The clear alternative to anecdotal evidence is to solve problems based on solid evidence, the so-called _____-based decision-making process.

Answers: **25-1.** remember **25-2.** generalized **25-3.** desirability **25-4.** hearsay **25-5.** sampling, evidence.

REVIEW OF KEY TERMS

Anecdotal evidence
Between-subjects design
Case study
Confounding of variables
Control group
Correlation
Correlation coefficient
Data collection techniques
Dependent variable
Descriptive statistics
Double-blind procedure
Experiment
Experimental group
Experimental bias
Extraneous variables
Field experiment
Frequency distribution
Frequency polygon

Halo effect
Hypothesis
Independent variable
Inferential statistics
Internet-mediated research
Journal
Mean
Median
Meta-analysis
Mode
Naturalistic observation
Operational definition
Participants
Placebo effects
Population
Qualitative research
Quantitative research
Random assignment

Range
Reactivity
Replication
Research methods
Response set
Sample
Sampling bias
Social desirability bias
Standard deviation
Statistical significance
Statistics
Subjects
Survey
Theory
Variability
Variables
Within-subjects design

_____ **1.** Any of the factors in an experiment that are controlled or observed by an experimenter or that in some other way affect the outcome.

_____ **2.** A tentative statement about the expected relationship between two or more variables.

_____ **3.** Precisely defines each variable in a study in terms of the operations needed to produce or measure that variable.

_____ **4.** Persons or animals whose behaviour is being studied; means the same thing as *participants*.

_____ **5.** Differing ways of conducting research, which include experiments, case studies, surveys, and naturalistic observation.

_____ **6.** A research method in which independent variables are manipulated and which permits causal interpretations.

_____ **7.** A condition or event that an experimenter varies in order to observe its impact.

_____ **8.** The variable that results from the manipulation in an experiment.

_____ **9.** The group in an experiment that receives a treatment as part of the independent variable manipulation.

_____ **10.** The group in an experiment that does not receive the treatment.

_____ **11.** Any variables other than the independent variables that seem likely to influence the dependent measure in an experiment.

_____ **12.** Distribution of subjects in an experiment in which each subject has an equal chance of being assigned to any group or condition.

_____ **13.** A link or association between variables such that one can be predicted from the other.

_____ **14.** The statistic that indicates the degree of relationship between variables.

_____ **15.** A research method in which the researcher observes behaviour in the natural environment without directly intervening.

_____ **16.** An in-depth, generally subjective, investigation of an individual subject.

_____ **17.** A questionnaire or interview used to gather information about specific aspects of subjects' behaviour.

_____ **18.** Procedures for making empirical observations, including questionnaires, interviews, psychological tests, and physiological recordings.

_____ **19.** Statistics helpful in organizing and summarizing (but not interpreting) data.

_____ **20.** Statistical procedures used to interpret data in an experiment and draw conclusions.

_____ **21.** The use of mathematics to organize, summarize, and interpret numerical data.

_____ **22.** A descriptive statistic and measure of central tendency that always falls in the exact half-way point of a distribution of data.

_____ **23.** The arithmetic average.

_____ **24.** The score that occurs most frequently.

_____ **25.** The spread or dispersion of data, including the extent to which scores vary from the mean.

_____ **26.** A measure of variability in data.

_____ **27.** A judgment inferred from statistics that the probability of the observed findings occurring by chance is very low.

_____ **28.** A repetition of a study to determine whether the previously obtained results can be duplicated.

_____ **29.** A group of subjects taken from a population.

_____ **30.** A larger group from which a sample is drawn and to which the researcher wishes to generalize.

_____ 31. Exists when a sample is not representative of the population from which it was drawn.

_____ 32. Also known as subjects, the individuals whose behaviour is systematically observed in a study.

_____ 33. Occurs when a researcher's expectations influence the results of the study.

_____ 34. Effects that occur when subjects experience a change due to their expectations (or to a "fake" treatment).

_____ 35. The tendency to respond in a particular way (e.g., agreeing) that is unrelated to the content of questions asked.

_____ 36. Occurs when an extraneous variable makes it difficult to sort out the effects of the independent variable.

_____ 37. The tendency to answer questions about oneself in a socially approved manner.

_____ 38. A research strategy in which neither the subjects nor the experimenters know which condition or treatment the subjects are in.

_____ 39. A periodical that publishes technical and scholarly material within a discipline.

_____ 40. A system of interrelated ideas used to explain a set of observations.

_____ 41. Support for a particular point of view through the use of personal (and frequently vivid) stories.

_____ 42. Studies in which data collection is done using the Web.

_____ 43. A type of research in which data consists of words and narratives of experiences

_____ 44. Research that involves empirical observations of the world reported as numeric quantities.

_____ 45. An experimental design in which subjects serve as their own control group.

_____ 46. An experimental design in which comparisons are made between two different groups of subjects.

_____ 47. An experiment conducted in a real-life setting.

_____ 48. When a subject's behaviour is altered by the presence of an observer.

_____ 49. A line figure used to present data from a frequency distribution.

_____ 50. An orderly arrangement of scores indicating the frequency of each score.

_____ 51. A measure of variability calculated by subtracting the lowest score from the highest score.

_____ 52. Combining the statistical results of many studies of the same question.

_____ 53. When an overall evaluation of a person (or thing) spills over to influence more specific ratings of that person (or thing)

Answers: 1. variables 2. hypothesis 3. operational definition 4. subjects 5. research methods
6. experiment 7. independent variable 8. dependent variable 9. experimental group 10. control group
11. extraneous variables 12. random assignment 13. correlation 14. correlation coefficient
15. naturalistic observation 16. case study 17. survey 18. data collection techniques 19. descriptive
statistics 20. inferential statistics 21. statistics 22. median 23. mean 24. mode 25. variability 26. standard

THE RESEARCH ENTERPRISE IN PSYCHOLOGY

deviation **27.** statistical significance **28.** replication **29.** sample **30.** population **31.** sampling bias **32.** participants **33.** experimenter bias **34.** placebo effects **35.** response set **36.** confounding of variables **37.** social desirability bias **38.** double-blind procedure **39.** journal **40.** theory **41.** anecdotal evidence. **42.** Internet-mediated research. **43.** qualitative research **44.** quantitative research **45.** within-subjects design **46.** between-subjects design **47.** field experiment **48.** reactivity **49.** frequency polygon **50.** frequency distribution **51.** range **52.** meta-analysis **53.** halo effect.

REVIEW OF KEY PEOPLE

Arthur Aron	Donald Dutton	David Wolfe
Neal Miller	Robert Rosenthal	Stanley Schachter

_____ **1.** Along with Dutton, studied the effects of arousal on sexual attraction.

_____ **2.** Co-investigator with Aron.

_____ **3.** Asserted that the benefits of animal research (e.g., the resulting treatments for mental and physical disorders) far outweigh the harm done.

_____ **4.** Argued that emotions can be re-labelled according to environmental cues.

_____ **5.** Studied experimenter bias, a researcher's unintended influence on the behaviour of subjects.

_____ **6.** Studied a psychological intervention for at-risk teens.

Answers: 1. Aron **2.** Dutton **3.** Miller. **4.** Schachter **5.** Rosenthal **6.** Wolfe.

SELF-QUIZ

1. A clinical psychologist works to reduce the suffering of individuals. What is the goal of this work?
   a. measurement
   b. understanding and prediction
   c. application and control
   d. description

2. An experimenter tests the hypothesis that physical exercise helps people's mood (makes them happier). Subjects in the experimental group participate on Monday and Tuesday, and those in the control group on Wednesday and Thursday. Which of the following is the independent variable?
   a. the hypothesis
   b. the day of the week
   c. the exercise
   d. the mood (degree of happiness)

3. Referring to the experiment described in question #2, what is the dependent variable?
   a. the hypothesis
   b. the day of the week
   c. the exercise
   d. the mood (degree of happiness)

4. Referring to the experiment described in question #2, what is an extraneous (confounding) variable?
   a. the hypothesis
   b. the day of the week
   c. the exercise
   d. the mood (degree of happiness)

5. What is the major advantage of the experimental method over the correlational approach?
   a. The experimental method permits one to make causal conclusions.
   b. The experimental method allows for prediction.
   c. The experimental method is generally less artificial than correlational procedures.
   d. The experimental method permits the study of people in groups.

6. In looking through some medical records, you find there is a strong relationship between depression and chronic pain. The stronger the physical pain that people report, the higher their scores on an inventory that measures depression. What conclusion can be justified?
   a. Depression tends to produce chronic pain.
   b. Chronic pain tends to produce depression.
   c. Both chronic pain and depression result from an unknown third factor.
   d. Depression and chronic pain are positively associated with each other.

7. What is the mode of the following data: 2, 3, 3, 3, 5, 5, 7, 12?
   a. 3
   b. 4
   c. 5
   d. 6

8. What is the median of the following data: 1, 3, 4, 4, 5, 6, 9?
   a. 3
   b. 4
   c. 4.57
   d. 6

9. Researchers find a negative relationship between alcohol consumption and speed of response: the more alcohol consumed, the slower the response speed. Which of the following fictitious statistics could possibly represent that correlation?
   a. –4.57
   b. –0.87
   c. 0.05
   d. 0.91

10. What does the term *statistical significance* refer to?
    a. how important the data are for future research on the topic
    b. the conclusion that there are no reasonable alternative explanations
    c. the inference that the observed effects are unlikely to be due to chance
    d. the representativeness of the sample

11. An instructor wants to conduct an experiment to find out whether a new teaching method is better than his usual procedures. His students are quite excited about the prospect of learning under the new procedure, but he cannot administer the new teaching method to everyone. A random selection of half of the students receives the new method, and the remaining half receives the old. What is the most obvious flaw in this experiment?
    a. Subjects should have been systematically assigned to groups.
    b. The sample is not representative of the population.
    c. Placebo effects or experimenter bias are likely to affect results.
    d. Distortions in self-report will affect results.

12. What procedure helps correct for experimenter bias?
    a. extraneous or confounding variables
    b. sleep learning or hypnosis
    c. a higher standard for statistical significance
    d. use of the double-blind procedure

13. With regard to the topic of deception in research with human subjects, which of the following statements is true?
   a. Researchers are careful to avoid deceiving subjects.
   b. Some topics could not be investigated unless deception was used.
   c. Deception does not resemble lying.
   d. All psychological research must involve some deception.

14. Which of the following is NOT one of the four Key Principles of Psychological Research according to the Canadian Psychological Association's ethical guidelines?
   a. Respect for the Dignity of Persons
   b. Responsible Caring
   c. Integrity in Relationships
   d. Responsibility to Oneself

15. In the Featured Study by Dutton and Aron (1974), what was one of the independent variables?
   a. sexual imagery in TAT responses
   b. the sex of participants
   c. making a telephone call to the experimental confederate
   d. the sex of the experimental confederates

16. Which of the following is one of the six standard parts of a psychological journal article?
   a. conclusions
   b. bibliography
   c. data summary
   d. discussion

17. What is contained in the PsycINFO computerized database?
   a. standard diagnostic information for classifying behaviour disorders
   b. abstracts of and bibliographic references for journal articles
   c. psychological profiles of known felons
   d. names of authors who specialize in abstractions

18. You view your friend as being, overall, a really great person. As a result, when considering his or her specific trait of outspokenness, you view it as a positive characteristic. What phenomenon does this demonstrate?
   a. halo effect
   b. placebo effect
   c. experimenter bias
   d. reactivity

19. All participants in an experiment complete trials on a reaction-time task. In some trials they are given a cue just before a stimulus is presented; in others they receive no cue. What kind of experiment is this?
   a. within-subjects design
   b. independent groups design
   c. between-subjects design
   d. multivariate design

Answers: 1. c **2.** c **3.** d **4.** b **5.** a **6.** d **7.** a **8.** b **9.** b **10.** c **11.** c **12.** d **13.** b **14.** d **15.** d. **16.** d **17.** b **18.** a. **19.** a.

Chapter Three

THE BIOLOGICAL BASES OF BEHAVIOUR

REVIEW OF KEY IDEAS

COMMUNICATION IN THE NERVOUS SYSTEM

1. **Describe the various parts of the neuron and their functions.**

   1-1. The neuron has three basic parts: the dendrites; the cell body, or soma; and the axon. The major mission of the average neuron is to receive information from one neuron and pass it on to the next neuron. The receiving part is the job of the branchlike parts called _____. They then pass the message along to the nucleus of the cell, called the cell body, or _____. From there the message is sent down the _____to be passed along to other neurons.

   1-2. Many axons are wrapped in a fatty jacket called the _____ _____, which permits for faster transmission of information and prevents messages from getting on the wrong track. Like the covering on an electrical cord, myelin acts as an _____ material.

   1-3. When the neural message reaches the end of the axon, it excites projections called terminal _____, which then release a chemical substance into the junction that separates them from other neurons. This junction between neurons is called the _____.

   1-4. Identify the major parts of a neuron in the figure below. Note that the arrow indicates the direction of the flow of information.

   (a) _____ (b) _____ (c) _____ (d) _____

Answers: 1-1. dendrites, soma, axon **1-2.** myelin sheath, insulating **1-3.** buttons, synapse **1-4.** (a) dendrites, (b) cell body or soma, (c) axon, (d) terminal buttons.

2. Describe the main functions of glia.

2-1. Glia are a second category of nervous system cells. Glia are much _____ than neurons, and they outnumber neurons by a ratio of about _____ to 1.

2-2. Glia supply _____ to neurons, help remove neurons' _____ products, and provide _____ around the axon of neurons.

2-3. More recently, glia cells have been shown to _____ and _____ chemical signals. They have also been implicated in such diseases as Alzheimer's disease, chronic pain, schizophrenia, and mood disorders.

Answers: 2-1. smaller, 10 **2-2.** nourishment, waste, insulation **2-3.** send, receive.

3. Describe the neural impulse.

3-1. When it is at rest, the neuron is like a tiny battery in that it contains a weak (negative/positive) charge. When the neuron is stimulated, the cell membrane becomes more permeable. This allows positively charged _____ ions to flow into the cell, thus lessening the cell's negative charge.

3-2. The change in the charge of the cell caused by the inflow of positively charged sodium ions, called an _____ potential, travels down the _____ of the neuron. After the firing of an action potential, there is a brief period in which no further action potentials can be generated. This brief period is called the absolute _____ period.

3-3. The text likens the neuron to a gun in that it either fires or does not fire. This property of the neuron is called the _____ law. Neurons transmit information about the strength of a stimulus by variations in the number of action potentials generated. For example, in comparison to a weak stimulus, a strong stimulus will generate a (higher/lower) rate of action potentials.

Answers: 3-1. negative, sodium **3-2.** action, axon, refractory **3-3.** all or none, higher.

4. Describe how neurons communicate at chemical synapses.

4-1. A neuron passes its message on to another neuron by releasing a chemical messenger into the gap or _____ that separates it from other neurons. The sending neuron, called the _____, releases a chemical messenger into the synaptic cleft, which then excites the _____ neuron.

4-2. The chemical messenger that provides this transmitting service is called a _____. The chemical binds with specifically tuned receptor sites on the postsynaptic neurons. In other words, the receptor sites accept some neurotransmitters and reject _____.

5. **Describe the two types of postsynaptic potentials and how neurons integrate and form neural circuits.**

   5-1. When the neurotransmitter combines with a molecule at the receptor site it causes a voltage change at the receptor site called a _____ potential (PSP). One type of PSP is excitatory, and it (<u>increases/decreases</u>) the probability of producing an action potential in the receiving neuron. The other type is inhibitory, and it _____ the probability of producing an action potential.

   5-2. Whether or not a neuron fires depends on the number of excitatory PSPs it is receiving and the number of _____ PSPs it is receiving. PSPs (<u>do/do not</u>) follow the all or none law.

   5-3. Put the five steps of communication at the synapse in their correct order (by using the numbers 1 through 5):

   _____ (a) The reuptake of transmitters by the presynaptic neuron.

   _____ (b) The enzyme inactivation or drifting away of transmitters in the synapse.

   _____ (c) The synthesis and storage of transmitters.

   _____ (d) The binding of transmitters at receptor sites on the postsynaptic membrane.

   _____ (e) The release of transmitters into the synaptic cleft.

   5-4. Whether or not a neuron fires depends upon the balance between excitatory PSPs and _____ PSPs.

   5-5. Most neurons are interlocked in complex networks that are constantly changing, eliminating old networks and adding new ones. Which process, adding networks or pruning, plays the larger role in moulding the neural networks?

   5-6. Hebb described learning as involving changes that take place at the _____. Specifically, he postulated that "When an axon of Cell A is near enough to excite a cell B and repeatedly or persistently takes part in firing it, some growth process or metabolic change takes place in one or both cells such that A's efficiency, as one of the cells firing B, is _____."

6. **Discuss some of the functions of acetylcholine and the monoamine neurotransmitters.**

   6-1. Our moods, thoughts, and actions all depend on the action of neurotransmitters. For example, the movement of all muscles depends on _____ (ACh). Like other neurotransmitters, ACh can only bind to specific sites, much like a lock and _____. However, other chemical substances can fool the receptor sites. For example, an agonist such as nicotine can (<u>block/mimic</u>) the action of ACh, while an antagonist such as curare can (<u>block/mimic</u>) the action of ACh.

6-2. Three neurotransmitters, dopamine, norepinephrine, and serotonin, are collectively known as _____. Both Parkinson's and schizophrenia have been linked with alterations in _____ activity, while the mood changes found in depression have been linked to receptor sites for norepinephrine and _____. Serotonin also plays a key role in the regulation of _____and wakefulness and perhaps _____ behaviour in animals.

Answers: 6-1. acetylcholine, key, mimic, block **6-2.** monoamines, dopamine, serotonin, sleep, aggressive.

7. Discuss how GABA, glycine, glutamate, and endorphins are related to behaviour.

7-1. GABA and its partner glycine are peculiar in that they appear to produce only (<u>excitatory/inhibitory</u>) PSPs.

7-2. Glutamate is a major _____ neurotransmitter and contributes to learning and memory.

7-3. Endorphins are chemicals internally produced by the body that have effects similar to those produced by the drug _____and its derivatives. That is, they are able to reduce pain and also to induce _____, such as the "runner's high" sometimes experienced by joggers.

Answers: 7-1. inhibitory **7-2** excitatory **7-3.** opium, pleasure (or euphoria).

ORGANIZATION OF THE NERVOUS SYSTEM

8. Provide an overview of the peripheral nervous system, including its subdivisions.

With approximately 100 billion individual neurons to control, it is important that the central nervous system has some kind of organizational structure. This organizational structure is depicted in Figure 3.6 of the text (page 87), and it will prove helpful if you have this figure in front of you while answering the following questions.

8-1. Answer the following questions regarding the organization of the peripheral nervous system:

(a) What constitutes the peripheral nervous system?

(b) What two subdivisions make up the peripheral nervous system?

(c) What is the role of the afferent and efferent nerve fibres?

(d) What two subdivisions make up the autonomic nervous system?

(e) Describe the opposing roles of the sympathetic and parasympathetic nervous systems.

Answers: 8-1. (a) All of the nerves that lie outside of the brain and spinal cord. (b) The somatic nervous system and the autonomic nervous system. (c) Afferent fibres carry information inward from the periphery, while efferent fibres carry information outward to the periphery. (d) The sympathetic nervous system and the parasympathetic nervous system. (e) The sympathetic system prepares the body for fight or flight, and the parasympathetic system conserves the body's resources.

9. **Distinguish between the central nervous system and the peripheral nervous system.**

9-1. What are the two parts of the central nervous system?

9-2. What is the name given to all of the nerves that lie outside of the central nervous system?

Answers: 9-1. the brain and the spinal cord **9-2.** the peripheral nervous system.

LOOKING INSIDE THE BRAIN: RESEARCH METHODS

10. **Describe how the EEG, lesioning, ESB, and transcranial magnetic stimulation are used to investigate brain function.**

10-1. The electroencephalograph, or _____, is a device that can measure the brain's _____ activity. Electrodes are placed on the scalp, and the brain's electrical activity is then monitored by the EEG machine and transformed into line tracings called _____waves.

10-2. Answer the following questions regarding the use of lesioning and ESB to investigate brain function:

(a) What are some limitations of studying people such as H.M., who have suffered naturally occurring brain damage?

(b) What technique involves the actual destruction of brain tissue in order to examine the resulting effect on behaviour?

(c) What technique would most likely be employed by a neurosurgeon to map the brain of a patient?

(d) Which techniques employ the use of electrodes and electrical currents?

(e) In what fundamental way does lesioning differ from ESB?

(f) Who is the well-known Canadian neurosurgeon who mapped functions of the brain with mild electrical probes?

10-3. _____ _____ _____ is a technique that allows scientists to temporarily increase or decrease activity in a specific area of the brain. This allows, for example, the creation of "_____ _____" using a painless, noninvasive method, which in turns allows investigators to examine the function of various brain areas.

Answers: 10-1. EEG, electrical, brain **10-2.** (a) Few subjects are available, the location and severity of the damage can't be controlled, and numerous extraneous variables are present. (b) lesioning, (c) ESB, (d) lesioning and ESB, (e) Lesioning is used to actually destroy tissue, whereas ESB is used to merely elicit behaviour. (f) Penfield **10- 3.** Transcranial magnetic stimulation, virtual lesions.

11. Describe the new brain imaging methods that are used to study brain structure and function.

11-1. There are three new kinds of brain-imaging procedures that have come into recent use. One of these procedures consists of a computer-enhanced X-ray machine that compiles multiple X-rays of the brain into a single, vivid picture. The resulting images are called _____ scans. An even newer device that produces clearer three-dimensional images of the brain goes by the name of magnetic resonance imaging scanner, and the images it produces are known as _____ scans.

11-2. Unlike CT and MRI scans, which can show only the structure of the brain, the positron emission tomography scanner can portray the brain's actual _____ across time. The images produced by this procedure are called _____ scans. Newer variations of MRI scans can also monitor brain activity, such as blood and oxygen flow, and thus provide both functional and structural information. These scans are called _____ magnetic images (fMRI).

Answers: **11-1.** CT, MRI **11-2.** activity, PET, functional.

THE BRAIN AND BEHAVIOUR

12. Summarize the key functions of the medulla, pons, cerebellum, and midbrain.

12-1. Three separate structures make up the hindbrain: the cerebellum, the pons, and the medulla. Identify these structures from the descriptions given below.

(a) This structure is essential for executing and coordinating physical movement.

(b) This structure attaches to the top of the spinal cord and controls many essential functions, such as breathing and circulation.

(c) This structure forms a bridge of fibres between the brainstem and cerebellum and plays an important role in both sleep and arousal.

12.2 Helping to locate objects in space is one of the major roles of the _____. In addition, dopamine-releasing neurons originate here and help to regulate the performance of _____ movements carried out by higher brain centres. It also shares a structure with the hindbrain that is essential for the regulation of sleep and wakefulness as well as modulation of muscular reflexes, breathing, and pain perception. This structure is called the _____ formation.

Answers: **12-1.** (a) cerebellum, (b) medulla, (c) pons **12-2.** midbrain, voluntary, reticular.

13. Summarize the key functions of the thalamus and hypothalamus.

13-1. The structure that serves as a way station for all sensory information headed for the brain is called the _____. The thalamus also appears to play an active role in _____ sensory information.

13-2. In addition to its role in controlling the autonomic nervous system and linking the brain to the endocrine system, the hypothalamus also plays a major role in regulating basic biological drives, such as fighting, _____, feeding, and _____.

Answers: **13-1.** thalamus, integrating **13-2.** fleeing, mating.

14. **Describe the nature and location of the limbic system, and summarize some of its key functions.**

   14-1. An interconnected network of structures involved in the control of emotion, motivation, and memory is collectively known as the _____ system. The hippocampus, for example, appears to play a key role in the formation of _____. However, the limbic system is best known for its role as the seat of _____. Electrical stimulation of particular areas of the limbic system in rats (particularly in the medial forebrain bundle) appears to produce intense _____. These "pleasure centres" actually appear to be neural circuits that release the neurotransmitter _____.

   Answers: 14-1. limbic, memories, emotion, pleasure, dopamine.

15. **Name the four lobes in the cerebral cortex, and identify some of their key functions.**

   15-1. The cerebrum is the brain structure that is responsible for our most complex _____ activities. Its folded outer surface is called the _____ cortex. The cerebrum is divided into two halves, known as the right and _____ cerebral hemispheres. The two hemispheres communicate with each other by means of a wide band of fibres called the _____ _____.

   15-2. Each cerebral hemisphere is divided into four parts called lobes. Match these four lobes (frontal, parietal, occipital, temporal) with their key function: (Hint: you can remember these, in order starting from the front of the hemisphere and going around clockwise, with the acronym "FPOT").

   _____ (a) Contains the primary motor cortex, which controls the movement of muscles.

   _____ (b) Contains the primary visual cortex, which initiates the processing of visual information.

   _____ (c) Contains the primary auditory cortex, which initiates the processing of auditory information.

   _____ (d) Contains the primary somatosensory cortex, which registers the sense of touch.

   15-3. The prefrontal cortex seems to play an active role in higher order functions involving working memory and relational reasoning, suggesting to some that it serves as an "executive _____ system."

   Answers: 15-1. mental, cerebral, left, corpus callosum 15-2. (a) frontal, (b) occipital, (c) temporal, (d) parietal 15-3. control.

16. **Summarize evidence on the brain's plasticity.**

   16-1. The brain's ability to change structure and function is known as plasticity. One line of evidence supporting plasticity is that _____ can sculpt the brain, as when string musicians show an enlarged representation of left-hand fingers in the somatosensory cortex.

16-2. A second line of evidence for plasticity is that neural reorganization often follows _____ of brain tissue.

16-3. A third line of evidence is _____, or the formation of new neurons. Adults have been shown to form new neurons in the olfactory bulb and the _____. Some researchers believe that neurogenesis helps contribute to the natural repair processes that occur after brain damage.

Answers: **16-1.** experience **16-2.** destruction **16-3.** neurogenesis, hippocampus.

RIGHT BRAIN/LEFT BRAIN: CEREBRAL LATERALITY

17. **Explain why scientists viewed the left hemisphere as the dominant hemisphere, and describe how split-brain research changed this view.**

17-1. Until recent years, it was believed that the left hemisphere dominated a submissive right hemisphere. Evidence for this belief came from several sources which all seemed to indicate that the left hemisphere played the dominant role with respect to the use of _____. For example, damage to an area in the frontal lobe known as _____ area was associated with speech deficits. Also, damage to another area, located in the temporal lobe, was found to be associated with difficulty in speech comprehension. This area is called _____ area. Both of these areas are located in the _____ cerebral hemisphere.

17-2. Answer the following questions regarding split-brain research:

(a) What was the result of severing the corpus callosum in these patients?

(b) Which hemisphere was found to be primarily responsible for verbal and language tasks in general?

(c) Which hemisphere was found to be primarily responsible for visual and spatial tasks?

17-3. What can be concluded with respect to hemispheric domination from split-brain studies?

Answers: **17-1.** language, Broca's, Wernicke's, left **17-2.** (a) The two cerebral hemispheres could no longer communicate with each other. (b) the left cerebral hemisphere. (c) the right cerebral hemisphere **17-3.** Neither hemisphere dominates; rather, each has its own specialized tasks.

18. **Describe how neuroscientists conduct research on cerebral specialization in normal subjects and what this research has revealed.**

18-1. Canadian researchers have compared younger and older children on their ability to perform a task involving integration across the two hemispheres. They showed that _____ children, who have a less mature _____ _____, performed less well on such a task, suggesting that a mature corpus callosum is necessary for integration of information across the two hemispheres.

18-2. Researchers have looked at left-right imbalances in the speed of visual or auditory processing in the two hemispheres and (have/have not) observed perceptual asymmetries in normal subjects.

18-3. Answer the following questions regarding the conclusions that can be drawn from the research on hemispheric asymmetry:

(a) Are you more likely to identify verbal stimuli quickly and accurately when presented to the right visual field (left hemisphere) or when presented to the left visual field (right hemisphere)?

(b) Are you more likely to identify visual-spatial information quickly and accurately, such as recognizing a face, when the stimuli are presented to the right visual field (left hemisphere) or when presented to the left visual field (right hemisphere)?

(c) What conclusions can be drawn from the research on normal subjects regarding hemispheric specialization with respect to cognitive tasks?

Answers: **18-1.** younger, corpus callosum **18-2.** have **18-3.** (a) when presented to the right visual field (left hemisphere), (b) when presented to the left visual field (right hemisphere), (c) The two hemispheres are specialized to handle different cognitive tasks.

THE ENDOCRINE SYSTEM: ANOTHER WAY TO COMMUNICATE

19. **Describe some of the ways in which hormones regulate behaviour.**

19-1. Answer the following questions regarding the workings of the endocrine system:

(a) What is the role played by the hormones in the endocrine system?

(b) While many glands comprise the endocrine system, which one functions as a master gland to control the others?

(c) What structure is the real power behind the throne here?

19-2. Fill in the boxes in the diagram below showing the role of the pituitary gland in the "fight or flight" response to stress.

Hypothalamus	⇨		⇨	ACTH hormone	⇨	

19-3. What is the role of sexual hormones

(a) Prior to birth?

(b) At puberty?

19-4. Research has examined whether circulating hormones are associated with behaviour. For example, there is evidence that levels of _____ regulate reproductive and pair-bonding behaviours, including feelings of _____ and _____ toward others.

Answers: 19-1. (a) They serve as chemical messengers. (b) the pituitary gland, (c) the hypothalamus **19-2.** pituitary, adrenal gland **19-3.** (a) They direct the formation of the external sexual organs. (b) They are responsible for the emergence of the secondary sexual characteristics. **19-4.** oxytocin, empathy, trust.

HEREDITY AND BEHAVIOUR: IS IT ALL IN THE GENES?

20. Describe the structures and processes involved in genetic transmission.

20-1. When a human sperm and egg unite at conception they form a one-celled organism called a _____. This cell contains 46 chromosomes, half of which are contributed by each _____, thus making 23 pairs. Each member of a pair operates in conjunction with its _____ member. The zygote then evolves to form all of the cells in the body, each of which have _____ pairs of chromosomes.

20-2. Each chromosome is actually a threadlike strand of a _____ molecule, and along this threadlike structure are found the individual units of information, called _____, that determine our biological makeup. Like chromosomes, genes operate in _____. For example, type of ear lobe is determined by a pair of genes. If both parents contribute a gene for the same type, the child will inherit this type, and the two genes are said to be _____. If the parents contribute two different genes for the type of ear lobe, the genes are said to be _____, and the child will inherit the type carried by the dominant gene. When heterozygous genes are paired, the dominant gene masks the _____ gene.

Answers: **20-1.** zygote, parent, opposite, 23 **20-2.** DNA, genes, pairs, homozygous, heterozygous, recessive.

21. Explain the difference between genotype and phenotype and the meaning of polygenic inheritance.

21-1. Answer the following questions about the difference between genotype and phenotype:

(a) What are the two genes that make up your ear lobe type said to be?

(b) What is your resulting ear lobe type said to be?

(c) Can your genotype or phenotype change over time?

21-2. What is meant when it is said that most human traits are polygenic?

Answers: **21-1.** (a) your genotype, (b) your phenotype, (c) Only your phenotype can change.
21-2. They are determined by two or more pairs of genes.

22. Explain the special methods used to investigate the influence of heredity on behaviour.

22-1. If a trait is due to heredity, then more closely related members of a family should show (lesser/greater) resemblance on this trait than less closely related family members. Studies using this method are called _____ studies. Data gathered from family studies (can/cannot) furnish conclusive proof as to the heritability of a specific trait. Even when it is demonstrated that a particular trait is highly related to the degree of family relationship, the cause for this relationship could be either heredity or _____.

22-2. A second method in this line of investigation is to compare specific traits across identical twins and fraternal twins. This method, called _____ studies, assumes that inherited traits are much more likely to be found among (identical/fraternal) twins. These studies do in fact show that for many characteristics, such as intelligence and extraversion, the resemblance is closest for _____ twins. However, since identical twins are far from identical on these characteristics, _____factors must also play a role here.

22-3. A third method in this line of investigation is to study children who have been separated from their biological parents at a very early age and raised by adoptive parents. The idea behind these _____ studies is that if the adoptive children more closely resemble their biological parents with respect to a specific trait, then it can be assumed that _____ plays a major role. On the other hand, if the adoptive children more closely resemble their adoptive parents with respect to a specific trait it would indicate that _____ plays a major role. Studies using this method to study the heritability of intelligence have found that adoptive children _____ resemble their biological and adoptive parents on this particular trait. This would indicate that a trait such as intelligence is influenced by both heredity and _____.

22-4. The process of determining the location and chemical sequence of genes on specific chromosomes is called _____ _____. While single genes responsible for certain medical conditions have been identified, behavioural traits such as intelligence likely involve multiple genes. Such traits are said to be _____.

22-5. An emerging field which studies heritable changes in gene expression that do not involve modification to DNA is called _____. For example, environmental events can alter gene expression in a manner that (can/cannot) be passed on to successive generations.

Answers: 22-1. greater, family, cannot, environment **22-2.** twin, identical, identical, environmental **22-3.** adoption, heredity, environment, equally, environment **22-4.** genetic mapping, polygenic **22-5.** epigenetics, can.

23. Explain the four key insights that represent the essence of Darwin's theory.

23-1. Darwin's four key insights are listed below. Match each one with the statement that best reflects the essence of the insight.

1. Organisms vary in endless ways.

2. Some of these characteristics are heritable.

3. Organisms tend to reproduce faster than the available resources necessary for their survival.

4. If a specific heritable trait contributes to survival or reproductive fitness its prevalence will increase over generations.

_____ (a) The gazelle that runs the fastest is most likely to leave offspring behind.

_____ (b) Members of most species die from starvation or other side effects of overcrowding.

_____ (c) Birds fly, fish swim, and lions roar.

_____ (d) We all have some traits that are very similar to our grandparents'.

Answers: 23-1. 1 (c), 2 (d), 3 (b), 4 (a).

24. Describe some subsequent refinements to evolutionary theory.

24-1. Although contemporary theorists accept Darwin's basic theory of natural selection, they have found that natural selection operates on a gene pool that is also influenced by genetic drift, mutations, and gene flow. Match these terms with the definitions given below.

(a) Spontaneous, heritable changes in a piece of DNA can occur in an individual organism.

_____

(b) Gene frequencies in a population can shift because of emigration (out flow) and immigration (in flow). _____

(c) There can be random fluctuations in a gene pool. _____

Answers: 24-1. (a) mutation, (b) gene flow, (c) genetic drift.

25. Provide some examples of animal behaviour that represent adaptations.

25-1. Answer the following questions about behavioural adaptations:

(a) What advantage do grasshoppers gain by being camouflaged? _____

(b) What advantage do gazelles that stop gain when spotting a cheetah? _____

Answers: 25-1. (a) It makes detection by a predator more difficult. (b) It increases their chances of escaping.

PUTTING IT IN PERSPECTIVE

26. Explain how this chapter highlighted three of the text's unifying themes.

26-1. Indicate which of the three unifying themes (heredity and environment jointly influence behaviour, behaviour is determined by multiple causes, and psychology is empirical) is particularly illustrated in each of the following situations:

(a) The discovery of the numerous factors that lead to the development of schizophrenia disorders.

(b) The development of many new techniques and instruments that led to the discovery of cerebral specialization.

(c) A new look at the two major factors that influence the development of personal characteristics such as intelligence and temperament.

Answers: 26-1. (a) Behaviour is determined by multiple causes. (b) Psychology is empirical. (c) Heredity and environment jointly influence behaviour.

EVALUATING THE CONCEPT OF "TWO MINDS IN ONE"

27. Critically evaluate each of the five ideas on cerebral specialization and cognitive processes discussed in the chapter.

27-1. Your text lists five popular ideas that have found support among some neuroscientists and psychologists. These ideas are:

(a) The two hemispheres are _____ to process different cognitive tasks.

(b) Each hemisphere has its own independent stream of _____.

(c) The two hemispheres have _____ modes of thinking.

(d) People vary in their _____ on one hemisphere as opposed to the other.

27-2. We will now proceed through each of these five assumptions to show how each has to be qualified in light of currently available evidence.

(a) The idea that the left and right brains are specialized to handle different kinds of information (is/is not) supported by research. However, there is evidence that this specialization hardly occurs in some persons, while in other persons the specialization is reversed, particularly among _____handed persons. Moreover, most tasks require the ongoing cooperation of _____ hemispheres.

(b) The evidence that each hemisphere has its own mind, or stream of consciousness, is actually very weak, except for persons who have undergone _____-_____surgery. The resulting "two minds" in these patients appears to be a by-product of the surgery.

(c) The assertion that each hemisphere has its own mode of thinking is (plausible/confirmed). A big problem here, however, is that mode of thinking, or cognitive style, has proven difficult to both define and _____.

(d) The assertion that some people are left-brained while others are right-brained (is/is not) conclusive at this time. Abilities and personality characteristics (do/do not) appear to be influenced by brainedness.

(e) The notion that most schooling overlooks the education of the right brain (does/does not) really make sense. Since both hemispheres are almost always sharing in accomplishing an ongoing task, it would be _____ to teach only one hemisphere at a time.

Answers: 27-1. (a) specialized, (b) consciousness, (c) different, (d) reliance (dependence)
27-2. (a) is, left-, both, (b) split-brain, (c) plausible, measure, (d) is not, do not, (e) does not, impossible.

28. Explain how neuroscience research has been overextrapolated by some education and child care advocates who have campaigned for infant schooling.

28-1.   Answer the following questions regarding neuroscience research:

(a) What happened to kittens deprived of light to one eye for the first four to six weeks of life?

(b) What happened to kittens deprived of light to one eye for the same amount of time after four months of age?

(c) What is the name given to that early period in the kitten's life when light is essential for the normal development of vision?

(d) What difference was found in synapses in rats that were raised in "enriched" environments when compared to rats raised in "impoverished" environments?

28-2. Answer the following questions regarding the overextrapolation of neuroscience findings:

(a) What findings argue against the notion that brain development is more malleable during the first three years of life?

(b) There are findings that argue against the notion that greater synaptic density is associated with greater intelligence. Which of the following is correct?

    1. Infant animals and human beings begin life with an overabundance of synaptic connections.

    2. Infant animals and human beings begin life with an insufficient number of synaptic connections.

    3. Learning involves the pruning of inactive synapses and reinforcing heavily used neural pathways.

Answers: 28-1. (a) They became blind in the light-deprived eye. (b) They did not suffer blindness in that eye. (c) critical period, (d) They had more synapses. **28-2.** (a) It has been found that the brain remains malleable throughout life. (b) 1 and 3 are correct.

REVIEW OF KEY TERMS

Absolute refractory period
Action potential
Adaptation
Adoption studies
Afferent nerve fibres
Agonist
Antagonist
Autonomic nervous system (ANS)
Axon
Behavioural genetics
Central nervous system (CNS)
Cerebral cortex
Cerebral hemispheres
Cerebrospinal fluid (CSF)
Chromosomes
Corpus callosum
Critical period
Dendrites
Dominant gene
Efferent nerve fibres
Electrical stimulation of the brain (ESB)
Electroencephalograph (EEG)
Endocrine system

Endorphins
Epigenetics
Excitatory PSP
Family studies
Fitness
Forebrain
Fraternal (dizygotic) twins
Genes
Genetic mapping
Genotype
Glia
Heterozygous condition
Hindbrain
Homozygous condition
Hormones
Hypothalamus
Identical (monozygotic) twins
Inclusive fitness
Inhibitory PSP
Lesioning
Limbic system
Midbrain
Mutation
Myelin sheath
Natural selection
Nerves

Neurogenesis
Neurons
Neurotransmitters
Oxytocin
Parasympathetic division
Perceptual asymmetries
Peripheral nervous system
Phenotype
Pituitary gland
Polygenic traits
Postsynaptic potential (PSP)
Recessive gene
Resting potential
Reuptake
Soma
Somatic nervous system
Split-brain surgery
Sympathetic division
Synapse
Synaptic cleft
Terminal buttons
Testosterone
Thalamus
Transcranial magnetic stimulation
Twin studies
Zygote

_____   1. An inherited characteristic that increased in a population (through natural selection) because it helped solve a problem of survival or reproduction during the time it emerged.

_____   2. A limited time span for the development of an organism that is optimal for certain capacities to emerge because the organism is especially responsive to certain experiences.

_____   3. Refers to the reproductive success of an individual organism relative to the average reproductive success in the population.

_____   4. Individual cells in the nervous system that receive, integrate, and transmit information.

_____   5. Neuron part that contains the cell nucleus and much of the chemical machinery common to most cells.

_____   6. Branchlike parts of a neuron that are specialized to receive information.

_____   7. A long, thin fibre that transmits signals away from the soma to other neurons, or to muscles or glands.

_____   8. An insulating jacket, derived from glia cells, that encases some axons.

_____   9. Small knobs at the end of the axon that secrete chemicals called neurotransmitters.

_____ 10. A junction where information is transmitted between neurons.

_____ 11. The stable, negative charge of an inactive neuron.

_____ 12. A brief change in a neuron's electrical charge.

_____ 13. The minimum length of time after an action potential during which another action potential cannot begin.

_____ 14. A microscopic gap between the terminal buttons of the sending neuron and the cell membrane of another neuron.

_____ 15. Chemicals that transmit information from one neuron to another.

_____ 16. A voltage change at the receptor site of a neuron.

_____ 17. An electric potential that increases the likelihood that a postsynaptic neuron will fire action potentials.

_____ 18. An electric potential that decreases the likelihood that a postsynaptic neuron will fire action potentials.

_____ 19. A technique for assessing hereditary influence by examining blood relatives to see how much they resemble each other on a specific trait.

_____ 20. A chemical that mimics the action of a neurotransmitter.

_____ 21. A chemical that opposes the action of a neurotransmitter.

_____ 22. An entire family of internally produced chemicals that resemble opiates in structure and effects.

_____ 23. System that includes all those nerves that lie outside the brain and spinal cord.

_____ 24. Bundles of neuron fibres (axons) that travel together in the peripheral nervous system.

_____ 25. System made up of the nerves that connect to voluntary skeletal muscles and sensory receptors.

_____ 26. Axons that carry information inward to the central nervous system from the periphery of the body.

_____ 27. Axons that carry information outward from the central nervous system to the periphery of the body.

_____ 28. System made up of the nerves that connect to the heart, blood vessels, smooth muscles, and glands.

_____ 29. The branch of the autonomic nervous system that mobilizes the body's resources for emergencies.

_____ 30. The branch of the autonomic nervous system that generally conserves bodily resources.

_____ 31. System that consists of the brain and spinal cord.

_____ 32. A solution that fills the hollow cavities (ventricles) of the brain and circulates around the brain and spinal cord.

_____ 33. A device that monitors the electrical activity of the brain over time by means of recording electrodes attached to the surface of the scalp.

_____ 34. Assessing hereditary influence by comparing the resemblance of identical twins and fraternal twins on a trait.

_____ 35. Method that involves destroying a piece of the brain by means of a strong electric current delivered through an electrode.

_____ 36. Method that involves sending a weak electric current into a brain structure to stimulate (activate) it.

_____ 37. Part of the brain that includes the cerebellum and two structures found in the lower part of the brainstem, the medulla and the pons.

_____ 38. The segment of the brainstem that lies between the hindbrain and the forebrain.

_____ 39. Part of the brain encompassing the thalamus, hypothalamus, limbic system, and cerebrum.

_____ 40. A structure in the forebrain through which all sensory information (except smell) must pass to get to the cerebral cortex.

_____ 41. A structure found near the base of the forebrain that is involved in the regulation of basic biological needs.

_____ 42. A densely connected network of structures located beneath the cerebral cortex, involved in the control of emotion, motivation, and memory.

_____ 43. The convoluted outer layer of the cerebrum.

_____ 44. The right and left halves of the cerebrum.

_____ 45. The structure that connects the two cerebral hemispheres.

_____ 46. Assessing hereditary influence by examining the resemblance between adopted children and both their adoptive and their biological parents.

_____ 47. Surgery in which the corpus callosum is severed to reduce the severity of epileptic seizures.

_____ 48. System of glands that secrete chemicals into the bloodstream that help control bodily functioning.

_____ 49. The chemical substances released by the endocrine glands.

_____ 50. The "master gland" of the endocrine system.

_____ 51. Threadlike strands of DNA molecules that carry genetic information.

_____ 52. A one-celled organism formed by the union of a sperm and an egg.

_____ 53. DNA segments that serve as the key functional units in hereditary transmission.

_____ 54. A gene that is expressed when the paired genes are different (heterozygous).

_____ 55. A gene that is masked when paired genes are heterozygous.

_____ 56. A person's genetic makeup.

_____ 57. The ways in which a person's genotype is manifested in observable characteristics.

_____ 58. Characteristics that are influenced by more than one pair of genes.

_____ 59. The sum of an individual's own reproductive success, plus the effects the organism has on the reproductive success of related others.

_____ 60. Left–right imbalances between the cerebral hemispheres in the speed of visual or auditory processing.

_____ 61. A spontaneous, inheritable change in a piece of DNA that occurs in an individual organism.

_____ 62. An interdisciplinary field that studies the influence of genetic factors on behavioural traits.

_____ 63. The two genes in a specific pair are the same.

_____ 64. The two genes in a specific pair are different.

_____ 65. Twins that emerge from one zygote that splits.

_____ 66. Twins that result when two eggs are fertilized simultaneously by different sperm cells, forming two separate zygotes.

_____ 67. The process of determining the location and chemical sequence of specific genes on specific chromosomes.

_____ 68. Posits that heritable characteristics that provide a survival or reproductive advantage are more likely than alternative characteristics to be passed on to subsequent generations and thus come to be selected over time.

_____ 69. A process in which neurotransmitters are sponged up from the synaptic cleft by the presynaptic neuron.

_____ 70. Cells that provide various types of support for neurons.

_____ 71. The formation of new neurons.

_____ 72. A male sex hormone produced by the testes.

_____ 73. A technique that allows scientists to temporarily increase or decrease activity in an area of the brain.

_____ 74. Influences on gene expression that do not involved changes to the DNA sequence.

_____ 75. A hormone involved in mating behaviour.

Answers: 1. adaptation **2.** critical period **3.** fitness **4.** neurons **5.** soma **6.** dendrites **7.** axon **8.** myelin sheath **9.** terminal buttons **10.** synapse **11.** resting potential **12.** action potential **13.** absolute refractory period **14.** synaptic cleft **15.** neurotransmitters **16.** postsynaptic potential (PSP) **17.** excitatory PSP **18.** inhibitory PSP **19.** family studies **20.** agonist **21.** antagonist **22.** endorphins **23.** peripheral nervous system **24.** nerves **25.** somatic nervous system **26.** afferent nerve fibres **27.** efferent nerve fibres **28.** autonomic nervous system (ANS) **29** sympathetic division **30.** parasympathetic division **31.** central nervous system (CNS) **32.** cerebrospinal fluid (CSF) **33.** electroencephalograph (EEG) **34.** twin studies **35.** lesioning **36.** electrical stimulation of the brain (ESB) **37.** hindbrain **38.** midbrain **39.** forebrain **40.** thalamus **41.** hypothalamus **42.** limbic system **43.** cerebral cortex **44.** cerebral hemispheres **45.** corpus callosum **46.** adoption studies **47.** split-brain surgery **48.** endocrine system **49.** hormones **50.** pituitary gland **51.** chromosomes **52.** zygote **36.** genes **54.** dominant gene **55.** recessive gene **56.** genotype **57.** phenotype **58.** polygenic traits **59.** inclusive fitness **60.** perceptual asymmetries **61.** mutation **62.** behavioural genetics **63.** homozygotic condition **64.** heterozygotic condition **65.** identical (monozygotic) twins **66.** fraternal (dizygotic) twins **67.** genetic mapping **68.** natural selection **69.** reuptake **70.** glia **71.** neurogenesis. **72.** testosterone. **73.** transcranial magnetic stimulation **74.** epigenetics **75.** oxytocin.

REVIEW OF KEY PEOPLE

John Connelly
Charles Darwin
Alan Hodgkin and Andrew Huxley
Roger Sperry and Michael Gazzaniga
Doreen Kimura

Sandra Witelson
James Olds
Candice Pert and Solomon Snyder
Donald Hebb
Bryan Kolb

Maryse Lassonde
Robert Plomin
Wilder Penfield
Brenda Milner
Doug Crawford

_____ **1.** Unlocked the mystery of the neural impulse.

_____ **2.** Known for their work with the split-brain.

_____ **3.** Showed that morphine works by binding to specific receptors.

_____ **4.** Discovered "pleasure-centres" in the limbic system.

_____ **5.** One of the leading behaviour genetics researchers in the past decade.

_____ **6.** Identified natural selection as the mechanism that orchestrates the process of evolution.

_____ **7.** Studied H.M., who experienced anterograde amnesia.

_____ **8.** Described the "cell-assembly."

_____ **9.** Studied the effects of sex hormones on brain organization.

_____ **10.** Mapped the brain of epilepsy patients during neurosurgery.

_____ **11.** Compared the functioning of the corpus callosum in younger and older children.

_____ **12.** Studied the role of the parietal cortex in visual control of reaching.

_____ **13.** Has contributed significantly to the study of brain plasticity.

_____ **14.** Known for his work on "locked-in" syndrome using EEG.

_____ **15.** Studied the brain of Einstein.

Answers: 1. Hodgkin and Huxley **2.** Sperry and Gazzaniga **3.** Pert and Snyder **4.** Olds and Milner **5.** Plomin **6.** Darwin **7.** Milner **8.** Hebb **9.** Kimura **10.** Penfield **11.** Lassonde **12.** Crawford **13.** Kolb **14.** Connelly. **15.** Witelson.

1. How do most neurons transmit information?
   a. from one neuron to another
   b. from the outside world to the brain
   c. from the brain to the muscles
   d. from the brain to the glands

2. Which part of the neuron is responsible for receiving information from other neurons?
   a. cell body
   b. soma
   c. axon
   d. dendrites

3. What is the function of the myelin sheath?
   a. It permits faster transmission of the neural impulse.
   b. It releases the neurotransmitter substance.
   c. It adds structural strength.
   d. It receives the neurotransmitter substance.

4. What term refers to the change in polarity of a neuron that results from the inflow of positively charged ions and the outflow of negatively charged ions?
   a. presynaptic potential
   b. postsynaptic potential
   c. synaptic potential
   d. action potential

5. Which of the following carries out the task of passing a message from one neuron to another?
   a. myelin sheath
   b. glia cells
   c. action potential
   d. neurotransmitters

6. Which of the following techniques is often used by neurosurgeons to map the brain when performing brain surgery?
   a. EEG recordings
   b. ESB
   c. lesioning
   d. transcranial magnetic stimulation

7. What is the seat of emotion?
   a. reticular formation
   b. hindbrain
   c. limbic system
   d. forebrain

8. What part of the brain is most likely damaged in people who have difficulty with language and speech following an accident that resulted in injury to the brain?
   a. right cerebral hemisphere
   b. left cerebral hemisphere
   c. right cerebellum
   d. left cerebellum

9. During the fight-or-flight response, which of the following takes on the role of supervisor?
   a. adrenal gland
   b. pituitary gland
   c. hypothalamus
   d. parasympathetic nervous system

10. What is exemplified by a person's current weight and height?
    a. genotype
    b. phenotype
    c. psychotype
    d. biotype

11. Which of the following kinds of studies can reveal the specific genes that influence a particular trait?
    a. family studies
    b. twin studies
    c. adoption studies
    d. genetic mapping studies

12. What did the Featured Study describing the use of PET-scan technology to examine memory processing suggest about self-related tasks?
    a. They uniquely involved left prefrontal brain activity.
    b. They had no unique brain activity associated with them.
    c. They uniquely involved right prefrontal brain activity.
    d. They uniquely involved left and right parietal brain activity.

13. Which of the following hormones are involved in empathy and trust?
    a. oxytocin
    b. leptin
    c. endorphin
    d. melatonin

14. Which of the following statements about right and left brain is correct?
    a. The right side of the brain is the creative side.
    b. The right and left brains are specialized to handle different kinds of information.
    c. Language tasks are always handled by the left side of the brain.
    d. Most schooling overlooks the education of the right brain.

15. Which of the following is NOT one of Darwin's four key insights?
    a. Some characteristics are heritable.
    b. Organisms vary in endless ways.
    c. Genetic drift is a major factor in the evolution of species.
    d. Organisms tend to reproduce faster than available resources.

16. What term refers to the ability of the brain to alter its structure and function?
    a. elasticity
    b. plasticity
    c. flexibility
    d. alterability

17. Which of the following is represented by the evolution of species?
    a. a fact
    b. a theory with a few flaws
    c. a theory with many flaws
    d. a speculation not open to empirical verification

18. What do evolutionary analyses assume?
    a. Organisms are controlled by genetic determinism.
    b. Organisms have a motive to maximize reproductive fitness.
    c. Only the physically strongest organisms will survive.
    d. Organisms have a motive to copulate.

19. Which of the following statements about synaptic connections in the brain is correct?
    a. Human beings begin life with an insufficient number of synapses.
    b. Human beings begin life with an overabundance of synapses.
    c. All synaptic connections are present from birth.
    d. Brain development is only malleable during the first three years of life.

20. What term applies to the growth of new neurons?
    a. neurogenesis
    b. neurogrowth
    c. rejuvenation
    d. neural reinstatement

Answers: 1. a **2.** d **3.** a **4.** d **5.** d **6.** b **7.** c **8.** b **9.** c **10.** b **11.** d **12.** c **13.** a **14.** b **15.** c **16.** b **17.** a **18.** d **19.** b **20.** a.

Chapter Four

SENSATION AND PERCEPTION

REVIEW OF KEY IDEAS

PSYCHOPHYSICS: BASIC CONCEPTS AND ISSUES

1. **Explain how stimulus intensity is related to absolute thresholds.**

   1-1.   You are sitting on a secluded beach at sundown with a good friend. You make a bet as to who will first detect an evening star. Since you have just recently covered this chapter in your text, you explain to your friend that doing so involves the detection of a stimulus threshold. In this case, the first star that provides the minimal amount of stimulation that can be detected is said to have crossed the _____. All of our senses have thresholds, but research clearly shows that the minimal amount of stimulation necessary to be detected by any one of our senses (is/is not) always the same. Therefore, the absolute threshold is defined as the stimulus intensity that can be detected _____ % of the time.

   Answers: **1-1.** threshold, is not, 50.

2. **Explain Weber's law and Fechner's law.**

   2-1.   Weber's law states that the size of a just noticeable difference (JND) is a constant proportion of the intensity (size) of the initial stimulus. This means that as a stimulus increases in intensity, the JND increases proportionally as well. Therefore, it would be more difficult to detect a slight increase in the length of a (2-centimetre [1-inch]/40-centimetre [20-inch]) line, a slight decrease in a (quiet/loud) tone, or a slight increase in the weight of a (500-gram [30-ounce]/1500-gram[90-ounce]) object.

   2-2.   Fechner's law states that larger and larger increases in stimulus intensity are required to produce perceptible increments, or _____, in the magnitude of sensation. What this means is that as the intensity of a stimulus increases, the size of the JND we are able to detect (decreases/increases).

   Answers: **2-1.** 40-centimetre [20-inch], loud, 1500-gram[90-ounce] **2-2.** JNDs, increases.

3. **Explain the basic thrust of signal-detection theory.**

   3-1.   The major idea behind signal detection theory is that our ability to detect signals depends not only on the initial intensity of a stimulus, but also on other sensory and decision processes. One factor that is particularly important here is the criterion you set for how certain you must feel before you react (what are the gains from being correct and what are the losses from being incorrect). What other factor is particularly important here?

   3-2.   Define each of the four possible outcomes in signal-detection theory:

   (a) Hit: _____

   (b) Miss: _____

   (c) False alarm: _____

   (d) Correct rejection: _____

   Answers: 3-1. background noise **3-2.** (a) detecting a signal when it is present, (b) failing to detect a signal when it is present, (c) detecting a signal when it is absent, (d) not detecting a signal when it is absent.

4. **Describe some evidence on perception without awareness, and discuss the practical implications of subliminal perception.**

   4-1.   Answer the following questions about the study conducted by Karremans, Stroebe, and Claus (2006):

   (a) How did the researchers manipulate subliminal perception?

   (b) What was their major finding?

   4-2.   What general conclusions can be drawn from the research on subliminal perception with respect to its potential persuasive effects?

   Answers: 4-1. (a) During a task requiring visual detection, they subliminally presented the words "LIPTON ICE" to half of the participants, whereas others were subliminally presented with neutral words. (b) The group exposed to the "LIPTON ICE" stimulus later rated Lipton Iced tea more favourably in comparison with the other group. **4-2.** The effects are weak.

5. **Discuss the meaning and significance of sensory adaptation.**

    5-1.   Which of the following examples best illustrates what is meant by sensory adaptation?

        (a) You are unable to clearly hear the conversation at the next table even though it sounds intriguing, and you are straining to listen.

        (b) The strawberries you eat at grandma's farm at the age of 20 seem not to taste as good as those you ate at the age of 6.

        (c) The wonderful smell you encounter upon first entering the bakery seems to have declined considerably by the time you make your purchase and leave.

    5-2.   If you answered *c* to the above question you are right on track and understand that sensory adaptation involves a gradual _____ in sensitivity to prolonged stimulation. This automatic process means that we are likely to be less sensitive to the constants in our sensory environments as we are to the _____.

Answers: 5-1. c **5-2.** decrease, changes.

OUR SENSE OF SIGHT: THE VISUAL SYSTEM

6. **List the three properties of light and the aspects of visual perception that they influence.**

    6-1.   Before we can see anything, _____ must be present. There are three characteristics of light waves that directly affect how we perceive visual objects; match each of these characteristics with its psychological effect.

        _____ (a) wavelength   1. colour

        _____ (b) amplitude   2. saturation (or richness)

        _____ (c) purity   3. brightness

Answers: 6-1. light waves (or light), (a) 1, (b) 3, (c) 2.

7. **Describe the role of the lens and pupil in the functioning of the eye.**

    7-1.   Getting light rays entering the eye to properly focus on the retina is the job of the _____. It accomplishes this task by either thickening or flattening its curvature, a process called _____. Controlling the amount of light entering the eye is the job of the _____. It accomplishes this task by opening or closing the opening in the centre of the eye called the _____.

    7-2.   Eye movements, or _____, are considered necessary for optimal visual experience. For example, sensory adaptation would occur without such movements, causing objects to seem to disappear.

Answers: 7-1. lens, accommodation, iris, pupil. **7-2.** saccades.

8. **Describe the role of the retina in light sensitivity and in visual information processing.**

8-1. The structure that transforms the information contained in light rays into neural impulses that are then sent to the brain is called the _____. All of the axons carrying these neural impulses exit the eye at a single opening in the retina called the optic _____. Since the optic disk is actually a hole in the retina, this part of the retina cannot sense incoming visual information, and for this reason it is called the _____ spot.

8-2. The specialized receptor cells that are primarily responsible for visual acuity and colour vision are called the _____. The cones are mainly located in the centre of the retina in a tiny spot called the _____. The specialized receptor cells that lie outside of the fovea and toward the periphery of the retina are called the _____. The rods are primarily responsible for peripheral vision and for _____vision.

8-3. Both dark and light adaptation are primarily accomplished through _____ reactions in the rods and cones. This chemical reaction occurs more quickly in the _____, so they are quicker to show both dark adaptation and light adaptation.

8-4. Light rays striking the rods and cones initiate neural impulses that are then transmitted to _____ cells and then to _____cells. From here the visual information is transmitted to the brain via the axons running from the retina to the brain, collectively known as the _____ nerve.

8-5. The processing of visual information begins within the receiving area of a retinal cell, called the _____ field. Stimulation of the receptive field of a cell causes signals to be sent inward toward the brain and sideways, or _____, to nearby cells, thus allowing them to interact with one another. The most basic of these interactive effects, lateral antagonism, allows the retina to compare light falling in a specific area against the general lighting. This allows the visual system to compute the (relative/absolute) levels of light.

Answers: 8-1. retina, disk, blind **8-2.** cones, fovea, rods, night **8-3.** chemical, cones **8-4.** bipolar, ganglion, optic **8-5.** receptive, laterally, relative.

9. **Describe the routing of signals from the eye to the brain and the brain's role in visual information processing.**

9-1. Visual information from the right side of the visual field (Figure 4-13 in the text) exits from the retinas of both eyes via the optic nerves and meets at the _____ chiasm, where it is combined and sent to the _____ side of the brain. Visual information from the left side of the visual field follows a similar pattern, meeting at the optic chiasm, and is then sent on to the _____ side of the brain.

9-2. After leaving the optic chiasm on their way to the visual cortex, the optic nerve fibres diverge along two pathways. Fill in the missing parts of the pathways below.

Main pathway

(a) Optic chiasm>>>_____ _____ _____ (part of the thalamus)>>>Visual Cortex

Secondary pathway

(b) Optic chiasm>>> _____ >>> _____>>>Visual cortex

9-3. The main pathway is subdivided into the magnocellular and parvocellular pathways, which simultaneously extract _____ kinds of information from the same input.

(a) Which channel handles the perception of colour?

(b) Which channel handles the perception of brightness?

9-4. Because the cells in the visual cortex respond very selectively to specific features of complex stimuli, they have been described as _____detectors. There are two major types of cells in the visual cortex: simple cells and complex cells. Identify them from their descriptions below.

(a) These cells are particular about the width and orientation of a line but respond to any position in their receptive field.

(b) These cells are very particular about the width, orientation, and position of a line.

9-5. There is evidence that cats raised in an environment in which they are never exposed to horizontal lines experience a perceptual deficit on discrimination tasks involving horizontal lines, presumably because development of the _____ is responsive to visual input.

9-6. As signals move further along in the visual processing system the neurons become (less/more) specialized as to what turns them on, and the stimuli that will activate them become (less/more) complex. For example, cells in the temporal lobe along the "what" pathway best respond to pictures of human _____, which may reflect an evolved adaptation. Conditions such as visual _____, or the inability to recognize objects, as well as prosopagnosia, or the inability to recognize familiar faces, likely involve damage to the "what" pathway.

Answers: 9-1. optic, left, right **9-2.** (a) lateral geniculate nucleus, (b) superior colliculus, thalamus
9-3. different, (a) parvocellular, (b) magnocellular **9-4.** feature, (a) complex cells, (b) simple cells
9-5. cortex **9-6.** more, more, faces, agnosia.

10. **Identify different methods used in vision research and describe the McCollough Effect.**

   10-1.   Research methods used by vision researchers include scanning techniques such as

   _____, microelectrodes, and the study of _____ _____ individuals.

   10-2.   The McCollough Effect is an afterimage phenomenon that reflects both _____ and

   _____ (i.e., line orientation). The fact that some individuals with agnosia (who

   lacked awareness of line orientation) still experience the McCollough Effect suggests that

   the effect (does/does not) depend on conscious form perception.

   Answers: 10-1. *f*MRI, brain-damaged **10-2.** colour, pattern/form, does not.

11. **Discuss the trichromatic and opponent process theories of colour vision and the modern reconciliation of these theories.**

   11-1.   The trichromatic theory of colour vision, as its name suggests, proposes three different

   kinds of receptors (channels) for the three primary colours: red, _____, and

   _____. The opponent process theory of colour vision also proposes three

   channels for colour vision, but these channels are red versus _____, yellow

   versus _____, and black versus _____.

   11-2.   These two theories of colour vision can be used to explain different phenomenon. Use T

   (trichromatic) or O (opponent process) to indicate which theory best explains the following

   phenomena.

   _____ (a) The colour of an afterimage is the complement of the original colour.

   _____ (b) The different kinds of colour blindness suggest three different kinds of receptors.

   _____ (c) People describing colours often require at least four different names.

   11-3.   The evidence is now clear that both theories are (incorrect/correct). Each is needed to

   explain all of the phenomena associated with colour vision. Three different kinds of cones

   have been found in the retina, which are sensitive to each of the three primary colours; this

   supports the _____ theory. It has also been found that visual cells in the retina,

   the LGN, and the visual cortex respond in opposite (antagonistic) ways to complementary

   colours, thus supporting the _____ theory.

   Answers: 11-1. green, blue, green, blue, white **11-2.** (a) O, (b) T, (c) O **11-3.** correct, trichromatic, opponent process.

12. **Discuss examples of how colour can affect behaviour.**

   12-1.   People's psychological response to specific colours likely reflects both _____ and

   _____ processes. The colour red may signify danger for humans. Research has

   shown that the colour red (helps/hinders) performance by evoking avoidance tendencies.

   Other studies have shown that the colour red fosters greater _____.

   Answers: 12-1. learning, evolutionary, hinders, attraction.

13. Distinguish between top-down processing and bottom-up processing.

13-1. The same visual stimulus can result in radically different perceptions, and thus our perceptions of the world are (<u>subjective/objective</u>). We perceive what we expect to perceive (perceptual set) and we may not perceive the unexpected, a phenomenon called _____ blindness.

13-2. Answer the following questions regarding top-down and bottom-up processing:

(a) Which process appears to assume feature analysis, the process of detecting specific elements in visual input and assembling them into a more complex whole?

(b) Which process appears to account for our ability to rapidly recognize and read long strings of words?

(c) What does the text conclude about which theory is correct?

Answers: 13-1. subjective, inattentional **13-2.** (a) bottom-up processing, (b) top-down processing, (c) Both theories have a place in form perception.

14. Explain the basic premise of Gestalt psychology, and describe Gestalt principles of visual perception.

14-1. The Gestalt view of form perception assumes that form perception is not constructed out of individual elements; rather, the form, or whole, is said to be _____ than the sum of its individual elements. The illusion of movement, called the _____ phenomenon, is used to support the Gestalt view of form perception because the illusion of movement (<u>is/is not</u>) completely contained in the individual chunks of stimuli that give rise to it. In other words, the illusion, or whole, appears to be _____ than the sum of its parts.

14-2. Five Gestalt principles of visual perception are illustrated below. Match each illustration with its correct name.

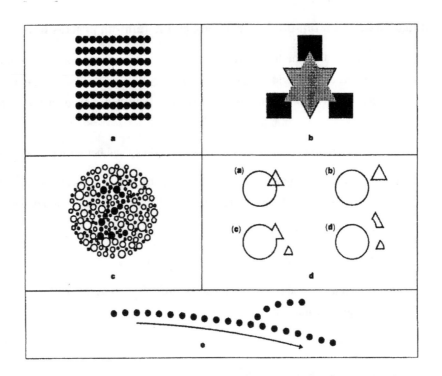

Proximity	(a) _____
Similarity	(b) _____
Continuity	(c) _____
Closure	(d) _____
Simplicity	(e) _____

14-3. What Gestalt principle is illustrated by the following:

(a) The words printed on this page appear to stand out from the white paper they are printed on?.

(b) Things moving in the same direction together get grouped together?.

Answers: 14-1. greater (or more), phi, is not, greater (or more) **14-2.** (a) proximity, (b) closure, (c) similarity, (d) simplicity, (e) continuity **14-3.** (a) figure and ground (b) common fate.

15. Explain how form perception can be a matter of formulating perceptual hypotheses.

15-1. The objects that surround us in the world outside of our bodies are called _____stimuli; the images the objects project on our retinas are called _____ stimuli. When perceived from different angles or distances, the same distal stimulus projects (<u>similar/different</u>) proximal images on the retina. This forces us to make perceptual _____ about the distal stimulus.

CHAPTER FOUR

Answers: 15-1. distal, proximal, different, hypotheses (or guesses).

16. Describe the monocular and binocular cues employed in depth perception.

16-1. There are two general kinds of cues that allow us to perceive depth. They are easy to remember because one kind involves the use of both eyes and is called _____ cues; the other kind requires the use of only one of the eyes and is called _____ cues. Depth perception (<u>does/does not</u>) require the use of both binocular and monocular cues.

16-2. Here are examples of two different kinds of binocular cues, retinal disparity and convergence. Identify each from these examples:

(a) As a person walks toward you your eyes turn inward.

(b) The images are slightly different on each retina and the differences change with distance.

16-3. There are two general kinds of monocular cues. One kind involves the active use of the eye, such as in the phenomenon of motion _____. The other general kind is used to indicate depth in flat pictures and thus is called _____ depth cues.

16-4. Identify the following pictorial cues:

(a) Parallel lines appear to grow closer as they recede into the distance.

(b) More distant objects appear to be higher in the field than nearer objects.

(c) When objects appear to be of the same size, closer ones appear larger than more distant ones.

(d) Near objects block or overlap more distant ones.

(e) Texture appears to grow finer as viewing distance increases.

(f) Patterns of light and dark suggest shadows that can create an impression of three-dimensional space.

17. **Describe perceptual constancies and illusions in vision, and discuss cultural variations in susceptibility to certain illusions.**

   17-1.   The tendency to experience stable perceptions in spite of constantly changing sensory input

   is called perceptual _____. For example, even though the retinal image

   shrinks as a friend walks away, she continues to appear her usual height. This is an example

   of _____ constancy.

   17-2.   Being fooled by the discrepancy between the appearance of a visual stimulus and its

   physical reality is what is meant by an optical _____. Both perceptual

   constancies and optical illusions illustrate the point that we are continually formulating

   _____ about what we perceive and also that these perceptions can be quite

   (subjective/objective).

   17-3.   What do the variations in cultural susceptibility to certain illusions tell us about our

   perceptual inferences?

18. **Describe the concepts of and the neuroanatomical correlates of vision for perception and vision for action.**

   18-1.   What are the two functions that vision serves?

   18-2.   The research of Goodale identified two visual pathways in the brain: The _____

   pathway is for perception of the external world, whereas the _____ pathway is for the

   visual control of action.

OUR SENSE OF HEARING: THE AUDITORY SYSTEM

19. **List the three properties of sound and the aspects of auditory perception that they influence.**

   19-1.   Name the perceived qualities that are associated with the following properties of sound

   waves.

Physical property	Description	Perceived Quality
(a) purity	kind of mixture	_____
(b) amplitude	wave height	_____
(c) wavelength	wave frequency	_____

Answers: 19-1. (a) timbre, (b) loudness, (c) pitch.

20. Summarize the information on human hearing capacities, and describe how sensory processing occurs in the ear.

20-1. Below are questions concerning human hearing capacities. Match the questions with their correct answers.

Answers	Questions
1. 90 to 120 decibels (dB)	___ (a) What is the frequency range of human hearing?
2. 1000 to 5000 Hz	___ (b) How loud do sounds have to be to cause damage to human hearing?
3. 20 to 20 000 Hz	___ (c) To what frequency range is human hearing the most sensitive?

20-2. Below is a scrambled sequence of events that occurs when a sound wave strikes the ear. Put these events in their correct order using the numbers 1 through 4.

_____ Fluid waves travel down the cochlea, causing the hair cells on the basilar membrane to vibrate.

_____ The pinna directs air to the eardrum.

_____ The hair cells convert fluid motion into neural impulses and send them to the brain.

_____ The motion of the vibrating eardrum is converted to fluid motion by the ossicles.

Answers: 20-1. (a) 3, (b) 1, (c) 2 **20-2.** 3, 1, 4, 2.

21. Compare and contrast the place and frequency theories of pitch perception, and discuss the resolution of the debate.

21-1. One theory of pitch perception assumes that the hair cells respond differentially to pitch depending on their location along the basilar membrane. This is the main idea of the _____ theory of pitch perception. A second theory assumes a one-to-one correspondence between the actual frequency of the sound wave and the frequency at which the entire basilar membrane vibrates. This is the main idea of the _____ theory of pitch perception.

21-2. Below are several facts uncovered by research. Tell which theory of pitch is supported by each of these facts.

(a) The hair cells vibrate in unison and not independently.

(b) Low frequency tones employ frequency coding to encode pitch.

(c) A wave pattern caused by the vibrating basilar membrane peaks at a particular place along the membrane.

21-3. The above facts mean that the perception of pitch depends on both _____ and _____ coding.

Answers: 21-1. place, frequency **21-2.** (a) frequency theory, (b) frequency theory, (c) place theory **21-3.** place, frequency.

22. Discuss the cues employed in auditory localization.

22-1. The sound shadow cast by the head is in a large part responsible for enhancing two important cues used for auditory localization. What are these two cues?

Answers: 22-1. The differences in the intensity and time of arrival of sound waves reaching each ear.

23. Describe the role of music experience in decoding speech prosody.

23-1. Musical aspects of speech, such as its intonation (melody) and stress and timing (rhythm) are referred to as _____ _____.

23-2. In the Featured Study, Thompson and his colleagues examined whether _____ _____ would enhance the ability to decode emotions from speech prosody. Overall, results of a series of studies suggested that musical training _____ participants' ability to decode emotions in speech.

Answers: 23-1. speech prosody **23-2.** musical training (Note: Other forms of training were also included), enhanced.

OUR CHEMICAL SENSES: TASTE AND SMELL

24. Describe the stimuli and receptors for taste, and discuss individual differences in taste perception.

24-1. The stimuli for taste perception are _____ absorbed in the saliva that stimulate taste cells located in the tongue's _____ _____. It is generally thought that there are four fundamental tastes; these are _____, _____, _____, and _____. Recently, a fifth primary taste has been identified, called _____.

24-2. What accounts for much of the wide variations in taste preferences among people?

24-3. What are some findings concerning "supertasters"?

Answers: **24-1.** chemicals; taste buds; sweet, sour, salty, bitter (in any order); umami. **24-2.** what they have been exposed to **24-3.** Supertasters are much more sensitive to sweet and bitter tastes. Supertasters are less fond of sweet and high-fat foods; they react more negatively to alcohol and tobacco; and they respond more negatively to many vegetables.

25. Describe the stimuli and receptors for smell, discuss how well people perform in odour identification tasks, and discuss the role of pheromones.

25-1. The stimuli for the sense of smell are _____ molecules floating in the air. The receptors for smell are hairlike structures located in the nasal passages called

_____ _____. In humans, the number of different types of olfactory receptors has been estimated to be _____. Specific odours probably trigger responses in different combinations of receptors. Human sensitivity to smell (does/does not) compare favourably with that of many other animals, although some animals surpass us in this respect.

25-2. _____ are imperceptible chemical messages sent by one organism to another member of the same species. Evidence of pheromones in humans includes the findings of McClintock, who showed that the menstrual cycles of women living together tend to

_____.

Answers: **25-1.** chemical, olfactory cilia, 350, does. **25-2.** Pheromones, converge.

OUR SENSE OF TOUCH: SENSORY SYSTEMS IN THE SKIN

26. Describe processes involved in the perception of pressure and temperature.

26-1. The statements below pertain to either the sense of pressure (P) or the sense of temperature (T). Indicate the correct answers below using the letters P or T.

_____ (a) The somatosensory area of the cortex is the primary receiving area for this sense.

_____ (b) Has receptors specific for either warmth or cold.

_____ (c) The free nerve endings in the skin are in patches that act like receptive fields in vision.

_____ (d) The free nerve endings in the skin fire spontaneously when no stimulus change is being experienced.

Answers: **26-1.** (a) P, (b) T, (c) P, (d) T.

27. Describe the two pathways along which pain signals travel, and discuss evidence that the perception of pain is subjective.

27-1. Pain signals travel to the brain by two slightly different pathways. One pathway sends signals directly and immediately through myelinated neurons to the cortex and is called the _____ pathway. The other sends signals to the cortex through unmyelinated neurons and is called the _____ pathway. The _____ pathway mediates lingering, less localized pain.

27-2. Many studies have demonstrated that the perception of pain can be affected by such factors as mood, ethnicity, culture, and context. Thus, the perception of pain is

_____.

Answers: 27-1. fast, slow, slow **27-2.** subjective.

28. Explain the gate-control theory of pain perception and recent findings related to it.

28-1. Answer the following questions regarding the perception of pain:

(a) What phenomenon did the gate-control theory of pain perception attempt to explain?

(b) What effect do endorphins have with respect to pain?

(c) What seems to be the role of the descending neural pathway that appears to originate in the periaqueductal grey (PAG) area in the midbrain?

28-2. Recent evidence has implicated _____ cells, such as astrocytes and microglia, in pain modulation.

Answers: 28-1. (a) why the perception of pain is so subjective, (b) an analgesic, or pain-relieving, effect, (c) It mediates the suppression of pain. **28-2.** glial.

OUR OTHER SENSES

29. Describe the perceptual experiences mediated by the kinaesthetic and vestibular senses.

29-1. The system that monitors the positions of various parts of the body is called the _____ system. This system sends information to the brain about body position and movement obtained from receptors located in the joints and _____.

29-2. The system that monitors the body's location in space is called the _____ system. The receptors for the vestibular system are primarily hair cells contained within the _____ canals in the inner ear.

29-3. What point does the text make about the kinaesthetic and vestibular systems, and indeed all sensory systems, in carrying out their tasks?

Answers: 29-1. kinaesthetic, muscles **29-2.** vestibular, semicircular **29-3.** They integrate information from other senses (in carrying out their tasks).

30. Explain how this chapter highlighted three of the text's unifying themes.

30-1. The fact that competing theories of both colour vision and pitch were eventually reconciled attests to the value of theoretical diversity. Why is this?

30-2. Why must our experience of the world always be highly subjective?

30-3. What do cultural variations in depth perception, taste preferences, and pain tolerance tell us about the physiological basis of perception?

Answers: **30-1.** They drove and guided the research that resolved the conflicts. **30-2.** The perceptual processes themselves are inherently subjective. **30-3.** That it is subject to cultural influences.

31. Discuss how the Impressionists, Cubists, and Surrealists used various principles of visual perception.

31-1. After reading the Application section in your text, try to answer the following questions by only looking at the paintings:

_____ (a) Which cubist painting depends particularly on the Gestalt principles of continuity and common fate for its effect?

_____ (b) Which surrealist painting makes use of a reversible figure to enhance a feeling of fantasy?

_____ (c) Which two impressionist paintings make use of colour mixing to illustrate how different spots of colours can be blended into a picture that is more than the sum of its parts?

_____ (d) Which cubist painting uses proximity, similarity, and closure to allow you to see its abstract subject (feature analysis applied to canvas)?

Answers: **31-1.** (a) Figure 4.57, (b) Figure 4.58, (c) Figures 4.54 and 4.55, (d) Figure 4.56.

32. Discuss how Escher, Vasarely, and Magritte used various principles of visual perception.

32-1. After reading the Application section in your text, try to answer the following questions by only looking at the paintings.

_____ (a) Which painting uses variations in context to make identical triangles appear very different?

_____ (b) Which two paintings incorporate impossible figures to achieve their effect?

_____ (c) Which painting makes particular use of texture gradient and light and dark shadow to convey the impression of depth?

Answers: 32-1. (a) Figure 4.62, (b) Figures 4.59 and 4.60, (c) Figure 4.61.

33. Explain how contrast effects can be manipulated to influence or distort judgments.

33-1. Which of the following contrast strategies, the door-in-the-face technique or employing comparitors, is being illustrated in the following situations:

(a) You want to hit the Florida beaches for spring break, but you need extra money from home. Realizing this is going to be a hard sell, you first ask for a week in Paris and then try to settle for the beaches.

(b) When your lover catches you in an indiscretion, you quickly point out many more serious infractions by friends and acquaintances.

33-2. Both of these strategies illustrate the point that our perceptions and judgments are _____.

Answers: 33-1. (a) the door-in-the-face technique, (b) employing comparitors **33-2.** subjective.

REVIEW OF KEY TERMS

Absolute threshold
Additive colour mixing
Afterimage
Auditory localization
Basilar membrane
Binocular depth cues
Bottom-up processing
Cochlea
Colour blindness
Comparitors
Complimentary colours
Cones
Convergence
Dark adaptation
Depth perception
Distal stimuli
Door-in-the-face technique
Farsightedness
Feature analysis
Feature detectors
Fechner's law
Fovea
Frequency theory
Gate-control theory

Gustatory system
Impossible figures
Just noticeable difference (JND)
Kinaesthetic system
Lateral antagonism
Lens
Light adaptation
Monocular cues
Motion parallax
Nearsightedness
Olfactory system
Opponent process theory
Optic chiasm
Optic disk
Optical illusion
Parallel processing
Perception
Perceptual constancy
Perceptual hypothesis
Perceptual set
Pheromones
Phi phenomenon
Pictorial depth cues
Place theory

Prosopagnosia
Proximal stimuli
Psychophysics
Pupil
Receptive field of a visual cell
Retina
Retinal disparity
Reversible figure
Rods
Saccades
Sensation
Sensory adaptation
Signal-detection theory
Subjective contours
Subliminal perception
Subtractive colour mixing
Threshold
Top-down processing
Trichromatic theory
Vestibular system
Visual agnosia
Weber's law

_____   1. The stimulation of sense organs.

_____   2. The selection, organization, and interpretation of sensory input.

_____   3. The study of how physical stimuli are translated into psychological (sensory) experience.

_____   4. A dividing point between energy levels that do and do not have a detectable effect.

_____   5. The minimum amount of stimulation that can be detected by an organism for a specific type of sensory input

_____   5. The minimum amount of stimulation that can be detected by an organism for a specific type of sensory input.

_____   6. The smallest amount of difference in the amount of stimulation that can be detected in a sense.

_____   7. States that the size of a just noticeable difference is a constant proportion of the size of the initial stimulus.

_____   8. Proposes that sensory sensitivity depends on a variety of factors besides the physical intensity of the stimulus.

_____   9. Involves a gradual decline in sensitivity to prolonged stimulation.

_____   10. States that larger and larger increases in stimulus intensity are required to produce perceptible increments in the magnitude of sensation.

_____   11. The transparent eye structure that focuses the light rays falling on the retina.

_____   12. The opening in the centre of the iris that helps regulate the amount of light passing into the rear chamber of the eye.

_____   13. The neural tissue lining the inside back surface of the eye that absorbs light, processes images, and sends visual information to the brain.

_____   14. Specialized receptors that play a key role in daylight vision and colour vision.

_____   15. Specialized receptors that play a key role in night vision and peripheral vision.

_____   16. A tiny spot in the centre of the retina that contains only cones, where visual acuity is greatest.

_____   17. The process in which the eyes become more sensitive to light in low illumination.

_____   18. The process in which the eyes become less sensitive to light in high illumination.

_____   19. A variety of deficiencies in the ability to distinguish among colours.

_____   20. The retinal area that, when stimulated, affects the firing of a particular cell.

_____   21. A hole in the retina where the optic nerve fibres exit the eye (the blind spot).

_____   22. Neurons that respond selectively to very specific features of more complex stimuli.

_____   23. Works by removing some wavelengths of light, leaving less light than was originally there.

_____   24. Works by superimposing lights, leaving more light in the mixture than in any one light by itself.

_____ 25. Proposes that the human eye has three types of receptors with differing sensitivities to different wavelengths.

_____ 26. Pairs of colours that can be added together to produce grey tones.

_____ 27. A visual image that persists after a stimulus is removed.

_____ 28. Proposes that colour is perceived in three channels, where an either-or response is made to pairs of antagonistic colours.

_____ 29. A drawing compatible with two different interpretations that can shift back and forth.

_____ 30. A readiness to perceive a stimulus in a particular way.

_____ 31. A process in which we detect specific elements in visual input and assemble these elements into a more complex form.

_____ 32. A progression from individual elements to the whole.

_____ 33. A progression from the whole to the individual elements.

_____ 34. An apparently inexplicable discrepancy between the appearance of a visual stimulus and its physical reality.

_____ 35. The illusion of movement created by presenting visual stimuli in rapid succession.

_____ 36. Stimuli that lie in the distance (in the world outside us).

_____ 37. The stimulus energies that impinge directly on our sensory receptors.

_____ 38. An inference about what distal stimuli could be responsible for the proximal stimuli sensed.

_____ 39. Involves our interpretation of visual cues that tell us how near or far away objects are.

_____ 40. Clues about distance that are obtained by comparing the differing views of two eyes.

_____ 41. Clues about distance that are obtained from the image in either eye alone.

_____ 42. A tendency to experience a stable perception in the face of constantly changing sensory input.

_____ 43. Locating the source of a sound in space.

_____ 44. A fluid-filled, coiled tunnel that makes up the largest part of the inner ear.

_____ 45. A membrane running the length of the cochlea that holds the actual auditory receptors, called hair cells.

_____ 46. Holds that our perception of pitch corresponds to the vibration of different portions, or places, along the basilar membrane.

_____ 47. Holds that our perception of pitch corresponds to the rate, or frequency, at which the entire basilar membrane vibrates.

_____ 48. Allows the retina to compare light falling in a specific area against the general lighting.

_____ 49. Our sense of taste.

_____ 50. Occurs when neural activity in a cell opposes activity in surrounding cells.

_____ 51. Objects that can be represented in two-dimensional figures but cannot exist in three-dimensional space.

_____ 52. Holds that incoming pain sensations pass through a "gate" in the spinal cord that can be opened or closed.

_____ 53. The sense that monitors the positions of the various parts of the body.

_____ 54. The system that provides the sense of balance.

_____ 55. The point at which the optic nerves from the inside half of each eye cross over and then project to the opposite half of the brain.

_____ 56. Clues about distance that can be given in a flat picture.

_____ 57. The registration of sensory input without conscious awareness.

_____ 58. Involves simultaneously extracting different kinds of information from the same input.

_____ 59. A case in which close objects are seen clearly but distant objects appear blurry.

_____ 60. A case in which distant objects are seen clearly but close objects are blurry.

_____ 61. A depth cue which refers to the fact that objects within 25 feet project images to slightly different locations on your right and left retinas, so the right and left eyes see slightly different images.

_____ 62. A binocular cue which involves sensing the eyes converging toward each other as they focus on closer objects.

_____ 63. A monocular depth cue which involves images of objects at different distances moving across the retina at different rates.

_____ 64. The inability to recognize familiar faces.

_____ 65. An inability to recognize familiar objects.

_____ 66. People, objects, events, and other standards that are used as a baseline for comparison in judgments.

_____ 67. Involves making a very large request that is likely to be turned down to increase the chances that people will agree to a smaller request.

_____ 68. Chemical messages sent by one organism to another member of the same species.

_____ 69. Brief fixations by the eyes as we scan the visual environment.

_____ 70. The perception of contours where none actually exist.

Answers: 1. sensation **2.** perception **3.** psychophysics **4.** threshold **5.** absolute threshold **6.** just noticeable difference (JND) **7.** Weber's law **8.** signal detection theory **9.** sensory adaptation **10.** Fechner's law **11.** lens **12.** pupil **13.** retina **14.** cones **15.** rods **16.** fovea **17.** dark adaptation **18.** light adaptation **19.** colour blindness **20.** receptive field of a visual cell **21.** optic disk **22.** feature detectors **23.** subtractive colour mixing **24.** additive colour mixing **25.** trichromatic theory of colour vision **26.** complementary colours **27.** afterimage **28.** opponent process theory of colour vision **29.** reversible figure **30.** perceptual set **31.** feature analysis **32.** bottom-up processing **33.** top-down processing **34.** optical illusions **35.** phi phenomenon **36.** distal stimuli **37.** proximal stimuli **38.** perceptual hypothesis **39.** depth perception **40.** binocular cues **41.** monocular cues **42.** perceptual constancy **43.** auditory localization **44.** cochlea **45.** basilar membrane **46.** place theory **47.** frequency theory **48.** lateral antagonism **49.** gustatory system **50.** olfactory system **51.** impossible figures **52.** gate-control theory **53.** kinaesthetic sense **54.** vestibular system **55.** optic chiasm **56.** pictorial depth cues **57.** subliminal perception **58.** parallel processing **59.** nearsightedness **60.** farsightedness **61.** retinal disparity **62.** convergence **63.** motion parallax **64.** prosopagnosia **65.** visual agnosia **66.** comparitors **67.** door-in-the-face technique **68.** pheromones **69.** saccades **70.** subjective contours illusion.

REVIEW OF KEY PEOPLE

Linda Bartoshuk   Herman von Helmholtz   Mel Goodale
Ronald Melzack and Patrick Wall   Gustav Fechner   Max Wertheimer
David Hubel and Torston Wiesel

_____   **1.** Pioneered the early work in the detection of thresholds.

_____   **2.** These two men won the Nobel prize for their discovery of
                                     feature detector cells in the retina.

_____   **3.** One of the originators of the trichromatic theory of colour
                                     vision.

_____   **4.** Made use of the phi phenomenon to illustrate some of the basic
                                     principles of Gestalt psychology.

_____   **5.** A leading authority on taste research.

_____   **6.** Proposed a gate-control theory of pain.

_____   **7.** Studied vision for perception and vision for action.

Answers: 1. Fechner **2.** Hubel and Wiesel **3.** Helmholtz **4.** Wertheimer **5.** Bartoshuk **6.** Melzack and
Wall **7.** Goodale.

SELF-QUIZ

1. We have gathered 50 people together to determine the absolute threshold of a particular tone. When
    will the absolute threshold have been reached?
    a. when the first person reports hearing the tone
    b. when all 50 people report hearing the tone
    c. when 25 people report hearing the tone
    d. when no one is able to hear the tone

2. What does research show about subliminal perception?
    a. It cannot be reliably demonstrated.
    b. It produces only weak effects.
    c. It can exert powerful effects.
    d. It does not show adaptation effects.

3. Which of the following places a major emphasis on subjective factors in the perception of
    thresholds?
    a. Weber's law
    b. Fechner's law
    c. Steven's power factor
    d. signal detection theory

4. What is the receiving area of a retinal cell called?
    a. cone
    b. fovial field
    c. rod
    d. receptive field

5. Typically, we are much more aware of the changes in our sensory environment than of the constants. This fact represents the general idea behind what concept?
   a. signal detection theory
   b. sensory adaptation
   c. the method of constant stimuli
   d. sensory equalization

6. What causes the major difference between a green light and a blue light?
   a. wave frequency
   b. wave purity
   c. wavelength
   d. wave saturation

7. Which theory of colour vision best explains why the colour of an afterimage is the complement of the original colour?
   a. the trichromatic theory
   b. the opponent process theory
   c. the pitch theory
   d. the frequency theory

8. Which of the following is the making of movies based upon?
   a. parallel processing
   b. lateral processing
   c. bottom-up processing
   d. phi phenomenon

9. Which of the following is NOT one of the pictorial depth cues?
   a. convergence
   b. linear perspective
   c. relative height
   d. texture gradients

10. Which of the following is an example of what is meant by perceptual constancy?
    a. Moths are always attracted to light.
    b. A round pie tin always appears to us as round.
    c. Proximal and distal stimuli are always identical.
    d. Absolute thresholds always remain the same.

11. What does gate-control theory attempt to explain?
    a. why the perception of pain is so subjective
    b. how subliminal perception works
    c. how receptive fields influence one another
    d. how the optic chiasm directs visual information

12. Considering human reactions to specific colours, which of the following is suggested by an evolutionary perspective?
    a. People learn to associate certain colours with particular experiences.
    b. Colour has had no influence on human behaviour.
    c. Certain colours have had adaptive significance for survival or reproduction.
    d. Men are more sensitive than women to the influence of colour on behaviour.

13. Which of the following is NOT considered to be a fundamental taste?
    a. sour
    b. sweet
    c. burnt
    d. bitter

14. Which of the following does NOT affect our sense of balance?
    a. semicircular canals
    b. kinesthetic sense
    c. visual cues
    d. umami detectors

15. Which of the following terms might best describe human perception?
    a. accurate
    b. objective
    c. subjective
    d. unknowable

16. What ability does musical experience possibly affect?
    a. detection of emotion conveyed in the speech of another person
    b. perception of certain objects
    c. smelling of certain odours
    d. experiencing of certain visual illusions, such as the Muller-Lyer illusion

17. What is the correct relationship between visual pathway and visual function?
    a. ventral stream and vision for perception
    b. rostral stream and vision for action
    c. dorsal stream and vision for perception
    d. rostral stream and vision for perception

18. When politicians point out that their misdeeds are miniscule when judged against their competitors, what procedure for affecting judgements is being used?
    a. the door-in-the-face technique
    b. the use of comparators
    c. the use of bottom-up processing
    d. the use of top-down processing

19. What evidence is associated with the convergence of the menstrual cycle among women who live together?
    a. pheromones
    b. hormones
    c. social learning
    d. sensory adaptation

Answers: 1. c **2.** b **3.** d **4.** d **5.** b **6.** c **7.** b **8.** d **9.** a **10.** b **11.** a **12.** c **13.** c **14.** d **15.** c **16.** a **17.** a **18.** b.
19. a.

Chapter Five

VARIATIONS IN CONSCIOUSNESS

REVIEW OF KEY IDEAS

ON THE NATURE OF CONSCIOUSNESS

1. **Discuss the nature of consciousness and the nature of unconscious thought effects.**

    1-1.   The personal awareness of internal and external events is how psychologists define
    _____. Consciousness is like a moving stream in that it is
    constantly_____.

    1-2.   _____-_____ describes people's experience of task-unrelated thoughts, which may
    take up 15–50% of people's time. Features of mind-wandering are that it is less likely to
    occur during tasks that require significant cognitive _____, it is associated with
    (more/less) accurate awareness of external information, and it may be associated with
    _____.

    1-3.   We control some mental processes, but others just seem to happen. _____ processes
    refer to thoughts or judgments that we exert some control over, whereas _____
    processes occur without intentional control or effort.

    1-4.   Unconscious thought involves less _____ than conscious thought. An advantage
    of unconscious thought is that is does not have the limitations in _____
    characteristic of conscious thought.

    1-5.   In the Featured Study on unconscious thought, it was predicted that unconscious thought
    might be superior to conscious thought when making _____ decisions. In the study,
    participants were given 12 pieces of information (some positive, some negative) about each
    of 3 roommates. One roommate was described very positively, one neutrally, and one
    negatively. Participants were either asked to choose their preferred roommate immediately,
    or were given either 4 minutes to think carefully about each potential roommate or 4
    minutes of distracting activity to prevent them from reflecting on their choice. Results
    showed that the distracted participants (who would rely on _____ thought) were most
    likely to choose the most favourable roommate, which seemed to reflect their ability to
    make more _____ judgments (i.e., ability to take more information into account).

Answers: 1-1. consciousness, changing **1-2.** Mind-wandering, resources, less, creativity **1-3.** Controlled,
automatic **1-4.** attention, capacity **1-5.** complex, unconscious, global.

2. Discuss the relationship between consciousness and EEG activity.

2-1. EEG recordings reveal that there (is/is not) some relationship between brain waves and levels of consciousness. There are four principal bands of brain wave activity, based on the frequency of the wave patterns. These are alpha, beta, delta, and theta. Identify these wave patterns from their descriptions given below.

_____ (a) alert (13–24 cps)   _____ (c) asleep (4–7 cps)

_____ (b) relaxed (8–12 cps)   _____ (d) deepest sleep (1–4 cps)

2-2. While variations in consciousness are correlated with variations in brain activity, the causal basis of this relationship remains _____.

Answers: 2-1. is, (a) beta, (b) alpha, (c) theta, (d) delta 2-2. unknown.

BIOLOGICAL RHYTHMS AND SLEEP

3. Summarize what is known about our biological clocks and their relationship to sleep.

3-1. One of the biological rhythms, the daily, or 24-hour, circadian rhythm, is influential in the regulation of sleep and wakefulness. This is accomplished through the regulation of several bodily processes, including body temperature. Describe below what happens to body temperature when we

(a) begin to fall asleep.

(b) continue into deeper sleep.

(c) begin to awaken.

3-2. There is evidence that exposure to _____ is responsible for regulating the 24-hour circadian clock. Sunlight affects the suprachiasmatic nucleus in the hypothalamus, which in turn signals the _____ gland. The pineal gland then secretes the hormone melatonin, which is a major player in adjusting biological clocks. Getting out of sync with the circadian rhythm is more likely to occur when the days are (shortened/lengthened). Shift work may also disrupt the circadian rhythm, as evidenced by increased _____ rates and poorer mental and physical health.

Answers: 3-1. (a) temperature decreases, (b) temperature continues to decrease, (c) temperature begins to increase 3-2. light (or sunlight), pineal, shortened, accident.

4. **Summarize the evidence on the value of melatonin and bright light for resetting biological clocks.**

    4-1. Research has shown that low doses of melatonin can (check those that apply):

        a. sometimes alleviate the effects of jet lag

        b. serve as an effective sedative for some people

        c. slow the aging process

        d. enhance sex

    4-2 Exposure to _____ _____ can also improve the sleep quality and alertness in shift workers, although the effects are modest.

Answers: 4-1. Only a and b are correct. **4-2.** bright light.

THE SLEEP AND WAKING CYCLE

5. **Describe how sleep research is conducted.**

    5-1. Sleep research is conducted by electronically monitoring various bodily activities, such as brain waves, muscular activity, eye movements, and so on, while persons actually _____ in a specially prepared laboratory setting. Through the use of a television camera or a window, researchers also _____ the subjects during sleep.

Answers: 5-1. sleep, observe (or watch).

6. **Describe how the sleep cycle evolves through the night.**

    6-1. Answer the following questions regarding the sleep cycle.

        (a) How many stages are there in one sleep cycle?

        (b) Which two stages make up slow-wave sleep?

        (c) Which brain waves are prominent during slow-wave sleep?

Answers: 6-1. (a) four (or five if you've included REM sleep), (b) 3 and 4, (c) delta.

7. **Compare and contrast REM and NREM sleep.**

    7-1. What particularly differentiates NREM sleep from rapid eye movement sleep, or _____ sleep, is that during REM sleep the brain wave pattern resembles that of a person who is wide _____. However, REM sleep is actually a fifth stage of sleep in which the muscle tone is extremely relaxed and the sleeper is almost _____. It is also during REM sleep that vivid _____ is most likely to occur.

    7-2. Research suggests that sleep may be important for consolidation of information acquired during the day. In addition, different sleep stages may be related to different types of

_____.

7-3. The sleep cycle is repeated approximately _____ times during an average night of sleep. NREM sleep dominates the early part of the sleep period, but _____ sleep and dreaming dominate the later stages of sleep. As one progresses through the night, the depth of NREM sleep tends to progressively (<u>increase/decrease</u>).

Answers: 7-1. REM, awake, paralyzed, dreaming **7-2.** learning **7-3.** four, REM, decrease.

8. Summarize age trends in patterns of sleep.

8-1. Not only do newborns sleep more frequently and for more total hours during a day than do adults, they also spend a greater proportion of time in _____ sleep. As they grow older, children move toward longer but (<u>more/less</u>) frequent sleep periods, and the total proportion of REM sleep declines from about 50% to the adult level of about _____%. During adulthood there is a gradual shift toward the (<u>lighter/deeper</u>) stages of sleep. Older adults appear to need _____ sleep, and they show a better tolerance for sleep deprivation.

Answers: 8-1. REM, less, 20, lighter, less.

9. Summarize how culture influences sleep patterns.

9-1. Answer the following questions regarding sleeping patterns across cultures.

(a) Which pattern, children sleeping with their parents (co-sleeping) or children sleeping alone, is the most widely practiced?

(b) Where are the "siesta" cultures generally located?

Answers: 9-1. (a) co-sleeping (b) tropical regions.

10. Discuss the neural basis of sleep.

10-1. Sleep and wakefulness is apparently under the control of several neural structures, but one that appears to be particularly essential for both sleep and wakefulness is the reticular _____. When a part of this system, called the ascending _____ _____ system (ARAS), is severed in cats, the cats remain in continuous _____. When the ARAS is stimulated in normal cats, they act _____.

Answers: 10-1. formation, reticular activating, sleep, alert (or awake).

11. Summarize evidence on the effects of complete and partial sleep deprivation.

11-1. Answer the following questions regarding the effects of different kinds of sleep deprivation.

(a) While both complete and partial sleep deprivation have a negative effect on mood and also on performance on both cognitive and perceptual-motor tasks, what is rather surprising about the degree of these negative effects?

(b) In what way might increased sleepiness be a major problem with respect to the workplace?

11-2. Pilcher and Walters showed that sleep-deprived students performed substantially worse on a cognitive task than nondeprived students. How did the sleep-deprived students rate their own effort, concentration, and performance?

11-3. Walker showed that sleep-deprived individuals show more activity in the _____ in response to negative photographs, and (more/less) connectivity between that structure and prefrontal control areas. This suggests that sleep-deprived individuals are more _____.

Answers: **11-1.** (a) The effects tend to be modest. (b) It can lead to increased accidents. **11-2.** They were unaware of these deficits. **11-3.** amygdala, less, emotional.

12. Discuss the effects of selective deprivation of REM sleep and slow-wave sleep, and the relationship between sleep loss and health.

12-1. Evidence suggests that REM sleep and slow-wave sleep (SWS) are necessary for memory consolidation of recent experiences. For example, there is a correlation between length of time spent in REM and SWS, on the one hand, and increments in _____, on the other. Reactivation of memories during sleep may also enhance memories in the brain, and sleep may foster _____ in relation to learning that took place the previous day. Finally, REM sleep may also be involved in the process of _____, or the forming of new neurons.

12-2. Sleep restriction has been shown to (increase/decrease) hunger and obesity. Sleep loss has also been associated with impaired _____ system functioning and increased inflammatory responses. Shorter sleep deprivation has also been linked with _____, hypertension, and cardiovascular disease. Mortality risk has been associated with either too little or too much sleep.

Answers: **12-1.** learning, creativity, neurogenesis **12-2.** increase, immune, diabetes.

13. Discuss the prevalence, causes, and treatments of insomnia.

13-1. As practically everybody will suffer from occasional bouts of insomnia, it is estimated that about _____ of adults will suffer from occasional insomnia, and of these about _____ will suffer from chronic problems with insomnia. There are three basic types of insomnia, which are easily remembered because one type occurs at the beginning of sleep, one type during sleep, and the third type at the end of sleep. Thus, one type involves difficulty in initially _____ asleep; one type involves difficulty in _____ asleep; and one type involves persistent _____ awakening.

13-2. While there are a number of different causes of insomnia, most of them appear to revolve around the anxiety and emotional reactions that result from the _____ of everyday living. Health problems and taking certain _____ can also be a factor. According to the _____ model of insomnia, some people are predisposed to insomnia due to their higher level of physiological arousal.

13-3. Two main classes of drugs for insomnia are _____ sedatives (e.g., Halcion) and _____ sedatives (e.g., Ambien). Unfortunately, these drugs can impair daytime functioning, and their effectiveness can weaken with prolonged use. Increased insomnia can be part of withdrawal symptoms when insomnia drugs are discontinued.

13-4. Longer-lasting benefits may occur with behavioural or _____-behavioural therapy (CBT). A recent meta-analysis suggests that between _____ and _____% of people with insomnia may benefit from CBT.

Answers: 13-1. 34–35%, 15–17%, falling, remaining, early 13-2. stress (or problems), drugs, hyperarousal 13-3. benzodiazepine, nonbenzodiazepine 13-4. cognitive, 70, 80.

14. Describe the symptoms of narcolepsy, sleep apnea, night terrors, nightmares, and somnambulism.

14-1. Described below are five different case histories of persons suffering from five different sleep disorders. Make the appropriate diagnosis for each one.

(a) Throckmorton is a young child who frequently wakes up during the night with a loud, piercing cry, but cannot describe what happened to him; he usually returns quickly to sleep. A night spent at the sleep clinic discloses that the episodes generally occur during NREM sleep. Throckmorton is most likely suffering from _____ _____.

(b) Gazelda reports that occasionally, even when typing a term paper or driving a car, she will quickly drop into a deep sleep. The sleep is often accompanied by dreams, which indicates REM sleep. Gazelda is most likely suffering from _____.

(c) Ajax is a young child who frequently wakes up terrified and relates vivid dreams to his parents, who rush to comfort him. The family physician tells the parents there is probably nothing to worry about unless these episodes persist, and that the child will most likely outgrow this problem. The diagnosis here is probably _____.

(d) Mr. Whistletoe will occasionally get up late at night and walk around the house. Unfortunately, Mr. Whistletoe is completely unaware of this behaviour and usually returns to bed without awakening. Upon awakening the next morning he is surprised by a new bruise on his leg, and he wonders how the chair in the living room got tipped over. Mr. Whistletoe would be diagnosed as suffering from _____, or sleep walking.

(e) Henrietta complains that during a night's sleep, she frequently wakes up gasping for breath. A visit to the sleep clinic discloses that, indeed, she does stop breathing for brief periods all through the night. Henrietta undoubtedly suffers from _____ _____.

(f) Frank, who is 52, yells and flails about during his REM dreams, sometimes becoming quite violent.

Answers: 14-1. (a) night terrors, (b) narcolepsy, (c) nightmares, (d) somnambulism, (e) sleep apnea, (f) REM sleep behaviour disorder.

THE WORLD OF DREAMS

15. Discuss the nature of dreams.

15-1. The conventional view of dreams is that they are mental experiences during REM sleep and often have a bizarre, story-like quality and vivid imagery. What do many theorists now think of this view?

15-2. In what way do nonREM dreams appear to differ from REM dreams?

Answers: 15-1. They question many aspects of this view. **15-2.** They are less vivid and less story-like.

16. Summarize findings on dream content.

16-1. Calvin Hall, who analyzed the contents of more than 10 000 dreams, concluded that the content of most dreams is (exotic/mundane). They tend to involve _____ settings and people.

16-2. A survey of first-year Canadian university students revealed that the most frequent types of dreams related to being _____ and to _____ experiences. Dreams distinctive to women tended to have (negative, positive) themes, including dreams related to phobias and anxiety. Nightmare frequency was about once every _____ _____.

16-3. What did Freud mean when he stated that our dreams reflect day residue?

16-4. What other factor has an inconsistent effect on our dreams?

Answers: 16-1. mundane, familiar **16-2.** chased (or pursued), sexual, negative, two weeks **16-3.** They are influenced by what happens to us in our daily lives. **16-4.** external stimuli (dripping water, ringing phones, etc.).

17. **Describe some cultural variations in beliefs about the nature and importance of dreams.**

17-1. Say which of the following statements about dreams is more characteristic of Western cultures (W) or nonWestern cultures (NW).

_____ (a) Little significance paid to the meaning of dreams.

_____ (b) Remembering dreams is important.

_____ (c) Dreams can be the focal point of existence.

_____ (d) Are likely to report frequent dreams involving food.

Answers: 17-1. (a) W, (b) NW, (c) NW, (d) persons from any culture who are chronically hungry.

18. **Describe the three theories of dreaming covered in the chapter.**

18-1. The text mentions three theories as to why we need to dream. Tell what cognitive purpose, if any, each of these theories proposes as to the purpose of dreaming.

(a) This was Sigmund Freud's theory about the need to dream.

(b) This theory proposed by Rosalind Cartwright is cognizant of the fact that dreams are not restricted by logic or reality.

(c) The activation-synthesis theory of Hobson and McCarley proposes that dreams occur as side effects of neural activation of the cortex by lower brain centres.

Answers: 18-1. (a) Dreams serve the purpose of wish fulfillment. (b) Dreams allow for creative problem-solving. (c) Dreams serve no cognitive purpose.

HYPNOSIS: ALTERED CONSCIOUSNESS OR ROLE PLAYING?

19. **Discuss hypnotic susceptibility, and list some prominent effects of hypnosis.**

19-1. While there are many different hypnotic induction techniques, they all lead to a heightened state of _____. Research shows that individuals (do/do not) vary in their susceptibility to hypnotic induction. In fact, approximately ____ – ____ % of the population do not respond at all, and approximately ____ – ____ % are highly susceptible to hypnotic induction. High hypnotizability comprises three components: _____, which is the capacity to reduce peripheral awareness and narrow the focus of one's attention; _____, which is the capacity to separate aspects of conscious experience; and _____, which is the tendency to uncritically accept directions and information.

19-2. The text lists several of the more prominent effects that can be produced by hypnosis.

Identify these effects from their descriptions given below.

(a) Reducing awareness of pain. _____

(b) Engaging in acts one would not ordinarily do. _____

(c) Perceiving things that do not exist or failing to perceive things that do exist.

_____

(d) Claiming that sour foods taste sweet. _____ _____

(e) Carrying out suggestions following the hypnotic induction session. _____

_____

(f) Claiming to forget what occurred during the induction session. _____

Answers: 19-1. suggestibility, do, 10–20, 10–15, absorption, dissociation, suggestibility **19-2.** (a) anaesthetic, (b) disinhibition, (c) hallucinations, (d) sensory distortions, (e) posthypnotic suggestions, (f) amnesia.

20. Explain the role-playing and altered-states theories of hypnosis.

20-1. A theory of hypnosis proposed by Barber and Spanos is that hypnosis is really a form of acting or role playing in which the subjects are simply acting as if they are hypnotized. What two lines of evidence support this theory?

20-2. A theory of hypnosis proposed by Hilgard is that hypnosis does in fact result in an altered state of consciousness. This theory holds that hypnosis results in a dissociation or _____ of consciousness into two parts. One half of the divided consciousness communicates with the hypnotist, while the other half remains _____, even from the hypnotized subject. In this case, pain perceived by the "hidden" part of the consciousness (is/is not) reported to the "aware" part of consciousness. The divided state of consciousness proposed by Hilgard (is/is not) a common experience in everyday life. One such example of this commonly experienced state is appropriately called highway _____.

Answers: 20-1. Nonhypnotized subjects can duplicate the feats of hypnotized subjects, and it has been shown that hypnotized subjects are often merely acting out their expectations of how hypnotized subjects should act. **20-2.** splitting (or dividing), hidden, is not, is, hypnosis.

MEDITATION: PURE CONSCIOUSNESS OR RELAXATION?

21. Summarize the evidence on the physiological correlates and long-term benefits of meditation.

21-1. Two types of meditation have been described: In _____ _____ approaches, such as Transcendental Meditation, attention is concentrated on a specific object or bodily sensation. In _____ _____ approaches, such as mindfulness meditation, attention is directed to the contents of one's moment-to-moment experiences. **21-2.** Certain short-term physiological changes may occur during meditation. One of the most prominent of these changes is that EEG brain waves change from the rapid beta waves to the slower _____ and theta waves. This change to slower waves is accompanied by (an increase/a decrease) in metabolic activity such as heart rate and oxygen consumption.

21-3. The claims made for the long-term effects of meditation may have some merit in that some studies have shown that subjects had lower levels of some stress hormones, improved mental health, and reduced anxiety and drug abuse. These changes can (also/not) be induced by other commonly used methods for inducing relaxation. Recent experiments show that meditation can _____ pain tolerance, perhaps reflecting increased brain thickness in brain regions that register pain.

Answers: 21-1. focused attention, open monitoring **21-2.** alpha, a decrease **21-3.** also, increase.

ALTERING CONSCIOUSNESS WITH DRUGS

22. List and describe the major types of abused drugs and their effects.

22-1. The 2004 Canadian Addiction Survey reported that 79% of Canadians had used _____ over the past year and 14% had used _____. More recent data from Health Canada shows that the use of cannabis by 15–24-year -olds has (increased/decreased) from 2004 to 2009. A major concern among youth is _____ drinking.

22-2. The text lists six different categories of psychoactive drugs; identify these drugs from the descriptions given below.

(a) This drug is the most widely used, and abused, of all psychoactive drugs and produces a relaxed euphoria that temporarily boosts self-esteem. Wine and beer are both examples of the drug _____.

(b) While this class of drugs derived from opium is effective at relieving pain, it can also produce a state of euphoria, which is the principal reason that opiates, or _____, are attractive to recreational users. A new drug in this class is oxycodone.

(c) The drugs in this class, such as LSD, mescaline, and psilocybin, are known for their ability to distort sensory and perceptual experiences, which is why they are given the collective name of _____.

(d) The drugs in this class include marijuana, hashish, and THC. Although they vary in potency, each of them can produce a mild and easygoing state of euphoria along with enhanced sensory awareness and a distorted sense of time. This class of drugs gets its name from the hemp plant _____, from which they are all derived.

(e) This class of drugs is known for its sleep-inducing (sedation) and behavioural depression effects, resulting in tension reduction and a relaxed state of intoxication. While there are several different drugs in this class, the barbiturates are the most widely abused. Commonly known as "downers," they are more properly called

_____.

(f) This class of drugs produces arousal in the central nervous system and ranges from mildly arousing drugs, such as caffeine and nicotine, to strongly arousing drugs, such as cocaine and the amphetamines. Known for their ability to produce an energetic euphoria, the drugs in this class go by the name of _____.

(g) This drug, also known as ecstasy, is a compound related to both amphetamines and mescaline and other hallucinogens. It produces a short-lived high.

Answers: 22-1. alcohol, cannabis, decreased, binge **22-2.** (a) alcohol, (b) narcotics, (c) hallucinogens, (d) cannabis, (e) sedatives, (f) stimulants, (g) MDMA.

23. **Explain why drug effects vary and how psychoactive drugs exert their effects in the brain.**

23-1. Taking a specific drug (<u>will/will not</u>) always have the same effect on the same person. This is because drug effects have _____ causation; individual, environmental, and drug factors can combine in many ways to produce the final effect. For example, one's expectations can strongly affect reactions to a drug. This is known as the _____ effect. Moreover, as one continues to take a specific drug, it requires a greater amount of the drug to achieve the same effect. This phenomenon is called drug _____.

23-2. Psychoactive drugs affect the CNS by selectively influencing _____ systems in a variety of ways. The action takes place at the juncture between neurons, called the _____. Amphetamines affect the neurotransmitters _____ (NE) and _____ (DA). Opiates bind to _____ receptors, which elevate the dopamine pathways that modulate _____. Receptors in the brain for THC, the active ingredient in marijuana, are called _____ receptors, which are normally activated by endocannabinoids.

23-3. It is now believed that virtually all abused drugs gain their reward effect by (<u>increasing/decreasing</u>) activity in the mesolimbic dopamine pathway, which has been characterized as the "_____ pathway."

Answers: 23-1. will not, multifactorial, placebo, tolerance **23-2.** neurotransmitter, synapse, norepinephrine, dopamine, reward, cannabinoid **23-3.** increasing, reward.

24. **Summarize which drugs carry the greatest risk of tolerance, physical dependence, and psychological dependence.**

24-1. When a person must continue taking a drug to avoid withdrawal illness, addiction, or _____ dependence is said to occur. Withdrawal symptoms may be seen as _____ responses triggered by stimuli paired with drug use in the past. When a person must continue taking a drug to satisfy intense emotional craving for the drug, then _____ dependence is said to occur.

24-2. The three riskiest drugs in terms of tolerance and physical and psychological dependence are

24-3. What physiological change in the brain appears to facilitate both physical and psychological dependence?

Answers: 24-1. physical, conditioned, psychological **24-2.** narcotics/opiates, sedatives, stimulants **24-3.** alterations in synaptic transmission.

25. Summarize evidence on the major physical health risks associated with drug abuse.

25-1. What two physical effects were found in the study in which rats were allowed unlimited access to heroin or cocaine, and which drug was the most deadly?

25-2. There are three major ways in which drugs may affect physical health. The most dramatic way is when a person takes too much of a drug, or drugs, and dies of an _____. Another way is when drug usage directly damages bodily tissue; this is referred to as a _____ effect. The third way is when drug usage results in accidents, improper eating and sleeping habits, infections, etc. These effects are collectively called _____effects. For example, alcohol can increase students' likelihood of engaging in _____ sexual behaviour.

Answers: 25-1. loss of body weight and death, cocaine **25-2.** overdose, direct, indirect, risky.

26. Discuss controversies about marijuana's health risks and preliminary evidence on the risks associated with MDMA use.

26-1. Say whether the following statements concerning marijuana are true or false.

_____ (a) Marijuana produces only a slight and insignificant decrease in the immune response.

_____ (b) Marijuana can have lasting effects on a male smoker's sexual functioning.

_____ (c) Heavy use of marijuana can produce measurable impairments in attention and memory.

_____ (d) A link has been discovered between cannabis use and schizophrenia.

26-2. Say whether the following statements regarding the long-term use of MDMA are true or false.

_____ (a) There is evidence linking heavy MDMA use with sleep disorders, depression, anxiety, or hostility.

_____ (b) There is no evidence linking MDMA use with subtle effects on cognitive function and memory deficits.

Answers: 26-1. (a) true, (b) false, (c) true, (d) true **26-2.** (a) true, (b) false.

PUTTING IT IN PERSPECTIVE

27. Explain how the chapter highlighted four of the text's unifying themes.

27-1. Identify which of the underlying themes (psychology evolves in a sociohistorical context, experience is subjective, cultures mould some aspects of behaviour, and psychology is theoretically diverse) is illustrated by the following statements.

(a) Psychologists have followed many different approaches and developed many different theories in their attempt to understand consciousness.

(b) The study of consciousness by psychologists followed rather than preceded renewed public interest in this topic.

(c) There are striking individual differences in the way people respond to hypnosis, meditation, and drugs.

(d) The significance given to dreams and sleep patterns can be influenced by this factor.

Answers: 27-1. (a) Psychology is theoretically diverse. (b) Psychology evolves in a sociohistorical context. (c) Experience is subjective. (d) Culture moulds some aspects of behaviour.

APPLICATION: ADDRESSING PRACTICAL QUESTIONS ABOUT SLEEP AND DREAMS

28. Summarize evidence on common questions about sleep discussed in the Application.

28-1. Answer the following questions about sleep and napping.

(a) How much sleep do we require?

(b) While napping can be refreshing for most people, in what way can it prove inefficient?

(c) Why are drugs such as sedatives and alcohol likely to interfere with refreshing sleep?

28-2. In addition to developing sensible daytime habits to combat insomnia, there are numerous methods for facilitating actually going to sleep. A common feature in all of them is that they generate a feeling of _____. Some methods generate a feeling of boredom, which is akin to relaxation. The important point here is that one (does/does not) ruminate on the heavy events in life when attempting to go to sleep.

Answers: 28-1. (a) It varies across individuals. (b) Insufficient time is spent in deeper sleep. (c) They interfere with REM and slow-wave sleep. **28-2.** relaxation (or calmness), does not.

29. **Summarize evidence on the common questions about dreams discussed in the Application.**

   29-1. While there are some persons who claim they never dream, what is really happening is that they cannot _____ their dreams. Dreams are best recalled when waking occurs during or immediately following (REM/NREM) sleep. Determination and practice (can/cannot) improve one's ability to recall dreams. A dream whose action takes place over a 20-minute period will actually last for approximately _____ minutes.

   29-2. Freud believed that dreams (do/do not) require interpretation because their true meaning is symbolically encoded in the obvious plot of the dream. Freud's theory that dreams carry hidden symbolic meaning would mean that dream interpretation (is/is not) a very complicated affair. More recent researchers now believe that dreams are (more/less) complicated than Freud believed. Calvin Hall makes the point that dreams require some interpretation simply because they are mostly (visual/verbal).

   29-3. In what way does lucid dreaming differ from regular dreaming?

   29-4. Indicate whether the following statements are "true" or "false."

   _____ (a) Evidence shows that some control over one's dreams is possible, but it is not easy, and results are not always consistent.

   _____ (b) There have been several reported cases of persons reporting their own deaths as the result of fatal dreams.

   _____ (c) It has been shown that subjects can communicate with researchers using prearranged eye signals during lucid dreaming.

Answers: 29-1. remember (or recall), REM, can, 20 **29-2.** do, is, less, visual **29-3.** In lucid dreaming one is aware that one is dreaming. **29-4.** (a) true, (b) false, (c) true.

CRITICAL THINKING APPLICATION

30. **Discuss the influence of definitions and how they are sometimes misused as explanations for the phenomena they describe.**

   30-1. Whether alcoholism is a disease or a result of personal failure depends on _____ gets to make up the definition. In fact, there is (only one/no) conclusive way to determine if alcoholism is a disease.

   30-2. To say that someone drinks too much because she is alcoholic is an example of _____ reasoning. Definitions can never serve as _____ of the thing they are defining.

REVIEW OF KEY TERMS

Alcohol	Insomnia	Physical dependence
Ascending reticular activating system (ARAS)	Lucid dreams	Psychoactive drugs
Biological rhythms	MDMA (ecstasy)	Psychological dependence
Cannabis	Meditation	REM sleep
Circadian rhythms	Mind wandering	REM sleep behaviour disorder
Dissociation	Narcolepsy	Sedatives
Electroencephalograph (EEG)	Narcotics	Sleep apnea
Electromyograph (EMG)	Nightmares	Slow-wave sleep (SWS)
Electrooculograph (EOG)	Night terrors	Somnambulism
Hallucinogens	NonREM (NREM) sleep	Stimulants
Hypnosis	Opiates	Tolerance

_____ **1.** A device that monitors the electrical activity of the brain.

_____ **2.** A device that records muscle activity and tension.

_____ **3.** A device that records eye movements.

_____ **4.** Periodic fluctuations in physiological functioning.

_____ **5.** The 24-hour biological cycles found in humans and many other species.

_____ **6.** Sleep involving rapid eye movements.

_____ **7.** Sleep stages 1 through 4, which are marked by an absence of rapid eye movements.

_____ **8.** Consists of the afferent fibres running through the reticular formation that influence physiological arousal.

_____ **9.** Drugs that are derived from opium that are capable of relieving pain. These drugs are also called narcotics.

_____ **10.** Involves chronic problems in getting adequate sleep.

_____ **11.** A disease marked by sudden and irresistible onsets of sleep during normal waking hours.

_____ **12.** Reflexive gasping for air that awakens a person and disrupts sleep.

_____ **13.** Abrupt awakenings from NREM sleep accompanied by intense autonomic arousal and feelings of panic.

_____ **14.** Anxiety-arousing dreams that lead to awakening, usually from REM sleep.

_____ **15.** Occurs when a sleeping person arises and wanders about in deep NREM sleep.

_____ **16.** A systematic procedure that typically produces a heightened state of suggestibility.

_____ **17.** Involves a splitting off of mental processes into two separate, simultaneous streams of awareness.

_____ **18.** A family of medical exercises in which a conscious attempt is made to focus attention in a nonanalytical way.

_____ **19.** Chemical substances that modify mental, emotional, or behavioural functioning.

_____ **20.** Sleep stages 3 and 4, in which low-frequency delta waves become prominent in EEG recordings.

_____ 21. Drugs that have sleep-inducing and behavioural depression effects.

_____ 22. Drugs that tend to increase central nervous system activation and behavioural activity.

_____ 23. A diverse group of drugs that have powerful effects on mental and emotional functioning, marked most prominently by distortions in sensory and perceptual experience.

_____ 24. The hemp plant, from which marijuana, hashish, and THC are derived.

_____ 25. A variety of beverages containing ethyl alcohol.

_____ 26. A progressive decrease in a person's responsiveness to a drug.

_____ 27. A condition that exists when a person must continue to take a drug to avoid withdrawal illness.

_____ 28. A condition that exists when a person must continue to take a drug to satisfy mental and emotional craving for the drug.

_____ 29. People's experience of task-unrelated thoughts.

_____ 30. Dreams in which persons are aware that they are dreaming.

_____ 31. A drug compounded from both amphetamine and hallucinogens that produces a short-lived high.

_____ 32. These drugs are also referred to as opiates.

_____ 33. A sleep disorder in which a person yells and moves during REM dreams.

Answers: 1. electroencephalograph (EEG) **2.** electromyograph (EMG) **3.** electrooculograph (EOG) **4.** biological rhythms **5.** circadian rhythms **6.** REM sleep **7.** nonREM sleep **8.** ascending reticular activating system (ARAS) **9.** opiates **10.** insomnia **11.** narcolepsy **12.** sleep apnea **13.** night terrors **14.** nightmares **15.** somnambulism **16.** hypnosis **17.** dissociation **18.** meditation **19.** psychoactive drugs **20.** slow-wave sleep (SWS) **21.** sedatives **22.** stimulants **23.** hallucinogens **24.** cannabis **25.** alcohol **26.** tolerance **27.** physical dependence **28.** psychological dependence **29.** mind wandering **30.** lucid dreams. **31.** MDMA (ecstasy) **32.** narcotics **33.** REM sleep behaviour disorder.

REVIEW OF KEY PEOPLE

Theodore Barber	Calvin Hall	William James
Rosalind Cartwright	Ernest Hilgard	Nicholas Spanos
William Dement	J. Alan Hobson	Shepard Siegel
Sigmund Freud		

_____ 1. Originated the term "stream of consciousness."

_____ 2. Argued for the existence of the unconscious and the hidden meaning of dreams.

_____ 3. As one of the pioneers in early sleep research, he coined the term REM sleep.

_____ 4. After analyzing thousands of dreams, he concluded that their contents are generally quite mundane.

_____ 5. Argued that withdrawal effects can be seen as conditioned responses triggered by stimuli associated with drug use.

_____ 6. Argued (along with Barber) that hypnotized individuals act out the role of a hypnotic subject.

_____ 7. Proposed a problem-solving view as a reason for dreaming.

_____ 8. Along with Spanos, one of the authors of the role playing theory of hypnosis.

9. A proponent of the altered state (divided consciousness) theory of hypnosis.

10. His activation-synthesis model proposes that dreams are only side effects of neural activation.

Answers: 1. James **2.** Freud **3.** Dement **4.** Hall **5.** Siegel **6.** Spanos **7.** Cartwright **8.** Barber **9.** Hilgard **10.** Hobson.

SELF-QUIZ

1. What brain wave is probably operating while you are taking this quiz?
   a. alpha
   b. beta
   c. theta
   d. delta

2. What did William James mean by his term "stream of consciousness"?
   a. Consciousness always remains at the same level.
   b. Consciousness never stops.
   c. Consciousness is constantly changing.
   d. Consciousness is beyond personal control.

3. What is the time period of the circadian rhythm?
   a. 1-year cycle
   b. 28-day cycle
   c. 24-hour cycle
   d. 90-minute cycle

4. When do the most vivid dreams generally occur?
   a. during REM sleep
   b. during NREM sleep
   c. during the early hours of sleep
   d. when alpha brain waves are present

5. What appears to be responsible for regulating the circadian rhythm?
   a. amount of time spent sleeping
   b. amount of time spent awake
   c. cultural practices
   d. exposure to light

6. What happens to cats after their ascending reticular activating system has been severed?
   a. They become very aggressive.
   b. They become very fearful.
   c. They remain in continuous wakefulness.
   d. They remain in continuous sleep.

7. Typically, what characterizes the content of most dreams?
   a. They are mundane.
   b. They are exotic.
   c. They are exciting.
   d. They are erotic.

8. What sleep disorder involves frequent stoppage of breathing?
   a. nightmares
   b. narcolepsy
   c. sleep apnea
   d. somnambulism

9. People can be made to act as if they are hypnotized even without the use of hypnotic induction. Is this statement true or false?
   a. true
   b. false

10. Which of the following is NOT associated with REM sleep?
    a. sleep walking
    b. dreaming
    c. high-frequency beta waves
    d. eye movements

11. How do psychoactive drugs exert their effect on the brain?
    a. by decreasing blood supply to the brain
    b. by altering neurotransmitter activity
    c. by breaking down essential brain amino acids
    d. by penetrating the nucleus of the neurons

12. What percentage of Canadians report problematic alcohol use?
    a. 5 to 10%
    b. 10 to 20%
    c. more than 30%
    d. more than 40%

13. Which of the following is a sleep disorder that involves acting out one's dreams?
    a. narcolepsy
    b. sleep apnea
    c. insomnia
    d. REM sleep-related disorder

14. Which of the following statements about dreaming is correct?
    a. Most people do not dream in colour.
    b. Practice will not improve the ability to recall dreams.
    c. From birth until death, everyone dreams.
    d. Dreams generally last only one or two minutes.

15. What was found in the study regarding the effects of sleep deprivation in college students?
    a. Sleep deprivation had little effect on their ability to perform cognitive tasks.
    b. Sleep deprivation had a substantial negative effect on their mood.
    c. Sleep deprivation had a substantial positive effect on their ability to perform cognitive tasks because the students compensated by increasing their effort.
    d. The students were unaware of the actual negative effect of the deprivation.

16. What psychological treatment provides long-term, lasting improvement for those with insomnia?
    a. dream analysis
    b. client-centred therapy
    c. psychoanalytic therapy
    d. cognitive-behavioural therapy

17. What hypothesis was tested in the Featured Study?
    a. Conscious thought is beneficial for especially complex problems.
    b. Unconscious thought is beneficial for especially complex problems.
    c. Conscious thought is beneficial for simple problems.
    d. Unconscious thought is beneficial for simple problems.

Answers: 1. b **2.** c **3.** c **4.** a **5.** d **6.** d **7.** a **8.** c **9.** a **10.** a **11.** b **12.** c **13.** d **14.** c **15.** d **16.** d **17.** b.

Chapter Six

LEARNING

REVIEW OF KEY IDEAS

1. **Define learning and conditioning, and explain their relevance for understanding the behaviour of humans and other animals.**

   1-1. Learning is a _____ _____ change in behaviour or _____ that is due to experience. Conditioning is a type of learning in which an organism learns _____ between events that occur in its environment.

   1-2. These types of learning are relevant to our understanding of behaviour, because they reflect how we acquire knowledge and _____ (such as shooting a puck), and also how we develop habits, personality traits, emotional responses, and personal preferences. Much of our behaviour and the behaviour of other animals reflects _____, and by studying simple forms of learning such as conditioning, we develop the foundation for understanding more complex types of learning.

   Answers: 1-1. relatively durable, knowledge, connections **1-2.** skills, learning.

CLASSICAL CONDITIONING

2. **Describe Pavlov's demonstration of classical conditioning and the key elements in this form of learning.**

   2-1. Classical conditioning is a type of learning that occurs when two stimuli are paired or associated closely in time. In Pavlov's initial demonstration, the two stimuli were a bell and _____.

   2-2. The response to one of the two stimuli occurs naturally and does not have to be learned or acquired through conditioning. This "unlearned" stimulus, in this case the food, is technically known as the _____ stimulus.

   2-3. The other stimulus is said to be neutral in the sense that it does not initially produce a response. When a response to this neutral stimulus is *acquired* or *learned*, the technical name for it is the _____ stimulus. In Pavlov's initial study, the conditioned stimulus was the sound of a _____.

2-4. The unconditioned stimulus in Pavlov's original study was the _____, and the conditioned stimulus was the _____. Salivation to the meat powder is known as the _____ response; salivation to the bell is termed the _____ response.

2-5. Label the parts of the classical conditioning sequence. Place the commonly used abbreviations for these terms in the parentheses.

(a) meat: _____

(b) salivation to meat: _____

(c) bell: _____

(d) salivation to bell: _____

2-6. Classical conditioning can also involve _____ conditioning, where a change in the liking of a stimulus results from pairing that stimulus with other positive or negative stimuli. Advertising campaigns take advantage of this type of learning, pairing their product with an _____ _____ that elicits pleasant emotions.

Answers: **2-1.** meat powder (or food) **2-2.** unconditioned **2-3.** conditioned, bell **2-4.** meat powder, bell, unconditioned, conditioned **2-5.** (a) unconditioned stimulus (UCS), (b) unconditioned response (UCR), (c) conditioned stimulus (CS), (d) conditioned response (CR) **2-6.** evaluative, unconditioned stimulus (US).

3. Discuss how classical conditioning may shape phobias and physiological processes, including drug effects.

3-1. The kids in the neighbourhood where one of us (R.S.) grew up used to dig tunnels in a neighbour's backyard. One day, someone got stuck in the tunnel and couldn't get out. Eventually he got out, but after that he didn't want to play in tunnels again. To this day, that person still has an intense fear, not only of tunnels, but of closed-in spaces in general. Label the parts of the classical conditioning process involved in the acquisition of the phobia of closed-in spaces. Use the abbreviations CS, CR, UCS, and UCR. (Hint: Even though "getting stuck" certainly involves a behaviour or response, it also has stimulus components.)

_____ getting stuck

_____ fear produced by getting stuck

_____ tunnels and closed-in spaces

_____ fear of tunnels and closed-in spaces

3-2. The individual described above had developed an intense fear, or phobia, acquired in part through the process of _____ conditioning. Other emotions can be conditioned as well. For example, the playing of a particular song you haven't heard in a while could produce a pleasant emotional response. The song would be considered a _____ stimulus.

3-3. Similarly, certain physiological responses can be conditioned. Label the parts of the conditioning process in the study on immunosuppression in rats described in the text. (Use the abbreviations CS, CR, UCS, and UCR.)

_____ the immunosuppressive drug

_____ unusual taste

_____ decreased antibody production produced by the drug

_____ decreased antibody production produced by the taste

3-4. Evidently sexual arousal can be classically conditioned as well. For example, quail can be conditioned to become sexually aroused by a neutral stimulus such as a red light, if the light has been paired with opportunities to copulate. The red light would be a _____ _____. Conditioned arousal produces more sperm, which enhances the likelihood of fertilization and the passing on of one's genes.

3-5. Probably in humans, as in quail, stimuli routinely paired with sex (e.g., lingerie, dim lighting) become _____ stimuli for sexual arousal.

3-6. According to Siegel, a drug and its effects can be considered an _____ stimulus, and the body's compensatory response to the drug can be considered an _____ response. Any contextual cue that the drug user is frequently exposed to prior to taking the drug (e.g., nighttime) can come to be a _____ stimulus, such that over time such stimuli can trigger their own _____ response. Because this conditioned compensatory response will grow in strength with repeated drug use under the same conditions, tolerance to the drug may develop. An overdose may occur if drugs are taken in new settings, because of a weaker _____ response. Also, exposure to cues that have come to be associated with drug use on occasions when the drug is not used may promote _____ symptoms.

Answers: **3-1.** UCS, UCR, CS, CR **3-2.** classical, conditioned **3-3.** UCS, CS, UCR, CR. **3-4.** conditioned stimulus **3-5.** conditioned **3-6.** unconditioned, unconditioned, conditioned, conditioned, conditioned, withdrawal.

4. Describe the classical conditioning phenomena of acquisition, extinction, and spontaneous recovery.

4-1. _Acquisition_ of a conditioned response occurs when the CS and UCS are contiguous, or paired. Not all pairings result in conditioning, however. What characteristics of a CS are more likely to produce acquisition of a CR?

4-2. Acquisition refers to the formation of a conditioned response. What is the term that refers to the weakening or disappearance of a CR? _____

4-3. Extinction in classical conditioning occurs when the _____ stimulus is presented _alone_, without the _____ stimulus.

4-4. After CRs are extinguished they may reappear, even without further conditioning.

(a) For example, after extinction of a response, a dog may again show the conditioned response (e.g., salivation to a bell) when returned to the apparatus in which it was originally conditioned. What is the name of this type of "reappearance" of the CR?

_____ _____

(b) When, or under what circumstance, is spontaneous recovery likely to occur?

(c) If an animal's CR is extinguished in a different environment from the one in which conditioning took place, it is likely to again show a CR when returned to the original environment. What is the name of this effect? _____ _____

Answers: **4-1.** A novel or particularly intense CS is more likely to produce conditioning. **4-2.** extinction **4-3.** conditioned, unconditioned **4-4.** (a) spontaneous recovery, (b) after extinction, following a period of nonexposure to the CS, (c) renewal effect.

5. Describe the processes of generalization and discrimination.

5-1. The more similar the stimuli are to the CS, the more likely the organism will _____ from the CS to the other stimuli. The less similar the stimuli are to the CS, the more likely the organism is to _____ them from the CS.

5-2. Casey (R.S.'s cat, now deceased) salivated when she heard the sound of food being dumped into her bowl. The process by which this salivary response was learned is _____ conditioning. The food is a(n) (CS/UCS/CR/UCR). The sound of the food is a(n) (CS/UCS/CR/UCR). Salivation to the sound is a(n) (CS/UCS/CR/UCR).

5-3. Pets are also likely to salivate when they hear other, similar sounds, like bags rustling in the kitchen or dishes being pulled from the cupboard. Salivation to these other sounds represents stimulus _____.

5-4. The case of _____ _____ demonstrates stimulus generalization, in that he initially learned to fear a white rat (by pairing the rat with a loud sound). Days later, his fear was shown to generalize to other white furry things, such as a dog.

5-5. With continued training, in which food is paired only with the sound of food entering the bowl and not with the other sounds, the animal will learn to salivate only to the rattling bowl. The process of learning to respond only to one particular stimulus, and not to a range of similar stimuli, is termed

_____.

Answers: **5-1.** generalize, discriminate **5-2.** classical, UCS, CS, CR **5-3.** generalization
5-4. Little Albert **5-5.** discrimination.

6. **Explain what happens in higher-order conditioning.**

   6-1.   Suppose that a *bell* and *meat powder* are paired, as in the original Pavlovian study. At some point, a conditioned salivary response will occur to the bell. Suppose that in a new series of trials a *clicking sound* (a new, neutral stimulus) is paired with the bell. Assuming that the stimuli are potent enough, that the timing is right, and so on, a _____ response will occur to the clicking sound.

   6-2.   The process described above, in which a stimulus that previously functioned as a *conditioned* stimulus was used as an *unconditioned* stimulus, is known as _____ conditioning.

   6-3.   In our example, in which the clicking sound and bell were paired, which stimulus acted as the UCS? _____

   Answers: **6-1.** conditioned **6-2.** higher-order **6-3.** the bell.

OPERANT CONDITIONING

7. **Discuss the nature of operant responding in comparison to the types of responding typically governed by classical conditioning.**

   7-1.   A major feature of Pavlovian or classical conditioning is that conditioned responses occur when two stimuli are paired or associated. For example, when a sound and food are paired together, a conditioned salivary response occurs to the _____.

   7-2.   In contrast, in operant conditioning, learning or conditioning occurs from stimuli that (precede/follow) the response, the stimuli that are the "payoff" or _____ of that particular behaviour.

   7-3.   Learning theorists originally supposed that the two types of conditioning controlled different types of responses: that classical conditioning controlled reflexive or (voluntary/involuntary) responses (such as salivation or leg flexion), while operant conditioning controlled voluntary responses. While this distinction holds up (all of the time/much of the time), it is now clear that the only absolute distinction is in terms of procedure.

   Answers: **7-1.** sound **7-2.** follow, reinforcers (or consequence) **7-3.** involuntary, much of the time.

8. **Describe Thorndike's work, and explain his law of effect.**

   8-1.   E.L. Thorndike's pioneering work on what he referred to as _____ learning provided the foundation for Skinner's _____ conditioning.

   8-2.   According to Thorndike's law of _____, if a response leads to a *satisfying effect* in the presence of a stimulus, the association between the stimulus and response is strengthened. Thorndike's law of effect is similar to Skinner's concept of reinforcement; both emphasize the _____ of behaviour.

   Answers: **8-1.** instrumental, operant **8-2.** effect, consequences.

9. **Describe Skinner's principle of reinforcement and the prototype experimental procedures used in studies of operant conditioning.**

9-1. A reinforcer is a stimulus or event that (1) is presented *after* a response and that (2) increases the tendency for the response to be repeated. Apply that definition to this example: Grundoon, a captive monkey, occasionally swings on a bar in his cage. Suppose that at some point Grundoon's trainers decide to give him a spoonful of applesauce whenever he swings. Is the applesauce a reinforcer? In terms of the definition above, how do you know that applesauce is a reinforcer?

9-2. The trainers switch to vinegar. Grundoon, an unusual primate, swings quite frequently when this behaviour is followed by vinegar. Is vinegar a reinforcer here? How do you know?

9-3. The trainers try another approach. They present Grundoon with fresh fruit *just before* they think he is likely to jump. It so happens that Grundoon's rate of jumping does increase. Is the fruit a reinforcer here? Why or why not?

9-4. The prototypical apparatus used in operant conditioning studies is the operant chamber, better known as the _____. On one wall of the chamber is mounted a manipulandum, a device that makes for an easily discernible response. For rats, the manipulandum is usually a small _____; for pigeons, the device is a _____ that the bird learns to peck.

9-5. A press of the lever or peck at the disk may produce a reinforcer, generally a small bit of food dispensed into the food cup mounted to one side or below the manipulandum. Each of these responses is recorded on a _____ _____, a device that creates a graphic record of the number of responses per unit time.

9-6. The cumulative recorder records the *rate* of the behaviour, that is, the number of _____ made per unit _____.

9-7. Below is a highly stylized version of a cumulative record. About how many responses were made during the first 40 seconds? _____ Which section of the graph (a, b, c, d, or e) has the steepest slope? _____ Which section of the graph illustrates the fastest rate of responding? _____ About how many responses were made between the 40th and 70th seconds? _____

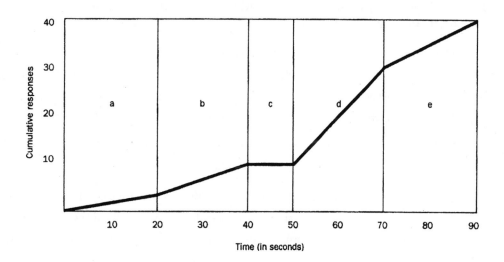

Answers: 9-1. Yes. If the animal's rate of swinging increases when followed by applesauce, then applesauce is a reinforcer. **9-2.** Yes. Because the vinegar is presented *after the response*, and because the *response rate increases*. (Note that this is an imaginary example to illustrate the point that *reinforcement is defined in terms of consequences*, not by subjective judgments about pleasantness and unpleasantness. I don't know of any monkeys that will respond for vinegar.) **9-3.** No. Reinforcing stimuli, by definition, *follow* the response. (Again, this is a contrived example just to illustrate the definition.) **9-4.** Skinner box, lever (or bar), disk **9-5.** cumulative recorder **9-6.** responses, time **9-7.** 10, d, d, 20.

10. Describe the operant conditioning phenomena of acquisition, shaping, and extinction.

10-1. Acquisition refers to the formation of new responses. In classical conditioning, acquisition occurs through a simple pairing of the CS and UCS. In operant conditioning, acquisition usually involves the procedure known as _____.

10-2. What is shaping? When is it used?

10-3. Extinction in classical conditioning involves removing the UCS while still presenting the CS.

(a) What is the extinction procedure in operant conditioning?

(b) What is the effect of extinction on behaviour (response rate)?

(c) What does the term *resistance to extinction* mean?

Answers 10-1. shaping **10-2.** Shaping is the process of reinforcing closer and closer approximations to the desired behaviour. It is used in the formation of a new response. **10-3.** (a) no longer presenting the reinforcers after a response, (b) Response rate decreases and may eventually stop. (c) Animals may continue to respond, for a period of time, even when reinforcers are no longer presented. The extent to which they will *continue to respond during extinction* is referred to as *resistance* to extinction.

11. Explain how stimuli govern operant behaviour and how generalization and discrimination occur in operant conditioning.

11-1. Suppose that a rat has been shaped so that when it presses a lever it receives a food pellet. With further training, the rat may respond only when a light (or sound, etc.) in the chamber is on and not when it is off. The food pellet (which follows the response) is a _____. The light (which precedes the response) is a _____ stimulus.

11-2. Reinforcers occur (<u>after/before</u>) the response occurs. Discriminative stimuli occur _____ the response occurs.

11-3. To create a discriminative stimulus, one reinforces a response only in the presence of a particular stimulus and not in its absence. In time, that stimulus will gain control of the response: animals will tend to emit the response only if the discriminative stimulus is (<u>present/absent</u>) and not if it is

_____.

11-4. For example, rats can be trained to press a lever when a light comes on and not to press when the light is off. Lever presses that occur when the light is on are followed by a food pellet; those that occur in the dark are not. Label each component of this operant-conditioning process by placing the appropriate letters in the blanks below.

_____ light   a. discriminative stimulus

_____ lever press   b. response

_____ food   c. reinforcer

11-5. "Heel, Fido!" says Ralph. Fido runs to Ralph's side. Fido gets a pat on the head. Label the parts of the operant conditioning sequence by placing the appropriate letters in the blanks. (To avoid confusion, the behaviour or response of interest in this example is already labelled.)

_____ "Heel, Fido!"   a. discriminative stimulus

_____ Fido gets a pat on the head.   b. response

__b__ Fido runs to Ralph's side.   c. reinforcer

11-6. Phyllis will lend money to Ralph, but only after Ralph promises to pay her back. Ralph is also careful to thank Phyllis for her help. The behaviour we are looking at here is Phyllis's lending behaviour.

_____ "Thank you very much, Phyllis."   a. discriminative stimulus

__b__ Phyllis lends.   b. response

_____ "I promise I'll pay you back."   c. reinforcer

11-7. Generalization occurs in operant as well as classical conditioning. For example, when I put dishes in the sink, our cat would *run to her bowl* looking for food. In technical terms, our cat _____ between the sound of food dropping in her bowl and the *similar* sound of dishes going into the sink. Despite the fact that food does not follow the sound of clattering dishes, our cat did *not* learn to _____ between the sounds in our kitchen.

Answers: 11-1. reinforcer, discriminative 11-2. after, before 11-3. present, absent 11-4. a, b, c
11-5. a, c, [b] 11-6. c, [b], a 11-7. generalizes, discriminate.

12. Discuss primary and secondary (conditioned) reinforcement in operant conditioning.

12-1. Define the following:

(a) Primary reinforcer:

(b) Secondary or conditioned reinforcer:

Answers: 12-1. (a) A primary reinforcer satisfies biological needs, such as needs for food, water, warmth, and sex. (b) A secondary, or conditioned, reinforcer is one that is learned or acquired through association with a primary reinforcer. For humans, secondary reinforcers include praise, attention, and money.

13. Discuss superstitious behaviour in relation to reinforcement and cognitive biases.

13-1. Skinner viewed superstitious behaviour as reflecting _____ reinforcement (i.e., reinforcement that did not actually depend on the organism's behaviour). Contemporary research on superstitious behaviour emphasizes _____ biases and errors. Recent research also shows that superstitions (can/cannot) enhance performance.

Answers: 13-1. noncontingent, cognitive, can.

14. Identify various types of schedules of reinforcement, and discuss their typical effects on responding.

14-1. Schedules of reinforcement are either continuous or intermittent. If reinforcers follow each response, the schedule is referred to as a(n) _____-reinforcement schedule, abbreviated CRF. If reinforcers only follow some responses and not others (e.g., FR, VR), or occur as a function of the passage of time (e.g., FI, VI), the schedule is referred to as a(n) _____ schedule.

14-2. Identify the following schedules of reinforcement by placing the appropriate abbreviations in the blanks: continuous reinforcement (CRF), fixed ratio (FR), variable ratio (VR), fixed interval (FI), variable interval (VI).

_____ A pigeon is reinforced whenever it has pecked a disk exactly 20 times.

_____ A pigeon is reinforced for pecking a disk, on the average, 20 times.

_____ A rat is always reinforced for the first response that follows a two-minute interval.

_____ A slot machine delivers a payoff, on the average, after every 10th pull of the lever.

_____ Every time the pigeon pecks a disk, it receives a pellet of food.

_____ A rat is reinforced, on the average, for the first response following a two-minute interval.

_____ A pig is reinforced for the first response after 30 seconds, then for the first response after 42 seconds, then for the first response after 5 seconds, and so on at variable intervals.

_____ Every two weeks Ralph picks up his payroll cheque at the office.

_____ A rat is reinforced after the 73rd response, then after the 22nd response, then after the 51st response, and so on at variable intervals.

14-3. Resistance to extinction refers to the extent to which responses occur during a period of extinction. What is the general effect of the intermittent schedules of reinforcement on resistance to extinction?

14-4. In terms of the effect on *rate* of responding, what is the general difference between the *ratio* schedules (FR and VR) and the *interval* schedules (FI and VI)?

14-5. In terms of the effect on *pattern* of responding, what is the general difference between *fixed* schedules and *variable* schedules?

Answers: 14-1. continuous, intermittent (or partial) **14-2.** FR, VR, FI, VR, CRF, VI, VI, FI, VR
14-3. The intermittent schedules increase resistance to extinction. **14-4.** The ratio schedules tend to produce more rapid responding than the interval schedules. **14-5.** Variable schedules tend to produce more regular patterns of responding, without pauses or scalloping, than do their fixed counterparts. They also result in more resistance to extinction.

15. Explain the distinction between positive and negative reinforcement.

15-1. Some Skinner boxes may be set up so that a moderate electric shock can be delivered to the feet of the animal through the floor of the box. Suppose that whenever the animal presses the bar, the shock is turned *off* for a period of time. Will the lever-pressing behaviour be *strengthened* or *weakened*? _____

15-2. By definition, what effect does reinforcement have on behaviour? What is the effect of positive reinforcement on behaviour? Of negative reinforcement?

15-3. With positive reinforcement, a stimulus is *presented* after the response. What is the procedure with negative reinforcement?

Answers: **15-1.** strengthened **15-2.** Reinforcement strengthens (increases the frequency of) behaviour. Both positive and negative reinforcement strengthen behaviour. **15-3.** The stimulus (an aversive stimulus) is *removed* after the response.

16. Describe and distinguish between escape learning and avoidance learning.

16-1. Review the section on escape and avoidance learning. In escape learning, the animal first experiences the aversive stimulus and then makes a response that escapes it. In avoidance learning, the animal responds to a cue that permits it to respond *before* the aversive stimulus is delivered, thereby avoiding it altogether. Label the following examples E for escape and A for avoidance.

_____ The weather has changed, and Fred is getting cold. He goes inside.

_____ Little Sandra rapidly removes her hand from the hot stove.

_____ A cue light comes on in a shuttle box. The rat rapidly runs to the other chamber.

_____ Randolph has been told that he will be mugged if he goes outside, so he stays inside.

_____ Sue has learned some new verbal behaviour. If she simply says, "No, I don't want that" shortly after a salesman starts his pitch, the salesman will stop bothering her.

_____ Alice sees Rupert in the distance. If Rupert sees her he will ask for her course notes, which she doesn't want to lend him. She heads in the other direction.

16-2. What is the major difference between escape learning and avoidance learning?

Answers: **16-1.** E, E, A, A, E, A **16-2.** The major difference is that with escape learning there is no cue stimulus, so that the animal must first experience the aversive stimulus and then *escape* it. In the case of avoidance learning, a cue preceding the aversive stimulus permits the animal to *avoid* the aversive event altogether.

17. Explain the role of classical conditioning and the role of negative reinforcement in avoidance behaviour.

17-1. Fear of the cue stimulus in avoidance learning is acquired through (classical/operant) conditioning, the association of the stimulus and shock. The running behaviour, on the other hand, is maintained by (classical/operant) conditioning, escape from the conditioned fear.

17-2. Escape increases the strength of a response through (negative/positive) reinforcement. The reason that phobic responses are particularly resistant to extinction is because each time an avoidance response is made, the internal _____ stimulus is reduced. For example, when people avoid contact with things that they are afraid of (e.g., spiders, elevators, airplanes), they are _____ reinforced by the removal of conditioned fear. Also, avoidance responses prevent the opportunity to _____ the conditioned response because the organism is never exposed to the conditioned stimulus.

Answers: **17-1.** classical, operant **17-2.** negative, fear, negatively, extinguish.

18. Describe punishment and its effects.

18-1. Punishment involves *weakening* a response by presenting an aversive stimulus after the response has occurred or by removal of a rewarding stimulus. Review the concepts of reinforcement and punishment by labelling each of the following with one of these terms: *positive reinforcement, negative reinforcement, punishment.*

(a) A stimulus is *presented* after the response; response rate *increases*: _____

(b) A stimulus is *presented* after the response; response rate *decreases*: _____

(c) A stimulus is *removed* after the response; response rate *increases*: _____

(d) A stimulus is *removed* after the response; response rate *decreases*: _____

18-2. Response rate *increases*. Which of the following procedures may have been used?

a. positive reinforcement

b. negative reinforcement

c. punishment

d. either a or b above

18-3. Response rate *decreases*. Which of the following procedures may have been used?

a. negative reinforcement

b. positive reinforcement

c. punishment

d. either *b* or *c* above

18-4. When a rat presses a bar in an operant chamber, the electric shock stops. Bar pressing increases. What procedure has been used?

a. positive reinforcement

b. negative reinforcement

c. punishment

d. extinction

18-5. Whenever the dog ran after a car, his master immediately threw a bucket of water on him. The dog stopped running after cars. What procedure was used?

a. positive reinforcement

b. negative reinforcement

c. punishment

d. extinction punishment

18-6. When Randolph spoke back to his parents, they took away his favourite toy. If Randolph stops talking back to his parents, what has occurred?

a. positive reinforcement

b. negative reinforcement

c. punishment

d. bribery

18-7. The use of punishment as a disciplinary procedure for children has drawbacks. For example, punishment is associated with poor parent–child relationships, elevated _____, delinquency, and an increased likelihood of child _____. Some of these difficulties will persist into adulthood. Critics of this research have pointed out that the findings should be interpreted as _____, not _____. However, the most recent studies do reveal that early experience of spanking is associated with negative outcomes, such as increased aggression and lower cognitive ability scores.

18-8. When punishment is used, the text suggests the following guidelines: (a) Apply punishment (<u>immediately/after a delay</u>). (b) Use a level of punishment that is (<u>severe/least severe</u>) to be effective. (c) Punish the behaviour consistently (<u>each time/only occasionally</u>) when it occurs. (d) When administering punishment, (<u>explain/do not explain</u>) why it is being given. (e) In general, when employing punishment, try to use (<u>physical punishment/withdrawal of privileges</u>).

Answers: **18-1.** (a) positive reinforcement, (b) punishment, (c) negative reinforcement, (d) punishment **18-2.** d **18-3.** c **18-4.** b **18-5.** c **18-6.** c **18-7.** aggression, abuse, correlational, causal **18-8.** (a) immediately, (b) least severe, (c) each time, (d) explain, (e) withdrawal of privileges.

CHANGING DIRECTIONS IN THE STUDY OF CONDITIONING

19. Discuss the phenomena of instinctive drift, conditioned taste aversion, preparedness, and ecological conditioned stimuli.

19-1. What is instinctive drift?

19-2. Why was the occurrence of instinctive drift surprising to operant psychologists? Discuss this question in terms of the supposed *generality* of the laws of learning.

19-3. What is conditioned taste aversion?

19-4. Why is the occurrence of conditioned taste aversion surprising? Discuss this question in terms of classical conditioning relating to: (1) CS-UCS delays and (2) the sense of taste compared with other senses.

19-5. Preparedness is Seligman's idea that there are *species-specific* tendencies to be conditioned in some ways and not in others. Both of the findings discussed above, the phenomena of

_____ _____and _____ _____ _____ involve the

concept of _____.

19-6. People are much more likely to die in a car than in an airplane, but phobias related to flying are much more common than phobias about driving. Why is that the case? Try to account for this oddity using Seligman's notion of preparedness.

19-7. Evidence suggests that humans would more quickly acquire a fear of snakes than a fear of guns, and that such learning would be more resistant to _____. Mineka's research on preparedness has suggested that we possess an _____ _____ for fear learning.

Answers: 19-1. It is the tendency for instinctive or innate behaviour to interfere with the process of conditioning. **19-2.** Before the 1960s, operant psychologists assumed that any response that animals could emit could readily be conditioned. This turned out not to be true. Animals may exhibit instinctive drift, the tendency to respond with certain innate behaviours that actually interfere with the process of conditioning. **19-3.** It refers to the somewhat unusual conditioning involving taste and nausea. If the distinctive taste of a particular food is followed some hours later by sickness (nausea, vomiting, etc.), that taste will become aversive and will itself come to elicit the response of nausea. **19-4.** It is surprising because (1) classical conditioning generally does not occur if there are long CS-UCS delays and (2) taste is only one of several senses stimulated in this situation. Garcia concluded that animals have an innate tendency to associate taste (rather than sight, sound, etc.) with sickness, even though the sickness may occur much later. **19-5.** instinctive drift, conditioned taste aversion, preparedness **19-6.** Seligman's notion of preparedness includes the idea that we are genetically predisposed to develop phobic responses to some stimuli more than to others—to spiders, rodents, and heights more readily than to baseballs, lamps, and backyards. Probably because of the heights that are part of flying, flying seems to be more conditionable than driving. **19-7.** extinction, evolved fear.

20. Explain the evolutionary perspective on learning.

20-1. Learning was traditionally viewed as involving basic mechanisms highly similar across species, such that learning was viewed as a very _____ process. Evolutionary views on learning emphasize that because different animals face different adaptive problems, learning has evolved in (different/similar) paths in different species.

Answers: 20-1. general, different.

21. Describe research on latent learning, signal relations and response–outcome relations, and explain their theoretical importance.

21-1. Tolman's work highlighted the importance of _____ learning, which describes learning that is not apparent from behaviour when it first occurs. This form of learning suggests that learning can take place in the absence of _____ and that learning can involve the formation of a _____ representation or map.

21-2. In the example of the signal relations study described, the number of conditioning trials in which CS and UCS were paired was the same for two groups, that is, 20 trials. The difference between the two treatment groups was that for one group the (CS/UCS) was presented *alone* for an additional series of 20 trials.

21-3. Theorists originally assumed that classical conditioning is an automatic, reflexive phenomenon that does not depend at all on higher mental processes. If that actually were true, then what should have been the effect of presenting the UCS alone for additional trials? Remember that both groups received exactly the same number of conditioning trials (CS–UCS pairings).

a. Extinction would occur.

b. The UCS-alone trials would weaken conditioning.

c. The UCS-alone trials would have no effect on conditioning.

21-4. In fact, what did occur in the signal relations studies?

a. Extinction.

b. The UCS-alone trials weakened conditioning.

c. The UCS-alone trials had no effect on conditioning.

21-5. These results suggest that the CS *signals* the occurrence of the UCS, and that additional trials with the UCS alone weaken the _____ value of the CS. What is surprising about these results? Rather than being an automatic, mechanical process, these studies suggest that classical conditioning involves _____ processes.

21-6. Response–outcome relations refers to the connection between an operant response and its consequences. For example, for a rat in a Skinner box, the relationship between the lever press (the response) and the food pellet (the outcome) is this: the rat gets the food *only if* it presses the lever. In other words, the reinforcer is (contingent/not contingent) on the response.

21-7. But does the animal "know" the connection between the response and reinforcer, or is the connection stamped in automatically? That is the crux of the response–outcome relations issue. Evidence suggests that (choose one of the following):

a. reinforcement and punishment are relatively automatic, mindless processes

b. cognition is not involved in an organism's responding in an operant chamber

c. humans and other animals actively try to figure out the contingencies, the relationship between response and outcome

21-8. Thus, research on signal relations and response–outcome relations has forced the development of new theories that emphasize a much more _____ explanation of conditioning, an explanation in which organisms actively attempt to detect the *relationship* between their behaviours and environmental events.

21-9. Why are the signal relations studies in classical conditioning and response–outcome relations studies in operant conditioning surprising and of theoretical importance?

Answers: 21-1. latent, reinforcement, cognitive **21-2.** UCS! (If the CS were presented alone, it would be extinction.) **21-3.** c **21-4.** b **21-5.** signalling, cognitive (or higher mental) **21-6.** contingent **21-7.** c **21-8.** cognitive **21-9.** These studies indicate that conditioning is not, as assumed earlier, an automatic process, but instead depends to a considerable degree on higher mental (cognitive) processes.

OBSERVATIONAL LEARNING

22. Discuss the nature and importance of observational learning.

22-1. Observational learning occurs when an organism learns by observing others, who are called

_____. This type of learning occurs in (<u>humans/animals/both humans and</u>

<u>animals</u>).

22-2. Why is the concept of observational learning so important? For one thing, the idea was surprising

to theorists who assumed that all learning could be accounted for by operant and classical

conditioning. For another, it extends classical and operant conditioning to include not only *direct*

experience, but also _____ or vicarious experience. We learn not only when we

behave, but also when we _____ the behaviour of others.

22-3. Bandura's theory has helped explain some puzzling aspects of conditioning in human behaviour.

For example, what happens when parents physically punish aggressive behaviour in their

children? While punishment by definition (<u>increases/decreases</u>) the behaviour it follows, a parent

using physical punishment also serves as a _____ for aggressiveness. In this

way, events intended to decrease aggression may, in the longer run, _____

aggression through the process of _____ learning.

Answers: 22-1. models, both humans and animals **22-2.** indirect, observe **22-3.** decreases, model, increase, observational.

23. List the basic processes in observational learning and discuss Bandura's view on whether reinforcement affects learning or performance.

23-1. In the space below, list and define the four processes that Bandura has identified as crucial

components of observational learning. The first letter of each concept is listed at the left.

A_____:

R_____:

R_____:

M_____:

23-2. Is reinforcement essential for learning? Many learning theorists used to think so, but in Bandura's

view reinforcement is essential only for (<u>learning/performance</u>). Bandura asserts that we may

learn, without being reinforced, simply by _____ the behaviour of a model, but

we are unlikely to perform the response unless we are _____ for doing so.

Answers: 23-1. Attention: Paying attention to a model's behaviour and consequences. Retention: Retaining in memory a mental representation of what one has observed. Reproduction: Having the ability to reproduce what one sees, to convert the image to behaviour. Motivation: Having the inclination, based on one's assessment of the likely payoff, to reproduce the observed behaviour. **23-2.** performance, observing, reinforced.

24. Describe research on observational learning and the media violence controversy, including the Featured Study.

24-1. In the Featured Study, Huesmann and colleagues examined whether early exposure to _____ on television predicted later _____. Television viewing habits were assessed during childhood, and many years later the amount of aggression and antisocial behaviour of participants was assessed through various measures, including self-report and report by significant others. Results showed that childhood viewing of violent TV correlated significantly with adult aggressive behaviour, for both male and female participants. These findings were upheld even when the researchers controlled for participants' level of _____ during childhood.

24-2. In the "Bobo Doll" experiment, children who saw a model get rewarded for being aggressive were more likely to be aggressive themselves compared to children who saw a model get punished for being aggressive. This demonstrated the effecting of observational learning on _____ of a behaviour. However, all the children behaved aggressively if they were offered a reward for imitating the model's behaviour (i.e., all children revealed evidence of the _____ of the behaviour).

24-3. Recent research suggests that exposure to media violence can _____ people to real-world violence. One study showed that those assigned to play violent video games for 20 minutes showed smaller _____ reactions to aggression (i.e., "numbing"). These effects may involve brain areas that decrease their activation levels following repeated exposure to violence.

Answers: **24-1.** violence, aggression, aggression **24-2.** performance, acquisition **24-3.** desensitize, physiological.

25. Describe research on mirror neurons and their role in observational learning.

25-1. Mirror neurons are neurons that are activated by performing an _____ or by seeing another person perform the same action. Therefore, mirrors neurons are believed to _____ _____ actions. They are found in the frontal and parietal lobes within humans, and may be relevant to our understanding of facial expressions, emotion recognition, empathy, autism, and language learning.

Answers: **25-1.** action, internally represent.

PUTTING IT IN PERSPECTIVE

26. Explain how the chapter highlighted two of the text's unifying themes.

26-1. Skinner emphasized the importance of *environmental* events (reinforcers, punishers, discriminative stimuli, schedules of reinforcement) as the determinants of behaviour. One of our unifying themes, however, is that heredity and environment interact. In support of this theme, list the names of three phenomena that show that *biology* has a powerful effect on *conditioning*.

26-2. The second theme well illustrated in this chapter is that psychology evolves in a sociohistorical context. Discuss one concept from operant psychology that appears to have influenced our everyday lives.

Answers: **26-1.** instinctive drift, conditioned taste aversion, preparedness **26-2.** Operant psychology has probably influenced the trend in our society toward relying more on the use of positive reinforcement than punishment—in child-rearing, in educational settings (e.g., the use of programmed learning), and as a management technique in business.

PERSONAL APPLICATION * ACHIEVING SELF-CONTROL THROUGH BEHAVIOUR MODIFICATION

27. **Describe how to specify your target behaviour and gather baseline data for a self-modification program.**

   27-1. What behaviour do you want to change? The question sounds simple, but the task of defining a _____ behaviour is often quite tricky.

   27-2. The behaviour that you select must be defined in terms of observable events, so that you will know if and when it changes. For example, for the problem of anger control, which of the following would be the most *directly observable* definition of "anger"?
   a. inner turmoil
   b. intense hostility
   c. loud voice and clenched fists

   27-3. Once you specify the target behaviour, you must gather _____ data on your behaviour prior to the intervention. At this time you should also keep track of events that precede the target behaviour, the _____ events, and also the positive and negative reinforcers that follow it, the _____ of your behaviour.

   Answers: **27-1.** target (or specific) **27-2.** c. Although even those behaviours would have to be further described in a behaviour modification program. Alternative a is not really observable. Alternative b could be behaviourally defined, but as it stands, it is hard to know precisely which behaviours intense hostility refers to. **27-3.** baseline, antecedent, consequences.

28. **Discuss your options for increasing or decreasing a response in designing a self-modification program.**

   28-1. To increase a target behaviour, you would use _____. The reinforcer (can/cannot) be something that you already are receiving. For example, you probably already watch TV, go to movies, or buy things for yourself, so you could make one of these events _____ on an increased frequency of the target behaviour.

   28-2. You would specify exactly what behavioural goals must be met before you receive the reinforcer; that is, you would arrange the _____. If your goal is to increase your studying, you might specify that TV watching for one hour is _____ on having studied for two hours.

28-3. Or you might specify that for each hour you studied you would earn points that could be "spent" for watching TV, going to movies, talking with friends, and so on. This type of arrangement is referred to as a _____ economy.

28-4. A fairly obvious way to decrease a target behaviour is to use _____. The problem with this approach is that it is difficult to follow through with self-punishment. So, there are two guidelines to keep in mind when using punishment in a self-control program: (1) Use punishment only in conjunction with _____ reinforcement; and (2) use a relatively _____ punishment that you, or perhaps a third party, will be able to administer.

28-5. It is also possible to use reinforcement to alter a problematic behaviour. For example, if you want to gradually reduce the amount that you smoke, you could reinforce yourself whenever you smoke fewer than a particular number of cigarettes per day. In this case, the behaviour being reinforced is "_____ _____."

28-6. For some situations you may be able to identify events that reliably precede the behaviours you are trying to stop. For example, for some people smoking is at least under partial control by certain types of social events. So, one strategy for decreasing a behaviour is to identify, and then avoid, the (antecedent/consequent) events that may control the behaviour.

Answers: **28-1.** reinforcement, can, contingent **28-2.** contingency, contingent **28-3.** token **28-4.** punishment, positive, mild **28-5.** smoking less **28-6.** antecedent.

29. Discuss how to execute, evaluate, and end a self-modification program.

29-1. Successful execution of the program depends on several factors. To avoid cheating, try creating a formal, written, behavioural _____. Or make an arrangement so that (only you/someone else) delivers the reinforcers and punishments.

29-2. If your program isn't working, some small revision may turn it around. Try increasing the strength of the reinforcer, or else try _____ the delay between the behaviour and delivery of the reinforcer.

29-3. It is generally a good idea to specify in advance the conditions under which you would end the program. You may wish to phase it out by having a(n) (gradual/immediate) reduction in the frequency or potency of reinforcers, although for some successful programs the new behaviours become self-maintaining on their own.

Answers: **29-1.** contract (or agreement), someone else **29-2.** decreasing **29-3.** gradual.

CRITICAL THINKING APPLICATION * MANIPULATING EMOTIONS: PAVLOV AND PERSUASION

30. Describe how classical conditioning is used to manipulate emotions.

30-1. It is easy to forget that Pavlovian conditioning involves more than salivating dogs. It involves emotion, and in that respect it is important for a range of reactions—from phobias to sexual arousal to the effects of advertising. For practice with conditioning concepts, label each of the following:

(a) A glamorous woman is shown entering an automobile. Label each of the following with CS, UCS, CR, and UCR. (Assume, for the sake of this example, that the target audience is initially more attracted to the woman than to the car. It could work the other way too.)

_____ the woman

_____ the car

_____ attraction to the car

_____ attraction to the woman

(b) A politician stands in front of a Stanley Cup–winning hockey team.

What is the CS? _____

The UCS? _____

(c) A salesperson takes you to lunch.

What is the CS? _____

The UCS? _____

The CR? _____

30-2. Of course, there's more going on in these examples than just classical conditioning. When we receive a favour, we are not only being conditioned; we may also feel obliged to pay back or _____ the person's favour.

30-3. While the examples we've used involve liking or attraction, other emotions may be conditioned as well—such as feelings of masculinity and femininity. Want to be more masculine? Drink this beer, ads may suggest. Not that we must be conscious of manipulation attempts, for conditioning (does/does not) seem to require our awareness.

30-4. How do we protect ourselves against attempts to manipulate our emotions? One suggestion from research on persuasion is that merely being _____ of the pervasiveness of conditioning will by itself provide some protections against manipulation strategies.

Answers: 30-1. (a) UCS, CS, CR, UCR, (b) the politician, the winning team, (c) the salesman (or his product), the lunch, liking of the salesman (or his product) **30-2.** reciprocate **30-3.** does not **30-4.** forewarned (or aware).

Acquisition
Antecedents
Avoidance learning
Behavioural contract
Behaviour modification
Classical conditioning
Conditioned reinforcers
Conditioned response (CR)
Conditioned stimulus (CS)
Conditioning
Continuous reinforcement
Cumulative recorder
Discriminative stimuli
Elicit
Emit
Escape learning
Extinction
Fixed-interval schedule

Fixed-ratio (FR) schedule
Higher order conditioning
Instinctive Drift
Instrumental learning
Intermittent reinforcement
Latent learning
Law of effect
Learning
Mirror neurons
Negative reinforcement
Observational learning
Operant chamber
Operant conditioning
Partial reinforcement
Pavlovian conditioning
Phobias
Positive reinforcement
Preparedness

Primary reinforcers
Punishment
Reinforcement
Reinforcement contingencies
Resistance to extinction
Schedule of reinforcement
Secondary reinforcers
Shaping
Skinner box
Spontaneous recovery
Stimulus discrimination
Stimulus generalization
Token economy
Trial
Unconditioned response (UCR)
Unconditioned stimulus (UCS)
Variable-interval (VI) schedule
Variable-ratio (VR) schedule

1. A relatively durable change in behaviour or knowledge that is due to experience.

2. Irrational fears of specific objects or situations.

3. The most common name for a type of learning in which a neutral stimulus acquires the ability to evoke a response that was originally evoked by another stimulus.

4. Another name for classical conditioning, derived from the name of the person who originally discovered the conditioning phenomenon.

5. Reducing the rate of a behaviour by following occurrence of the behaviour with presentation of an aversive stimulus or by removal of a positive stimulus.

6. A stimulus that evokes an unconditioned response.

7. The response to an unconditioned stimulus.

8. A previously neutral stimulus that has acquired the capacity to evoke a conditioned response.

9. A learned reaction to a conditioned stimulus that occurs because of previous conditioning.

10. To draw out or bring forth, as in classical conditioning.

11. Any presentation of a stimulus or pair of stimuli in classical conditioning.

12. The formation of a new response tendency.

13. Neurons that are activated by performing an action or seeing another person performing an action.

14. The gradual weakening and disappearance of a conditioned response tendency.

15. The reappearance of an extinguished response after a period of nonexposure to the conditioned stimulus.

16. Occurs when an organism responds to new stimuli that are similar to the stimulus used in conditioning.

_____ 17. Occurs when an organism learns not to respond to stimuli that are similar to the stimulus used in conditioning.

_____ 18. Occurs when a conditioned stimulus functions as if it were an unconditioned stimulus.

_____ 19. This term, introduced by Skinner, refers to learning in which voluntary responses come to be controlled by their consequences.

_____ 20. Another name for operant conditioning, this term was introduced earlier by Edward L. Thorndike.

_____ 21. Law stating that if a response in the presence of a stimulus leads to satisfying effects, the association between the stimulus and the response is strengthened.

_____ 22. Occurs when an event following a response strengthens the tendency to make that response.

_____ 23. A standard operant chamber in which an animal's responses are controlled and recorded.

_____ 24. Production of voluntary responses in responding in operant conditioning.

_____ 25. The circumstances or rules that determine whether responses lead to presentation of reinforcers; or, the relationship between a response and positive consequences.

_____ 26. Device that creates a graphic record of operant responding as a function of time.

_____ 27. The reinforcement of closer and closer approximations of the desired response.

_____ 28. Occurs when an organism continues to make a response after delivery of the reinforcer for it has been terminated.

_____ 29. Cues that influence operant behaviour by indicating the probable consequences (reinforcement or nonreinforcement) of a response.

_____ 30. Stimulus events that are inherently reinforcing because they satisfy biological needs.

_____ 31. Stimulus events that acquire reinforcing qualities by being associated with primary reinforcers.

_____ 32. A specific pattern of presentation of reinforcers over time.

_____ 33. Occurs when every instance of a designated response is reinforced.

_____ 34. The name for all schedules of reinforcement in which a designated response is reinforced only some of the time.

_____ 35. The schedule in which the reinforcer is given after a fixed number of nonreinforced responses.

_____ 36. The schedule in which the reinforcer is given after a variable number of nonreinforced responses.

_____ 37. The schedule in which the reinforcer is given for the first response that occurs after a fixed time interval has elapsed.

_____ 38. The schedule in which the reinforcer is given for the first response that occurs after a variable time interval has elapsed.

_____ 39. Occurs when a response is strengthened because it is followed by the arrival of a rewarding (presumably pleasant) stimulus.

_____ 40. Occurs when a response is strengthened because it is followed by the removal of an aversive (unpleasant) stimulus.

_____ 41. Occurs when an organism engages in a response that brings aversive stimulation to an end.

_____ 42. Occurs when an organism engages in a response that prevents aversive stimulation from occurring.

_____ 43. Learning associations between events that occur in an organism's environment.

_____ 44. Occurs when an animal's innate response tendencies interfere with conditioning processes.

_____ 45. Occurs when an organism's responding is influenced by the observation of others, who are called models.

_____ 46. A systematic approach to changing behaviour through the application of the principles of conditioning.

_____ 47. Events that typically precede your target behaviour and may play a major role in governing your target response; also, another term for discriminative stimuli.

_____ 48. A system for distributing symbolic reinforcers that are exchanged later for a variety of genuine reinforcers.

_____ 49. A written agreement outlining a promise to adhere to the contingencies of a behaviour-modification program.

_____ 50. When a designated response is reinforced only some of the time; another name for intermittent reinforcement.

_____ 51. Another name for secondary reinforcers.

_____ 52. A species-specific predisposition to be conditioned in certain ways and not in others.

_____ 53. A small enclosure in which an animal's responses are recorded and followed by specified consequences; a Skinner box.

_____ 54. Learning that is not apparent from behaviour when it first occurs.

Answers: 1. learning **2.** phobias **3.** classical conditioning **4.** Pavlovian conditioning **5.** punishment **6.** unconditioned stimulus (UCS) **7.** unconditioned response (UCR) **8.** conditioned stimulus (CS) **9.** conditioned response (CR) **10.** elicit **11.** trial **12.** acquisition **13.** mirror neurons **14.** extinction **15.** spontaneous recovery **16.** stimulus generalization **17.** stimulus discrimination **18.** higher-order conditioning **19.** operant conditioning **20.** instrumental learning **21.** law of effect **22.** reinforcement **23.** Skinner box **24.** emit **25.** reinforcement contingencies **26.** cumulative recorder **27.** shaping **28.** resistance to extinction **29.** discriminative stimuli **30.** primary reinforcers **31.** secondary reinforcers **32.** schedule of reinforcement **33.** continuous reinforcement **34.** intermittent reinforcement **35.** Fixed-ratio (FR) schedule **36.** variable-ratio (VR) schedule **37.** Fixed-interval (FI) schedule **38.** variable-interval (VI) schedule **39.** positive reinforcement **40.** negative reinforcement **41.** escape learning **42.** avoidance learning **43.** conditioning **44.** instinctive drift **45.** observational learning **46.** behaviour modification **47.** antecedents **48.** token economy **49.** behavioural contract **50.** partial reinforcement **51.** conditioned reinforcers **52.** preparedness **53.** operant chamber **54.** latent learning.

REVIEW OF KEY PEOPLE

Albert Bandura	Robert Rescorla	E.L. Thorndike
John Garcia	Martin Seligman	
Ivan Pavlov	B.F. Skinner	

_____ 1. The first to describe the process of classical conditioning.

_____ 2. Developed a principle known as the law of effect; coined the term "instrumental learning."

_____ 3. Elaborated the learning process known as operant conditioning; investigated schedules of reinforcement; developed programmed learning.

4. Asserted that environmental stimuli serve as signals and that some stimuli in classical conditioning are better signals than others.

5. Described and extensively investigated the process of observational learning.

6. Discovered that taste aversion was conditioned only through taste and nausea pairings and not through other stimulus pairings, such as taste and shock.

7. Proposed the theory of preparedness, the notion that there are species-specific predispositions to condition to certain stimuli and not to others.

Answers: 1. Pavlov **2.** Thorndike **3.** Skinner **4.** Rescorla **5.** Bandura **6.** Garcia **7.** Seligman.

SELF-QUIZ

1. In Pavlov's original demonstration of classical conditioning, what did salivation to the bell represent?
   a. conditioned stimulus
   b. conditioned response
   c. unconditioned stimulus
   d. unconditioned response

2. Sally developed a fear of balconies after she almost fell from a balcony on several occasions. In her case, what was the conditioned response?
   a. the balcony
   b. fear of the balcony
   c. almost falling
   d. fear resulting from almost falling

3. When the unconditioned stimulus (UCS) is removed and the conditioned stimulus (CS) is presented alone for a period of time, what will occur?
   a. classical conditioning
   b. generalization
   c. acquisition
   d. extinction

4. Sally developed a fear of balconies after almost falling. Although she has had no dangerous experiences on bridges, cliffs, or tall buildings, she now fears these situations as well. What likely produced a fear of these other situations?
   a. instinctive drift
   b. spontaneous recovery
   c. generalization
   d. discrimination

5. When a researcher reinforces closer and closer approximations to the target behaviour, what procedure is being used?
   a. shaping
   b. classical conditioning
   c. discrimination training
   d. extinction

6. John says, "Please pass the salt." Ralph passes the salt. "Thank you," says John. John's request precedes a behaviour (salt passing) that is reinforced ("Thank you"). In what terms does the request "Please pass the salt" relate to the passing of the salt?
   a. as a discriminative stimulus
   b. as a response
   c. as a positive reinforcer
   d. as a conditioned stimulus (CS)

7. A rat is reinforced for the first lever-pressing response that occurs, on the average, after 60 seconds. Which schedule is the rat on?
   a. fixed ratio
   b. variable ratio
   c. fixed interval
   d. variable interval

8. When the rat presses a lever, the mild electric shock on the cage floor is turned off. What procedure is being used?
   a. punishment
   b. escape
   c. discrimination training
   d. avoidance

9. A cue light comes on in the dog's shuttle box. It jumps the hurdle to the other side. What procedure is being used?
   a. punishment
   b. escape
   c. discrimination training
   d. avoidance

10. In avoidance learning, by what process does the cue stimulus acquire the capacity to elicit fear?
    a. operant conditioning
    b. classical conditioning
    c. generalization
    d. discrimination

11. The contingencies are as follows: if the response occurs, a stimulus is *presented*; if the response does not occur, the stimulus is not presented. Under this procedure, the strength of the response *increases*. What procedure is being used?
    a. positive reinforcement
    b. negative reinforcement
    c. punishment
    d. avoidance training

12. In terms of the traditional view of conditioning, what are the two main reasons why research on conditioned taste aversion was surprising?
    a. There was a long delay between CS and UCS, and cues other than taste did not condition.
    b. The dislike of a particular taste was operantly conditioned, and nontaste cues were classically conditioned.
    c. Conditioning did not occur to taste cues, but conditioning did occur to all other stimuli present when the food was consumed.
    d. The sense of taste and smell seem to be relatively weak.

13. Animal trainers (the Brelands) trained pigs to put coins in a piggy bank for a food reward. The animals learned the response, but instead of depositing the coins immediately in the bank, the pigs began to toss them in the air, drop them, push them on the ground, and so on. What had occurred that interfered with conditioning?
   a. conditioned taste aversion
   b. blocking
   c. instinctive drift
   d. signal relations

14. Which of the following produces strong resistance to extinction?
   a. a continuous reinforcement schedule
   b. an intermittent reinforcement schedule
   c. optimal foraging behaviour
   d. discrimination and differentiation

15. In the case of Little Albert, which was the unconditioned stimulus?
   a. the white rat
   b. the loud sound
   c. all white furry animals
   d. the fear toward the rat

16. According to Siegel, what might happen to cues in the environment that are repeatedly associated with the taking of a drug?
   a. They may become conditioned responses.
   b. They may become unconditioned stimuli.
   c. They may become conditioned stimuli.
   d. They may become conditioned responses.

Answers: 1. b **2.** b **3.** d **4.** c **5.** a **6.** a **7.** d **8.** b **9.** d **10.** b **11.** a **12.** a **13.** c **14.** b **15.** b **16.** c.

Chapter Seven
HUMAN MEMORY

Review of Key Ideas

ENCODING: GETTING INFORMATION INTO MEMORY

1. Describe the three basic human memory processes.

1-1.   The three basic human memory processes are:

(a) Putting the information in, a process called _____.

(b) Holding on to the information, a process called _____.

(c) Getting the information back out, a process called _____.

Answers: **1-1.** (a) encoding, (b) storage, (c) retrieval.

2. Discuss the role of attention in memory.

2-1.   If you are being introduced to a new person and you want to remember her name, it is first necessary to give selective _____ to this information. This requires _____ out irrelevant sensory input. The debate between early and late selection theories of attention is an argument over when this filtering takes place, before or after _____ is given to the arriving material.

2-2.   Although there is ample evidence to support both early- and late-selection theories of attention, what conclusion have some been led to?

2-3.   What effect does divided attention have on memory and many other tasks, such as using a cellphone while driving?

2-4.   Canadian psychologists Hasher and Zacks distinguished between _____ (intentional) processing of information and _____ (nonintentional) processing of information. This distinction means that, at times, people can know information but not remember how they acquired the knowledge.

Answers: **2-1.** attention, filtering, meaning **2-2.** The location of the attention filter may be flexible rather than fixed. **2-3.** It decreases performance. **2-4.** effortful, automatic.

3. Describe the three levels of information processing proposed by Craik and Lockhart and how processing relates to memory.

3-1.   Craik and Lockhart proposed three levels for encoding incoming information, with ever-increasing retention as the depth of processing increases. In their order of depth these three levels are

(a) _____   (b) _____   (c) _____

3-2. Below are three-word sequences. Tell which level of processing each sequence illustrates and why.

(a) cat   IN   tree   _____

(b) car   BAR   czar   _____

(c) CAN CAP   CAR   _____

3-3. If this theory is correct, then we would expect most persons to best remember the sequence in _____. This is because the words in this sequence have greater_____ than do the other two sequences. It has been found that processing time (is/is not) a reliable index of depth of processing, and thus what constitutes "levels" remains vague.

Answers: **3-1.** (a) structural, (b) phonemic, (c) semantic **3-2.** (a) Semantic because we immediately give meaning to the words. (b) Phonemic because the words sound alike. (c) Structural because the words look alike. **3-3.** a (cat in tree); meaning; is not.

4. Describe three techniques for enriching encoding and research on each.

4-1. Elaboration helps us to better remember the words RUN FAST CAT than the words WORK SLOW TREE. Why is this?

4-2. According to Paivio's dual-coding theory, why is it easier to remember the word APPLE than the word PREVAIL?

4-3. What is the general idea behind self-referent encoding?

Answers: **4-1.** Because the words RUN FAST CAT allow us to make richer and more elaborate associations among them than do the other three words (for example, you can imagine a cat running fast). **4-2.** Because it is easier to form a visual image of the word APPLE, thus allowing for storage of both the word and the image. **4-3.** We are more likely to remember information when it is relevant to ourselves.

STORAGE: MAINTAINING INFORMATION IN MEMORY

5. Describe the role of the sensory store in memory.

5-1. Sensory memory allows for retention of information for a very (brief/long) period of time. The retention time for sensory memory for both vision and audition is about _____ _____. During this brief period the information (remains in/is changed from) its original sensory form.

Answers: **5-1.** brief, 1/4 second, remains in.

6. Discuss the characteristics of short-term memory (STM).

6-1. Indicate whether the following statements regarding short-term memory are true or false.

_____(a) Has a virtually unlimited storage capacity.

_____(b) Has a storage capacity of seven, plus or minus two, items (or, according to recent evidence, perhaps as low as four plus or minus one).

_____(c) Requires continuous rehearsal to maintain information in store for more than 20 or 30 seconds.

_____(d) Stores information more or less permanently.

_____(e) Chunking can help to increase the capacity of this system.

_____ (f) Experts chunk information differently and more efficiently than nonexperts.

Answers: 6-1. (a) false, (b) true, (c) true, (d) false, (e) true, (f) true.

7. Discuss Baddeley's model of working memory.

7-1. According to Baddeley, *working memory* is a limited capacity storage system that temporarily maintains and stores information, providing an interface between perception, memory, and _____.

7-2. Say which component of Baddeley's working memory (phonological rehearsal loop, visuospatial sketchpad, executive control system, or episodic buffer) is operating in the following situations.

(a) You successfully divide your attention between the TV and a friend's conversation.

(b) You continue to recite a phone number as you walk toward the phone.

(c) You are describing the location of a restaurant to a friend.

(d) You are able to compare your memory of what an old friend looked like with his or her current appearance.

7-3. Research has supported Baddeley's model of working memory. For example, tasks that involve the visuospatial _____ do not interfere with tasks that engage in the phonological _____.

7-4. *Working memory capacity* is one's ability to hold and manipulate information in _____ _____. It is thought to play a role in complex cognitive abilities, such as reading comprehension, reasoning, intelligence, and musical ability.

8. **Evaluate the hypothesis that all memories are stored permanently in long-term memory (LTM).**

   8-1.   There are two views regarding the durability of information in LTM. One is that no information is ever lost, and the other is that _____ information is lost. Those who favour the permanent view explain forgetting as a failure of _____. The information is still there, we just cannot get it out.

   8-2.   How do those who doubt the permanency of long-term memory counter the following two lines of evidence cited by the permanent proponents?

   (a) Flashbulb memories of previous events?

   (b) Penfield's electrically triggered memories?

9. **Describe conceptual hierarchies, schemas, and semantic networks, and their role in long-term memory.**

   9-1.   Group the following words into two groups, or categories:

           rose   dog   grass   cat   tree   rat

   You probably grouped the words into plants and animals, which is the general idea behind _____. Thus, clustering leads to forming categories (concepts), and in turn the categories are organized into _____ hierarchies. For example, the categories of plants and animals can be placed under the higher category (hierarchy) of _____ things.

   9-2.   It also appears that LTM stores information in clusters of knowledge about particular objects or events, called _____. For example, in the study cited by the text, the subjects who falsely recalled seeing books did so because of their schema of what a professor's _____ looks like. Although people are (more/less) likely to remember things consistent with their schemas, this is not always true, particularly with objects that contrast (dramatically/casually) with their schema-based expectations. It has also been suggested that people can possess _____ schemas, which are representations of events that surround interpersonal interactions. These are thought to affect how we process information about others and ourselves.

9-3. In addition to conceptual categories, it appears that LTM also stores information in terms of semantic networks. If you understand the idea behind semantic networks and its related idea of spreading activation, you should be able to answer the questions below.

Person A attends an urban university and frequently studies while riding a bus to and from school.

Person B attends a university located in a rural area and frequently studies outside in one of the many parklike areas surrounding the school.

(a) When asked to think of words associated with the word STUDY, which of the students is most likely to think of the word GRASS?_____

(b) Which person is most likely to think of the word TRAFFIC?_____

(c) Which person is most likely to think of the word PEACEFUL?_____

Answers: 9-1. clustering, conceptual, living **9-2.** schemas, office, more, dramatically, relational **9-3.** (a) person B, (b) person A, (c) person B.

10. Explain how parallel distributed processing (PDP) models view the representation of information in memory.

10-1. Parallel distributed processing (PDP) models assume that a piece of knowledge is represented by a particular _____ of activation across an entire system of interconnected neural networks. This approach is called "connectionism" because the information lies in the strengths of the _____.

Answers: 10-1. pattern, connections.

RETRIEVAL: GETTING INFORMATION BACK OUT OF MEMORY

11. Explain how retrieval cues and context cues influence retrieval.

11-1. Tulving distinguished between poor retrieval that is due to a lack of _____ of the information (the information is no longer in the memory system) versus poor retrieval that reflects lack of _____ of the information (available but not accessible at the moment).

11-2. In the following examples, indicate whether retrieval cues or context cues are being used to retrieve information from long-term memory.

(a) In trying to recall the name of a high school classmate, you get the feeling that his first name began with an "L," and begin saying names like Larry, Leroy, Lionel, etc.

(b) Or you may attempt to recall the high school classmate by imagining the history class in which he sat in the row next to you.

11-3. The term used to refer to situations in which memory is improved because the conditions during encoding and retrieval are similar is the "_____ _____ principle." Even matching a person's _____ state at encoding and retrieval, such as a state of intoxication or a particular mood-state, may facilitate memory.

Answers: 11-1. availability, accessibility **11-2.** (a) retrieval cues, (b) context cues **11-3.** encoding specificity, internal.

12. Discuss Bartlett's work and research on the misinformation effect.

12-1. Bartlett's work with "The War of the Ghosts" found that the subjects reconstructed the original tale to fit with their already established _____. Since we use schemas to move information into and out of long-term memory, it is not too surprising that retrieved information may be altered by these schemas.

12-2. For example, Elizabeth Loftus found that subjects who were originally asked, "How fast were the cars going when they (hit/smashed) into each other?" were much more likely to falsely recall having seen broken glass on a videotaped scene when tested at a later date. In this case the word "smashed" resulted in a different _____ than did the word "hit." The distortion of memory by the word "smashed" is an example of how post-event information can result in the _____ of an original memory. This phenomenon has been called the _____ effect.

12-3. Even the process of retelling a story can introduce _____ into memory. This reflects the fact that when telling a story, people adjust it to their goals, audience, or context. These distortions can then reshape their later recollections of the same events.

Answers: 12-1. schemas **12-2.** smashed, schema, reconstruction, misinformation **12-3.** inaccuracies (or errors).

13. Discuss the implications of evidence on source monitoring and reality monitoring, and identify what is meant by destination memory.

13-1. A third explanation for distorted memory retrieval involves reality monitoring and source monitoring. Reality monitoring involves judging whether memories come from _____ or _____ events. Source monitoring concerns attributions about the _____ of memories. Errors in memory from both kinds of monitoring are (rare/common).

13-2. Say whether the situations below are examples of source monitoring (S) or reality monitoring (R).

_____ (a) You become convinced that you broke your arm when you were five years old, but your mother tells you that it never happened.

_____ (b) You attribute a funny story to your good friend Tom when in fact it was Fred, whom you don't really care for, who told you the story.

_____ (c) You believe that you received an A in high school algebra, but your transcript shows a C.

13-3. Recalling that you have told your mother but not recalling that you have told your sister about your A grade on your psychology exam is an example of _____ memory.

Answers: 13-1. external, internal, origins, common **13-2.** (a) R, (b) S, (c) R **13-3.** destination memory.

FORGETTING: WHEN MEMORY LAPSES

14. Describe Ebbinghaus's forgetting curve and three measures of retention.

14-1. Ebbinghaus's forgetting curve, using nonsense syllables and himself as the subject, showed that forgetting was most rapid in the (first/second) nine hours after learning the material. Later research has shown that the dramatic decline is (the same/much less) when more meaningful material is involved.

14-2. Which of the three different methods of measuring forgetting is illustrated in each of the following situations?

(a) You are asked to identify a suspect in a police line-up.

(b) You time yourself while learning 20 new French words. After a week you find you have forgotten some of the words, and you again time yourself while learning the list a second time.

(c) You are asked to draw a floor plan of your bedroom from memory.

Answers: 14-1. first, much less **14-2.** (a) recognition, (b) relearning, (c) recall.

15. **Explain how forgetting may be due to ineffective encoding.**

   15-1. Why are most people unable to recognize things that they have seen on many occasions, such as a Canadian penny?

   15-2. What is another name for information loss due to ineffective coding of this kind?

   15-3. Why is semantic coding better than phonemic coding for enhancing future recall of written material?

   Answers: **15-1.** They never encoded the correct figure in their memories. **15-2.** pseudoforgetting
   15-3. Semantic coding will lead to deeper processing and more elaborate associations.

16. **Compare and contrast decay and interference as potential causes of forgetting.**

   16-1. Two other theories of forgetting propose additional factors that may be involved in retrieval failure. One theory holds that retrieval failure may be due to the impermanence of the memory storage itself. This is the notion behind the _____ theory of forgetting. Decay theory is best able to explain retrieval failure in _____ _____ memory and to a lesser extent in (short-term/long-term) memory.

   16-2. The other theory attributes retrieval failure to other information already in the memory or to information arriving at a later time. This is the notion behind the _____ theory of forgetting. According to interference theory, the failure may be caused by interference from information already in the memory, a phenomenon called _____ interference, or the failure may be caused by interference occurring after the original memory was stored, a phenomenon called _____ interference. Interference is most likely to occur when the materials being stored are very (similar/different).

   Answers: **16-1.** decay, sensory store, short-term **16-2.** interference, proactive, retroactive, similar.

17. **Explain how forgetting may be due to factors in the retrieval process.**

   17-1. Breakdowns in the retrieval process can occur when the encoding specificity principle is violated. This means there has been a mismatch between the original memory code and the _____ cue being used to retrieve the information. A common instance of this violation is seen when one attempts to retrieve a semantically coded word with (semantic/phonemic) retrieval cues.

17-2. Retrieval failure may also occur when there is a poor fit between initial encoding processing and the processing required by the measure of retention. In other words, the two kinds of processing are not transfer-_____.

17-3. Sigmund Freud felt that some breakdowns in the retrieval process could be attributed to purposeful suppression of information by unconscious forces, a phenomenon called _____ forgetting. Freud called motivated forgetting _____.

Answers: 17-1. retrieval, phonemic **17-2.** appropriate **17-3.** motivated, repression.

18. Summarize evidence for the view that most recovered memories of childhood sexual abuse are genuine.

18-1. Those who argue that most of these recovered memories are genuine assert that the frequency of sexual abuse in childhood is (less/more) widespread than most people realize.

18-2. What did the 17-year follow-up study find regarding 129 female children who had had emergency treatment for sexual abuse?

Answers: 18-1. more **18-2.** 38% failed to report the original incident.

19. Summarize evidence for the view that most recovered memories of childhood sexual abuse are inaccurate.

19-1. How do the sceptics of these recovered memories of childhood sexual abuse explain their origin?

19-2. What is the only way to tell for certain if a recovered memory is genuine or a pseudomemory?

Answers: 19-1. Some suggestible people are convinced by persuasive therapists (that these events must have happened). **19-2.** through independent corroborative evidence.

20. Identify the seven sins of memory.

20-1. According to Schachter, the sins of transience, absentmindedness, and blocking are sins of _____. _____ involves memories weakening over time, absentmindedness reflects failing to pay attention, and _____ is revealed in the tip-of-the-tongue phenomenon.

20-2. The sins of misattribution, suggestibility, bias, and persistence are sins of _____. Misattribution would be demonstrated in a source monitoring error, _____ may reflect the influence of misleading questions, bias refers to the influence of current feelings or knowledge on how we reconstruct past events, and _____ describes being unable to forget unwanted memories (e.g., of trauma).

Answers: 20-1. omission, Transience, blocking **20-2.** commission, suggestibility, persistence.

IN SEARCH OF THE MEMORY TRACE: THE PHYSIOLOGY OF MEMORY

21. **Summarize evidence on the neural circuitry underlying memory.**

    21-1.   Which of the following changes have been implicated in the physiology of memory?

            (a) alterations in synaptic transmission at specific sites

            (b) induced changes in RNA

    21-2.   Answer the following questions regarding the neural circuitry of memory.

            (a) What caused a rabbit to lose its memory of a conditioned eye blink?

            (b) What neural changes were found in rats that learned to run a series of mazes?

            (c) What does research with long-term potentiation (LTP) tell us about how memory is stored?

            (d) What is long-term depression (LTD), and what is it relevant to?

            (e) What is thought to be the relevance of neurogenesis to memory?

Answers: 21-1. a **21-2.** (a) destruction of an area in the cerebellum, (b) increased growth of neuronal dendritic trees, (c) Specific memories may have specific localized dedicated neural circuits. (d) Long-term depression involves a decrease in neural excitability along a pathway, and it may be related to forgetting. (e) Neurogenesis may enhance memory, and a lack of neurogenesis may impair memory. Also, it is speculated that neurogenesis allows memories to be "time-stamped" (i.e., newer cells are associated with newer memories).

22. **Distinguish between two types of amnesia, and identify the anatomical structures implicated in memory.**

    22-1.   Amnesia cases due to head injury provide clues about the anatomical basis of memory. There are two basic types of head-injury amnesia. When the memory loss is for events prior to the injury, it is called _____ amnesia. When the memory loss is for events following the injury, it is called _____ amnesia.

22-2. What general region of the brain appears to play a major role in the consolidation of memories?

22-3. Consolidation is a hypothesized process that involves the gradual conversion of information into durable memory _____ stored in long-term memory. These memories are consolidated in the hippocampal region and then stored (<u>in the hippocampus/all over the cortex</u>).

22-4. The neural basis for working memory may involve several areas. The central executive may especially involve the _____ cortex, whereas the phonological loop and the visuospatial sketchpad may involve areas within the left and right hemispheres, respectively.

Answers: 22-1. retrograde, anterograde **22-2.** the entire hippocampal region (also referred to as the medial temporal lobe memory system) **22-3.** codes, all over the cortex **22-4.** prefrontal.

ARE THERE MULTIPLE MEMORY SYSTEMS?

23. Distinguish between implicit versus explicit memory and between declarative and procedural memory.

23-1. Label the two following situations as to whether they are examples of implicit or explicit memory.

(a) After studying for your history test, you were able to easily recall the information during the exam.

(b) While studying for your history exam, you unexpectedly recall an incident from the previous summer.

23-2. Another division of memory systems has been hypothesized for declarative memory and procedural memory. Identify these two divisions from their descriptions given below.

(a) This system allows you to drive a car or play a piano with minimal attention to the execution of movements that are required.

(b) This system allows you to explain how to drive a car or play a piano to a friend.

23-3. Describe at least two lines of evidence supporting the distinction between procedural and declarative memory.

Answers: **23-1.** (a) explicit, (b) implicit **23-2.** (a) procedural, (b) declarative **23-3.** Declarative memory depends on conscious, effortful processes; it declines over time; and it is severely impaired in amnesiacs. These aren't generally true for procedural memory.

24. Explain the distinctions between episodic versus semantic memory and prospective versus retrospective memory.

24-1. It has also been hypothesized that declarative memory can be further subdivided into semantic and episodic memory. Identify these two kinds of memory from the following descriptions:

(a) This kind of memory acts like an encyclopedia, storing all of the factual information you possess.

(b) This kind of memory acts like an autobiography, storing all of your personal experiences.

24-2. According to the Featured Study, episodic memory may be intimately related to our ability to imagine the _____. According to the constructive _____ _____ hypothesis, remembering the past and simulating the future (are/are not) highly similar and therefore utilize similar neural processes. Schachter and Addis showed that participants using words to remember a past event and those using words to imagine a future event both showed activation in similar brain regions when measured on an _____ machine.

24-3. Still another possibility is that we have separate memory systems for prospective and retrospective memory. The distinction here is between our ability to remember events from the past or previously learned information, _____ memory, and our ability to remember or perform actions in the future, _____ memory.

Answers: **24-1.** (a) semantic, (b) episodic **24-2.** future, episodic simulation, are, MRI **24-3.** retrospective, prospective.

PUTTING IT IN PERSPECTIVE

25. Explain how this chapter highlighted three of the text's unifying themes.

25-1. Three unifying themes were especially noteworthy in this chapter: the subjectivity of experience, psychology's theoretical diversity, and multifactorial causation. The text mentions two areas in which subjectivity may influence memory. Identify them as follows.

(a) We often see only that which gets the focus of our _____.

(b) Every time we tell about a particular experience, details are added or subtracted because of the _____ nature of memory.

25-2. The numerous debates about the nature of memory storage, the causes of forgetting, and the existence of multiple memory systems nicely illustrate psychology's _____

_____.

25-3. Since the memory of a specific event can be influenced by many factors, operating in each of the three memory stores, it is obvious that memory, like most behaviour, has

_____ _____.

Answers: 25-1. (a) attention, (b) reconstructive **25-2.** theoretical diversity **25-3.** multifactorial causation.

APPLICATION: IMPROVING EVERYDAY MEMORY

26. Discuss the importance of rehearsal, distributed practice, and interference in efforts to improve everyday memory.

26-1. The text lists three general strategies for improving everyday memory. Identify which strategy is being employed in the following examples.

(a) Most persons can remember their phone number because of extensive_____.

(b) Willie always takes breaks between study periods when changing subject matter. Willie must realize the importance of _____ practice.

(c) Ajax never studies any other material besides mathematics on the day of his math exams in order to minimize _____.

26-2. The serial position effect means that words in the middle of a list will need (more/less) of our attention.

Answers: 26-1. (a) rehearsal, (b) distributed, (c) interference **26-2.** more.

27. Discuss the value of deep processing and good organization in efforts to improve everyday memory.

27-1. Answering questions such as these is much better than simply underlining the same material in the text because it forces you to engage in _____ _____.

27-2. Outlining material from textbooks can enhance retention because it leads to better _____ of the material.

Answers: 27-1. deep processing **27-2.** organization.

28. Describe some verbal and visual mnemonic devices that can be used to improve everyday memory.

28-1. Specific strategies for enhancing memory are called _____ devices. Examples of strategies that do not employ visual images are listed below. See if you can identify which strategy is being employed in each illustration.

(a) Using the phrase "My Very Excellent Mother Just Sells Nuts Under Protest" to remember the names and positions of the planets illustrates the use of an _____.

(b) International Business Machines is easily identified by its _____, IBM.

(c) The phrase "One two three four, I left my keys in the drawer" illustrates the use of

_____.

(d) Since you are going to the store, your roommate asks you to bring her a bar of Ivory soap, a box of Kleenex, and a Snickers bar. You then make up a story which begins, "On my way to the Ivory Coast to check on the latest shipment of Kleenex, I...." Here you're making use of a _____ method as a mnemonic device.

28-2. Three techniques involving visual imagery can also serve as helpful mnemonic devices: the link method, the method of loci, and the keyword method. Identify these examples:

(a) You want to remember the name of your bus driver, Ray Blocker, who has especially large forearms. You form an image of a man using his large arms to block light rays from his face.

(b) You want to remember to buy bananas, eggs, milk, and bread. You visualize walking in your front door and tripping on a bunch of bananas. Stumbling forward into the hallway you notice broken eggs on the table, etc.

(c) You imagine yourself using a banana to break eggs, which you then pour into a bowl of milk and bread.

Answers: 28-1. mnemonic, (a) acrostic, (b) acronym, (c) rhyming, (d) narrative **28-2.** (a) keyword method, (b) method of loci, (c) link method.

CRITICAL THINKING APPLICATION

29. Explain how hindsight bias and overconfidence contribute to the frequent inaccuracy of eye-witness testimony.

29-1. The frequent inaccuracy of eye-witness testimony is due in part to the reconstructive nature of memory, source monitoring, and the misinformation effect. In addition, the text points out that still another factor is our tendency to mould our interpretation of the past to fit how events actually turned out. This is called _____ _____.

29-2. The failure to seek disconfirming evidence can often lead to the _____ effect, which is still another reason for the frequent inaccuracy of eye-witness testimony.

Answers: 29-1. hindsight bias **29-2.** overconfidence.

Review of Key Terms

Anterograde amnesia	Keyword method	Retention
Attention	Levels-of-processing theory	Retrieval
Chunk	Link method	Retroactive interference
Clustering	Long-term memory (LTM)	Retrograde amnesia
Conceptual hierarchy	Long-term potentiation (LTP)	Retrospective memory
Connectionist models	Method of loci	Schema
Consolidation	Misinformation effect	Self-referent encoding
Decay theory	Mnemonic devices	Semantic memory system
Declarative memory system	Nondeclarative memory system	Semantic network
Dual-coding theory	Overlearning	Sensory memory
Elaboration	Parallel distributed processing (PDP) models	Serial-position effect
Encoding	Proactive interference	Short-term memory
Encoding specificity principle	Procedural memory system	Source monitoring
Episodic memory system	Prospective memory	Source-monitoring error
Explicit memory	Reality monitoring	Storage
Flashbulb memories	Recall	Tip-of-the-tongue
Forgetting curve	Recognition	Transfer-appropriate processing
Hindsight bias	Rehearsal	Working memory
Implicit memory	Relearning	Working memory capacity
Interference theory	Repression	

_____ 1. Putting coded information into memory.

_____ 2. Maintaining coded information in memory.

_____ 3. Recovering information from memory stores.

_____ 4. The process of focusing awareness on a narrowed range of stimuli or events.

_____ 5. Involves remembering to perform actions in the future.

_____ 6. Involves remembering events from the past or previously learned information.

_____ 7. The initial processing of information is similar to the type of processing required by the subsequent measure of retention.

_____ 8. Assume that cognitive processes depend on patterns of activation in highly interconnected computational networks that resemble neural networks. (Note: *Two* key terms apply to this definition.)

_____ 9. Memory that involves the intentional recollection of previous experiences.

_____ 10. A theory that proposes that deeper levels of processing result in longer-lasting memory codes.

_____ 11. Involves linking a stimulus to other information at the time of encoding.

_____ 12. A theory that memory is enhanced by forming both semantic and visual codes since either can lead to recall.

_____ 13. Preserves information in the original sensory form for a very brief time.

_____ 14. A limited capacity memory store that can maintain unrehearsed information for 20 to 30 seconds.

_____ 15. The process of repetitively verbalizing or thinking about new information.

_____ 16. A group of familiar stimuli stored as a single unit.

_____ 17. An unlimited capacity memory store that can hold information over lengthy periods of time.

_____ 18. Unusually vivid and detailed recollections of momentous events.

_____ 19. Occurs when subjects show better recall of items at the beginning and end of a list than of items in the middle.

_____ 20. Memory for factual information.

_____ 21. Memory for actions, skills, and operations.

_____ 22. Memory made up of chronological, or temporally dated, recollections of personal experiences.

_____ 23. Memory that contains general knowledge that is not tied to the time when the information was learned.

_____ 24. The tendency to remember similar or related items in a group.

_____ 25. These consist of concepts joined together by links that show how the concepts are related.

_____ 26. A long-lasting increase in neural excitability at synapses along a specific neural pathway.

_____ 27. An organized cluster of knowledge about a particular object or sequence of events.

_____ 28. The attempt to mould our interpretation of the past to fit how it actually turned out.

_____ 29. A temporary inability to remember something you know accompanied by the feeling that it's just out of reach.

_____ 30. A curve graphing retention and forgetting over time

_____ 31. The proportion of material remembered.

_____ 32. The ability to remember information without any cues.

_____ 33. Requires the selection of previously learned information from an array of options (e.g., multiple-choice tests).

_____ 34. Requires the memorization of information a second time to determine how much time or effort is saved.

_____ 35. Attributes forgetting to the impermanence of memory storage.

_____ 36. Attributes forgetting to competition from other material.

_____ 37. Occurs when new information impairs the retention of previously learned information.

_____ 38. Occurs when previously learned information impairs the retention of new information.

_____ 39. States that the value of a retrieval cue depends on how well it corresponds to the memory code.

_____ 40. Involves purposeful suppression of memories (motivated forgetting).

_____ **41.** A theoretical process involving the gradual conversion of information into durable memory codes stored in long-term memory.

_____ **42.** The loss of memory for events that occurred prior to a brain injury.

_____ **43.** The loss of memory for events that occur after a brain injury.

_____ **44.** Strategies for enhancing memory.

_____ **45.** The continued rehearsal of material after it has apparently been mastered.

_____ **46.** Involves forming a mental image of items to be remembered in a way that connects them together.

_____ **47.** A mnemonic device that involves taking an imaginary walk along a familiar path.

_____ **48.** Involves associating a concrete word with an abstract word and generating an image to represent the concrete word.

_____ **49.** A multi-level classification system based on common properties among items (e.g., cats, animals, living things).

_____ **50.** Is apparent when retention is exhibited on a task that does not require intentional remembering.

_____ **51.** The process of deciding how or whether information is personally relevant.

_____ **52.** The process of making attributions about the origins of memories.

_____ **53.** The process of deciding whether memories are based on external or internal sources.

_____ **54.** An error that occurs when a memory derived from one source is attributed to another.

_____ **55.** Another term for the procedural memory system, which houses memory for actions, skills, and operations.

_____ **56.** When recall of an event is altered by introducing misleading post-event information.

_____ **57.** A limited capacity storage system that temporarily maintains and stores information, providing an interface between perception, memory, and action.

_____ **58.** The ability to hold and manipulate information in conscious attention.

Answers: 1. encoding **2**. storage **3**. retrieval **4**. attention **5**. prospective memory **6**. retrospective memory **7**. transfer-appropriate processing **8**. connectionist models and parallel distributed processing (PDP) **9**. explicit memory **10**. levels of processing theory **11**. elaboration **12**. dual-coding theory **13**. sensory memory **14**. short-term memory (STM) **15**. rehearsal **16**. chunk **17**. long-term memory (LTM) **18**. flashbulb memories **19**. serial position effect **20**. declarative memory system **21**. procedural memory system **22**. episodic memory system **23**. semantic memory system **24**. clustering **25**. semantic networks **26**. long-term potentiation **27**. schema **28**. script **29**. tip-of-the-tongue phenomenon **30**. forgetting curve **31**. retention **32**. recall **33**. recognition **34**. relearning **35**. decay theory **36**. interference theory **37**. retroactive interference **38**. proactive interference **39**. encoding specificity principle **40**. repression **41**. consolidation **42**. retrograde amnesia **43**. anterograde amnesia **44**. mnemonic devices **45**. overlearning **46**. link method **47**. method of loci **48**. keyword method **49**. conceptual hierarchy **50**. implicit memory **51**. self-referent encoding **52**. source monitoring **53**. reality monitoring **54**. source-monitoring error **55**. nondeclarative memory **56**. misinformation effect **57**. working memory **58**. working memory capacity.

Review of Key People

Richard Atkinson and Richard Shiffrin   Marcia Johnson   Brenda Milner
Fergus Craik and Robert Lockhart   Elizabeth Loftus   Endel Tulving
Herman Ebbinghaus   George Miller

_____ 1. Proposed three progressively deeper levels for processing incoming information.

_____ 2. Influential in the development of the model of three different kinds of memory stores (sensory, STM, and LTM).

_____ 3. She and her colleagues proposed the notions of source and reality monitoring.

_____ 4. Demonstrated that the reconstructive nature of memory can distort eyewitness testimony.

_____ 5. Used nonsense syllables to become famous for his forgetting curve.

_____ 6. One of his many contributions was the encoding specificity principle.

_____ 7. Proposed the concept of chunking for storing information in short-term memory.

_____ 8. Followed the case of HM, who had his hippocampus removed.

Answers: 1. Craik and Lockhart **2.** Atkinson and Shiffrin **3.** Johnson **4.** Loftus **5.** Ebbinghaus **6.** Tulving **7.** Miller **8.** Milner.

Self-Quiz

1. Which of the following is NOT one of the three basic human memory processes?
   a. storage
   b. retrieval
   c. decoding
   d. encoding

2. Which one of the three levels of processing would probably be employed when someone attempts to memorize the following three-letter sequences: WAB, WAC, and WAD?
   a. structural
   b. semantic
   c. phonemic
   d. chunking

3. Which of the following statements applies to Paivio's dual-coding theory?
   a. Words are easier to encode than images.
   b. Abstract words are easier to encode than concrete words.
   c. Visual imagery may hinder the retrieval of words.
   d. It should be easier to remember the word *banana* than the word *justice*.

4. Retrieval from long-term memory is usually best when the information has been stored at which level of processing?
   a. structural
   b. semantic
   c. phonemic
   d. chunking

5. Which of the memory stores can store the least amount of information?
   a. sensory store
   b. short-term memory
   c. long-term memory
   d. episodic memory

6. Which of the following sequences of words would be most subject to a clustering effect?
   a. FAN HEAVEN JUSTICE CHAIR
   b. HOUSE VACATION MOUSE STATISTIC
   c. BLUE DOG CAMEL YELLOW
   d. CONVERSE ICICLE CONCEPT THINKING

7. According to Hasher and Zacks, what are the two ways that we can process information?
   a. effortful versus automatic
   b. inattentive versus attentive
   c. sensory versus perceptual
   d. bottom-up versus top-down

8. When you attempt to recall the name of a high school classmate by imagining yourself back in English class with her, what information are you using?
   a. retrieval cues
   b. context cues
   c. schemas
   d. recognition cues

9. You recall being lost in a shopping mall at the age of five, but your parents assure you that it never happened. What most likely causes errors like this?
   a. ineffective encoding
   b. a reality monitoring error
   c. a source monitoring error
   d. limited short-term memory capacity

10. What is being measured when you take this particular self-test?
    a. constructive errors
    b. reconstructive errors
    c. recall
    d. recognition

11. What might result from ineffective encoding of information?
    a. primacy effect
    b. recency effect
    c. pseudoforgetting
    d. chunking

12. Which location of memory loss is decay theory best able to explain?
    a. sensory store
    b. long-term memory
    c. short-term memory
    d. repressed memory

13. What is the likely result of violating the encoding specificity principle?
    a. being unable to encode information
    b. being unable to store information
    c. being unable to retrieve information
    d. being unable to form a visual image of the material you want to retrieve

14. Research has shown a higher corroboration rate for which of the following types of abuse memories?
    a. those that are very emotionally charged
    b. those that involved events prior to age 3
    c. those that are recovered spontaneously
    d. those that are recovered in therapy

15. What types of memory appear to be intimately related?
    a. implicit and procedural memory
    b. implicit and semantic memory
    c. explicit and procedural memory
    d. implicit and declarative memory

16. Why is it very easy to recall the name of your high school?
    a. because it has been subjected to extensive deep processing
    b. because it has been subjected to extensive clustering
    c. because it has been subjected to extensive chunking
    d. because it has been subjected to extensive rehearsal

17. What is often the result of failing to seek out disconfirming evidence?
    a. overconfidence effect
    b. reconstructive bias
    c. hindsight bias
    d. source monitoring error

18. What may be the cause of the amnesia experienced by a perpetrator of a violent crime?
    a. encoding specificity
    b. elaborative rehearsal
    c. parallel distributed processing
    d. semantic networks

19. Which of the following is a "sin of memory" that refers to how one's current knowledge can affect one's recall of the past?
    a. suggestibility
    b. bias
    c. persistence
    d. misattribution

Answers: 1. c 2. a 3. d 4. b 5. b 6. c 7. a 8. b 9. b 10. d 11. c 12. a 13. c 14. c 15. a 16. d 17. a 18. a 19. b.

Chapter Eight

LANGUAGE AND THOUGHT

REVIEW OF KEY IDEAS

THE COGNITIVE REVOLUTION IN PSYCHOLOGY

1. **Describe the "cognitive revolution" in psychology.**

   1-1.   Answer the following questions regarding the cognitive revolution in psychology.

   (a) In what decade did this revolution get underway?

   (b) Why were earlier cognitive approaches abandoned?

   (c) What topics did the cognitive revolution open up for cognitive psychologists to study?

   Answers: 1-1. (a) the 1950s, (b) because of the limitations of introspection and the rise of behaviourism, (c) memory, language, problem solving, decision-making, and reasoning.

LANGUAGE: TURNING THOUGHTS INTO WORDS

2. **Outline the key properties of language.**

   2-1.   Language is characterized by four properties: it is symbolic, semantic, generative, and structured. Identify each of these properties in the following statements.

   (a) Applying rules to arrange words into phrases and sentences illustrates the_____ property of language.

   (b) Using words or geometric forms to represent objects, actions, or events illustrates the _____ property of language.

   (c) Making different words out of the same letters, such as NOW and WON, illustrates the _____ property of language.

   (d) Giving the same meaning to different words, such as CHAT, KATZ, and CAT, illustrates the _____ aspect of language.

2-2. Identify the following parts (units) of language.

(a) With around 40 of these basic sounds you can say all of the words in the English language. _____

(b) Phonemes are combined into these smallest units of meaning in a language, which may include root words as well as prefixes and suffixes. _____

(c) The component of language concerned with understanding the meaning of words and word combinations is called _____.

(d) These rules specify how words can be combined into phrases and sentences. _____

Answers: 2-1. (a) structured, (b) symbolic, (c) generative, (d) semantic **2-2.** (a) phonemes, (b) morphemes, (c) semantics, (d) syntax.

3. Outline the development of human language during the first year.

3-1. Answer the following questions regarding the development of language during the first year of life.

(a) Even at two months of age, infants show a preference for _____ sounds, reflecting what Werker has called a "perceptual bias."

(b) What are a child's three major vocalizations during the first six months of life?

(c) What is the range in months for the babbling stage of language development?

(d) What gradually occurs as the babbling stage progresses?

(e) One view of babbling is that it is a _____ achievement, reflecting the brain's increasing control over motor operations required for speech. Another view is that babbling is a _____ achievement, reflecting the infant's increased ability to produce natural language.

Answers: 3-1. (a) speech, (b) crying, laughing, and cooing, (c) 6 to 18 months, (d) The babbling increasingly resembles spoken language. (e) motor, linguistic.

4. Describe children's early use of single words and word combinations.

4-1. What does the text mean when it states that the receptive vocabulary of toddlers is much larger than their productive vocabulary?

4-2. Identify the following phenomena observed in children's early use of language.

(a) What phenomenon is illustrated when a child calls all four-legged creatures "doggie"? _____

(b) What phenomenon is illustrated when a child correctly communicates her desire to know where the family dog is simply by asking, "Doggie?"_____

(c) What phenomenon is illustrated when a child complains to her mother, "Doggie eat cookie"?_____

(d) What phenomenon is illustrated when a child says, "Doggie runned away"?

(e) What phenomenon is illustrated when a child puns, "I love your I's"?_____

(f) Children begin to appreciate irony and sarcasm between the ages of _____ and _____.

(g) Solve the following anagram, which best describes how children acquire language skills: WSYLIFT._____

Answers: 4-1. They can understand more spoken words than they can reproduce themselves. **4-2.** (a) overextensions, (b) holophrases, (c) telegraphic speech, (d) overregularization, (e) metalinguistic awareness, (f) 6, 8, (g) SWIFTLY.

5. Describe the purpose, findings, and interpretation of the Featured Study on infant babbling.

5-1. Petitto and Marentette (1991) tested whether the maturation of speech production mechanisms (i.e., a motor achievement) or the maturation of a brain-based language capacity (i.e., a linguistic achievement) was behind infant babbling. They tested these alternative possibilities by studying _____ infants who use a nonspeech language, American _____ _____, and comparing them with hearing infants.

5-2. They predicted that if babbling represents a linguistic achievement then it (should/should not) appear (albeit in a different form) in deaf infants.

5-3. Results revealed that deaf infants showed evidence of _____ babbling. In addition, the babbling by deaf infants resembled babbling for hearing infants in terms of progression through stages and time course. They concluded that babbling does not reflect _____ mechanisms involved in speech production but rather reflects the developing _____ _____ of the infant.

Answers: 5-1. deaf, Sign Language **5-2.** should **5-3.** manual, motor, language capacity.

6. Summarize the effect of bilingualism on language and cognitive development, and the factors that influence the learning of a second language.

6-1. What does research comparing monolingual and bilingual children show with respect to their language and cognitive development?

6-2. What are some disadvantages and advantages of bilingualism?

6-3. What are the three hypotheses that account for the cognitive advantages of bilingualism?

6-4. For minority students, what are drawbacks of immersion in the majority language?

6-5. What three factors positively influence the learning of a second language?

Answers: 6-1. They are largely similar in their rate of development (in both areas). **6-2.** On some tasks, bilinguals may have a slight disadvantage on language-processing speed, but they may have advantage on tasks emphasizing cognitive flexibility, analytical reasoning, selective attention, and metalinguistic awareness. **6-3.** First, bilingual children may develop control over executive processes earlier than monolingual children. Second, as adults, enhanced executive control of bilinguals should give them advantages on tasks emphasizing executive function. Third, bilinguals should show delayed decline of executive processes as a function of aging. **6-4.** undermining self-esteem and heritage language proficiency, **6-5.** starting at an early age, becoming acculturated, and one's motivation and attitude toward the group whose language is being learned.

7. Summarize evidence on language acquisition in animals.

7-1. Indicate whether each of the following is true or false.

_____ (a) Researchers have been able to teach chimpanzees to use symbols to communicate.

_____ (b) Kanzi the chimp appears to comprehend both words and their relations to one another as specified by the structure.

_____ (c) Language acquisition in chimpanzees appears to be very similar to language acquisition in children.

_____ (d) Research using PET scans suggests that chimpanzees have an area in the left hemisphere analogous to Broca's area in humans.

Answers: 7-1. (a) true, (b) true, (c) false, (d) true.

8. Discuss the possible evolutionary basis of language.

8-1. What evolutionary advantage might language have given human populations when compared to the Neanderthals (whom many believe lacked the language capabilities found in human beings)?

Answers: 8-1. The Neanderthals became extinct (and we're still here).

9. Compare and contrast the behaviourist, nativist, and interactionist perspectives on the acquisition of language.

9-1. Identify the following perspectives on the acquisition of language.

(a) This perspective places great emphasis on the role of reinforcement and imitation._____

(b) This perspective assumes that children make use of a language acquisition device (LAD) to acquire transformational rules which enable them to easily translate between surface structure and deep structure._____

(c) This interactionist perspective argues that language development is tied to progress in thinking and general cognitive development._____

(d) This interactionist perspective argues that language development is directed to some extent by the social benefits children derive from interaction with mature language users._____

_____

(e) This interactionist theory proposes that the neural circuits supporting language emerge gradually in response to language learning experiences._____

9-2. Which perspective places greatest emphasis on

(a) nurture _____

(b) nature _____

(c) nature interacting with nurture _____

Answers: 9-1. (a) behaviourist, (b) nativist, (c) cognitive theories, (d) social communication theories, (e) emergentist theories **9-2.** (a) behaviourist, (b) nativist, (c) interactionist.

10. Discuss culture and language and the status of the linguistic relativity hypothesis.

10-1. What is the major idea behind Benjamin Whorf's linguistic relativity hypothesis?

10-2. What did Eleanor Rosch's experiment show when she compared the colour recognition ability of English-speaking people and Dani people, who have only two words for colour?

10-3. While language does not appear to invariably determine thought, it may exert some influence over the way we approach an idea. In other words, one's language may make it either _____or more _____to think along certain lines.

Answers: 10-1. Language determines thought. **10-2.** She found no difference in the ability to deal with colours. **10-3.** easier, difficult.

PROBLEM SOLVING: IN SEARCH OF SOLUTIONS

11. List and describe the three types of problems proposed by Greeno.

11-1. Greeno has proposed three types of problems (arrangement, inducing structure, and transformation). Identify each of these types from descriptions given below.

(a) This type of problem requires the problem solver to discover the relations among the parts of the problem.

(b) This type of problem requires the problem solver to place the parts in a way that satisfies some specific criterion.

(c) This type of problem requires the problem solver to carry out a sequence of changes or rearrangements in order to reach a specific goal.

11-2. Which types of Greeno's problems are represented in the following situations?

(a) Which two three-letter English words can be made from the letters TBU?

(b) Fill in the missing word in, "Grass is to green as snow is to _____."

(c) You need to take your child to a paediatrician, your dog to the veterinarian, and your mother to the hairdresser, all within a limited time period. You think to yourself, "I'll take the kid and the dog and pick up Mom. Mom can stay with the kid at the doctor's office while I take the dog to the vet. Then I'll ..."

11-3. Which type of problems are often solved in a sudden burst of insight?

Answers: 11-1. (a) arrangement, (b) inducing structure, (c) transformation **11-2.** (a) inducing structure, (b) arrangement, (c) transformation **11-3.** arrangement.

12. Explain how irrelevant information and functional fixedness can hinder problem solving.

12-1. Which of the barriers to effective problem solving, irrelevant information or functional fixedness, are you overcoming when you

(a) make a financial decision without first consulting your horoscope?

(b) use a page of newspaper as a wedge to keep a door open?

13. Explain how mental set and unnecessary constraints can hinder problem solving.

13-1. Which of the barriers to effective problem solving, mental set or unnecessary constraints, are you overcoming when you

(a) colour outside the lines to create a more interesting picture?

(b) teach an old dog a new trick?

14. Describe a variety of general problem-solving strategies.

14-1. The text describes a variety of different problem-solving techniques, or_____. Which of these heuristics (means/ends analysis, forming subgoals, working backward, searching for analogies, or changing the representation of the problem) would be most applicable in solving the following problems?

(a) While opening your car door you drop the keys. The keys hit your foot and bounce underneath the car, too far to reach. It has stopped raining, so you close your umbrella and ponder how to get your keys.

(b) You have accepted the responsibility for chairing the homecoming celebration at your school.

(c) Alone at night in the office, you observe that the ink cartridge is missing from a printer you want to use. After obtaining a new cartridge, you can't figure out how to install it correctly. Glancing around, you see a similar printer with the cartridge installed.

(d) As an entering first-year student in college, you have already chosen a field of study and a specific graduate school you wish to attend. Now all you have to do is accomplish this goal.

(e) You have agreed to become the campaign chairwoman for a friend who wants to run for student body president. Obviously, your goal is to make your friend look like a good choice to students, but which heuristic do politicians often employ here?

(f) After thinking about how to resolve a difficult mathematics problem, you take a break for an hour or two. When you return to the problem, you now have a new solution that comes to mind. What is this effect called?

Answers: 14-1. heuristics, (a) search for analogies (the umbrella can be used as a rake), (b) form subgoals, (c) work backward (see how the cartridge comes out), (d) means/ends analysis, (e) change the representation of the problem (make the opponents look like a bad choice), (f) the incubation effect.

15. **Discuss the distinction between field independence and dependence.**

    15-1. Answer the following true-false questions regarding the distinctions between field-dependent and field-independent persons.

        _____ (a) Field-dependent persons are more likely to use internal cues to orient themselves in space.

        _____ (b) Field-independent persons are more likely to recognize the component parts of a problem rather than just seeing it as a whole.

    Answers: 15-1. (a) false, (b) true.

16. **Discuss cultural variations in cognitive style as they relate to problem solving.**

    16-1. Answer the following true-false questions regarding cultural variations in cognitive style.

        _____ (a) Persons living in cultures that depend on hunting and gathering for their subsistence are generally more field dependent than persons living in more sedentary, agricultural societies.

        _____ (b) Persons raised in cultures with lenient child-rearing practices and an emphasis on personal autonomy tend to be more field independent.

    16-2. Nisbett and others have proposed that East Asian cultures focus on context and relationships among elements in a field, which they call a _____ cognitive style, whereas people from Western cultures focus on objects and their properties, rather than context, which they call an _____ cognitive style. They conclude that these cultural disparities in cognitive style are (<u>substantial/minimal</u>).

    Answers: 16-1. (a) false, (b) true **16-2.** holistic, analytical, substantial.

DECISION-MAKING: CHOICES AND CHANCES

17. **Compare the additive and elimination by aspects approaches to selecting an alternative.**

    17-1. Indicate which of these two approaches to decision-making would be best when

    (a) The task is complex and there are numerous alternatives to choose from.

    (b) You want to allow attractive attributes to compensate for unattractive attributes.

    Answers: 17-1. (a) elimination by aspects, (b) additive.

18. **Identify some "quirks" to people's decisions, and explain the factors that individuals typically consider in risky decision-making.**

18-1. Answer the following true-false questions regarding various quirks in people's decision-making.

_____ (a)   Evaluations of the attributes of options being compared (e.g., features of two bicycles one is choosing between) tend to be very stable.

_____ (b)   Comparative evaluations tend to yield different results than separate evaluations.

_____ (c)   Decisions about products can be swayed by such features as brand familiarity.

_____ (d)   People are happy to grapple with uncertainty.

18-2. What differentiates risky decision-making from other kinds of decision-making?

18-3. What is the most you can know when making a risky decision?

18-4. What two things must be known in order to calculate the expected value of making a risky decision when gambling with money?

18-5. How does the concept of subjective utility explain why some persons still engage in risky decision-making when the expected value predicts a loss?

Answers: 18-1. (a) false, (b) true, (c) true, (d) false **18-2.** The outcome is uncertain. **18-3.** the probability of a particular outcome **18-4.** the average amount of money you could expect to win or lose with each play and the probability of a win or loss **18-5.** The personal worth of the outcome may outweigh the probability of losing.

19. Describe the availability and representativeness heuristics.

19-1. Estimating the probability of an event on the basis of how often one recalls it has been experienced in the past is what Tversky and Kahneman call a(n) _____ heuristic.

19-2. When most people are asked if there are more words that begin with N or words that have N as the third letter, they apply the availability heuristic and guess incorrectly. Explain why they do this.

19-3. Estimating the probability of an event on the basis of how similar it is to a particular model or stereotype of that event is what Tversky and Kahneman call a(n) _____ heuristic.

19-4. "Steve is very shy. He has a high need for structure and likes detail. Is Steve more likely to be a salesperson or a librarian?" When persons are given this problem, they usually guess that he is a librarian, even though there are many more salespersons than there are librarians. Explain why they do this.

Answers: 19-1. availability **19-2.** Because they can immediately recall many more words that begin with N than words having N as the third letter. **19-3.** representativeness **19-4.** Because they employ the representativeness heuristic and Steve fits the stereotype of a librarian.

20. Describe base rate neglect and the conjunction fallacy and their causes.

20-1. Identify which example of flawed reasoning—base rate neglect or the conjunction fallacy—is being described below.

(a) Estimating that the odds of two uncertain events happening together are greater than the odds of either event happening alone.

(b) Guessing that "Steve" is a librarian and not a salesperson.

(c) Which one of these two errors in judgment is a misapplication of the representativeness heuristic?

Answers: 20-1. (a) the conjunction fallacy, (b) base rate neglect, (c) base rate neglect.

21. Describe the focus of the field of behavioural economics.

21-1. Behavioural economics examines the effects of human's (actual/idealized) decision-making processes. Simons' "Theory of _____ _____" asserted that people often make irrational decisions that are less than optimal.

21-2. Kahneman and Tversky documented ways in which human decision-making departs from rational. For example, they demonstrated that how a problem is _____ can affect our choices.

Answers: 22-1. actual, Bounded Rationality **21-2.** framed.

22. Explain evolutionary theorists' evaluation of cognitive research on flaws in human decision strategies.

22-1. What are two arguments put forth by evolutionary psychologists concerning research conducted on humans' decision-making abilities?

22-2. According to Cosmides and Tooby, cognitive research may reveal poor human performance only because studies tend to involve _____ problems that have no _____ significance.

22-3. According to Gigerenzer, human employ "fast and frugal" heuristics in their reasoning, including the _____ heuristic, which leads us to infer that a recognized alternative has a higher value. These tend to be employed when people do not have the time, resources, or cognitive capacities to make optimal decisions.

22-4. According to _____-_____ theories, we sometimes employ short-cuts when making decisions, in line with Gigerenzer's fast and frugal heuristics, but at other times we engage in more elaborate, effortful, controlled judgments.

Answers: 22-1. They argue that such research has imposed an unrealistic standard of rationality and that such research has framed problems in ways incompatible with the evolved mind. **22-2.** artificial, adaptive **22-3.** recognition **22-4.** dual-process.

PUTTING IT IN PERSPECTIVE

23. Explain how this chapter highlighted four of the text's themes.

23-1. Indicate which one of the four unifying themes (the interaction of heredity and the environment, behaviour is shaped by cultural heritage, the empirical nature of psychology, and the subjectivity of experience) are best represented by the following statements.

(a) Psychologists developed objective measures for higher mental processes, thus bringing about the cognitive revolution.

(b) The manner in which questions are framed can influence cognitive appraisal of the questions.

(c) Neither pure nativist theories nor pure nurture theories appear to adequately explain the development of language.

(d) The ecological demands of one's environment appear to somewhat affect one's cognitive style.

Answers: 23-1. (a) the empirical nature of psychology, (b) the subjectivity of experience, (c) the interaction of heredity and the environment, (d) Behaviour is shaped by cultural heritage.

UNDERSTANDING PITFALLS IN DECISION-MAKING

24. Explain what is meant by the gambler's fallacy and the law of small numbers.

24-1. Identify which example of flawed reasoning, the gambler's fallacy or the law of small numbers, is being described below.

(a) The belief that a small sampling of cases can be as valid as a large sampling of cases.

(b) The belief that the odds of a chance event increase if the event hasn't occurred recently.

Answers: 24-1. (a) the law of small numbers, (b) the gambler's fallacy.

25. Describe the propensity to overestimate the improbable and seek confirming evidence.

25-1. What flaw in reasoning often results from intense media coverage of dramatic, vivid, but infrequent events?

25-2. What omission leads to the confirmation bias when making decisions?

25-3. How is the confirmation bias related to belief perseverance?

25-4. What is myside bias?

Answers: 25-1. the propensity to overestimate the improbable 25-2. failure to seek out disconfirming evidence 25-3. Disconfirming evidence is subjected to little or sceptical evaluation 25-4. Myside bias is the tendency to evaluate evidence in a manner slanted in favour of one's own opinions.

26. Discuss the overconfidence effect and the effects of framing and loss aversion on decisions.

26-1. Answer the following true-false questions regarding the overconfidence effect.

_____ (a) We are much less subject to this effect when making decisions about ourselves as opposed to about more worldly matters.

_____ (b) Scientists are not generally prone to this effect when making decisions about information in their own fields.

26-2. Asking persons if they would prefer their glass of wine to be half-full or half-empty illustrates the general idea behind the_____ of questions.

26-3. In general, losses loom _____ than gains of equal size. The problem with this phenomenon, called loss aversion, is that people tend to (over/under)estimate the intensity and duration of negative emotions they will experience after a loss.

Answers: 26-1. (a) false, (b) false 26-2. framing 26-3. larger, over.

27. Describe some language manipulation strategies that people use to shape others' thoughts.

27-1. State which language manipulation strategy is being used in each of the following situations.

(a) A politician says that his opponent "has an IQ somewhat below room temperature."

(b) Pet owners have their pets "put to sleep" when they become terminally ill.

(c) Only someone unbelievably stupid would be against more gun control legislation.

(d) Insurance companies sell "life insurance" policies rather than "death benefits" policies.

27-2. Research examining semantic slanting shows that an organization is best advised to slant its objectives so as to be (<u>for/against</u>) something when attempting to accomplish its goal.

Answers: 27-1. (a) name calling, (b) semantic slanting, (c) anticipatory name calling, (d) semantic slanting **27-2.** for

Acculturation
Algorithm
Availability heuristic
Behavioural economics
Belief perseverance
Bilingualism
Cognition
Confirmation bias
Conjunction fallacy
Decision-making
Fast mapping
Field dependence-independence
Framing

Functional fixedness
Gambler's fallacy
Heuristic
Incubation effect
Insight
Language
Language acquisition device (LAD)
Linguistic relativity
Loss aversion
Mental set
Metalinguistic awareness
Morphemes
Myside bias

Overextension
Overregularization
Phonemes
Problem solving
Problem space
Representativeness heuristic
Risky decision-making
Semantics
Syntax
Telegraphic speech
Theory of bounded rationality
Trial and error
Underextentions

_____ 1. The component of language concerned with understanding the meaning of words and word combinations.

_____ 2. A collection of symbols, and rules for combining those symbols, that can be used to create an infinite variety of messages.

_____ 3. The smallest units of sound in a spoken language.

_____ 4. The smallest units of meaning in a language.

_____ 5. The rules that specify how words can be combined into phrases and sentences.

_____ 6. Using a word incorrectly to describe a wider set of objects or actions than it is meant to.

_____ 7. Using a word to describe a narrower set of objects than it is meant to.

_____ 8. Single-word utterances that represent the meaning of several words.

_____ 9. The ability to reflect on the use of language.

_____ 10. Consists of the acquisition of two languages that employ different speech sounds, vocabulary, and grammatical rules.

_____ 11. The degree to which a person is socially and psychologically integrated into a new culture.

_____ 12. Basing the estimated probability of an event on the ease with which relevant instances come to mind.

_____ 13. Basing the estimated probability of an event on how similar it is to the typical prototype of that event.

_____ 14. The mental processes involved in acquiring knowledge.

_____ 15. The tendency to perceive an item only in terms of its most common use.

_____ 16. The sudden discovery of a correct solution to a problem following incorrect attempts.

_____ 17. A strategy for solving problems.

_____ 18. The process by which children map a word on an underlying concept after only one exposure to the word.

	19.	When new solutions for a problem surface after a period of not thinking about the problem.
_____	20.	Generalizing grammatical rules to irregular cases where they do not apply.
_____	21.	Making decisions under conditions of uncertainty.
_____	22.	A hypothetical innate mechanism or process that facilitates the learning of language.
_____	23.	Persisting in using problem-solving strategies that have worked in the past.
_____	24.	The theory that one's language determines one's thoughts.
_____	25.	The active efforts to discover what must be done to achieve a goal that is not readily attainable.
_____	26.	Trying possible solutions sequentially and discarding those that are in error until one works.
_____	27.	Evaluating alternatives and making choices among them.
_____	28.	How issues are posed or how choices are structured.
_____	29.	A methodical, step-by-step procedure for trying all possible alternatives in searching for a solution to a problem
_____	30.	The tendency to hang on to beliefs in the face of contradictory evidence.
_____	31.	The tendency to seek information that supports one's decisions and beliefs while ignoring disconfirming evidence.
_____	32.	Occurs when people estimate that the odds of two uncertain events happening are greater than the odds of either event happening alone.
_____	33.	Refers to individuals' tendency to rely primarily on either external or internal frames of reference when orienting themselves in space.
_____	34.	The belief that the odds of a chance event increase if the event hasn't occurred recently.
_____	35.	Refers to the set of possible pathways to a solution considered by the problem solver.
_____	36.	Asserts that people tend to use simple strategies in decision-making that focus only on a few facets of available options and often result in "irrational" decisions that are less than optimal.
_____	37.	A field of study that focuses on people's actual decision-making processes.
_____	38.	The tendency to evaluate evidence in a manner slanted in favour of one's own opinions.
_____	39.	The phenomenon that losses loom larger than gains of equal size.

Answers: 1. semantics **2.** language **3.** phonemes **4.** morphemes **5.** syntax **6.** overextensions **7.** underextensions **8.** telegraphic speech **9.** metalinguistic awareness **10.** bilingualism **11.** acculturation **12.** availability heuristic **13.** representativeness heuristic **14.** cognition **15.** functional fixedness **16.** insight **17.** heuristic **18.** fast mapping **19.** incubation effect **20.** overregularization **21.** risky decision-making **22.** language acquisition device (LAD) **23.** mental set **24.** linguistic relativity **25.** problem solving **26.** trial and error **27.** decision-making **28.** framing **29.** algorithm **30.** belief perseverance **31.** confirmation bias **32.** conjunction fallacy **33.** field dependence-independence **34.** gambler's fallacy **35.** problem space **36.** theory of bounded rationality **37.** behavioural economics **38.** myside bias **39.** loss aversion.

REVIEW OF KEY PEOPLE

Ellen Bialystok
Noam Chomsky
Sue Savage-Rumbaugh
Leda Cosmides and John Tooby

Wallace Lambert
Steven Pinker
Janet Werker
Daniel Kahneman and Amos Tversky

Laura-Ann Petitto
B.F. Skinner
Herbert Simon

_____ 1. Won the Nobel Prize for his research on decision-making and artificial intelligence.

_____ 2. Proposed that children learn language through the established principles of learning.

_____ 3. Proposed that children learn language through a biologically built-in language acquisition device.

_____ 4. Co-researchers who showed that people base probability estimates on heuristics that do not always yield reasonable estimates of success.

_____ 5. Along with her colleagues, she taught the chimp Kanzi to communicate in a way that made use of all the basic properties of language.

_____ 6. Argues that human language ability is a species-specific trait that is the product of natural selection.

_____ 7. Argue that the human mind has evolved to solve specific adaptive problems.

_____ 8. Showed that infants have a perceptual bias to selectively attend to speech sounds.

_____ 9. Studied babbling in deaf and hearing infants.

_____ 10. Studies the effects of bilingualism on children's cognition.

_____ 11. A McGill scholar who has studied French immersion.

Answers: 1. Simon **2.** Skinner **3.** Chomsky **4.** Kahneman and Tversky **5.** Savage-Rumbaugh **6.** Pinker
7. Cosmides and Tooby. **8.** Werker **9.** Petitto **10.** Bialystok **11.** Lambert.

SELF-QUIZ

1. In what decade did the cognitive revolution in psychology occur?
   a. 1920s
   b. 1970s
   c. 1950s
   d. 1990s

2. Which of the following is NOT one of the basic properties of language?
   a. generative
   b. symbolic
   c. structured
   d. alphabetical

3. What is the word *slow* an example of?
   a. a metalinguistic
   b. a phoneme
   c. a syntactical unit
   d. a morpheme

4. What does a child show awareness of when she says that *tub* and *but* are constructed of the same three letters?
   a. morphemes
   b. phonemes
   c. metalinguistics
   d. syntax

5. Which of the following statements about language is NOT correct?
   a. A chimp has learned to sign (in ASL) more than 150 words.
   b. Children and chimps appear to learn language in a similar manner.
   c. A chimp has shown comprehension for both words and their relation to one another.
   d. The ability to use language may not be unique to humans.

6. When acquiring language skills, children appear to learn rules rather than specific word combinations. This fact argues most strongly against which theory of language development?
   a. cognitive
   b. behaviourist
   c. nativist
   d. social communication

7. The anagram exemplifies which one of Greeno's problem types?
   a. arrangement problem
   b. inducing structure problem
   c. transformation problem
   d. chunking problem

8. When you use a piece of paperclip as a temporary replacement for the screw that fell out of your glasses, what barriers to problem solving are you overcoming?
   a. irrelevant information
   b. functional fixedness
   c. mental set
   d. unnecessary constraints

9. What heuristics would you probably employ if assigned the task of carrying out a school election?
   a. work backwards
   b. representativeness
   c. search for analogies
   d. form subgoals

10. What cultural context would a field-independent person most likely come from?
    a. one that encourages strict child-rearing practices
    b. one that has an agricultural base
    c. one that encourages personal autonomy
    d. one that stresses conformity

11. When faced with having to choose among numerous alternatives, what approach do most people opt for?
    a. an elimination by aspects approach
    b. an additive approach
    c. a means/end analysis approach
    d. a subjective-utility approach

12. Most people mistakenly believe that more people die from tornadoes than from asthma. This belief is based on the mistaken application of which of the following decision-making approaches?
    a. means/end analysis
    b. compensatory decision model
    c. availability heuristic
    d. representativeness heuristic

13. What may result from failure to actively seek out contrary evidence?
    a. overestimating the improbable
    b. conjunction fallacy
    c. gambler's fallacy
    d. confirmation bias

14. People generally prefer a choice that provides an 80% chance of success over one that provides a 19% chance of failure. What does this example illustrate?
    a. the effect of the availability heuristic
    b. the effect of the representativeness heuristic
    c. the effect of framing
    d. the effect of mental set

15. Owners of automobile junkyards prefer to use the term automobile recycling centres. What does the use of this term exemplify?
    a. framing
    b. semantic slanting
    c. anticipatory name calling
    d. subjective utility

16. The Featured Study shows that deaf infants babble (albeit with their hands) in a way that demonstrates a similar developmental progression and timing as hearing infants. According to this finding, what achievement does babbling reflect?
    a. motor achievement
    b. unimportant achievement
    c. linguistic achievement
    d. behavioural achievement

17. What do we call the tendency to evaluate evidence in a manner slanted in favour of one's own opinions?
    a. myside bias
    b. incubation effect
    c. uncertainty effect
    d. availability effect

18. John feels that the negative impact of losing $50 is greater than the positive impact of winning $50. What do we call this phenomenon?
    a. myside bias
    b. uncertainty effect
    c. loss aversion
    d. confirmation bias

Answers: 1. c **2.** d **3.** d **4.** c **5.** b **6.** b **7.** a **8.** b **9.** d **10.** c **11.** a **12.** c **13.** d **14.** c **15.** b **16.** c **17.** a **18.** c.

Chapter Nine

INTELLIGENCE AND PSYCHOLOGICAL TESTING

REVIEW OF KEY IDEAS

KEY CONCEPTS IN PSYCHOLOGICAL TESTING

1. **List and describe the principal categories of psychological tests.**

   1-1. Most psychological tests can be placed into one of two very broad categories. These two categories are _____ tests and _____ tests.

   1-2. There are three categories of mental abilities tests. Below are examples of each of these categories. Identify them.

   (a) The ACT and SAT tests you may have taken before entering college are examples of _____ tests.

   (b) The exams you frequently take in your introductory psychology class are examples of _____ tests.

   (c) Tests used to demonstrate general intellectual giftedness are examples of _____ tests.

   1-3. Personality tests allow an individual to compare himself or herself to other persons with respect to particular personality _____. Personality tests generally (do/do not) have right and wrong answers.

   Answers: 1-1. mental ability, personality (in either order) **1-2.** (a) aptitude, (b) achievement, (c) intelligence **1-3.** characteristics (or traits), do not.

2. **Explain the concepts of standardization and test norms.**

   2-1. Developing test norms and uniform procedures for use in the administration and scoring of a test is the general idea behind test _____.

   2-2. In order to interpret a particular score on a test, it is necessary to know how other persons scored on this test. This is the purpose of test _____. An easy method for providing comparisons of test scores is to convert the raw scores into _____ scores.

2-3.   The sample of people that the norms are based on is called the _____ group.

Answers: **2-1.** standardization **2-2.** norms, percentile **2-3.** standardization.

3. Explain the meaning of test reliability and how it is estimated.

3-1.   The ability of a test to produce consistent results across subsequent measurements of the same persons is known as its _____. Psychological tests (are/are not) perfectly reliable.

3-2.   Re-administering the same test to the same group of persons a week or two following the original testing (test-retest) allows one to estimate the _____ of a test. If a test is highly reliable, then a person's scores on the two different administrations will be very similar. The amount of similarity can be assessed by means of the _____ coefficient. The closer the correlation comes to 1.0 the (more/less) reliable the test is.

Answers: **3-1.** reliability, are not **3-2.** reliability, correlation, more.

4. Explain the three types of validity and how they are assessed.

4-1.   The ability of a test to actually measure what it claims to measure is known as its _____. The term *validity* is also used to refer to the accuracy or usefulness of the _____ based on a test.

4-2.   There are three general kinds of validity. Identify each of these kinds from the descriptions given below.

   (a)   This kind of validity will tend to be high when, for example, scores on the ACT and SAT actually predict success in college. _____

   (b)   This kind of validity will be of particular importance to you when taking your exams for this class. It will be high if the exam sticks closely to the explicitly assigned material. _____

   (c)   This kind of validity is more vague than the other two kinds and refers to the ability of a test to measure abstract qualities, such as intelligence. _____.

4-3.   As with the estimation of reliability, the estimation of validity makes use of the

   _____ _____.

Answers: **4-1.** validity, inferences (or decisions) **4-2.** (a) criterion-related validity, (b) content validity, (c) construct validity **4-3.** correlation coefficient.

THE EVOLUTION OF INTELLIGENCE TESTING

5. Summarize the contributions of Galton and Binet to the evolution of intelligence testing.

5-1.   Identify each of the above men from the descriptions of their contributions given on the next page.

(a) This man developed the first useful intelligence test. His tests were used to predict success in school, and scores were expressed in terms of mental age. _____

(b) This man began the quest to measure intelligence. He assumed that intelligence was mainly inherited and could be measured by assessing sensory acuity. He also invented correlation and percentile test scores._____

Answers: 5-1. (a) Binet, (b) Galton.

6. Summarize the contributions of Terman and Wechsler to the evolution of intelligence testing.

6-1. Identify each of the above men from the descriptions of their contributions given below.

(a) This man revised Binet's tests to produce the Stanford-Binet Intelligence Scale, the standard for all future intelligence tests. He also introduced the intelligence quotient (IQ). _____

(b) This man developed the first successful test of adult intelligence, the WAIS. He also developed new intelligence tests for children. _____

(c) In developing his new intelligence tests, this man added many nonverbal items which allowed for the separate assessment of both verbal and nonverbal abilities. He also replaced the IQ score with one based on the normal distribution. _____

Answers: 6-1. (a) Terman, (b) Wechsler, (c) Wechsler.

7. Describe some new trends in the assessment of intelligence.

7-1. The notion that intelligence is a function of general mental abilities (Spearman's "g") dominated the early thinking in test development. However, other researchers began to conclude that intelligence involves (few/multiple) abilities. Cattell and Horn believe that intelligence should be divided into intelligence that involves reasoning ability, memory capacity, and speed of information processing, which they call _____ intelligence, and intelligence that involves ability to apply acquired knowledge and skills in problem solving, which they call _____ intelligence.

7-2. As test developers have began to turn away from tests designed to measure general intelligence, what kinds of tests are replacing them?

Answers: 7-1. multiple, fluid, crystallized **7-2.** tests of specific mental abilities.

BASIC QUESTIONS ABOUT INTELLIGENCE TESTING

8. Explain the meaning of an individual's score on a modern intelligence test.

8-1. Answer the following questions regarding intelligence test scores.

(a) In what manner is human intelligence assumed to be distributed?

(b) What percentage of people have an IQ score below 100?

(c) What percentage of persons would score two or more standard deviations above the mean?

Answers: 8-1. (a) It forms a normal distribution. (b) 50% (c) 2%.

9. Describe the reliability and validity of modern IQ test scores.

9-1.   Answer the following questions about the reliability of modern intelligence tests.

(a) What reliability estimates (correlation coefficients) are found for most modern intelligence tests?

(b) What might be a problem here with respect to an individual's test score?

9-2.   Answer the following questions with respect to the validity of modern intelligence tests.

(a) What is the correlation between IQ tests and grades in school?

(b) What is the correlation between IQ tests and the number of years of schooling that people complete?

(c) What might be a general problem with assuming intelligence tests are a valid measure of general mental ability?

9-3.   Answer the following questions with respect to the stability over time of IQ scores.

(a) During the preschool years, IQ scores tend to be (<u>stable/unstable</u>).

(b) By about age _____, IQ scores tend to stabilize (and, therefore, are better predictors of adult IQ scores), although some people do show substantial changes.

Answers: 9-1. (a) They are in the low .90s. (b) Temporary conditions, such as high anxiety, could lower the score. **9-2.** (a) .40s and .50s, (b) around .70, (c) They principally focus on mental abilities conducive to academic success and ignore other kinds of intelligence, such as the ability to think critically. **9-3.** (a) unstable, (b) 9.

10. **Discuss how well intelligence tests predict vocational success.**

10-1. In what way is IQ related to occupational achievement?

10-2. What are some limitations concerning the ability of IQ scores to predict performance within a particular occupation?

Answers: 10-1. People who score high on IQ tests are more likely to end up in high-status jobs compared to those who score low. **10-2.** Only about 25% of variation in job performance is predicted by IQ; the validity of supervisor ratings as a measure of job performance has been questioned; and minority groups may be disadvantaged by the use of IQ tests for job performance.

11. **Discuss the use of IQ tests in nonWestern cultures.**

11-1. Which of the following statements best summarizes the history of IQ testing in nonWestern cultures?

(a) Most Western and nonWestern cultures have successfully adapted the IQ tests to their own cultures.

(b) Many nonWestern cultures have different conceptions of what intelligence is and do not necessarily accept Western notions as to how it can be measured.

Answer: 11-1. b.

EXTREMES OF INTELLIGENCE

12. **Describe how intellectual disability is defined and divided into various levels.**

12-1. In addition to having subnormal mental abilities (IQ scores of less than 70 to 75), what else is included in the definition of intellectual disability?

12-2. There are four levels of intellectual disability: mild, moderate, severe, and profound. Identify each of these levels from the descriptions given below:

(a) These persons have IQ scores below 20 and require total care.

(b) These persons have IQ scores between 50 and 75 and may become self-supporting after leaving school and becoming adults.

(c) These persons have IQ scores between 35 and 50 and can be semi-independent in a sheltered environment.

(d) These persons have IQ scores between 20 and 35 and can help to contribute to their self-support under total supervision.

Answers: 12-1. The individual must show deficiencies in adaptive (everyday living) skills originating before age 18. These skills include conceptual skills, social skills, and practical skills. **12-2.** (a) profound, (b) mild, (c) moderate, (d) severe.

13. Discuss what is known about the causes of intellectual disability.

13-1. Although there are more than 350 organic syndromes associated with intellectual disability, including Down syndrome, _____ X syndrome, phenylketonuria, and hydrocephaly, organic causes account for only about _____ % of cases.

13-2. There are two general hypotheses as to the causes of the remaining 75% of cases, most of which are diagnosed as mild. One theory is that intellectual disability results from subtle _____ defects that are difficult to detect. The other theory suggests that it is caused by a variety of unfavourable _____ conditions.

Answers: 13-1. fragile, 25 **13-2.** (a) physiological, environmental.

14. Discuss the role of IQ tests in the identification of gifted children.

14-1. Answer the following questions regarding gifted children:

(a) What method is used almost exclusively to identify gifted children?

(b) What is the lowest IQ score that is generally needed to qualify children as gifted?

Answers: 14-1. (a) scores on IQ tests, (b) 130.

15. Describe the characteristics of the gifted and factors relating to adult achievements of the gifted.

15-1. Answer the following questions regarding the characteristics of the gifted:

(a) What did Terman's long-term study of gifted children show with respect to the physical, social, and emotional development of these children?

(b) Ellen Winner took a special look at profoundly gifted children (IQ above 180). What did she estimate to be the incidence of interpersonal and emotional problems in these children when compared to other children?

(c) What three factors must interact and be present to an exceptional degree in order to produce the rarest form of giftedness, according to Renzulli?

(d) What is meant by the term "hidden gifted"?

(e) In addition to intensive training and hard work, what other factor may be necessary to achieve extraordinary achievement?

(f) To what does Simonton attribute the development of talent?

Answers: 15-1. (a) They were above average in all three areas. (b) It's about twice as high in the profoundly gifted children. (c) intelligence, motivation, creativity (in any order), (d) children with very high IQ scores but who are underachieving in school, (e) rare, innate talent, (f) Simonton argues for a combination of both innate ability and supportive environmental factors.

HEREDITY AND ENVIRONMENT AS DETERMINANTS OF INTELLIGENCE

16. **Summarize the empirical evidence that heredity affects intelligence.**

   16-1. Below are the mean correlations for the intelligence of four different groups of children: *siblings reared together, fraternal twins reared together, identical twins reared apart*, and *identical twins reared together*. Match the group with the appropriate correlation.

   .86 _____   .60 _____

   .72 _____   .44 _____

   16-2. What do the above correlations tell us about the role of heredity in intelligence?

Answers: 16-1. (.86) identical twins reared together, (.72) identical twins reared apart, (.60) fraternal twins reared together, (.44) siblings reared together **16-2.** that heredity plays a significant role in intelligence.

17. **Discuss estimates of the heritability of intelligence and their limitations.**

   17-1. The consensus estimate of experts is that the heritability ratio for human intelligence hovers around 50%. What does this mean?

   17-2. What are the limitations of heritability estimates?

Answers: 17-1. 50% of the variation in intelligence in a particular group is estimated to be due to heredity (leaving 50% due to environmental factors). **17-2.** Heritability is a group statistic and may give misleading results when applied to particular individuals; the heritability of a trait can vary from one group to another; and there really is no single value that represents any true heritability of IQ.

18. **Describe various lines of research that indicate that environment affects intelligence.**

    18-1. What cumulative effects on intelligence have been found among children reared in deprived environments?

    18-2. What effects on intelligence have been found among children moved from deprived environments to more enriched environments?

    18-3. Answer the following questions regarding the "Flynn effect."

        (a) What did Flynn's research show with respect to generational changes in IQ scores since 1930 in the industrialized world?

        (b) Can these generational changes be attributed to heredity?

Answers: 18-1. There is a gradual decrease in intelligence (across time). **18-2.** There is a gradual increase in intelligence (across time). **18-3.** (a) Scores have been steadily rising. (b) no.

19. **Using the concept of reaction range, explain how heredity and the environment interact to affect intelligence.**

    19-1. The notion behind the concept of reaction range is that heredity places an upper and lower _____ on how much an individual can vary with respect to a characteristic such as intelligence. This means that a child's IQ can vary significantly depending on the kind of _____ he or she experiences. The major point here is that the limits for intelligence are determined by _____ factors, and the movement within these limits is determined by _____ factors.

    19-2. Thus far, molecular genetics research (<u>has/has not</u>) advanced as quickly as expected, likely reflecting the fact that (<u>many/few</u>) genes are likely to influence intelligence and the fact that the influence of any one gene is likely to be (<u>small/large</u>).

Answers: 19-1. limit, environment, genetic (or hereditary), environmental. **19-2.** has not, many, small.

20. **Discuss heritability and socioeconomic disadvantage as alternative explanations for cultural differences in average IQ.**

    20-1. Two explanations for the cultural differences in IQ scores are listed below. Tell what each of these explanations means.

        (a) Jensen's heritability explanation.

        (b) Socioeconomic disadvantage.

20-2. What evidence is consistent with the socioeconomic disadvantage explanation?

Answers: 20-1. (a) The cultural differences are due to heredity. (b) The cultural differences are due to environmental factors. **20-2.** Average IQ scores among children from lower social classes tend to be about 15 points below those among children of middle- and upper-class homes.

21. Discuss the possible contributions of stereotype vulnerability and cultural bias to ethnic differences in average IQ.

21-1. Steele's theory of stereotype vulnerability holds that a widely held stereotype, that certain racial groups are mentally inferior, acts on the members of these groups so as to make them (more/less) vulnerable (they tend to under perform) when confronted with tests assessing intellectual ability. Steele believes that this same vulnerability (does/does not) exist for women entering domains dominated by men. Research so far (does/does not) support the theory of stereotype vulnerability.

21-2. Stereotype threat may impair performance because it leads people to expend mental _____ suppressing negative thoughts about the possible future. These thoughts hijack working _____, which is critical to success on complex cognitive tests.

21-3. What did the text conclude about the possible effects of cultural bias with respect to ethnic differences in IQ scores?

Answers: 21-1. more, does, does **21-2.** resources, memory **21-3.** The IQ gap may reflect differences in knowledge due to disparities in exposure to information. However, such cultural bias produces only weak and inconsistent effects.

NEW DIRECTIONS IN THE ASSESSMENT AND STUDY OF INTELLIGENCE

22. Describe biological correlates of intelligence.

22-1. There is a (positive/negative) correlation between brain volume and IQ scores. The volume of key areas of the brain, including the prefrontal cortex, visual association cortex, somatosensory association cortex, anterior cingulate, and Broca's and Wernicke's areas correlate with IQ scores. IQ scores also positively correlate with both _____ matter and _____ matter of the brain.

22-2. Intelligence also correlates with positively with _____. This may reflect good _____, which foster both high intelligence and good health. This may also reflect that smarter people take care of their health. Or it may reflect that intelligence fosters career success and _____, which allows better access to health care and lesser exposure to toxins and pathogens.

Answers: 22-1. positive, grey, white **22-2.** longevity, genes, affluence.

23. **Describe Sternberg's and Gardner's theories of intelligence and the concept of emotional intelligence.**

23-1. Sternberg's triarchic theory proposes that intelligence is composed of three basic parts. Match these parts with their individual functions.

SUBTHEORY   FUNCTION

____ Contextual   (a) Emphasizes the role played by society.

____ Experiential   (b) Emphasizes the cognitive processes underlying intelligence.

____ Componential   (c) Emphasizes the interplay between intelligence and experience.

23-2. Which of these three sub-theories also contains three underlying subcomponents (metacomponents, performance components, and knowledge-acquisition components)?

23-3. In a recent addition to his theory, Sternberg has proposed three facets of what he calls "successful intelligence." Match these three facets with their respective descriptions.

FACETS (INTELLIGENCE)   DESCRIPTIONS

____ Analytical   (a) Ability to deal effectively with everyday

                            problems.

____ Creative   (b) Ability to generate new ideas.

____ Practical   (c) Abstract reasoning, evaluation, and judgment.

23-4. Gardner has proposed eight relatively distinct human intelligences. What does his research show with respect to a "g" factor among these separate intelligences?

23-5. The ability to perceive and express emotion, assimilate emotion in thought, understand and reason with emotion, and regulate emotion is the general idea behind _____ intelligence. Parker has suggested that emotional intelligence may be particularly helpful when it comes to coping with _____ _____.

Answers: **23-1.** a, c, b **23-2.** componential **23-3.** c, b, a **23-4.** There does not appear to be a "g" factor; i.e., people display a mix of strong, weak, and intermediate abilities. **23-5.** emotional, stressful events.

PUTTING IT IN PERSPECTIVE

24. **Discuss how the chapter highlighted three of the text's unifying themes.**

24-1. Answer the following questions about the three unifying themes (cultural factors shape behaviour, psychology evolves in a sociohistorical context, and heredity and environment jointly influence behaviour).

(a) What theme is exemplified by the controversy over the book *The Bell Curve?*

(b) What theme is exemplified by the different views about the nature of intelligence held by Western and nonWestern cultures?

(c) What theme is exemplified by the extensive research using twin studies, adoption studies, and family studies?

Answers: 24-1. (a) Psychology evolves in a sociohistorical context. (b) Cultural factors shape behaviour. (c) Heredity and environment jointly influence behaviour.

APPLICATION: MEASURING AND UNDERSTANDING CREATIVITY

25. Discuss popular ideas about the nature of creativity.

25-1. Popular notions about creativity would have us believe that creative ideas arise from nowhere, occur in a burst of insight, are not related to hard work, and are unrelated to intelligence. What does the text say about these notions?

Answers: 25-1. They are all false.

26. Describe creativity tests, and summarize how well they predict creative achievement.

26-1. Most tests of creativity attempt to assess (conventional/divergent) thinking, for example, by asking subjects to list as many uses as they can for a book. Creativity scores are based on the _____ of alternatives generated and the originality and _____ of the suggested alternatives.

26-2. Creativity tests are rather (good/mediocre) predictors of creativity in the real world. One reason for this is that they attempt to treat creativity as a (specific/general) trait, while research evidence seems to show it is related to quite _____ particular domains.

Answers: 26-1. divergent, number, usefulness (or utility) **26-2.** mediocre, general, specific.

27. Discuss associations between creativity and personality, intelligence, and mental illness.

27-1. What two traits appear to be at the core of the personality characteristics common to creative people?

27-2. What is a recently discovered route to creativity?

27-3. The association between intelligence and creativity is _____, and perhaps as high as .40. According to the _____ hypothesis, creativity requires a minimum level of intelligence, such that most highly creative people are above average in intelligence.

27-4. What form of mental illness appears to be associated with creative achievement?

Answers: 27-1. openness to new experiences and nonconformity **27-2.** living abroad **27-3.** positive, threshold **27-4.** mood disorders.

CRITICAL THINKING APPLICATION

28. Explain how appeals to ignorance and reification have cropped up in numerous debates about intelligence.

28-1. Tell whether the following statements represent examples of appeals to ignorance or to reification.

(a) He doesn't do very well in college because he's lacking in intelligence.

(b) Since research has not clearly shown that environment can affect intelligence, then intelligence must be due to heredity.

(c) More money should be spent on research to find the accurate heritability coefficient of intelligence.

Answers: 28-1. (a) reification, (b) appeals to ignorance, (c) reification.

REVIEW OF KEY TERMS

Achievement tests
Aptitude tests
Construct validity
Content validity
Convergent thinking
Correlation coefficient
Creativity
Criterion-related validity
Crystallized intelligence
Deviation IQ scores

Divergent thinking
Emotional intelligence
Factor analysis
Fluid intelligence
Heritability ratio
Intelligence tests
Mental age
Mental retardation
Normal distribution
Percentile score

Personality tests
Psychological test
Reaction range
Reification
Reliability
Standardization
Test norms
Validity

_____ 1. A standardized measure of a sample of a person's behaviour.

_____ 2. Tests that measure general mental ability.

_____ 3. Tests that measure various personality traits.

_____ 4. Tests that assess talent for specific kinds of learning.

_____ 5. Tests that gauge the mastery and knowledge of various subject areas.

_____ 6. The development of uniform procedures for administering and scoring tests, including the development of test norms.

_____ 7. Data that provides information about the relative standing of a particular test score.

_____ 8. Number indicating the percentage of people who score above or below a particular test score.

_____ 9. The measurement consistency of a test.

_____ 10. The ability of a test to measure what it was designed to measure.

_____ 11. The degree to which the content of a test is representative of the domain it is supposed to measure.

_____ 12. The degree to which the scores on a particular test correlate with scores on an independent criterion (test).

_____ 13. The degree to which there is evidence that a test measures a hypothetical construct.

_____ 14. A score indicating the mental ability typical of a chronological age group.

_____ 15. Mental age divided by chronological age and multiplied by 100.

_____ 16. A symmetrical, bell-shaped curve that describes the distribution of many physical and psychological attributes.

_____ 17. Scores that translate raw scores into a precise location in the normal distribution.

_____ 18. Subnormal, general mental ability accompanied by deficiencies in everyday living skills originating prior to age 18. Also referred to as intellectual disability.

_____ 19. An estimate of the percentage of variation in a trait determined by genetic inheritance.

_____ 20. Genetically determined limits on intelligence.

_____ 21. Method that uses the correlation among many variables to identify closely related clusters.

_____ 22. The ability to apply acquired knowledge and skills to problem solving.

_____ 23. Includes reasoning ability, memory capacity, and speed of information processing.

_____ 24. The generation of ideas that are original, novel, and useful.

_____ 25. Thinking that attempts to narrow down a list of alternatives to a single best solution.

_____ 26. Thinking that attempts to expand the range of alternatives by generating many possible solutions.

_____ 27. A numerical index of the degree of relationship between two variables.

_____ 28. Occurs when a hypothetical abstract concept is given a name and then treated as though it were a concrete, tangible object.

_____ 29. The ability to perceive and express emotion, assimilate emotion in thought, understand and reason with emotion, and regulate emotion.

Answers: 1. psychological tests **2.** intelligence tests **3.** personality tests **4.** aptitude tests **5.** achievement tests **6.** standardization **7.** test norms **8.** percentile score **9.** reliability **10.** validity **11.** content validity **12.** criterion-related validity **13.** construct validity **14.** mental age **15.** intelligence quotient **16.** normal distribution **17.** deviation IQ scores **18.** mental retardation **19.** heritability ratio **20.** reaction range **21.** factor analysis **22.** crystallized thinking **23.** fluid thinking **24.** creativity **25.** convergent thinking **26.** divergent thinking **27.** correlation coefficient **28.** reification **29.** emotional intelligence.

REVIEW OF KEY PEOPLE

Alfred Binet   Sandra Scarr   Lewis Terman
Sir Francis Galton   Claude Steele   David Wechsler
Howard Gardner   Robert Sternberg   Ellen Winner
Arthur Jensen

_____ 1. Developed the Stanford-Binet Intelligence Scale.

_____ 2. Developed the first successful test of adult intelligence.

_____ 3. Postulated a cognitive triarchic theory of intelligence.

_____ 4. Proposed a reaction range model for human intelligence.

_____ 5. Developed the first useful intelligence test.

_____ 6. Postulated a heritability explanation for cultural differences in intelligence.

_____ 7. Began the quest to measure intelligence.

_____ 8. Proposed a stereotype vulnerability theory as an explanation for racial differences on IQ test scores.

_____ 9. Has suggested the existence of a number of relatively autonomous human intelligences.

_____ 10. Argued that moderately gifted children are quite different from profoundly gifted children.

Answers: 1. Terman **2.** Wechsler **3.** Sternberg **4.** Scarr **5.** Binet **6.** Jensen **7.** Galton **8.** Steele **9.** Gardner **10.** Winner.

SELF-QUIZ

1. What kind of test is this self-test you are now taking?
   a. aptitude test
   b. achievement test
   c. intelligence test
   d. criterion-related test

2. Which of the following statistics is generally used to estimate reliability and validity?
   a. correlation coefficient
   b. standard deviation
   c. percentile score
   d. median

3. What particular kind of validity do tests such as the SAT and ACT strive for?
   a. content validity
   b. construct validity
   c. absolute validity
   d. criterion-related validity

4. Which of the following statements best describes modern intelligence tests?
   a. Validity is generally higher than reliability.
   b. Reliability is generally poor.
   c. Reliability is generally higher than validity.
   d. Validity is generally poor.

5. Which group of adults who are mentally retarded (i.e., have an intellectual disability) can often pass for normal?
   a. those with mild disability
   b. those with moderate disability
   c. those with severe disability
   d. those with profound disability

6. What percentage of mental retardation cases have been definitely linked to organic causes?
   a. approximately 25%
   b. approximately 50%
   c. approximately 75%
   d. approximately 90%

7. According to Terman's long-term study of gifted children, which of the following areas of development was NOT demonstrated to be one in which these children tend to excel in?
   a. physical development
   b. social development
   c. emotional development
   d. spiritual development

8. Which of the following groups shows the highest correlation with respect to intelligence?
   a. fraternal twins reared together
   b. fraternal twins reared apart
   c. identical twins reared apart
   d. identical twins reared together

9. If the heritability ratio for intelligence is 80%, this means that, for you, heredity determines 80% of your intelligence and environment determines 20%. Is this statement true or false?
   a. true
   b. false

10. What observation underlies the "Flynn effect"?
    a. The general intelligence in industrialized societies has been rising across time.
    b. The general intelligence in industrialized societies has been declining across time.
    c. The general intelligence in industrialized societies is primarily affected by environment and not heredity.
    d. The general intelligence in industrialized societies is primarily affected by heredity and not environment.

11. What is the prevalence of mental retardation (or intellectual disability)?
    a. 0.01 to 0.05%
    b. 1 to 3%
    c. 6 to 10%
    d. 10 to 15%

12. What research evidence best supports explanations for racial differences in intelligence?
    a. Jensen's heritability theory
    b. cultural bias in IQ tests
    c. socioeconomic disadvantage
    d. Watson's differential conditioning theory

13. What does Steele's theory of stereotype vulnerability attempt to explain?
    a. why Asian-Americans score higher than average on IQ tests
    b. why African-Americans score lower than average on IQ tests
    c. why cultural bias must necessarily be inherent in all intelligence tests
    d. why the general intelligence in a population declines across time

14. What does Spearman's "g" imply?
    a. that most kinds of intelligence are highly related
    b. that most kinds of intelligence are not highly related
    c. that intelligence is highly correlated with personality characteristics
    d. that intelligence is uncorrelated with personality characteristics

15. What do most tests of creativity emphasize?
    a. convergent thinking
    b. divergent thinking
    c. bursts of insight
    d. getting at unconscious thought processes

16. What form of mental illness is often associated with outstanding creativity?
    a. anxiety disorders
    b. antisocial personality
    c. schizophrenia
    d. mood disorders

17. Which of the following statements is an example of reification?
    a. Birds of a feather flock together.
    b. Creative people are born, not raised.
    c. She gets good grades in school because she is intelligent.
    d. Intelligence tests are only moderate predictors of vocational success.

18. Which of the following terms means the same as mental retardation?
    a. mental disability
    b. intellectual disability
    c. cognitive limitation
    d. intellectual limitation

19. Recent research has identified which of the following as leading to creativity?

    a. living abroad
    b. exercising regularly
    c. reading newspapers
    d. eating well

Answers: 1. b **2.** a **3.** d **4.** c **5.** a **6.** a **7.** d **8.** d **9.** b **10.** a **11.** b **12.** c **13.** b **14.** a **15.** b **16.** d **17.** c **18.** b **19.** a.

Chapter Ten

MOTIVATION AND EMOTION

REVIEW OF KEY IDEAS

MOTIVATIONAL THEORIES AND CONCEPTS

1. **Define motivation and compare drive, incentive, and evolutionary approaches to understanding motivation.**

   1-1. Motivation is defined as involving _____-_____ behaviour.

   1-2. Drive theories are based on the idea that organisms strive to maintain a state of physiological equilibrium. For example, organisms are motivated to maintain water balance; when deprived of water they experience thirst. Thirst is a _____ to return to a state of water equilibrium.

   1-3. A drive is a state of tension. According to drive theories, organisms are motivated to seek drive or tension _____.

   1-4. Theories that emphasize the pull from the external environment are known as _____ theories. For example, we may be motivated to eat, not as a function of hunger, but as a result of the smell or appearance of food. Incentive theories (operate/do not operate) according to the principle of homeostasis.

   1-5. From the point of view of evolutionary theory, all motivations, such as the needs for affiliation, dominance, achievement, and aggression, as well as needs for food and water, occur because they have _____ value for the species. Organisms with adaptive sets of motivational characteristics are more likely to pass their _____ on to the next generation.

   1-6. Place the name of the theoretical approach described below (drive, incentive, or evolutionary) in the blanks.

   _____   Emphasizes the pressure to return to a state of equilibrium.

   _____   Actions result from attempts to reduce internal states of tension.

   _____   Emphasizes "pull" from the environment (as opposed to "push" from internal states).

   _____   Motivations arise as a function of their capacity to enhance reproductive success, to pass genes to the next generation.

   _____   Motivation to pursue a goal or object depends on the *value* of the object and one's *expectancy* of success at obtaining it.

   Answers: 1-1. goal-directed **1-2.** drive **1-3.** reduction **1-4.** incentive, do not operate **1-5.** adaptive (or survival, reproductive), genes **1-6.** drive, drive, incentive, evolutionary, incentive.

2. **Distinguish between the two major categories of motives found in humans.**

    2-1. Most theories of motivation distinguish between _____ motives (e.g., for food, water, sex, warmth) and _____ motives. Biological needs are generally essential for the _____ of the group or individual.

    2-2. Social motives (e.g., for achievement, autonomy, affiliation) are acquired as a result of people's experiences. While there are relatively few biological needs, people theoretically may acquire an unlimited number of _____ needs.

Answers: 2-1. biological, social, survival **2-2.** social.

THE MOTIVATION OF HUNGER AND EATING

3. **Summarize evidence of the physiological factors implicated in the regulation of hunger.**

    3-1. Within the brain, the major structure implicated in eating behaviour is the _____.

    3-2. Researchers used to think that eating was controlled by "on" and "off" centres in the hypothalamus. When the lateral hypothalamus (LH) was destroyed, animals stopped eating, as if hunger had been turned off like a switch. When the ventromedial hypothalamus (VMH) was destroyed, animals started to eat. While these structures are still considered important in hunger regulation, researchers now believe that eating is controlled to a greater extent by (complex neural circuits/simple anatomical centres).

    3-3. In addition, researchers have changed their conclusions about the relative importance of various structures. According to current thinking, the _____ nucleus and the _____ nucleus both play an important role in hunger.

    3-4. Much of the food we consume is converted into _____, a simple sugar that is an important source of energy.

    3-5. Based on research findings about glucose, Mayer proposed the theory that there are specialized neurons in the brain that function to monitor blood glucose. Lower levels of glucose, for example, are associated with a(n) (increase/decrease) in hunger.

    3-6. For cells to extract glucose from the blood, the hormone _____ must be present. Insulin will produce a(n) (increase/decrease) in the level of sugar in the blood, with the result that the person experiences a(n) (increase/decrease) in the sensation of hunger. Two hormones involved in the short-term regulation of hunger are _____ (which promotes feelings of hunger) and _____ (which signals fullness).

    3-7. More recently, a regulatory hormone called leptin has been discovered, a hormone produced by (fat cells/neurons) and circulated to the hypothalamus in the bloodstream. Higher levels of the hormone _____ reflect a higher level of fat in the body, which is associated with a (increase/decrease) in the sensation of hunger.

Answers: 3-1. hypothalamus **3-2.** complex neural circuits **3-3.** arcuate, paraventricular **3-4.** glucose **3-5.** increase **3-6.** insulin, decrease, increase, ghrelin, CCK **3-7.** fat cells, leptin, decrease.

4. **Summarize evidence on how the availability of food and other cues, culture, learning, and stress influence hunger.**

4-1. Hunger is based not only on a physiological need, but also on external factors, such as the appearance, tastiness, and availability of food. Thus, some aspects of hunger motivation support the (drive/incentive) approach to motivation. Sometimes we eat, according to this research, simply because food is available. Major cues associated with eating include _____, quantity available, _____, and the presence of others. For example, there is evidence that as you eat a specific food, its incentive value declines, a phenomenon called _____-_____ _____.

4-2. Social cues also play a role in our eating. The _____ _____ Model suggests that social norms, as revealed by the behaviour of others around us, affect our eating. Most typically, people eat (more/less) when others are nearby.

4-3. Although we have some innate taste preferences (e.g., for fat), it is also clear that _____ affects what we eat. For example, taste preferences and aversions may be learned by pairing a taste with pleasant or unpleasant experiences, the process of _____ conditioning.

4-4. In addition, we are more likely to eat food that we see others eating, especially if the others are parents or friends. Thus, food preferences are acquired not only through conditioning, but also through the process of _____ learning.

4-5. Our environments also provide frustrating circumstances that create _____, a factor that may also trigger eating in many people. Although stress and increased eating are linked, it's not clear why the relationship occurs.

Answers: 4-1. incentive, palatability, variety, sensory-specific satiety **4-2.** Inhibitory Norm, less **4-3.** learning (or environment, culture), classical **4-4.** observational **4-5.** stress.

5. **Discuss obesity and the factors that contribute to its development.**

5-1. Obesity is usually defined in relation to the _____ _____ index (BMI; weight in kilograms divided by height in metres squared). A BMI of over _____ is often used as an indicator of obesity. The overall rate of obesity in Canada is _____%. Obesity rates in Canada have _____ over the last two decades. A group revealing a substantially increasing rate of obesity is _____.

5-2. Evolutionary theorists propose that in our ancestral past, when faced with the likelihood of famine, people evolved a capacity to overeat. Overeating, as a hedge against food shortages, had _____ value. In many areas of the world food is no longer scarce, but our tendency to overeat remains. In terms of our physiological needs, (very few/most) people overeat, and because of differences in makeup some become overweight.

5-3. It is clear that many factors affect body weight and that some of the most important are genetic. For example, Stunkard et al. (1986) found that adopted children were much more similar in BMI to their (biological/adoptive) parents than to their (biological/adoptive) parents, even though they were brought up by the latter.

5-4. The most striking finding of the Stunkard et al. (1990) study with twins was that (identical/fraternal) twins reared apart were more similar in BMI than (identical/fraternal) twins reared in the same family environment. This research supports the idea that (genetics/environment) plays a major role in body weight.

5-5. The concept of set point may help explain why body weight remains so stable. The theory proposes that each individual has a "natural" body weight that is set, in large part, by the person's (genetics/environment).

5-6. According to Schachter's _____ hypothesis, obese people are extra sensitive to _____ cues that affect hunger and are less sensitive to _____ physiological signals. More recently, it has been suggested that obese individuals are especially sensitive to the (normative/sensory) type of external cues.

5-7. According to _____-_____ theory, individual differences in body weight are due in large part to differences in genetic makeup. This theory asserts that the body actively defends a (wide range/particular) body weight by, for example, increasing hunger or decreasing metabolism.

5-8. Settling-point theory is a bit more optimistic: individuals who make long-term changes in eating or exercise will drift downward to a lower _____ point without such active resistance. The settling-point view also asserts that this balance is achieved as a result of (a wide variety of/genetic) factors.

5-9. According to the dietary restraint concept, the world is divided into two types of people: unrestrained eaters, who eat as much as they want when they want, and _____ eaters, who closely monitor their food intake and frequently go hungry.

5-10. While restrained eaters are constantly on guard to control their eating, at times they may lose control and eat to excess. In other words, restraint may be disrupted or _____, with the result that people overeat. This may include overeating just before they initiate a _____ (i.e., in anticipation of food deprivation). Paradoxically, then, restraint in eating may contribute to obesity. Restrained eaters are also more sensitive to the media's portrayal of _____ images of the thin body type.

Answers: 5-1. Body Mass, 30, 15, doubled, children **5-2.** survival (or adaptive), most **5-3.** biological, adoptive **5-4.** identical, fraternal, genetics **5-5.** genetics **5-6.** externality, external, internal, sensory **5-7.** set-point, particular **5-8.** settling, a wide variety of **5-9.** restrained **5-10.** disinhibited, diet, idealized.

6. Describe eating disorders and some factors associated with them.

6-1. The disorder that involves self-starvation is _____ nervosa, and the disorder that involves binge eating and purging is _____ nervosa. About _____% of Canadian women will develop an eating disorder, and the prevalence is (increasing/decreasing).

6-2. Factors such as an overemphasized thin _____ and pressures to be _____ contribute to eating disorders, in addition to other biological, psychological, developmental, and social factors.

Answers: 6-1. anorexia, bulimia, 3, increasing **6-2.** ideal, thin.

SEXUAL MOTIVATION AND BEHAVIOUR

7. Describe survey findings concerning the sexual activities of young Canadians.

7-1. According to recent Canadian surveys, about _____% of 15–17-year-olds and _____% of 20–24-year-olds have engaged in sexual intercourse. Engaging in sex at an early age is correlated with _____ _____ partners and (among girls) weak _____-_____. Having sex without using a condom is (rare/not uncommon), with _____% of sexually active 20–24-year-olds reporting such behaviour.

Answers: 7-1. 28, 80, multiple sexual, self-concepts, not uncommon, 44.

8. Outline the four phases of the human sexual response.

8-1. Write the names of the four phases of the human sexual response in the order in which they occur. (Hint: I made up a mnemonic device that's hard to forget. The first letter of each phase name produces EPOR, which happens to be ROPE spelled backward.)

(a) _____

(b) _____

(c) _____

(d) _____

8-2. In the blanks below write the first letter of each phase name that correctly labels the descriptions below.

_____ Rapid increase in arousal (respiration, heart rate, blood pressure, etc.)

_____ Vasocongestion of blood vessels in sexual organs; lubrication in female

_____ Continued arousal, but at a slower place

_____ Tightening of the vaginal entrance

_____ Pulsating muscular contractions and ejaculation

_____ Physiological changes produced by arousal subside

_____ Includes a refractory period for men

Answers: 8-1. (a) excitement, (b) plateau, (c) orgasm, (d) resolution 8-2. E, E, P, P, O, R, R.

9. Discuss parental investment theory and findings on human gender differences in sexual activity.

9-1. Triver's parental investment theory asserts that a species' mating patterns are determined by the investment each sex must make to produce and nurture offspring. Since human females are the ones who are pregnant for nine months and breastfeed the offspring, their _____ in the child is, by this analysis, greater than that of human males.

9-2. According to this viewpoint, whichever sex makes the smaller investment will *compete* for mating opportunities with the sex that makes the larger investment, and the sex that makes the larger investment will be more *selective* of partners. Thus, males of many mammalian species, including human beings, seek to maximize their reproductive potential by mating with (as many/as few) females as possible. Females, on the other hand, optimize their reproductive potential by being (selective/unrestricted) in mating.

9-3. In line with predictions from parental investment theory and evolutionary theory in general, Buss's research showed that _____ placed a higher value on potential partners' status and financial prospects, whereas _____ placed a higher value on youthfulness and physical attractiveness. These findings (<u>did/did not</u>) emerge across cultures.

Answers: 9-1. investment **9-2.** as many, selective **9-3.** women, men, did.

10. Describe the Featured Study on judging mate potential.

10-1. The study by Roney and colleagues examined whether women could draw meaningful inferences about males' _____ and _____ _____ from facial cues. Women rated the level of masculinity, parental potential, and other attributes of a number of facial photos of men.

10-2. Results showed that ratings of masculinity correlated significantly with males' actual _____ levels, and that ratings of parental potential (e.g., how much the man liked children) correlated with males' scores on a test of interest in infants. Finally, women's ratings of masculinity correlated with their estimates of males' (<u>short/long</u>)-term mate potential, whereas women's ratings of parental interest correlated with their estimates of males' (<u>short/long</u>)-term mate potential.

Answers: 10-1. masculinity, parental potential **10-2.** testosterone, short, long.

11. Summarize evidence on the impact of erotic materials, including aggressive pornography, on human sexual behaviour.

11-1. Findings on the relationship between exposure to erotic materials and sexual activity have been inconsistent and open to interpretation. One fairly consistent finding, however, has been that erotic materials (<u>increase/decrease</u>) the likelihood of sexual activity for a few hours after exposure.

11-2. In the Zillman and Bryant study, male and female undergraduates who were exposed to relatively heavy doses of pornography over a period of weeks developed attitudes involving sexual practices that were more (<u>liberal/conventional</u>). Other research has found a correlation between the acceptance of pornography and a history of (<u>more/fewer</u>) sex partners.

11-3. In general researchers (<u>have/have not</u>) found a link between exposure to erotic materials and sex crimes.

11-4. Several studies have found that pornography depicting violence against women (<u>decreases/increases</u>) men's tendency to be aggressive toward women. In these laboratory studies, aggression is defined as willingness to deliver electric shock to other subjects.

11-5. Other studies have found that exposure to aggressive pornography makes sexual coercion or rape seem (<u>less/more</u>) offensive to the participants, a troublesome finding in view of current information about the prevalence of rape.

Answers: 11-1. increase **11-2.** liberal, more **11-3.** have not **11-4.** increases **11-5.** less.

12. Summarize evidence on the nature of sexual orientation and on how common homosexuality is.

12-1. Sexual orientation refers to a person's preference for emotional and sexual relationships with individuals of the other sex, the same sex, or either sex. Those who prefer relationships with the other sex are termed

_____, with the same sex _____, and with either sex _____.

12-2. Because people may have experienced homosexuality in varying degrees, it seems reasonable to consider sexual orientation as a(n) (<u>continuum/all-or-none distinction</u>). In part because of this definitional problem, and in part due to prejudice against homosexuals, it is difficult to determine precisely the proportion of homosexuals in the population. A frequently cited statistic is 10%, but recent surveys place the proportion somewhere between _____.

Answers: 12-1. heterosexuals (or straights), homosexuals (or gays or lesbians), bisexuals **12-2.** continuum, 5% and 8%.

13. Summarize evidence on the determinants of sexual orientation.

13-1. What factors determine sexual orientation? Psychoanalysts thought the answer involved some aspect of the parent–child relationship. Behaviourists assumed that it was due to the association of same-sex stimuli with sexual arousal. Thus, both psychoanalytic and behavioural theorists proposed (<u>environmental/biological</u>) explanations of homosexuality.

13-2. Extensive research on the upbringing of homosexuals has (<u>supported/not supported</u>) the idea that homosexuality is primarily explainable in terms of environmental factors.

13-3. Recent studies have produced evidence that homosexuality is in part genetic. Which of the following types of studies have supported this conclusion? (Place Y for yes or N for no in the blanks.)

_____ Studies of hormonal differences between heterosexuals and homosexuals.

_____ Studies of twins and adopted children.

_____ Autopsy studies of the hypothalamus.

13-4. Subjects in one of the studies described were gay men who had an identical twin brother, a fraternal twin brother, or an adopted brother. For each of the categories, what percentage of the brothers of the subjects were also gay? Place the appropriate percentages in the blanks: 11%, 22%, 52%.

_____ Identical twins

_____ Fraternal twins

_____ Adopted brothers

13-5. Many theorists also suspect that secretions of _____ during prenatal development may be involved. For example, some research has found that women exposed prenatally to high _____ levels are more likely to be homosexual.

13-6. While much of the evidence points toward biological factors, the fact that identical twins turn out to share sexual orientation only half of the time suggests that _____ factors are involved in some way. Exactly what those factors might be is unknown, however.

13-7. There is also some evidence of greater _____ (or malleability) in females' sexuality than in males. For example, lesbian and bisexual women may change their sexual orientation over the course of their adult years.

ACHIEVEMENT: IN SEARCH OF EXCELLENCE

14. **Describe the achievement motive, and discuss how individual differences in the need for achievement influence behaviour.**

   14-1. People with high achievement motivation have a need to

   a. master difficult challenges

   b. outperform others

   c. excel and compete

   d. all of the above

   14-2. What is the relationship between estimates of achievement motive in a country and the economic growth of that county?

   14-3. The procedure used for measuring need for achievement involves subjects telling stories about pictures shown in the _____ _____ _____.

   14-4. How do people who score high on need for achievement differ from those who score low?

15. **Explain how situational factors influence achievement strivings.**

   15-1. According to Atkinson's elaboration of McClelland's views, achievement-oriented behaviour is determined not only by (1) achievement motivation, but also by (2) the _____ that success will occur and (3) the _____ value of success.

   15-2. As the difficulty of a task increases, the _____ of success at the task decreases. At the same time, success at harder tasks may be more satisfying, so the _____ value of the task is likely to increase. When both the incentive value and probability of success are weighed together, people with a high need for achievement would tend to select tasks of (extreme/moderate) difficulty.

   15-3. In addition to success, Atkinson has included fear of failure as a factor. People vary not only in their motivation to succeed, but also in their motivation to avoid _____.

   15-4. The motivation to avoid failure may either stimulate achievement or inhibit achievement. Explain.

THE ELEMENTS OF EMOTIONAL EXPERIENCE

16. Describe the cognitive component of emotion.

16-1. The word *cognition* refers to thoughts, beliefs, or conscious experience. When faced with an ugly-looking insect (or, for some people, the edge of a cliff or making a speech in public), you might say to yourself, "This is terrifying" (or maybe disgusting). This thought or cognition has an evaluative aspect: we assess our emotions as pleasant or unpleasant. Thus, one component of emotion is the thinking, or _____ component, which includes _____ in terms of pleasantness-unpleasantness.

16-2. Recent research on _____ _____ has shown that we are not very good at anticipating our emotional reactions to future events. For example, people are not very accurate in predicting the intensity and durational of their emotional reactions.

Answers: 16-1. cognitive, evaluation **16-2.** affective forecasting.

17. Describe the physiological underpinnings of emotion.

17-1. The second component of emotion is the _____ component, primarily actions of the _____ nervous system. Your encounter with the insect might be accompanied by changes in heart rate, breathing, or blood pressure—or by increased electrical conductivity of the skin, known as the _____ skin response (GSR).

17-2. Lie detectors don't actually detect lies, they detect _____ reflected by changes in heart rate, respiration, and GSR. Emotion does not necessarily reflect lying: some people can lie without showing emotional arousal, and others show arousal when asked incriminating questions. Advocates claim that polygraphs are about 85% to 90% accurate; recent research (supports/does not support) this claim. In most courtrooms polygraph results (are/are not) considered reliable enough to be used as evidence.

17-3. Recent evidence suggests that the brain structure known as the _____ plays a central role in emotion.

17-4. The amygdala doesn't process emotion by itself but is at the core of a complex set of neural circuits. Sensory information relating to fear arrives at the thalamus and from there is relayed along two pathways, to the nearby _____ and also to areas in the _____.

17-5. The amygdala processes information extremely rapidly, which has clear _____ value for the organism in threatening situations. The cortex responds more slowly, but in greater detail, and relays potentially moderating information to the amygdala. While the hub of this vigilance system seems to be the _____, both pathways are useful in assessing threat.

17-6. Additional brain areas involved in emotion include the _____ cortex (which contributes to voluntary control of emotional reactions), the _____ cortex (implicated in pain-related emotional distress), and the _____ _____ pathway (which plays a major role in pleasurable emotions associated with rewarding events). Specialized neurons involved in empathy are called _____ neurons.

18. Discuss the body language of emotions and the facial feedback hypothesis.

18-1. We communicate emotions not only verbally but also _____, through our postures, gestures, and especially our facial _____.

18-2. Ekman and Friesen found that there are _____ fundamental facial expressions of emotion: happiness, sadness, anger, fear, surprise, and disgust. Children who have been blind since birth frown and smile just like sighted children, which supports the idea that basic facial expressions are largely (learned/innate).

18-3. According to some researchers, facial expressions not only reflect emotions but help create them. This viewpoint, known as the _____ hypothesis, asserts that facial muscles send signals to the brain that help produce the subjective experience of emotion. For example, turning up the corners of your mouth will tend to make you feel _____.

19. Discuss cross-cultural similarities and variations in emotional experience.

19-1. Ekman and Friesen asked people in different cultures to label the emotion shown on photographs of faces. What did they find?

19-2. Different cultures show striking similarities in other aspects of emotional experience as well. For example, regardless of culture, meeting with friends tends to trigger one emotion and encountering failure another. Thus, certain types of _____ trigger the same emotions across cultures.

19-3. While there are similarities in emotional expression across cultures, there are also striking differences. For example, certain word labels for emotion (e.g., sadness, anxiety, remorse) (occur/do not occur) in all cultures. However, recent evidence suggests that cultural disparities in naming emotions may not necessarily reflect differences in emotional processing.

19-4. Although people in different cultures tend to show the same basic expressions of emotion, when they do so is governed by different cultural norms. What emotions are you "supposed" to show at a funeral, or when watching a sporting event? The unwritten rules that regulate our display of emotion, known as _____ rules, vary considerably across cultures.

CHAPTER TEN

20. Compare and contrast the James-Lange and Cannon-Bard theories of emotion, and explain how Schachter reconciled these conflicting views in his two-factor theory.

20-1.   Suppose you saw a rat in your room (and assume that you are afraid of rats). Why would you be afraid? One would think that the process would be as follows: first you would be consciously aware of your fear of the rat, then you would experience the autonomic or visceral arousal that accompanies fear. The James-Lange theory reverses this process: we first experience the (<u>visceral arousal/conscious fear</u>), and then we experience (<u>visceral arousal/conscious fear</u>).

20-2.   According to the James-Lange theory, then, fear and other emotions occur not as a result of different conscious experiences but as a result of different patterns of _____ activation.

20-3.   The Cannon-Bard theory argued that a subcortical structure in the brain (they thought it was the thalamus) simultaneously sends signals to both the cortex and the autonomic nervous system. According to this theory

a. conscious fear would precede autonomic arousal.

b. autonomic arousal would precede conscious fear.

c. autonomic arousal and conscious fear would occur at the same time.

20-4.   According to Cannon-Bard, emotion originates in

a. subcortical structures.

b. the autonomic nervous system.

c. conscious awareness.

20-5.   The Cannon-Bard theory contends that different emotions (e.g., fear, joy, love, anger) are accompanied by

a. different patterns of autonomic arousal.

b. nearly identical patterns of autonomic arousal.

c. neither of the above.

20-6.   Schachter's two-factor view is similar to the James-Lange theory in that (<u>visceral arousal/conscious experience</u>) is thought to precede the mental awareness of an emotion. The theory is similar to the Cannon-Bard theory in that (<u>general autonomic arousal/different autonomic responses</u>) is assumed to account for a wide variety of emotions.

20-7.   Since arousal is in large part the same regardless of the emotion, according to Schachter, we feel different emotions as a result of *inferences* we make from events in the environment. Hence, the two factors in Schachter's theory are _____ (roughly the same for all emotions) and _____ (people's interpretation of the arousal based on the situation).

20-8.   To review the three theories, label each of the following with the name of a theory:

(a) _____ The subjective experience of emotion is caused by different patterns of autonomic arousal.

(b) _____ Emotions cannot be distinguished on the basis of autonomic arousal; general autonomic arousal causes one to look for an explanation or label.

(c) _____ Love is accompanied by a different autonomic pattern from hate.

(d) _____ The subjective experience of emotion is caused by two factors, namely, arousal and cognition.

(e) _____ Emotions originate in subcortical brain structures; different emotions produce almost identical patterns of autonomic arousal.

(f) _____ Ralph observes that his heart pounds and that he becomes a little out of breath at times. He also notices that these signs of arousal occur whenever Mary is around, so he figures that he must be in love.

20-9. In what sense does Schachter's theory reconcile the James-Lange and Cannon-Bard theories?

Answers: 20-1. visceral arousal, conscious fear **20-2.** autonomic (or visceral) **20-3.** c **20-4.** a **20-5.** b **20-6.** visceral arousal, general autonomic arousal **20-7.** arousal, cognition **20-8.** (a) James-Lange, (b) Schachter's two-factor, (c) James-Lange, (d) Schachter's two-factor, (e) Cannon-Bard, (f) Schachter's two-factor **20-9.** Schachter's view is similar to the James-Lange theory in that arousal is thought to precede the conscious experience of emotion; it is similar to the Cannon-Bard theory in that there is assumed to be just one general physiological arousal response rather than a different visceral response for each emotion. Since arousal is in large part the same regardless of the emotion, Schachter proposed that we feel different emotions as a result of inferences we make from events in the environment.

21. Summarize the evolutionary perspective on emotion.

21-1. By preparing an organism for aggression and defence, the emotion of anger helps an organism survive. The emotions of fear, surprise, and interest have similar functions. From an evolutionary perspective, all emotions developed because of the _____ value they have for a species.

21-2. Evolutionary theorists view emotions primarily as a group of (<u>innate/learned</u>) reactions that have been passed on because of their survival value. They also believe that emotions originate in subcortical areas, parts of the brain that evolved before the cortical structures associated with higher mental processes. In the view of evolutionary theorists, emotion evolved before thought and is largely (<u>dependent on/independent of</u>) thought.

21-3. How many basic, inherited emotions are there? The evolutionary writers assume that the wide range of emotions we experience are blends or variations in intensity of approximately _____ innate or prewired primary emotions.

21-4. As an example of an evolved emotion, disgust allows us to avoid _____, thereby increasing our chances of survival.

Answers: 21-1. survival (or adaptive) **21-2.** innate, independent of **21-3.** eight (or between six and ten) **21-4.** disease.

22. Explain how this chapter highlighted five of the text's unifying themes.

22-1. Five of the text's organizing themes were prominent in this chapter. Indicate which themes fit the following examples by writing the appropriate abbreviations in the blanks below: C for cultural context, SH for sociohistorical context, T for theoretical diversity, HE for heredity and environment, and MC for multiple causation.

(a) Achievement behaviour is affected by achievement motivation, the likelihood of success, the likelihood of failure, and so on. ____

(b) Display rules in a culture tell us when and where to express an emotion. ____

(c) Changing attitudes about homosexuality have produced more research on sexual orientation; in turn, data from the research has affected societal attitudes. ____

(d) Body weight seems to be influenced by set point, blood glucose, and inherited metabolism. It is also affected by eating habits and acquired tastes, which vary across cultures. ____, ____, and ____

(e) The James-Lange theory proposed that different emotions reflect different patterns of physiological arousal; Cannon-Bard theory assumed that emotions originate in subcortical structures; Schachter viewed emotion as a combination of physiological arousal and cognition. ____

Answers: 22-1. (a) MC, (b) C, (c) SH, (d) HE, MC, C, (e) T.

PERSONAL APPLICATION * EXPLORING THE INGREDIENTS OF HAPPINESS

23. Summarize information on factors that do not predict happiness.

23-1. Indicate whether each of the following statements is true or false.

(a) ____ There is very little correlation between income and happiness.

(b) ____ Younger people tend to be happier than older people.

(c) ____ People who have children tend to be happier than those without children.

(d) ____ People with high IQ scores tend to be happier than those with low IQ scores.

(e) ____ There is a negligible correlation between physical attractiveness and happiness.

23-2. List five factors discussed in your text that have little or no relationship to happiness.

Answers: 23-1. (a) T, (b) F, (c) F, (d) F, (e) T **23-2.** money (or income), age, parenthood (either having or not having children), intelligence, physical attractiveness.

24. Summarize information on factors that are moderately or strongly correlated with happiness.

24-1. Indicate whether each of the following statements is true or false.

(a) ____ One of the strongest predictors of happiness is good health.

(b) ____ Social support and friendship groups are moderately related to happiness.

(c) ____ Religious people tend to be somewhat happier than nonreligious people.

(d) ____ Marital status is strongly related to happiness; married people tend to be happier than single people.

(e) ____ Job satisfaction tends to be strongly related to general happiness; people who like their jobs tend to be happy.

(f) ____ Differences in personality have a negligible relationship to happiness; introverts, on the average, are just as happy as extraverts.

24-2. List four factors that are moderately correlated with happiness and three that are strongly correlated.

Answers: 24-1. (a) F (People adapt, so there is only a moderate relationship between health and happiness.), (b) T, (c) T, (d) T, (e) T, (f) F (People who are extraverted, are optimistic, and have high self-esteem tend to be happier.)
24-2. moderately related: health, social activity (friendship), religion, and culture. Strongly related: marriage, work (job satisfaction), and personality.

25. Explain three conclusions that can be drawn about the dynamics of happiness.

25-1. One conclusion about happiness is that how we feel about our health, wealth, job, and age are more important than the facts of our situation. In other words, the objective realities are less important than our _____ reactions.

25-2. In addition, the extent of our happiness depends on the comparison group. Generally, people compare themselves to others who are similar in some dimension, such as friends or neighbours. In the final analysis, our happiness is relative to the _____ to which we compare ourselves.

25-3. A third conclusion is that our baseline for judging pleasantness and unpleasantness constantly changes. When good things happen, we shift our baselines (what we feel we "need" or want) upward; when bad things happen, we shift down. In other words, people _____ to changing circumstances by changing their baselines of comparison, a process termed _____ adaptation.

Answers: 25-1. subjective **25-2.** group (or people) **25-3.** adapt (or adjust), hedonic.

CRITICAL THINKING APPLICATION * ANALYZING ARGUMENTS: MAKING SENSE OUT OF CONTROVERSY

26. Describe the key elements in arguments.

26-1. In logic, an *argument* is a series of statements that claims to prove something (whether it does or not). Arguments are comprised of two major parts, a *conclusion* and one or more *premises*. The _____ are statements intended to present evidence or proof. The _____ supposedly derives from or is proved by the premises.

26-2. Consider this logical argument: "Any field of study that uses the scientific method is a science. Psychology uses the scientific method. Thus, psychology is a science." Label the parts of the argument below (C for conclusion and P for premise).

____ Any field of study that uses the scientific method is a science.

_____ Psychology uses the scientific method.

_____ Thus, psychology is a science.

Answers: 26-1. premises, conclusion **26-2.** P, P, C. Note that this is an example of a valid argument. Other people may or may not agree with the premises (e.g., they may define science differently), but the conclusion logically follows from the premises.

27. Explain some common fallacies that often show up in arguments.

27-1. Read over the section on common logical fallacies described in your text. Then match the examples with the appropriate terms. (Suggestion: Use the abbreviations in parentheses for matching. Note that there are five fallacies and seven examples; two fallacies are used twice.)

irrelevant reasons (IR)

circular reasoning (CR)

slippery slope (SS)

weak analogies (WA)

false dichotomy (FD)

(a) _____ Trouble sleeping causes great difficulty in our lives because insomnia is a major problem for people.

(b) _____ People with insomnia should use the herb melatonin because insomnia is an enormous problem in our country.

(c) _____ Vitamin C is extremely effective in slowing the aging process. I know it is effective because I have taken it for many years. Obviously, the reason I take Vitamin C is that it works to reduce aging.

(d) _____ If we don't stop communism in Vietnam now, it will spread next to Laos, then to Cambodia, and then to the entire Southeast Asian Peninsula.

(e) _____ We saw what happened when Chamberlain gave in to Hitler. The same thing will happen again unless we stand up to the tyranny in the Middle East.

(f) _____ We can fight in the Balkans now, or we can prepare for World War III.

(g) _____ Ralph bought a blender on a Tuesday in Peoria and it lasted a long time. If I buy a blender on a Tuesday in Peoria, it should also last a long time.

Answers: 27-1. (a) CR. The premise and conclusion are the same. (b) IR. Insomnia may be a problem, but that does not lead to the conclusion that the herb melatonin should be taken. (c) CR. The conclusion, the first statement, is simply a restatement of the premise, which is the last statement. (d) SS. The argument is that if you allow one thing to happen, then a series of other things will inevitably happen. In fact, there may be no necessary connection between the events. (e) WA. While the two situations may have a degree of similarity, they are also likely to be sufficiently dissimilar to make the argument invalid. (f) FD. The choice seems to be between the two options, but, logically, these are not the only choices. We may also do both, or neither. (g) WA. While the situations share some elements in common, this does not mean that they share all elements or that some elements cause others.

REVIEW OF KEY TERMS

Achievement motive
Affective forecasting
Argument
Assumptions
Bisexuals
Body Mass Index (BMI)
Collectivism
Display rules
Drive
Emotion
Externality hypothesis

Galvanic skin response (GSR)
Glucose
Hedonic adaptation
Heterosexuals
Homosexuals
Incentive
Individualism
Insulin
Lie detector
Motivation

Obesity
Orgasm
Polygraph
Premises
Refractory period
Set-point theory
Settling-point theory
Sexual orientation
Subjective well-being
Vasocongestion

_____ 1. Goal-directed behaviour that may be affected by needs, wants, interests, desires, and incentives.

_____ 2. Cultural norms that regulate the expression of emotions.

_____ 3. One or more premises that are used to provide support for a conclusion.

_____ 4. The reasons presented in an argument to persuade someone that a conclusion is true.

_____ 5. Premises in an argument that are assumed, but for which no proof or evidence is offered.

_____ 6. A measure of weight that controls for variations in height; weight in kilograms divided by height in metres squared.

_____ 7. Refers to cultures that put group goals ahead of personal goals and defines a person's identity in terms of the groups to which a person belongs.

_____ 8. Blood sugar.

_____ 9. Schachter's idea that obese people are extra sensitive to external food-related cues.

_____ 10. A hormone secreted by the pancreas needed for extracting glucose from the blood.

_____ 11. Refers to cultures that put personal goals ahead of group goals and defines a person's identity in terms of the personal attributes.

_____ 12. The theoretical natural point of stability in body weight.

_____ 13. The condition of being overweight.

_____ 14. An internal state of tension that motivates an organism to reduce tension.

_____ 15. Engorgement of the blood vessels.

_____ 16. Sexual climax.

_____ 17. A time following orgasm during which males are unresponsive to sexual stimulation.

_____ 18. Whether a person prefers emotional–sexual relationships with members of the same sex, the other sex, or either sex.

_____ 19. People who seek emotional–sexual relationships with members of the same sex.

_____ 20. People who seek emotional–sexual relationships with members of the other sex.

_____ 21. People who seek emotional–sexual relationships with members of either sex.

_____ 22. Efforts to predict one's emotional reactions to future events.

_____ 23. Individuals' personal perceptions of their overall happiness and life satisfaction.

_____ 24. The need to master difficult challenges and to excel in competition with others.

_____ 25. An increase in the electrical conductivity of the skin related to an increase in sweat gland activity.

_____ 26. A reaction that includes cognitive, physiological, and behavioural components.

_____ 27. The technical name for the "lie detector."

_____ 28. The informal name for polygraph, an apparatus that monitors physiological aspects of arousal (e.g., heart rate, GSR).

_____ 29. An external goal that motivates behaviour.

_____ 30. The view that body weight is determined by a wide variety of factors and that the body does not defend a particular point.

_____ 31. When the mental scale that people use to judge the pleasantness or unpleasantness of their experience shifts so that their neutral point changes.

Answers: 1. motivation **2.** display rules **3.** argument **4.** premises **5.** assumptions **6.** body mass index (BMI) **7.** collectivism **8.** glucose **9.** externality hypothesis **10.** insulin **11.** individualism **12.** set point **13.** obesity **14.** drive **15.** vasocongestion **16.** orgasm **17.** refractory period **18.** sexual orientation **19.** homosexuals **20.** heterosexuals **21.** bisexuals **22.** affective forecasting **23.** subjective well-being **24.** achievement motive **25.** galvanic skin response (GSR) **26.** emotion **27.** polygraph **28.** lie detector **29.** incentive **30.** settling-point theory **31.** hedonic adaptation.

REVIEW OF KEY PEOPLE

John Atkinson   William James   Henry Murray
David Buss   Joseph LeDoux   Judith Rodin
Walter Cannon   William Masters and Virginia Johnson   Stanley Schachter
Paul Ekman and Wallace Friesen   David McClelland

_____ 1. Proposed that emotions arise in subcortical areas of the brain.

_____ 2. Compiled an influential catalogue of common social needs; also devised the TAT.

_____ 3. Prominent evolutionary theorist who explored, among many other topics, gender differences in human mate preferences.

_____ 4. Proposed that eating, on the part of obese people, is controlled by external cues; devised the two-factor theory of emotion.

_____ 5. Stressed the importance of the amygdala as the core of a set of interacting neural circuits that process emotion.

_____ 6. Did the ground-breaking work on the physiology of the human sexual response.

_____ 7. Is responsible for most of the early research on achievement motivation.

_____ 8. Emphasized additional factors in an elaboration of McClelland's theory of achievement motivation.

_____ 9. In a series of cross-cultural studies found that people can identify six or so basic emotions from facial expressions.

_____ 10. Thought that emotion arose from one's perception of variations in autonomic arousal.

_____ 11. Studied the cues that can elicit hunger processes.

SELF-QUIZ

1. Which of the following individuals are most likely to be similar in body mass?
   a. identical twins brought up in different family environments
   b. fraternal twins brought up in the same family environment
   c. parents and their adopted children
   d. adopted siblings brought up in the same family environment

2. What is the subjective feeling of hunger NOT influenced by?
   a. the amount of glucose in the bloodstream
   b. secretion of insulin
   c. external cues, including odour and appearance of food
   d. secretion of androgen

3. What hunger-related hormone is responsible for glucose being extracted from the blood?
   a. CCK
   b. insulin
   c. ghrelin
   d. leptin

4. The sex that makes the larger investment in offspring (bearing, nursing, etc.) will be more selective of partners than the sex that makes the smaller investment. Which of the following theories does that statement relate to?
   a. adaptation level theory
   b. parental investment theory
   c. investment differentiation theory
   d. social learning theory

5. Which of the following theories proposes that the body actively defends a particular body weight by adjusting metabolism and hunger?
   a. set-point theory
   b. settling-point theory
   c. adaptation level theory
   d. parental investment theory

6. Which of the following statements best represents the James-Lange theory of emotion?
   a. The subjective experience of emotion is caused by thinking about the cause of autonomic arousal.
   b. The conscious experience of emotion is caused by different patterns of autonomic arousal.
   c. Emotion originates in subcortical structures, which send signals to both the cortex and the autonomic nervous system.
   d. Cognitive awareness of emotion precedes autonomic arousal.

7. Consider the fact that identical twins are more likely to share sexual orientation than fraternal twins. What does that fact suggest about sexual orientation?
   a. It is due to the environment.
   b. It is in part genetic.
   c. It is largely chemical.
   d. It is primarily hormonal.

8. What is the term for cultural norms that indicate which facial expressions of emotion are appropriate on particular occasions?
   a. display rules
   b. parental investments
   c. investment differentiations
   d. social scripts

9. According to the evolutionary theories, what characterizes the women whom men seek as partners?
   a. They are similar to the men in important attitudes.
   b. They have a good sense of humour.
   c. They are beautiful, youthful, and in good health.
   d. They have good financial prospects.

10. What test is generally used to measure the need for achievement?
    a. the TAT
    b. the GSR
    c. the Rorschach
    d. the MMPI

11. What does evidence regarding facial expression in different cultures suggest?
    a. that two-factor theory accounts for nonverbal behaviour
    b. that facial expression of emotion is to some extent innate
    c. that emotions originate in the cortex
    d. that learning is the major factor in explaining basic facial expressions

12. Who proposed that emotion arises from one's perception or interpretation of autonomic arousal?
    a. Schachter
    b. Cannon-Bard
    c. LeDoux
    d. McClelland

13. Which of the following theories assert that thinking or cognition plays a relatively small role in emotion?
    a. two-factor theory
    b. James-Lange theory
    c. achievement theory
    d. evolutionary theory

14. What attribute is found to be most strongly associated with happiness?
    a. physical attractiveness
    b. health
    c. job satisfaction
    d. general intelligence

15. Someone who exhorts people to take action against company policy says, "We can oppose these changes, or we can live out our lives in poverty." Which of the following fallacies does this type of argument reflect?
    a. slippery slope
    b. weak analogy
    c. false dichotomy
    d. circular reasoning

16. What eating disorder involves binging and purging?
    a. obesity
    b. bulimia nervosa
    c. anorexia nervosa
    d. pica

17. What kind of measure is most often used to determine obesity?
    a. self-report obesity scale
    b. set-point scale
    c. weight in kilograms
    d. body mass index

18. What term applies to the attempt to predict one's emotional reactions to future events?
    a. emotional expectations
    b. affective forecasting
    c. emotionometer
    d. emotional predictions

19. What is the heritability of happiness?
    a. approximately 20%
    b. approximately 30%
    c. approximately 40%
    d. approximately 50%

20. Which of the following variables is NOT considered a cue which influences eating?
    a. palatability of food
    b. temperature of food
    c. variety of food available
    d. quantity of food available

Answers: 1. a **2.** d **3.** b **4.** b **5.** a **6.** d **7.** b **8.** a **9.** c **10.** a **11.** b **12.** a **13.** d **14.** c **15.** c **16.** b **17.** d **18.** b **19.** d **20.** b.

Chapter Eleven

HUMAN DEVELOPMENT ACROSS THE LIFE SPAN

REVIEW OF KEY IDEAS

1. **Define development.**

   1-1. Development is the sequence of _____-_____ changes that occur as a person progresses from conception to death. It includes both the _____ and _____ changes that take place as people grow older.

   Answers: 1-1. age-related, biological, behavioural.

PROGRESS BEFORE BIRTH: PRENATAL DEVELOPMENT

2. **Outline the major events of the three phases of prenatal development.**

   2-1. Each box below represents one month in the typical pregnancy; each short line at the top of the boxes represents one week. Indicate the beginning and end of each phase of prenatal development by placing the appropriate capital letters from the diagram in the blanks after the descriptions below.

   (a) The germinal stage begins at conception, represented by point _____ in the diagram, and ends at point _____.

   (b) The embryonic stage begins at point _____ and ends at point _____.

   (c) The fetal stage begins at point _____ and ends at point _____.

   2-2. List the names of the three phases of prenatal development in the order in which they occur. In the parentheses at the right, indicate the age ranges encompassed by each stage.

   (a) _____   (   )

(b) _____   (   )

(c) _____   (   )

2-3.   Match each stage in the previous question with the descriptions below. Use the letters G, E, and F to represent the germinal, embryonic, and fetal stages.

_____   The placenta begins to form.

_____   At the end of this stage the organism begins to have a human appearance; it is about 2.5 centimetres (1 inch) in length.

_____   The zygote begins to implant in the uterine wall; about one in five are rejected.

_____   Muscles and bones develop, and physical movements occur.

_____   Most major birth defects probably have their origins in this stage.

_____   The age of viability (about 22 to 26 weeks after conception) occurs during this stage.

Answers: 2-1. (a) G, E, (b) E, F, (c) F, N **2-2.** (a) germinal (birth to two weeks), (b) embryonic (two weeks to two months) (c) fetal (two months to nine months) **2-3.** G, E, G, F, E, F.

3. Summarize the impact of environmental factors on prenatal development.

3-1.   Indicate whether the following statements concerning environmental factors and fetal development are true (T) or false (F).

_____   Severe malnutrition increases the risk of birth complications and neurological deficits.

_____   Few, if any, drugs consumed by a pregnant woman are able to pass through the placental barrier.

_____   Recent studies indicate that moderate drinking during pregnancy produces no risk for the developing fetus.

_____   Marijuana use by a pregnant woman may lead to attention/impulsivity problems in the child.

_____   Heavy drinking of alcohol by a pregnant woman may produce microencephaly, heart defects, and retardation in her child.

_____   Smoking during pregnancy is related to increased risk of miscarriage and other birth complications.

_____   The placenta screens out many but not all infectious diseases.

_____   Genital herpes is usually transmitted during the birth process, when newborns come into contact with their mothers' lesions.

_____   HIV is transmitted primarily during the birth process, when newborns come into contact with their mothers' blood cells.

_____   Good quality prenatal care is associated with fewer premature births and higher infant survival rates.

_____   Maternal anxiety and depression are associated with behavioural problems of offspring.

_____   Prenatal malnutrition elevates risk for later development of schizophrenia.

Answers: 3-1. T, F, F, T, T, T, T, T, T, T, T, T.

4. **Describe general trends and principles and cultural variations in motor development.**

    4-1.   In the space below, describe the two basic trends in motor development described in the text.

        Cephalocaudal trend:

        Proximodistal trend:

    4-2.   The average ages at which children display various behaviours and abilities are referred to as developmental _____. While these averages provide useful information, they don't reflect variability, and the age at which children display certain behaviours or abilities varies (enormously/very little) across children.

    4-3.   Thus, with regard to the behaviour of walking up steps, for example, which of the following is true?

        a. Children walk up steps at approximately the same age.

        b. Many normal children walk up steps well after or well before the average age indicated.

    4-4.   The process that underlies the developmental norms is *maturation*. What is maturation? (Be specific with regard to the factors of heredity and environment.)

    4-5.   Cross-cultural research has revealed a considerable degree of consistency between cultures in terms of when and in what order motor skills appear. In general, early motor development is much more dependent on (maturation/culture) than is later motor development. As children in a culture grow older, however, the motor skills that they acquire depend to a greater extent on (maturation/culture).

Answers: 4-1. Head to foot: children tend to gain motor control of the upper body before the lower body. Centre outward: the tendency to gain control of the torso before the limbs. **4-2.** norms, enormously **4-3.** b **4-4.** Maturation refers to developmental changes that occur in an organism as a result of *genetic*, as opposed to environmental, factors. **4-5.** maturation, culture.

5. **Summarize the findings of Thomas and Chess's longitudinal study of infant temperament.**

    5-1.   Identify the following designs by indicating whether they are longitudinal or cross-sectional.

        (a) _____   In this experimental design, researchers compare groups of subjects of differing ages at a single point in time.

        (b) _____   This design measures a single group of subjects over a period of time.

    5-2.   Using a longitudinal design, Thomas and Chess identified three basic temperaments, described below. Place the names of these temperamental styles in the appropriate blanks.

(a) _____ Happy, regular in sleep and eating, adaptable.

(b) _____ Less cheery, less regular in sleep and eating, more wary of new experiences.

(c) _____ Glum, erratic in sleep and eating, irritable.

5-3. The largest group of children (about 40%) were of the _____ temperament, another 15% were _____, and 10% were in the _____ category. The remaining 35% showed mixtures of these three temperaments.

5-4. What is the major result and conclusion from the Thomas and Chess study?

Answers: 5-1. (a) cross-sectional, (b) longitudinal **5-2.** (a) easy, (b) slow-to-warm-up, (c) difficult **5-3.** easy, slow-to-warm-up, difficult **5-4.** Temperament remains somewhat stable across age. A child's temperament at three months tends to predict temperament at age 10 years.

6. Summarize theories of attachment and research on patterns of attachment, and their effects.

6-1. Newborn babies do not form attachments to their mothers immediately. They begin to show a strong preference for their mothers, often crying when they are separated, beginning at about _____ months of age.

6-2. The emotional distress that occurs when some infants are separated from their caregivers is called _____ anxiety. This distress peaks at about _____ months of age and then begins to decline.

6-3. Early research by Harlow questioned the behaviourist assumption that early attachment reflects reinforcement effects by showing that a "substitute mother" monkey that provides _____ _____ is preferred over one that provides food.

6-4. Bowlby argued that there was likely a _____ basis for attachment. He stated that infants are biologically programmed to emit behaviours that elicit protective, caring responses from adults, and that adults are biologically programmed to respond with warmth, love, and protection. In other words, attachment has _____ value. Contemporary theorists also emphasize _____ fitness as another adaptive advantage of attachment.

6-5. Attachment research by Ainsworth and her colleagues made use of the _____ _____ procedure. This research indicated that attachments between mothers and their infants tend to fall into three categories. Label each of the following with the pattern of attachment described: *secure, anxious-ambivalent, avoidant, or disorganized-disoriented.*

(a) _____ The infant is anxious even when the mother is near, becomes very agitated when she leaves, and is not comforted when the mother returns.

(b) _____ The infant seeks little contact with the mother and is not distressed when she leaves.

(c) _____ The infant plays comfortably when the mother is present, is upset when the mother leaves, but is quickly calmed by her when she returns.

(d) _____ The infant appears confused about whether he or she should approach or avoid his or her mother.

6-6. Although one cannot assume a causal relationship, attachment in infancy has been found to be related to behaviour in later childhood. For a number of desirable characteristics, including social skills, persistence, curiosity, leadership, and cognitive development, it appears that children who experienced a _____ attachment have the advantage.

Answers: 6-1. six to eight **6-2.** separation, 14 to 18 **6-3.** contact comfort **6-4.** biological, survival, reproductive **6-5.** strange situation, (a) anxious-ambivalent, (b) avoidant, (c) secure, (d) disorganized-disoriented **6-6.** secure.

7. Discuss culture in relation to attachment.

7-1. Separation anxiety occurs at roughly the same ages across different cultures. There are cross-cultural differences, however, in the proportion of infants who fall into the three attachment categories (see Figure 11.7 in your text).

(a) Which cultural sample (U.S.A., Germany, or Japan) showed the highest proportion of *avoidant* attachments? _____

(b) Which cultural sample evidenced virtually *no avoidant attachments* at all?
_____

(c) Which sample showed the highest levels of *anxious/ambivalent* attachments?
_____

(d) Which two countries had the highest proportion of *secure* attachments?
_____ and _____

Answers: 7-1. (a) Germany, (b) Japan, (c) Japan, (d) Japan, U.S.A.

8. Outline the basic tenets of Erikson's theory, and describe his stages of childhood personality development.

8-1. Erikson's theory is clearly derived from Freudian psychoanalytic theory. Freud asserted that there are five childhood stages that determine the adult's personality. In contrast, Erikson proposed that there are _____ stages that influence personality across an individual's (childhood/entire lifespan).

8-2. Erikson described four childhood stages and four adult stages. In the spaces below, write the names of the crises that mark the four *childhood* stages, and indicate in the parentheses the approximate ages at which the crises are supposed to occur.

(a) _____ vs. _____   (   )

(b) _____ vs. _____   (   )

(c) _____ vs. _____   (   )

(d) _____ vs. _____   (   )

8-3. Below are descriptions of several individuals. In what childhood stage would they have acquired these characteristics, according to Erikson? Use the letters from the question above to indicate the stages.

_____ Jack has trouble functioning effectively in the world outside his family; he is unproductive, and he lacks a sense of competence.

_____ Kristi is insecure and suspicious of everyone.

_____ Larry was torn between being independent of his family and avoiding conflict; as an adult, he feels guilty and lacks self-esteem.

_____ From an early age, Maureen's parents never seemed satisfied with what she did. Maureen is plagued by a sense of shame and self-doubt.

8-4. As you may have noted in responding to the previous item, a weakness of Erikson's theory is that it attempts to account for very (few/many) aspects of personality. Thus, the theory cannot explain the enormous individual _____ between people.

Answers: 8-1. eight, entire lifespan **8-2.** (a) trust vs. mistrust (first year), (b) autonomy vs. shame and doubt (second year), (c) initiative vs. guilt (ages three to six), (d) industry vs. inferiority (age six through puberty) **8-3.** d, a, c, b **8-4.** few, differences (or variation).

9. Outline Piaget's stages of cognitive development, and discuss the strengths and weaknesses of Piaget's theory.

9-1. The diagram on the next page represents Piaget's four main stages of development. Write the names of the stages in the appropriate blanks.

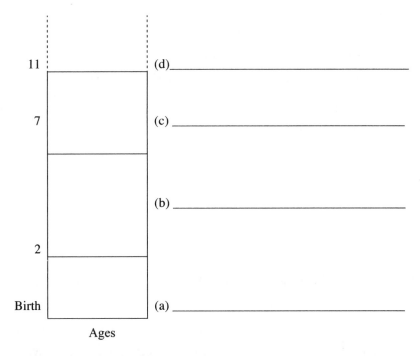

11	(d) _____
7	(c) _____
	(b) _____
2	
Birth	(a) _____

Ages

9-2. The stages of development are marked by changes in children's thinking processes brought about by two major processes. If the child interprets a new experience in terms of an *existing* mental structure, then _____ is operating. On the other hand, if the child interprets an experience by *changing* his or her thinking strategy, then the child has used _____.

9-3. Following is a list of characteristics of children's thinking during various stages. Identify the stage by placing the correct letter (from the diagram above) in the blanks.

_____ At the end of this stage, the child is beginning to develop the capacity for symbolic thought (to think terms of mental images).

_____ At the beginning of this stage, the child's behaviour is dominated by reflexes and the ability to coordinate sensory input and movement.

_____ The child understands conservation and can handle hierarchical classification but tends not to use abstractions.

_____ The child's thought processes are abstract and systematic.

_____ Object permanence occurs toward the end of this stage.

_____ During the first part of this stage, "out of sight, out of mind" might describe the child's reaction to hidden objects.

_____ When water is poured from a wide beaker into a taller beaker, children say there is now more water in the taller beaker.

_____ The child demonstrates a lack of understanding of conservation.

_____ The child shows the shortcomings of centration, irreversibility, egocentrism, and animism.

_____ For the first time, the child in this stage is mentally able to undo an action and also is able to focus on more than one feature of a problem at the same time.

9-4. When my (R.S.'s) daughter Vanessa was about five, I placed two rows of stones on the grass, as illustrated below. Each row contained the same number of stones.

Row A: * * * * * * *

Row B: * * * * * * *

I then spread out one row so that it took up more space:

Row A: * * * * * * * *

Row B: * * * * * * *

(a) I then asked Vanessa to point to the row that now had more stones. If Vanessa behaved like other preoperational children, which row would she point to? _____

(b) The preoperational child has not yet mastered the principle that physical quantities remain constant in spite of changes in their shape or, in this case, arrangement. What is the name of this principle? _____

9-5. Some research has demonstrated that certain aspects of Piaget's theory may be incorrect in detail. For example, while Piaget argued that development is discontinuous (i.e., made-up of discrete stages), some evidence points to _____ in development. Also, there is some evidence that object permanence and some aspects of conservation may develop (earlier/later) than Piaget had thought.

9-6. Piaget also had little to say about individual _____ in development or about so-called _____ of stages in which elements of an earlier stage may appear in a later one.

9-7. Piaget thought that people of all cultures would pass through the stages at the same time; subsequent research has found that this (is/is not) the case. While the *sequence* of stages appears to be relatively invariant across cultures, the _____ that children follow in passing through these stages varies considerably across cultures. Nonetheless, Piaget's brilliance, the novelty of his approach, and the wealth of research that his theory inspired assure his place in history.

Answers: 9-1. (a) sensorimotor, (b) preoperational, (c) concrete operations, (d) formal operations **9-2.** assimilation, accommodation **9-3.** a, a, c, d, a, a, b, b, b, c **9-4.** (a) Row A (at which point Samantha, then eight and in the stage of concrete operations, was astonished by her sister's choice and informed her that there were the same number in both!), (b) conservation **9-5.** continuity, earlier **9-6.** differences, mixing **9-7.** is not, timetable (or age, time).

10. Describe neo-Piagetian views on cognitive development.

10-1. Pascual-Leone used _____ _____ concepts in his re-interpretation of Piaget's developmental stages. He argued that cognitive development involves an increase in information processing capacity. _____-_____ (similar to working memory) refers to the maximum number of mental concepts that can be kept in mind at one time. Gifted children have (<u>higher/lower</u>) M-capacity than do non-gifted children.

10-2. Case presented a neo-Piagetian view in which he suggested that cognitive development does not involve a single general intellectual factor, but rather involves _____ skills that may show uneven development.

Answers: 10-1. information processing, M-capacity, higher. **10-2.** distinct (or discrete).

11. Describe how Vygotsky's Sociocultural Theory differs from Piaget's views.

11-1.   First, whereas Piaget argued that cognitive development is primarily fuelled by children's active exploration of the world, Vygotsky argued that cognitive development is fuelled by _____ _____.

11-2.   Second, whereas Piaget viewed cognitive development as a universal process, Vygotsky argued that _____ exerts a significant influence over how cognitive growth unfolds.

11-3.   Third, whereas Piaget viewed children's mastery of _____ as just another aspect of cognitive development, Vygotsky argued that language acquisition plays a central role. For example, he argued for an important role of _____ _____ in children's ability to plan strategies, regulate their actions, and accomplish their goals.

11-4.   According to Vygotsky, a child's zone of proximal development is the gap between what a learner can accomplish _____ and what he or she can achieve with guidance from more skilled partners. _____ occurs when the assistance provided to a child is adjusted as learning progresses.

Answers: 11-1. social interaction **11-2.** culture **11-3.** language, private speech **11-4.** alone, Scaffolding.

12. Summarize evidence that suggests that some cognitive abilities could be innate.

12-1. When infants look at a stimulus that is presented repeatedly, the strength of their responses gradually decreases. They spend less and less time looking at the stimulus, and their heart and respiration rates decrease. This reduction in response strength is known as _____. When a new stimulus is presented, response strength increases, a process known as _____.

12-2. By using the habituation-dishabituation technique, researchers can tell when a child is able to discriminate between different events. For example, at 3 to 4 months of age, infants understand that: (Write T or F for each of the following.)

____ Objects on slopes roll down rather than up.

____ One solid object cannot pass through another.

____ Objects move in continuous paths.

12-3. In another demonstration of the cognitive abilities of young children, five-month-old infants were shown a display in which an object was added to or subtracted from others behind a screen.

Remarkably, the children exhibited surprise, indicated by the response of (habituation/dishabituation), when the expected number of objects was not there. This result suggests that infants (are/are not) able to add and subtract small numbers.

12-4. Because these cognitive abilities occur at such an early age, before infants would have had much chance to learn them, some theorists have concluded that these capacities are largely (acquired/innate).

12-5. Two groups of theorists favour an explanation in terms of innate cognitive abilities: the *nativists* and the *evolutionary* psychologists. Of these theoretical positions, it is primarily the (nativists/evolutionary theorists) who are interested in explaining why these abilities are innately programmed.

12-6. Why would we be prewired to understand addition and subtraction? The (nativists/evolutionary theorists) assert that basic addition and subtraction abilities had clear _____ value in a hunting, foraging, and social-bargaining society.

Answers: 12-1. habituation, dishabituation **12-2.** T, T, T **12-3.** dishabituation, are **12-4.** innate
12-5. evolutionary theorists **12-6.** evolutionary theorists, survival (or adaptive).

13. Describe the concepts of critical and sensitive periods in development.

13-1. A critical period is a limited time span when it is optimal for certain capacities to emerge because the organism is especially _____ to certain experiences. A sensitive period suggests an optimal period for acquisition, but acquisition could occur at a later point. Many argue that these periods may apply to our acquisition of _____ and _____ abilities.

Answers: 13-1. responsive, language, musical.

14. Describe what is meant by a child's theory of mind.

14-1. "Theory of mind" refers to children's understanding about the mind and how it works, and how children conceive of _____ _____ thought processes, knowledge, beliefs, and feelings.

14-2. An experimenter shows a child a candy box and asks what it contains. The child responds, "Candy." In fact, when the box is opened, the child sees that it contains crayons. The child is then asked what he would expect another child to say, when the other child is shown the closed box.

(a) Suppose the first child is five years old. What does he say that the second child will say when shown the closed box, candy or crayons? _____

(b) Suppose a three-year-old child is asked the same question. He says that candy is in the box, and when the box is opened, he sees it is crayons. What does he say the second child will say is in the closed box? _____

(c) Once shown that the box contains crayons, the three-year-old is also asked what he originally said. What does he say he said, candy or crayons? _____

14-3. Why does the three-year-old child respond this way? Because most children under four years do not understand that there can be a difference between *beliefs* and *external reality*. In other words, they cannot yet appreciate the possibility that people can hold _____ beliefs that do not accurately reflect reality.

14-4. Between ages three and four, children make the connection between mental states and external reality. They develop the understanding that beliefs (<u>may not/will always</u>) reflect external reality. The understanding of false belief is a necessary condition for the child moving from a _____ theory of mind (i.e., viewing the mind like a recording device) toward the more mature _____ theory of mind (i.e., viewing the mind as a constructive interpreter of reality).

Answers: 14-1. another person's **14-2.** (a) candy, (b) crayons, (c) crayons **14-3.** false **14-4.** may not, copy, interpretive.

15. Outline Kohlberg's stages of moral development, and summarize the strengths and weaknesses of Kohlberg's theory.

15-1. Kohlberg's theory includes three moral levels, each with two stages, for a total of six stages. Indicate which of the three moral levels is described in each of the following statements.
   (a) Acts are considered wrong because they are punished or right because they lead to positive consequences. _____
   (b) Individuals at this level conform very strictly to society's rules, which they accept as absolute and inviolable. _____
   (c) This level is characterized by situational or conditional morality, such that stealing might be considered wrong in one circumstance but permissible in another. _____

15-2. The central ideas of Kohlberg's theory have received a fair amount of support. Research has found that children (<u>do/do not</u>) tend to progress through Kohlberg's stages in the order that he indicated. As children get older, stages 1 and 2 reasoning tend to decrease, while stages 3 and 4 reasoning tend to _____.

15-3. There have also been several criticisms of Kohlberg's theory. First, individuals may show characteristics of several different stages at the same time. In other words, as was true of other stage theories, there tends to be a "_____" of stages.

15-4. Second, it may be the case that Kohlberg's theory is much more (<u>value-free/culture-specific</u>) than he had supposed. The theory may reflect a liberal, individualistic ideology most characteristic of modern _____ nations.

15-5. Third, Kohlberg's theory emphasized moral _____; as a result, other aspects of moral development, such as the development of empathy and the development of moral emotions, received less attention.

15-6. Fourth, Gilligan has argued that males and females are socialized differently, such that women develop a morality of _____ and men a morality of _____. Because the latter is classified within a higher stage of reasoning, Gilligan argues that Kohlberg's stages are biased in favour of _____.

Answers: 15-1. (a) preconventional, (b) conventional, (c) postconventional **15-2.** do, increase **15-3** mixing **15-4.** culture-specific, Western **15-5.** reasoning **15-6.** care, justice, males.

THE TRANSITION OF ADOLESCENCE

16. Describe the major events of puberty.

16-1. Match the descriptions with one of the appropriate terms: pubescence, puberty, secondary sex characteristics, menarche, and adolescence.

(a) _____   The approximately two-year span preceding puberty that is marked by rapid growth in height and weight and during which secondary sex characteristics appear.

(b) _____   Physical features that distinguish one sex from another but that are not essential for reproduction (e.g., facial hair in males, breasts in females).

(c) _____   The stage during which sexual functions essential for reproduction reach maturity; includes menarche in females and the production of sperm in males.

(d) _____   The first occurrence of menstruation.

(e) _____   The transitional period between childhood and adulthood that includes early physical changes (puberty) and later cognitive and social changes.

Answers: 16-1. (a) pubescence, (b) secondary sex characteristics, (c) puberty, (d) menarche, (e) adolescence.

17. Describe changes taking place in the teen brain.

17-1. There is evidence that growth of the _____ matter seems to increase steadily from childhood into puberty, reflecting the fact that neurons are becoming more _____. Grey matter decreases in volume, reflecting synaptic _____.

17-2. Most of these changes appear to take place in the _____ _____, which has been characterized as an _____ _____ centre crucial to planning, emotional regulation, and inhibition of responses. Immaturity of the prefrontal cortex may be related to adolescents' tendency to engage in risky behaviour.

Answers: 17-1. white, myelinated, pruning **17-2.** prefrontal cortex, executive control.

18. **Evaluate the assertion that adolescence is a time of turmoil.**

18-1. How tumultuous is adolescence? With regard to suicide and other indicants of stress, current data indicate that: (Mark T or F for each of the following statements.)

_____ Most 12- to 13-year-old Canadian youth report being happy with their lives.

_____ Suicide among adolescents has increased over the past few decades.

_____ The rate of adolescent suicide attempts is greater for males than females.

_____ The suicide rate among First Nations Canadians is higher than for the general Canadian population.

_____ In general, adolescents encounter somewhat more storm and stress than do people in other periods of life.

Answers: 18-1. T, T, F, T, T.

19. **Describe the Featured Study on Canadian First Nations youth.**

19-1. Chandler and Lalonde examined whether differences in suicide rates across various groups of First Nations Canadians reflected differences in cultural _____ between these groups. A lack of cultural continuity could contribute to a lack of _____ continuity, thereby leading to higher suicide rates.

19-2. Chandler and Lalonde used a set of cultural _____ (e.g., self-governance; land claims; and control over education, health, or emergency services) to determine the degree of cultural continuity in various First Nations communities. They found that suicide rates were (higher/lower) in those communities whose cultural practices helped to preserve and restore Native culture. That is, cultural continuity promoted _____ continuity and the ability to inhibit self-destructive thoughts and actions.

Answers: 19-1. continuity, personal (or self) **19-2.** markers, lower, personal.

20. **Discuss some common patterns of identity formation in adolescence.**

20-1. Adolescence is a period of change, so it is readily understandable that adolescents tend to focus on the struggle for _____, the question of "Who am I?"

20-2. Recall that Erik Erikson described four crises that mark childhood. What is the crisis that marks adolescence, according to Erikson? _____ vs. _____

20-3. Marcia (1966, 1980) has described four orientations or statuses that individuals may adopt in attempting to resolve identity. In order of increasing maturity these are identity diffusion, foreclosure, achievement, and moratorium.

(a) One possible status is simply to take on the values and roles prescribed by one's parents, the status of identity _____. While this may temporarily resolve the crisis, in the long run, the individual may not be comfortable with the adopted identity.

(b) Another status involves a period of experimentation with various ideologies and careers and a delay in commitment to any one, termed identity _____.

(c) If the experimentation and lack of commitment become permanent, the individual is said to be in a status of identity _____.

(d) On the other hand, if the consideration of alternatives leads to conviction about a sense of self, one takes on the status referred to as identity _____.

20-4. The statuses are not stages that adolescents pass through in an orderly manner. In fact, recent research has found that (very few/most) adolescents shift back and forth among the four identity statuses. In addition, most individuals reach the last stage, identity _____, at a later age than Marcia had supposed.

Answers: **20-1.** identity **20-2.** identity, confusion **20-3.** (a) foreclosure, (b) moratorium, (c) diffusion, (d) achievement **20-4.** most, achievement.

21. Summarize arguments for "emerging adulthood" as a new developmental stage.

21-1. Arnett has argued that a transitional stage of life occurs between the ages of _____ and _____. The features of this stage include a subjective sense that one is between the stages of adolescence and adulthood, a sense of great _____, a tendency toward self-_____, and identity formation.

Answers: **21-1.** 18, 25, optimism, focus.

THE EXPANSE OF ADULTHOOD

22. Summarize evidence on the stability of personality.

22-1. Do people change throughout their lifetimes, or does personality tend to remain the same? Research evidence supports the conclusion that

a. personality is stable across one's lifetime

b. personality changes across one's lifetime

c. both of the above

d. neither of the above

22-2. Both stability and change occur. This reflects the fact that one's _____ standing on personality traits doesn't tend to change much, but _____ scores do change (e.g., adults' mean raw scores on agreeableness and conscientiousness tend to increase).

Answers: **22-1.** c **22-2.** relative, raw.

23. Outline Erikson's stages of development in adulthood.

23-1. In the spaces below, write the names of the crises that mark Erikson's three stages of adulthood. In the parentheses, indicate the approximate period of adulthood during which the crises are supposed to occur.

(a)_____ vs. _____   (   )

(b)_____ vs. _____   (   )

(c)_____ vs. _____   (   )

23-2. Following are descriptions of the crises occurring in each of the above stages. Indicate the stages by placing the appropriate letters (a, b, or c from the previous question) in the blanks.

_____ Concern for helping future generations versus a self-indulgent concern for meeting one's own desires.

_____ Concern to find meaning in the remainder of one's life versus a preoccupation with earlier failures and eventual death.

_____ Concern for developing a capacity for intimacy with others versus a strategy in which others are manipulated as a means to an end.

Answers: 23-1. (a) intimacy vs. isolation (early adulthood), (b) generativity vs. self-absorption (middle adulthood), (c) integrity vs. despair (aging years) **23-2.** b, c, a.

24. Describe typical transitions in family relations during the adult years.

24-1. In part due to shifting social and economic trends, remaining single or postponing marriage is a much more acceptable option today than it was a few decades ago. Nonetheless, over _____ percent of Canadian adults eventually marry. Since the 1980s, the number of common-law relationships in Canada has been (decreasing/increasing). Since 1997, the rate of divorce in Canada has been (increasing/decreasing).

24-2. In general, most new couples are happy, but a source of conflict is the negotiation of marital roles in relation to _____ commitments. Men's careers continue to take priority, and women still do the bulk of household chores.

24-3. Most couples have children and rate it as a highly _____ experience. However, parenthood is associated with lower _____ _____.

24-4. Adolescence is not as _____ a time as once believed, but it can generate conflict with parents.

24-5. Most parents adjust (well/poorly) to the empty nest and marital satisfaction often goes (up/down).

Answers: 24-1. 90, increasing, decreasing **24-2.** career **24-3.** positive, marital satisfaction **24-4.** turbulent **25-5.** well, up.

25. Describe the physical changes associated with aging and the evidence on Alzheimer's disease.

25-1. As we age, our physical and cognitive characteristics change. Indicate which of the following physical traits *increase* and which *decrease* by placing checkmarks in the appropriate blanks.

Physical changes	Increases	Decreases
Proportion of body fat	_____	_____
Overall weight	_____	_____
Number of neurons in the brain	_____	_____
Visual acuity	_____	_____
Ability to see close	_____	_____
Hearing	_____	_____

25-2. The ending of the menstrual cycle and loss of fertility among women is referred to as
_____. Most women experience some physical discomfort during menopause (e.g.,
hot flashes), but the emotional distress (does/does not) appear to be especially severe.

25-3. An abnormal condition marked by loss of memory and other cognitive abilities is termed a
_____. Dementia occurs in approximately _____ % of individuals over age 75.
Thus, dementia (is/is not) a normal part of the aging process.

25-4. The disorder known as _____ disease accounts for approximately 60% of
dementia. This disease is accompanied by a (slight/widespread) loss of neurons, beginning in the
hippocampus and spreading to other areas of the brain.

25-5. Alzheimer's usually begins (before/after) age 65 and is initially marked by the rapid forgetting of
newly acquired information. Eventually, victims may fail to recognize familiar people and become
disoriented and unable to care for themselves. A cure for Alzheimer's (does/does not) appear to be
close at hand. Causes likely include genetic factors, and protective factors are thought to include
regular _____ and participation in stimulating _____ activities.

Answers: 25-1. Body fat and overall weight increase (except that overall weight may decrease somewhat after the mid-50s); the rest decrease **25-2.** menopause, does not **25-3.** dementia, 15–20, is not **25-4.** Alzheimer's, widespread **25-5.** after, does not, exercise, cognitive.

26. Describe how intelligence and memory change in later adulthood.

26-1. With regard to changes in cognitive ability that may accompany aging, which of the following is/are true? (Mark T or F.)

_____ Average test scores in cognitive ability show some decline after age 60.

_____ For the majority of people, the decline in general intelligence that occurs in later years is relatively slight.

_____ Crystallized intelligence is more likely to decline with aging than fluid intelligence.

_____ The memory loss that accompanies aging is relatively severe for the majority of people.

_____ The type of general cognitive loss that occurs with aging is thought to involve processing speed.

_____ Problem solving ability generally remains unimpaired as people age if older people are given additional time to compensate for reduced speed.

_____ Computerized cognitive training may enhance memory performance.

Answers: 26-1. T, T, F, F, T, T, T.

PUTTING IT IN PERSPECTIVE

27. Explain how this chapter highlighted the text's unifying themes.

27-1. The behaviour of a child is the result of the child's genetic inheritance and its environment, which includes the behaviour of the child's parents. In turn, the behaviour of the parents toward the child is affected both by their inherited characteristics and by the behaviour of the child. Thus, behaviour is the result not of heredity or environment operating separately but of an _____ between the two factors.

27-2. To understand the concept of *interaction*, consider this problem: There is a form of mental retardation that results from phenylketonuria, an inherited inability to metabolize a common amino acid in milk. When fed milk, children born with phenylketonuria become mentally retarded. Is this type of retardation an inherited disorder?

a. Yes, it's genetic.

b. No, it's caused by the environment.

c. A certain proportion of the causal factors are hereditary, and the remainder are due to the environment.

d. The disorder results from heredity and environment operating jointly.

27-3. This chapter has been concerned with changes in human behaviour across the life span. The theme being stressed here is that these changes result from an *interaction* of heredity and environment. In your own words, explain how the interaction operates.

Answers: 27-1. interaction **27-2.** d. (This disorder might at first seem to be inherited, since there is a genetic trait involved. But the retardation does not occur if the infant is not fed milk products, which involves the environment. The point is that this disorder, like behaviour in general, cannot be attributed solely to nature or to nurture or even to relative weights of each; it is a function of an *interaction* between the two.) **27-3.** The interaction of heredity and environment refers to the fact that we are a product of both factors. It means more than that, however. Heredity and environment don't operate separately. Interaction means that the genetic factors affect the operation of the environment and that environmental factors affect genetic predispositions. The influence of one factor *depends on* the effects of the other.

28. Summarize evidence on gender differences in behaviour, and discuss the significance of these differences.

28-1. Which gender tends to show more of (or score higher on tests of) the following abilities or traits? Circle the correct answer at the right.

Cognitive

verbal skills	Males	Females	Neither
mathematical skills	Males	Females	Neither
visual-spatial skills	Males	Females	Neither

Personality

Extraversion	Males	Females	Neither
Agreeableness	Males	Females	Neither
Conscientiousness	Males	Females	Neither
Neuroticism	Males	Females	Neither

Social

aggression	Males	Females	Neither
sensitivity to nonverbal cues	Males	Females	Neither
risk-taking	Males	Females	Neither
sexually permissive attitudes	Males	Females	Neither
assertiveness	Males	Females	Neither
anxiety	Males	Females	Neither
nurturance	Males	Females	Neither

28-2. There is an enormous overlap between the genders with regard to these traits. There are, of course, many females who are more aggressive than the average male and many males who are more sensitive to nonverbal cues than the average female. Thus, it is important to note that the differences referred to in this section are differences between group _____, and that the size of the differences is relatively _____. And, there is recent evidence that the gender gap in math has (widened/disappeared) in the United States.

Answers: 28-1. cognitive: females, males, males; personality: females, females, females, females; social: males, females, males, males, males, females, females **28-2.** averages (or means), small, disappeared.

29. Explain how biological factors are thought to contribute to gender differences.

29-1. For evolutionary theorists, the relative invariance of gender differences found across cultures reflects natural selection. From this perspective, males are more sexually active and permissive than females because reproductive success for males is maximized by seeking (few/many) sexual partners. Greater aggressiveness has survival value for males because it enhances their ability to acquire material _____ sought by females selecting a mate.

29-2. Evolutionary theorists also assert that ability differences between the genders reflect the division of labour in our ancestral past. Males were primarily the hunters and females the gatherers, and the adaptive demands of hunting may have produced males' superiority at most _____ tasks.

29-3. The evolutionary view of gender is certainly an interesting and plausible explanation of the remarkable similarity in gender differences across cultures. The viewpoint has its critics, however. For one thing, there are reasonable _____ theories of gender differences; for another, the evolutionary explanation is relatively (<u>easy/difficult</u>) to test empirically.

29-4. Concerning other biological factors, several studies indicate that hormones contribute to shaping gender differences. For example, females exposed prenatally to high levels of an _____-like drug given to their mothers during pregnancy tend to show more male-typical behaviour than do other females.

29-5. Recent studies have also found that normal aging men given testosterone to enhance their sexual function tend to show increases in _____ perception. While these correlational studies involving hormones support the role of biology in gender development, it is important to note that they are based on (<u>small/large</u>) samples of people who have (<u>normal/abnormal</u>) conditions.

29-6. Other biological evidence indicates that males depend more heavily on the left hemisphere for verbal processing and on the right for spatial processing than is the case with females. That is, males may tend to exhibit more cerebral _____ than females. This finding has been linked to another finding, that females have larger _____ callosums (the connecting sheath of axons between hemispheres) than do males.

29-7. Results from studies of specialization and of gender differences in the corpus callosum have not been consistent, however. In addition, it would be difficult to see how gender differences in *specialization* could account for gender differences in *ability*, that is, the superiority of males on _____ tasks and the superiority of females on _____ tasks.

Answers: 29-1. many, resources **29-2.** spatial (or visual-spatial) **29-3.** alternative, difficult **29-4.** androgen **29-5.** spatial (or visual-spatial), small, abnormal **29-6.** specialization, corpus **29-7.** visual-spatial, verbal.

30. Explain how environmental factors are thought to contribute to gender differences.

30-1. Many researchers remain convinced that gender differences are largely shaped by the environment. One of the ways that children learn gender roles is from the consequences for their behaviour, the rewards and punishments that they receive in the process known as _____ conditioning.

30-2. Children also acquire information by seeing what others do, the process of _____ learning. While children imitate both males and females, they are more likely to imitate the behaviour of (<u>same-sex/opposite-sex</u>) models.

30-3. In addition to operant conditioning and observational learning, children are active participants in their own gender-role socialization, the process referred to as _____-socialization. First, once they discover (at age five or six) that being a boy or girl is a permanent condition, they will then _____ themselves as boys or girls. Second, following classification in terms of gender, children will _____ characteristics and behaviours associated with their gender. Third, they will bring their _____ in line with their values by engaging in "sex-appropriate" behaviours.

30-4. Whether through operant conditioning, observational learning, or self-socialization, the major forces for gender-role socialization occur in three main areas of the child's environment, namely, in their _____, in _____, and in the _____.

Answers: 30-1. operant **30-2.** observational (or modeling), same-sex **30-3.** self, classify (or categorize), value, behaviour **30-4.** families, schools, media.

CRITICAL THINKING APPLICATION * ARE FATHERS ESSENTIAL TO CHILDREN'S WELL-BEING?

31. Explain the argument that fathers are essential for healthy development and some criticism of this line of reasoning.

31-1. Over the past several decades in the U.S.A., the percentage of children brought up without fathers in the home has steadily increased, from about 17% in 1960 to more than 35% today. During the same period, there has also been a dramatic (<u>decrease/increase</u>) in teen pregnancy, juvenile delinquency, violent crime, drug abuse, eating disorders, and family dysfunction in general.

31-2. Further, fatherless children are two to three times more likely than fathered children to drop out of high school, become a teenage parent, or become a juvenile delinquent. In other words, father absence (<u>causes/is correlated with</u>) a host of unfortunate cultural trends.

31-3. Based on the association between father absence and social problems, some writers have asserted that the presence of a father is essential for a child's well-being. As you are by now well aware, however, one (<u>can/cannot</u>) infer causation on the basis of correlational data alone.

31-4. Among the reasonable alternative explanations for the correlational relationship described are the following. Father absence frequently occurs when the parents _____, so it is possible that this factor, rather than father absence, may cause the negative effects referred to.

31-5. Or, since father absence is much more frequent in (<u>low-income/high-income</u>) families, it is possible that poverty, rather than father absence, may cause some (or all) of the negative effects.

31-6. Also there is contradictory evidence, including the fact that children raised by lesbian parents are (<u>inferior to/similar to</u>) those raised by heterosexual parents.

31-7. In your continued critical thinking about the assertions discussed, recall also the fallacies in reasoning introduced in Chapter 10: irrelevant reasons, circular reasoning, slippery slope, weak analogies, and false dichotomy. Which of these apply to the following assertions? Use the abbreviations IR, CR, SS, WA, or FD.

(a) _____ "If present trends continue, our society could be on the verge of social suicide."

(b) _____ "To tolerate the trend of fatherlessness is to accept the inevitability of continued societal recession."

Answers: 31-1. increase **31-2.** is correlated with **31-3.** cannot **31-4.** divorce **31-5.** low-income **31-6.** similar to **31-7.** (a) SS. The argument is that if we allow one event to happen, then other events will inevitably follow on this slippery slope that will lead to disaster. (b) FD. The quote may have elements of more than one fallacy, but the author really is posing a dichotomy: either we reduce father absence, or else we will face social decline. Of course, we could do both (reduce father absence and face social decline) or neither.

REVIEW OF KEY TERMS

Accommodation
Age of viability
Animism
Assimilation
Attachment
Centration
Cephalocaudal trend
Cognitive development
Conservation
Cross-sectional design
Dementia
Development
Developmental norms
Dishabituation
Egocentrism
Embryonic stage

Family life cycle
Fetal alcohol syndrome
Fetal stage
Gender
Gender differences
Gender roles
Gender stereotypes
Germinal stage
Habituation
Irreversibility
Longitudinal design
Maturation
Menarche
Mid-life crisis
Motor development
Object permanence

Placenta
Prenatal period
Primary sex characteristics
Proximodistal trend
Puberty
Pubescence
Scaffolding
Secondary sex characteristics
Separation anxiety
Sex
Socialization
Stage
Temperament
Zygote

_____ 1. The sequence of age-related changes that occurs as a person progresses from conception to death.

_____ 2. The period of pregnancy, extending from conception to birth.

_____ 3. The first two weeks after conception.

_____ 4. The structure that connects the circulation of the fetus and the mother but that blocks passage of blood cells.

_____ 5. The second stage of prenatal development, lasting from two weeks after conception until the end of the second month.

_____ 6. The third stage of prenatal development, lasting from two months after conception through birth.

_____ 7. The age at which the baby can first survive in the event of a premature birth.

_____ 8. A collection of congenital problems associated with a mother's excessive use of alcohol during pregnancy.

_____ 9. Changing existing mental structures to explain new experiences, a concept from Piaget's theory of cognitive development.

_____ 10. Developmental changes in muscular coordination required for physical movement.

_____ 11. The head-to-foot direction of motor development.

_____ 12. The centre-outward direction of motor development.

_____ 13. The average ages at which people display certain behaviours and abilities.

_____ 14. Characteristic mood, energy level, and reactivity.

_____ 15. One group of subjects is observed over a long period of time.

_____ 16. Investigators compare groups of subjects of differing ages at a single point in time.

_____ 17. A difficult, turbulent period of doubt and reappraisal of one's life that may occur at midlife.

_____ 18. Emotional distress displayed by an infant when separated from a person with whom it has formed an attachment.

_____ 19. Culturally constructed distinctions between femininity and masculinity.

_____ 20. Widely held beliefs about females' and males' abilities, personality traits, and social behaviour.

_____ 21. Development of thinking, reasoning, remembering, and problem solving.

_____ 22. The gradual reduction in response strength that occurs when people are repeatedly exposed to some event.

_____ 23. The increase in response strength that occurs when people are exposed to a new stimulus event.

_____ 24. A mental capacity that involves recognizing that objects continue to exist even when they are no longer visible.

_____ 25. Piaget's term for the awareness that physical quantities remain constant in spite of changes in their shape or appearance.

_____ 26. The Piagetian term for the tendency to focus on just one feature of a problem and neglect other important features.

_____ 27. The inability to cognitively visualize reversing an action.

_____ 28. Thinking characterized by a limited ability to share another person's viewpoint.

_____ 29. A sequence of stages that families tend to progress through.

_____ 30. Interpreting new experiences in terms of mental structures already available, a concept from Piaget's theory of cognitive development.

_____ 31. The attribution of lifelike qualities to inanimate objects.

_____ 32. A developmental period during which certain behaviours and capacities occur.

_____ 33. The biologically based categories of male and female.

_____ 34. A close, emotional bond of affection between an infant and its caregiver.

_____ 35. Physical features associated with gender that are not directly needed for reproduction.

_____ 36. The physical structures necessary for reproduction.

_____ 37. The two-year span preceding puberty, marked by the appearance of secondary sex characteristics and by rapid growth.

_____ 38. The first occurrence of menstruation.

_____ 39. The stage during which reproductive functions reach maturity.

_____ 40. An abnormal condition marked by multiple cognitive deficits; more prevalent in older adults but not a product of normal aging.

	41.	Developmental changes that reflect one's genetic blueprint rather than environment.
	42.	A one-celled organism created by the process of fertilization, the union of sperm and egg.
	43.	Behavioural differences between females and males.
	44.	When the assistance provided to a child is adjusted as learning progresses.
	45.	The acquisition of norms, roles, and behaviours expected of people in a particular group.
	46.	Expectations concerning what is the appropriate behaviour for each sex.

Answers: 1. development **2.** prenatal period **3.** germinal stage **4.** placenta **5.** embryonic stage **6.** fetal stage **7.** age of viability **8.** fetal alcohol syndrome **9.** accommodation **10.** motor development **11.** cephalocaudal trend **12.** proximodistal trend **13.** developmental norms **14.** temperament **15.** longitudinal design **16.** cross-sectional design **17.** mid-life crisis **18.** separation anxiety **19.** gender **20.** gender stereotypes **21.** cognitive development **22.** habituation **23.** dishabituation **24.** object permanence **25.** conservation **26.** centration **27** irreversibility **28.** egocentrism **29.** family life cycle **30.** assimilation **31.** animism **32.** stage **33.** sex **34.** attachment **35.** secondary sex characteristics **36.** primary sex characteristics **37.** pubescence **38.** menarche **39.** puberty **40.** dementia **41.** maturation **42.** zygote **43.** gender differences **44.** scaffolding **45.** socialization **46.** gender roles.

REVIEW OF KEY PEOPLE

Mary Ainsworth
Jay Belsky
John Bowlby

Robbie Case
Jean Piaget
Alexander Thomas and Stella Chess

Erik Erikson
Lawrence Kohlberg
Juan Pascual-Leone

	1.	Conducted a major longitudinal study in which they identified three basic styles of children's temperament.
	2.	Conducted research on daycare.
	3.	Theorized that there are critical periods in human infants' lives during which attachments must occur for normal development to take place.
	4.	Partitioned the life span into eight stages, each accompanied by a psychosocial crisis.
	5.	Pioneered the study of children's cognitive development.
	6.	Developed a stage theory of moral development.
	7.	Described three categories of infant–mother attachment.
	8.	A neo-Piagetian theorist who used the concept of M-capacity.
	9.	A neo-Piagetian theorist who emphasized that cognitive capacity involves numerous discrete skills that may show uneven development.

Answers: 1. Thomas and Chess **2.** Belsky **3.** Bowlby **4.** Erikson **5.** Piaget **6.** Kohlberg **7.** Ainsworth **8.** Pascual-Leone **9.** Case.

SELF-QUIZ

1. Which prenatal stage begins at the second week and ends at the second month of pregnancy?
   a. germinal stage
   b. embryonic stage
   c. fetal stage
   d. seminal stage

2. In which prenatal stage do most major birth defects probably originate?
   a. germinal stage
   b. embryonic stage
   c. fetal stage
   d. seminal stage

3. A child is shown a candy box. When asked what he thinks is in it, he says, "Candy." He is then shown that the candy box actually contains crayons. He is then asked what he thinks another child will say when shown the same closed box. He says that he thinks the next child will say, "Crayons." What would be the best guess about the age of the child?
   a. three years
   b. five years
   c. six years
   d. seven years

4. In their Featured Study, what did Chandler and Lalonde examine concerning a lack of cultural continuity within First Nations communities in B.C.?
   a. whether it would be associated with suicide
   b. whether it would be associated with violence
   c. whether it would be associated with educational attainment
   d. whether it would be associated with economic prosperity

5. What is the major conclusion from Thomas and Chess's longitudinal study of temperament?
   a. Children's temperaments tend to go through predictable stages.
   b. A child's temperament is not a good predictor of the temperament of the adult.
   c. The most common childhood temperament is "slow-to-warm-up children."
   d. Children's temperaments tend to be consistent over the years.

6. According to Erikson, what does the crisis that occurs in the first year of life involve?
   a. trust versus mistrust
   b. initiative versus guilt
   c. industry versus inferiority
   d. identity versus conformity

7. During which stage in Piaget's system is the child first able to handle conservation problems and hierarchical classification problems?
   a. sensorimotor
   b. preoperational
   c. concrete operations
   d. formal operations

8. A child in the early sensorimotor period is shown a ball, which she watches intensely. The ball is then hidden under a pillow. What will the child do?
   a. ask, "Where is the pillow?"
   b. stare at the pillow but not pick it up
   c. move the pillow and pick up the ball
   d. ignore the pillow, as if the ball didn't exist

9. Who developed a stage theory of moral development?
   a. Piaget
   b. Kohlberg
   c. Gould
   d. Bowlby

10. Which of the following cognitive capacities is most likely to decline as a function of aging?
    a. fluid intelligence
    b. crystallized intelligence
    c. problem-solving ability
    d. specialized intelligence

11. Some researchers have found that very young children (e.g., five months old) appear to be aware of the addition or subtraction of objects from behind a screen. What technique was used in these studies?
    a. sensory preconditioning
    b. self-socialization
    c. classical conditioning
    d. habituation-dishabituation

12. What factor tends to be accompanied by a drop in ratings of marital satisfaction?
    a. childlessness during early married life
    b. the birth of the first child
    c. the first child's departure for college
    d. when the last child leaves home

13. On what kind of tests do females tend to score higher than males?
    a. verbal ability tests
    b. mathematical ability tests
    c. visual-spatial ability tests
    d. cerebral specialization tests

14. What characteristic tends to be shown by females who were exposed to high levels of androgen during prenatal development?
    a. more male-typical behaviour than other females
    b. more stereotypic female behaviour than other females
    c. less cerebral specialization than other females
    d. a larger corpus callosum than other females

15. Once children discover that their gender is permanent, they are likely to want to engage in behaviour that is "sex appropriate" as defined by their culture. What is the name for this process?
    a. operant conditioning
    b. observational learning
    c. self-socialization
    d. classical conditioning

16. According to Lalonde and Chandler, what idea must a child understand to develop an interpretive theory of mind?
    a. conservation
    b. permanence
    c. false belief
    d. reversibility

17. Who advanced the idea of a zone of proximal development?
    a. Piaget
    b. Erikson
    c. Harlow
    d. Vygotsky

18. What area of the brain is believed to mature through adolescence and be related to the willingness of teens to engage in risky behaviour?
    a. prefrontal cortex
    b. hippocampus
    c. cingulate cortex
    d. mesolimbic dopamine pathway

19. According to Arnett, which of the following are NOT characteristic of emerging adulthood?
    a. pessimism about the future
    b. self-focus
    c. a subjective feeling of being between adolescence and adulthood
    d. identity formation

Answers: 1. b 2. b 3. a 4. a 5. d 6. a 7. c 8. d 9. b 10. a 11. d 12. b 13. a 14. a 15. c 16. c 17. d 18. a 19. a.

Chapter Twelve

PERSONALITY: THEORY, RESEARCH, AND ASSESSMENT

REVIEW OF KEY IDEAS

THE NATURE OF PERSONALITY

1. Define the construct of personality in terms of consistency and distinctiveness.

1-1. I could always tell when my colleague across the hall (now retired) had finished for the day, because I could hear squeaking as he carefully moved his computer table under his bookcase. And I knew what followed: he closed and re-shelved his books, sorted the papers on his desk into two piles, and slid the pens and pencils into his desk drawer bin. The fact that my colleague engaged in the *same behaviours* every day illustrates the feature of personality termed _____.

1-2. When I'm done, on the other hand, I usually just stand up and walk out, leaving my somewhat (some would say very) messy desk behind. The fact that my colleague and I *differ* with respect to office neatness illustrates the feature of personality termed _____.

Answers: 1-1. consistency (or stability) **1-2.** distinctiveness (or behavioural differences).

2. Explain what is meant by a personality trait, and describe the five-factor model of personality.

2-1. A consistent or durable disposition to behave in a particular way is referred to as a personality _____. Personality trait descriptions frequently consist of a series of _____, such as anxious, excitable, shy, aggressive, and so on.

2-2. There are an enormous number of trait words that could be used to describe people. Gordon Allport, for example, listed several thousand. Raymond Cattell reduced Allport's list to just _____ traits. More recently, McCrae and Costa have described an even simpler model involving only _____ traits, the so-called Big Five theory.

2-3. Research has shown that the Big Five traits do correlate with important life outcomes. For example, _____ correlates with higher grades and reduced mortality, and _____ correlates with a greater likelihood of divorce.

2-4. Some researchers maintain that more than five factors are needed to describe personality. Of the various models, however, the dominant conception of personality structure is currently the _____ theory.

2-5. Below are listed some of the adjectives that describe each of the five factors: neuroticism, extraversion, openness to experience, agreeableness, and conscientiousness. List the name of each of the factors next to the descriptions. (The five factors are relatively easy to remember using the acronym OCEAN).

_____: outgoing, sociable

_____: imaginative, nonconforming

_____: anxious, insecure

_____: dependable, disciplined

_____: sympathetic, trusting

Answers: 2-1. trait, adjectives **2-2.** 16, five **2-3.** conscientiousness, neuroticism **2-4.** Big Five (or five-factor)
2-5. extraversion, openness to experience, neuroticism, conscientiousness, agreeableness.

PSYCHODYNAMIC PERSPECTIVES

3. List and describe the three components into which Freud divided the personality, and indicate how these are distributed across three levels of awareness.

3-1. The following is a schematic illustration of the three Freudian structures of personality. Label each structure.

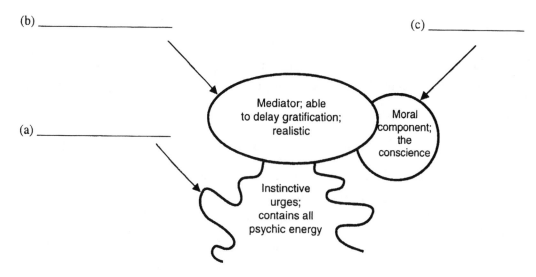

3-2. Freud superimposed levels of consciousness on the psychic structures. The following illustration makes clear that two of the structures exist at all three levels, while one is entirely unconscious. Label the levels.

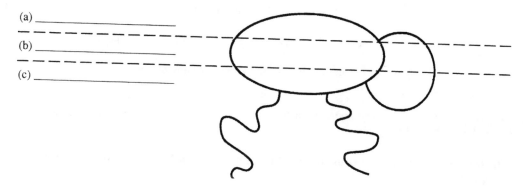

(a) _____

(b) _____

(c) _____

Answers: 3-1. (a) id, (b) ego, (c) superego **3-2.** (a) conscious, (b) preconscious, (c) unconscious. (The diagram shows that the ego emerges from the id, and that the superego grows out of the ego.)

4. **Explain the preeminence of sexual and aggressive conflicts in Freud's theory, and describe the operation of defence mechanisms.**

4-1. Freud believed that most of our conflicts arise from _____ and _____ urges. Conflicts relating to these areas were preeminent in his mind because (1) they are subject to subtle social _____ and, for that reason, are a source of confusion; and (2) they are less likely to be immediately gratified and more apt to be _____ than other urges.

4-2. Following is a list of the defence mechanisms. Match each with the correct description by placing the appropriate letters in the blanks.

A. rationalization	D. displacement	G. identification
B. repression	E. reaction formation	H. sublimation
C. projection	F. regression	

_____ A return to an earlier, less mature stage of development.

_____ Forming an imaginary or real alliance with a person or group; becoming like them.

_____ Creating false but reasonable-sounding excuses.

_____ Pushing distressing thoughts into the unconscious.

_____ Channelling unacceptable thoughts into socially acceptable behaviours.

_____ Attributing ones own thoughts, feelings, or conflicts to another.

_____ Expressing an emotion that is the exact opposite of the way one really, but unconsciously, feels.

_____ Diverting emotional feelings from their original source to a substitute target.

4-3. Using the letters from the previous question, match the defence mechanisms with the following examples.

_____ After John and Marsha break up, John says he hates Marsha; this statement helps him defend against his real feelings of affection.

_____ "Society is filled with perverts," says the preacher; but later evidence suggests that he is the one with the sexual conflicts.

_____ In reaction to the stress of entering college, Alice starts acting like a grade-school kid.

_____ Bruce acts like John Wayne, and he owns tapes of all the Duke's movies.

_____ Mary is angry at her mother, so she kicks her baby brother.

Answers: 4-1. sexual, aggressive, norms (or rules, controls), frustrated (or thwarted, unfulfilled) **4-2.** F, G, A, B, H, C, E, D **4-3.** E, C, F, G, D.

5. Outline Freud's psychosexual stages of development and their theorized relations to adult personality.

5-1. List Freud's stages of psychosexual development, in the order in which they are supposed to occur, in the blanks below. Place the ages in the parentheses.

(a) _____ (   )

(b) _____ (   )

(c) _____ (   )

(d) _____ (   )

(e) _____ (   )

5-2. The following behaviours or personality characteristics are supposed to result from fixation at a particular psychosexual stage. Place the names of the correct stages in the blanks.

(a) She has problems with anger control, is hostile toward people in authority, and defies any attempt at regulation of her behaviour. _____

(b) He eats too much, drinks too much, and smokes. _____

(c) He has occasional outbursts of hostility toward his father that he can't understand. In family arguments he sides with his mother. _____

5-3. The Oedipus complex occurs during the _____ stage, between the ages of _____ and _____. This complex theoretically involves an erotically tinged attraction toward the (<u>same-sex/opposite-sex</u>) parent and a strong hostility toward the (<u>same-sex/opposite-sex</u>) parent. Resolution of the Oedipus complex involves (<u>increasing/stopping</u>) both the child's erotic attraction and the child's hostility.

Answers: 5-1. (a) oral (first year), (b) anal (second year), (c) phallic (ages three through five), (d) latency (age five to puberty), (e) genital (puberty on) **5-2.** (a) anal, (b) oral, (c) phallic **5-3.** phallic, 3, 5, opposite-sex, same-sex, stopping.

6. Summarize the revisions of Freud's theory proposed by Jung and Adler.

6-1. Freud devised the theory and method of treatment termed *psychoanalysis*. To differentiate his approach from Freud's, Jung called his theory _____ _____. Like Freud, Jung emphasized the unconscious determinants of personality. Unlike Freud, he proposed that the unconscious consists of two layers, a _____ unconscious and a _____ unconscious. The personal unconscious is similar to Freud's unconscious, but it has less emphasis on sexuality. The

CHAPTER TWELVE

collective unconscious is a repository of inherited, ancestral memories that Jung termed

_____.

6-2. Jung's major contribution to psychology is considered by many to be his description of two major personality types: _____, reserved, contemplative people who tend to be concerned with their own internal world of thoughts, and _____, outgoing people who are more interested in the external world of others.

6-3. For Freud, the driving energy behind the human personality was sexuality; for Jung it may have been the collective unconscious. For Adler, it was striving for _____ and the attempt to overcome childhood feelings of inferiority. Efforts to overcome imagined or real inferiorities involve _____ through development of one's abilities. While Adler considered compensation to be a normal mechanism, he saw _____ as an abnormal attempt to conceal feelings of inferiority.

6-4. Adler is associated with the term _____ _____, an exaggerated feeling of inadequacy, supposedly caused by parental pampering or neglect in early childhood. Adler also thought that _____ _____ (that is, whether one is an only child, first-born, second-born, etc.) had a major effect on personality.

6-5. Adler's concept of birth order has created considerable interest. Initial data failed to support Adler's hypotheses, but Frank Sulloway's recent analyses of decades of research concludes that birth order (is/is not) a factor in personality. Referring to the _____ trait theory, Sulloway proposed, for example, that first-borns are more conscientious but less agreeable than later-borns. (Not all/All other) research on birth order has supported Sulloway's conclusions, and the topic is of current interest to many researchers.

Answers: 6-1. analytical psychology, personal, collective, archetypes **6-2.** introverts, extraverts **6-3.** superiority, compensation, overcompensation **6-4.** inferiority complex, birth order **6-5.** is, Big Five, Not all.

7. Summarize the strengths and weaknesses of the psychodynamic approach to personality.

7-1. Psychoanalytic formulations have had a major impact on the field of psychology. List the three contributions discussed in your text.

7-2. Psychoanalytic formulations have also been extensively criticized. After each of the following statements, list the particular criticism, from the discussion in your text, that the statement invites.

(a) Freud proposed that females develop weaker superegos and that they have a chronic sense of inferiority caused by penis envy. _____

(b) Although he discussed some characteristics associated with the psychosexual stages, Freud didn't really specify which events, occurring during which childhood stages, produce which sets of personality traits. _____

(c) Claims of support for the theories are based largely on clinical case studies and clinical intuition.

_____

(d) Freud's theories were based on a rather narrow, limited group of people. _____

Answers: 7-1. The discovery that *unconscious forces* can influence behaviour, that *internal conflict* may generate psychological distress, and that *early childhood experiences* influence the adult personality
7-2. (a) sexism, (b) vague (untestable ideas), (c) inadequate or weak evidence, (d) unrepresentative samples.

BEHAVIOURAL PERSPECTIVES

8. **Discuss how Skinner's principles of operant conditioning can be applied to the structure and development of personality.**

   8-1. Which of the following processes plays an important part in Skinner's ideas about human behaviour?

   a. mental conflict

   b. the mind

   c. free will

   d. none of the above

   8-2. According to Skinner, much of our behaviour is affected by reinforcement, punishment, or extinction—in other words, by the environmental _____ that follow our behaviour. For example, if some individuals behave in a consistently aggressive manner (i.e., have aggressive personality traits), they do so because they have been _____ for behaving aggressively in the past.

   8-3. Skinner recognized that there are differences between people and that people behave relatively consistently over time. Distinctiveness and consistency occur, however, not because of what's going on in an individual's *mind* but because of what has occurred previously in their _____.

   8-4. Thus, for Skinner, personality is not mental, but environmental. People's minds don't change, their environment changes. Skinner makes a strong case for the point of view that our behaviour is caused, or _____ rather than free, and that the determinants are largely _____ rather than genetic.

   Answers: 8-1. d **8-2.** consequences (stimuli, events), reinforced **8-3.** environment **8-4.** determined, environmental.

9. **Describe Bandura's social cognitive theory, and compare it to Skinner's viewpoint.**

   9-1. In what respect is Bandura's point of view similar to Skinner's?

   9-2. Three of the major differences between Bandura's and Skinner's viewpoints involve the concepts, listed below. Carefully define and explain these concepts and indicate how they represent a difference from Skinner's position.

(a) reciprocal determinism:

(b) observational learning:

(c) self-efficacy:

9-3. According to Bandura, whom do we imitate and in what circumstances?

Answers: 9-1. It is similar in that Bandura believes that personality is largely shaped through learning.
9-2. (a) *Reciprocal determinism* refers to the point of view that not only does environment determine behaviour, as Skinner asserted, but that behaviour determines environment, and further, that behaviour, environment, and mental processes all mutually affect one another. (b) *Observational learning* is the process through which we learn behaviours by observing the consequences of someone else's (i.e., a model's) behaviour. For example, we learn not only by being reinforced, as Skinner proposed, but by observing someone else being reinforced. (c) *Self-efficacy* is a belief in our ability to perform certain behaviours. This belief affects whether we undertake those behaviours and how well we perform them. Skinner makes no allowance for mentalistic concepts such as self-efficacy. **9-3.** We tend to imitate models whom we like, consider attractive and powerful, view as similar to ourselves, and whom we observe being reinforced.

10. Identify Mischel's major contribution to personality theory, and indicate why his ideas have generated so much controversy.

10-1. Mischel's major contribution to personality theory is his contention that human behaviour is determined to a much greater extent by the _____ than by _____

10-2. Why is this such a controversial idea for personality theory?

10-3. What do advocates of the *interactional* approach argue?

Answers: 10-1. situation (or situational factors), personality (or personality traits) **10-2.** The notion is controversial because the very definition of personality involves the word *consistency*. Mischel's findings suggest that behaviour is not as consistent as personality theorists may have thought, that it is strongly affected by an ever-changing situation. **10-3.** They argue that personality traits interact with situational factors to produce behaviour.

11. Summarize the strengths and weaknesses of the behavioural approach to personality.

11-1. The major strengths of the behavioural approach have been its commitment to empirical

_____ and its identification of important _____ determinants of behaviour.

11-2. The major weaknesses of the behavioural approach, according to its critics, have been its denial of free will and of the importance of _____ processes, and its dilution of the _____ approach.

Answers: 11-1. research, environmental (or empirical) **11-2.** cognitive, behavioural.

HUMANISTIC PERSPECTIVES

12. Explain how humanism was a reaction against both the behavioural and psychodynamic approaches, and discuss the assumptions of the humanistic view.

12-1. The humanistic movement reacted against the behavioural approach because of its mechanistic view of personality and its emphasis on _____ research, and against the psychoanalytic approach because of its emphasis on _____ drives.

12-2. The humanistic viewpoint found fault with both movements because they stressed _____, or absolute causation. The humanists also thought that the behaviourists and the Freudians failed to recognize the (unique/common) qualities of human behaviour.

12-3. Humanistic psychology emphasizes the (similarities/differences) between human beings and the other animal species, believes we (are controlled by/can rise above) our biological heritage, asserts that we are largely (rational/irrational) creatures, and maintains that a person's (subjective/objective) view of the world is more important than _____ reality.

Answers: 12-1. animal, primitive (or animalistic) **12-2.** determinism, unique **12-3.** differences, can rise above, rational, subjective, objective.

13. Identify the single structural construct in Rogers's person-centred theory, and summarize his view of personality development.

13-1. Who are you? What are you like? What are your unique qualities? What is your typical behaviour? Your answers to these questions are likely to reflect what Rogers called the _____.

13-2. Although Ralph tends to be a submissive and somewhat lazy person (and that is the way his friends, family, and co-workers describe him), he views himself as hard-working and dynamic, a leader both on the job and at home.

(a) What is Ralph's self-concept?

(b) Is his self-concept congruent or incongruent?

(c) According to Rogers, what parental behaviour may have led to this incongruence?

(d) According to Rogers, what parental behaviour would have resulted in Ralph's achieving congruence rather than incongruence?

13-3. Define the following Rogerian concepts.

(a) conditional love:

(b) unconditional love:

13-4. What is defensiveness for Rogers?

Answers: 13-1. self or self-concept **13-2.** (a) that he is hard-working, dynamic, and a leader, (b) incongruent, (c) conditional love or acceptance, (d) unconditional love or acceptance **13-3.** (a) affection given conditionally, the condition being that the child or adult must live up to another's expectations, (b) affection given without conditions, full acceptance of the person not dependent on what he or she is or does. **13-4.** Defensiveness is related to Rogers's incongruence. As with Freud, people defend against anxiety by distorting or denying reality. For Rogers, defensiveness arises when people defend their self-concepts against inconsistent experiences.

14. Identify the important concepts in Higgins's self-discrepancy theory.

14-1. Higgins identified two standards that we compare our actual self to: the _____ self and the _____ self. Higgins argues that anxiety occurs when there is a discrepancy between our actual and our _____ self. Depression occurs when there is a discrepancy between our actual and our _____ self.

Answers: 14-1. ought, ideal, ought, ideal.

15. Describe the results of the Featured Study on the effects of a "significant other" on self-concept.

15-1. Using the views of others to judge ourselves has been called reflective _____. Baldwin examined whether such a process operates even when we are _____ reminded of a significant person in our lives at the point of making such appraisals.

15-2. In the first study, graduate students rated the quality of their own research ideas after being subliminally primed with either a disapproving face of their _____ _____ or an approving face of another psychologist. Results showed that being exposed to a subliminally presented disapproving face of someone of significance led students to make more (<u>positive/negative</u>) ratings of their own research ideas.

15-3. In the second study, female Catholic students first read a passage that portrayed a permissive attitude toward sexuality. They were then exposed subliminally to a disapproving face of either the _____ or a stranger. They then rated themselves in the areas of anxiety, morality, and competency. Results showed that the participants rated themselves more (<u>positively, negatively</u>) when exposed to the disapproving face of the Pope compared to the disapproving stranger's face. These findings support the idea that our current self-concepts can be affected by evaluations of us provided by significant others.

Answers: **15-1.** appraisal, subliminally **15-2.** research supervisor, negative **15-3.** Pope, negatively.

16. Explain Maslow's hierarchy of needs, and summarize his findings on the characteristics of self-actualizing people.

16-1. Maslow proposed that human needs are arranged in a hierarchy, usually depicted as a pyramid, with the most basic, physiological needs at the _____ and higher-level needs closer to the _____.

16-2. The lower level needs would include needs for food, water, and factors related to survival and security. Next in the hierarchy would be a need for acceptance by others. Higher level needs, called _____ needs, would include the need for knowledge and aesthetic beauty. At the top of the pyramid is the need for _____, the need to express one's full potential.

16-3. A higher level need would be activated only after a lower level need is satisfied. For example, a need for knowledge would be activated (<u>before/after</u>) needs for esteem, belongingness, and several lower level needs had been reasonably well satisfied.

16-4. Maslow referred to a need to fulfill one's potential in his concept of _____. For example, if a woman had the talent and strong desire to become a mathematician, but followed the urging of others and became a nurse instead (or vice versa), she would not be _____.

16-5. Maslow proposed that people who are self-actualized have exceptionally healthy personalities. Which of the following, according to Maslow, are characteristic of self-actualized people? Place Y in the blank if the description applies, N if it does not.

_____ spontaneous

_____ has more profound emotional experiences than others

_____ uncomfortable being alone

_____ not dependent on others for approval

_____ thrive on their work

_____ extreme in personality (e.g., either conforming or rebellious)

16-6. Kenrick and colleagues have recently proposed that the highest human needs are related to _____ _____. Specifically, they propose that the top three needs should be the need to find a _____, the need to retain a mate, and the need to successfully _____ _____.

Answers: **16-1.** bottom, top **16-2.** growth, self-actualization **16-3.** after **16-4.** self-actualization, self-actualized **16-5.** Y, Y, N, Y, Y, N **16-6.** reproductive fitness, mate, parent offspring.

17. Summarize the strengths and weaknesses of the humanistic approach to personality.

17-1. To its credit, the humanistic movement called attention to the possibility that a person's _____ views may be more important than objective reality. The movement also emphasized the importance of the _____, or self-concept, and stressed the study of the (normal/abnormal) personality.

17-2. Critics have also identified several weaknesses of the humanistic formulations. Match the weaknesses listed below with the statements, by placing the appropriate letters in the blanks.

a. poor testability

b. unrealistic view of human nature

c. inadequate evidence

____ Humanistic psychologists tend to scorn research, so little experimental support for their views has emerged.

____ Even without research, some of the descriptions, such as of self-actualized personalities, have an idealized, perfectionistic ring.

____ Humanistic ideas are frequently difficult to define, so research on some concepts is difficult or impossible.

Answers: **17-1.** subjective, self, normal **17-2.** c, b, a.

BIOLOGICAL PERSPECTIVES

18. Describe Eysenck's theory of personality.

18-1. According to Eysenck, individual differences in personality can be understood in terms of a hierarchy of traits. At the top of the hierarchy are three fundamental higher-order traits from which all other traits derive: _____, _____, and _____.

18-2. Eysenck asserted that a major factor in personality involves the ease with which people can be _____. Eysenck believed that differences in conditionability, like personality differences in general, are to a large extent (environmentally/genetically) determined.

18-3. Conditionability, in turn, is related to extraversion-introversion. According to Eysenck, (extraverts/introverts) have higher levels of physiological arousal, a characteristic that makes them (more/less) readily conditioned.

18-4. Why would conditionability be related to introversion? Because easily conditioned people could be readily conditioned to fear social situations. People who fear social situations may be classified as

_____.

Answers: 18-1. extraversion, neuroticism, psychoticism (you can remember these with the acronym PEN) **18-2.** conditioned, genetically **18-3.** introverts, more **18-4.** introverts.

19. Summarize behavioural genetics research and neuroscience research on personality and their conclusions.

19-1. The most important and conclusive result from the various twin studies is the finding that the personalities of (identical/fraternal) twins reared (together/apart) were more similar than those of (identical/fraternal) twins reared (together/apart). This outcome has been found with several dependent measures, including the factors of the Big Five personality inventory as well as peer ratings.

19-2. Approximately what percentage of the variance in personality is assumed to be caused by genetic factors?

a. 10 to 20%

b. 20 to 40%

c. 40 to 60%

d. 60 to 80%

19-3. How important a determinant of personality is family environment, according to the results of these studies?

a. of very little importance

b. of about the same importance as heredity

c. more important than heredity

19-4. The twin studies have had a major impact on the way psychologists think about the causes of human behaviour. Why are the results so important and so surprising?

19-5. Recent neuroscience research using MRI technology has examined associated between the Big Five personality traits and the _____ of various brain structures. Extraversion correlated with the size of the brain's _____ regions. _____ correlated with the volume of brain areas involved in negative emotions and threat. Conscientiousness correlated with the size of brain areas involved in _____ and voluntary control.

Answers: 19-1. identical, apart, fraternal, together. This is the most important comparison because, even though the fraternal twins shared the same environment, their common environment did not make them nearly as similar as twins who did not have a common environment *but who shared the same genes*. **19-2.** c **19-3.** a **19-4.** Theories of development and personality have tended to stress the importance of the environment, especially the family environment; the recent twin studies find heredity to be very important and family environment to be of little importance. Thus, the results are contrary to the expectations of most of us and of much of the theorizing in the field of personality **19-5.** size, reward, neuroticism, planning.

20. Outline Buss's explanation for why the Big Five traits are important.

20-1. As group animals, we gain an advantage by being able to predict the behaviour of other human beings.

That is, the ability to recognize the "Big Five" characteristics in others has _____ value for our species.

20-2. The big five traits are: neuroticism, extraversion, openness to experience, agreeableness, and conscientiousness. In terms of survival value, it is useful to know who in a group will fulfill their commitments, the trait of _____ ; who will fall apart under stress, the trait of _____ ; who will be a good problem solver, the trait of _____ , and so on.

20-3. The fact that these traits appear as dimensions across a variety of cultures attests to their importance. For Buss, our ability to _____ these traits in others also has adaptive significance. MacDonald, also an evolutionary theorist, asserts that it is the traits themselves, not just the ability to _____ them, that had adaptive value in our evolutionary past.

Answers: 20-1. adaptive (or survival, evolutionary) **20-2.** conscientiousness, neuroticism, openness to experience **20-3.** recognize, recognize.

21. Summarize the strengths and weaknesses of the biological approach to personality.

21-1. People frequently blame parents for children's personalities. I recently asked a friend of mine why she thought a mutual acquaintance was so obnoxious. She said, "Well, raised with such crazy parents, what would you expect?" I asked, "Is that an argument for environment or heredity?" That is one of the benefits of the twin studies: they put data in place of speculation. But what are some of the weaknesses of the biological approach? First, heritability ratios should be regarded only as _____ that will vary depending on sampling and other procedures. Second, there is no truly comprehensive biological _____ of personality.

Answers: 21-1. estimates, theory.

A CONTEMPORARY EMPIRICAL APPROACH TO PERSONALITY

22. Discuss what is known about narcissism.

22-1. Narcissism is defined as having an inflated sense of _____, a need for attention and _____, a sense of entitlement, and a tendency to exploit others.

22-2. Symptoms of _____ _____ Disorder include having a grandiose sense of self-importance, a constant need for attention, difficulty dealing with criticism, and a sense of entitlement.

22-3. Narcissists have self-concepts that are easily _____. Narcissists also tend to be impulsive and are prone to unprovoked _____. They may initially be seen by others as charming, but eventually come across as arrogant and unlikeable. Interestingly, there is some evidence that narcissism is (increasing/decreasing) in recent generations. This trend may be related to an excessive focus on physical attractiveness among young people, and to materialism and overconsumption.

Answers: 22-1. importance, admiration **22-2.** Narcissistic Personality **22-3.** threatened, aggression, increasing.

23. **Discuss the essentials of terror management theory.**

23-1. According to terror management theory, because humans have the ability to be aware of the inevitability of death, feelings of _____, alarm, and terror arise when people think about their mortality.

23-2. This crisis is solved by _____. Worldviews give people a sense of being part of an enduring legacy, or a sense of meaning, that can soothe fear of death.

23-3. Confidence in the validity of one's cultural worldview and seeing oneself as living up to the standards of one's worldview provides a sense of _____-_____. Therefore, self-esteem serves as an _____ _____.

Answers: 23-1. anxiety **23-2.** culture **23-3.** self-esteem, anxiety buffer.

CULTURE AND PERSONALITY

24. **Summarize research on the cross-cultural validity of the five-factor model and on cultural variations in conceptions of self.**

24-1. For a decade or so after World War II, researchers using the Freudian model attempted to find a modal personality type representative of each culture. This attempt was (<u>successful/not successful</u>).

24-2. With the current increased attention to cultural factors, interest in the relationship between personality and culture has again surfaced, and the new data have revealed both cross-cultural similarities and differences. With regard to similarity, precisely the same "_____" personality factors tend to emerge in different cultures. With regard to differences, a comparison of 51 cultures revealed cultural disparities in average trait scores across different countries. For example, Brazilians scored high on _____, and Australians scored high on _____.

24-3. With regard to differences, research by Markus and Kitayama clearly indicates that the individualistic orientation characteristic of the West is not universal across cultures. While North Americans tend to value (<u>independence/connectedness</u>), Asians value (<u>interdependence/uniqueness</u>) among people. Similarly, while North American parents encourage their children to (<u>stand out/blend in</u>), Asian parents emphasize taking pride in the accomplishments of (<u>each individual/the group</u>).

24-4. _____ involves putting personal goals ahead of group goals and defining one's identity in terms of personal attributes, whereas _____ involves putting group goals ahead of personal goals and defining one's identity in terms of the groups one belongs to. (<u>Individualists/collectivists</u>) tend to engage in more self-enhancement.

Answers: 24-1. not successful **24-2.** Big Five, neuroticism, extraversion **24-3.** independence, interdependence, stand out, the group **24-4.** individualism, collectivism, Individualists.

PUTTING IT IN PERSPECTIVE

25. **Explain how the chapter highlighted three of the text's unifying themes.**

25-1. We've just discussed one of the three themes emphasized in this chapter, that our behaviour is influenced by our cultural heritage. Two other themes prominently demonstrated in the area of personality are that

the field is theoretically _____ and that psychology evolves in a
_____ context.

25-2. Freudian, behavioural, and biological perspectives of personality assume that behaviour is determined; the _____ perspective does not. The biological perspective stresses genetic inheritance; the behavioural perspective stresses (heredity/environment). As these examples illustrate, the study of personality has produced an enormous amount of theoretical _____.

25-3. Concerning sociohistorical context, it is clear that theories of personality have strongly affected our culture. For example, the surrealist art movement, begun in the 1920s, derives directly from _____ psychology, as do other movements in literature and the arts. And the current debate on the effects of media violence is, to a large extent, a product of research in social _____ theory.

25-4. In turn, culture has affected psychology. For example, it seems quite likely that the sexually repressive climate of Victorian Vienna caused Freud to emphasize the _____ aspects of human behaviour; and it is clear, from Freud's own description, that World War I influenced his development of the second Freudian instinct, the _____ instinct. Thus, psychology evolves in a _____ context.

Answers: 25-1. diverse, sociohistorical **25-2.** humanistic, environment, diversity **25-3.** psychoanalytic (or Freudian), learning **25-4.** sexual, aggression, sociohistorical.

PERSONAL APPLICATION * UNDERSTANDING PERSONALITY ASSESSMENT

26. Outline the four principal uses of personality tests.

26-1. List the four principal uses of personality tests in the blanks next to the correct descriptions.

(a) Psychological _____: Measuring personality traits in empirical studies.

(b) _____: Advising people on career plans and decisions.

(c) _____ selection: Choosing employees in business and government.

(d) Clinical _____: Assessing psychological disorders.

Answers: 26-1. (a) research, (b) Counselling, (c) Personnel, (d) diagnosis.

27. Describe the MMPI, 16PF, and NEO Personality Inventory, and summarize the strengths and weaknesses of self-report inventories.

27-1. The MMPI, 16PF, and NEO Personality Inventories are (projective/self-report) tests. All three tests are also used to measure (single/multiple) traits.

27-2. Identify which tests (MMPI, 16PF, or NEO) are described by each of the following.

(a) _____ Originally designed to diagnose psychological disorders.

(b) _____, _____ Originally designed to assess the normal personality.

(c) _____ Contains 187 items.

(d) _____ Contains 567 items.

(e) _____ Measures the "big five" personality traits.

(f) _____ Includes four validity scales to help detect deception.

27-3. The major strength of self-report inventories, in comparison with simply asking a person what they are like, is that they provide a more precise and more (<u>objective</u>/personal) measure of personality.

27-4. The major weakness of self-report inventories is that they are subject to several sources of error, including the following: (1) Test-takers may intentionally fake responses, that is, may engage in deliberate _____. (2) While not realizing it, people may answer questions in ways to make themselves "look good," the _____ _____ bias. (3) In addition, some people tend either to agree or to disagree with nearly every statement on a test, a source of error involving _____ sets.

Answers: **27-1.** self-report, multiple **27-2.** (a) MMPI, (b) 16PF, NEO, (c) 16PF, (d) MMPI, (e) NEO, (f) MPI **27-3.** objective **27-4.** deception, social desirability, response.

28. Describe the projective hypothesis, and summarize the strengths and weaknesses of projective tests.

28-1. If you have ever looked at clouds and described the images you've seen, you've done something similar to taking a projective test. If you thought that the images you saw reflected something about your personality, then you also accepted the *projective hypothesis*. The projective hypothesis is the idea that people will tend to _____ their characteristics onto ambiguous stimuli, so that what they see reveals something about their personalities and problems.

28-2. Two major projective tests are the Rorschach, a series of _____, and the TAT, a series of simple _____.

28-3. The advantages of projective tests are that (1) since the way the tests are interpreted is not at all obvious, it is difficult for people to engage in intentional _____; and (2) projective tests may help tap problems or aspects of personality of which people are _____.

28-4. The major weakness of projective tests concerns _____ scoring, inadequate norms, cultural bias, and poor _____ and validity. Clinicians often find information from projective tests to be (<u>useful</u>/useless). Some have suggested that, given their poor scientific evidence, projective tests should be referred to as instruments or techniques rather than tests.

Answers: **28-1.** project **28-2.** inkblots, pictures (or scenes) **28-3.** deception, unconscious (or unaware) **28-4.** inconsistent, reliability, useful.

29. Describe advantages and disadvantages of personality testing on the Internet.

29-1. Advantages of Internet-based testing include the fact that tests can be completed _____ with reduced _____. Also, information such as answer-_____ and how long questions are pondered before being answered can be measured. Online tests can also be completed by _____ residents who lack access to psychologists.

29-2. Disadvantages of online testing include _____ of test item content, verifying the _____ of respondents, and whether results obtained from online testing are equivalent to what is found from paper-and-pencil versions of the tests. With respect to this latter issue, results thus far suggest that results from online tests (are/are not) similar to those obtained from offline counterparts.

Answers: **29-1.** quickly, costs, changing, rural **29-2.** security, identity, are.

CRITICAL THINKING APPLICATION * HINDSIGHT IN EVERYDAY ANALYSES OF PERSONALITY

30. Discuss how hindsight bias affects everyday analyses of personality, as well as some theoretical analyses of personality.

30-1. I (R.S.) am writing this sentence following a period of very substantial decline in the stock market. Somewhat surprising, to me at least, is the fact that my colleagues say they saw it coming. If everyone saw it coming, why didn't everyone sell last year? Or the year before? Because we didn't see it coming. Rather, once exposed to information, we are inclined to believe that we already knew it, the cognitive tendency known as the _____.

30-2. You may recall from Chapter 11 the experiment with the three-year-old and the candy box. The child first guesses that candy is in the candy box. After the child sees that crayons are in the candy box, the three-year-old will usually insist that he always thought that there were crayons in the box. The five-year-old doesn't make this mistake, but these data suggest that the _____ begins early, that from a young age we reconstruct past events in terms of _____ information.

30-3. Suppose you meet someone who is achievement motivated and fiercely independent. You learn that this person was brought up by adoptive parents who were somewhat distant and undemonstrative. Would you connect the events, thinking that the parent's child-rearing style accounted for their child's independence? Or, suppose that the person brought up by these parents is depressed and chronically unemployed. Would you connect the parenting and personality in this case, too? You might, because people tend to interpret _____ events in terms of _____ _____, which is a definition of the hindsight bias.

30-4. What is the hindsight bias? Write a definition in the space below.

30-5. In what way might psychoanalytic interpretations involve the hindsight bias?

30-6. How might evolutionary theory's account of the emergence of the Big Five traits reflect the hindsight bias?

Answers: 30-1. hindsight bias (By the way, this week the market recovered a bit. I knew it would!)
30-2. hindsight bias, present (or current, outcome, recent) **30-3.** past (or previous), present information (or outcomes, current information) **30-4.** Once we know something, we tend to reinterpret past events in terms of that information. Or, once exposed to information, we tend to think we knew it all along. Or, knowing the outcome of events tends to bias our recall and interpretation of those events. **30-5.** Once the analyst is exposed to an individual's personality, he or she can easily explain how the person's childhood experiences could account for the present behaviour. **30-6.** Once exposed to the fact that the Big Five traits appear world-wide, a theorist can fairly easily explain why that might be the case. If a dozen entirely different traits had emerged, one could imagine that there could be an evolutionary explanation for that occurrence as well.

REVIEW OF KEY TERMS

Archetypes
Behaviourism
Collective unconscious
Compensation
Conscious
Defence mechanisms
Displacement
Ego
Extraverts
Factor analysis
Fixation
Hierarchy of needs
Hindsight bias
Humanism
Id
Identification
Incongruence

Introverts
Model
Narcissism
Need for self-actualization
Observational learning
Oedipal complex
Personal unconscious
Personality
Personality trait
Phenomenological approach
Pleasure principle
Preconscious
Projection
Projective tests
Psychodynamic theories
Psychosexual stages

Rationalization
Reaction formation
Reality principle
Reciprocal determinism
Regression
Repression
Self-actualizing persons
Self-concept
Self-efficacy
Self-enhancement
Self-report inventories
Striving for superiority
Sublimation
Superego
Terror management theory
Unconscious

_____ 1. An individual's unique constellation of consistent behavioural traits.

_____ 2. A characteristic that represents a durable disposition to behave in a particular way in a variety of situations.

_____ 3. A systematic arrangement of needs, according to priority, in which basic, physiological needs must be met before social or growth needs are aroused.

_____ 4. All the diverse theories, descended from the work of Sigmund Freud, that focus on unconscious mental forces.

_____ 5. The primitive, instinctive component of personality that operates according to the pleasure principle.

_____ 6. The id's demands for immediate gratification of its urges.

_____ 7. The decision-making component of personality that operates according to the reality principle.

_____ 8. The ego's delay of gratification of the id's urges until appropriate outlets and situations can be found.

_____ 9. The moral component of personality that incorporates social standards about what represents right and wrong.

_____ 10. Consists of whatever you are aware of at a particular point in time.

_____ 11. Contains material just beneath the surface of awareness that can be easily retrieved.

_____ 12. Contains thoughts, memories, and desires that are well below the surface of conscious awareness.

_____ 13. The series of largely unconscious Freudian reactions that protect a person from unpleasant emotions such as anxiety or guilt.

_____ 14. The defence mechanism that pushes distressing thoughts and feelings into the unconscious or keeps them from emerging into consciousness.

_____ 15. Attributing your own thoughts, feelings, or motives to another.

_____ 16. Creating false but plausible excuses to justify unacceptable behaviour.

_____ 17. Diverting emotional feelings (usually anger) from their original source to a substitute target.

_____ 18. Behaving in a way that is exactly the opposite of one's true (but unconscious) feelings.

_____   19. Reverting to immature patterns of behaviour.

_____   20. Bolstering self-esteem by forming an imaginary or real alliance with some person or group.

_____   21. Developmental periods with a characteristic sexual focus that leave their mark on adult personality.

_____   22. A failure to move forward from one stage to another as expected.

_____   23. Characterized by erotically tinged desires for one's opposite-sex parent and hostility toward one's same-sex parent.

_____   24. Jungian concept referring to the structure holding material that is not in one's awareness because it has been repressed or forgotten.

_____   25. A storehouse of latent memory traces inherited from our ancestral past.

_____   26. Emotionally charged images and thought forms that have universal meaning.

_____   27. People who tend to be preoccupied with the internal world of their own thoughts, feelings, and experiences.

_____   28. People who tend to be interested in the external world of people and things.

_____   29. An Adlerian concept referring to a universal drive to adapt, to improve oneself, and to master life's challenges.

_____   30. Efforts to overcome imagined or real inferiorities by developing one's abilities.

_____   31. Personality tests that ask people a series of questions about their characteristic behaviour.

_____   32. A statistical procedure that identifies clusters of variables that are highly correlated with one another.

_____   33. A theoretical orientation based on the premise that scientific psychology should study only observable behaviour.

_____   34. The assumption that internal mental events, external environmental events, and overt behaviour all influence one another.

_____   35. Learning that occurs when an organism's responding is influenced by the observation of others.

_____   36. A person whose behaviour is observed by another.

_____   37. Our belief about our ability to perform behaviours that should lead to expected outcomes.

_____   38. A theoretical orientation that emphasizes the unique qualities of humans, especially their freedom and potential for personal growth.

_____   39. Approach that assumes we have to appreciate individuals' personal, subjective experiences to truly understand their behaviour.

_____   40. A collection of beliefs about one's own nature, unique qualities, and typical behaviour.

_____   41. A Rogerian concept referring to the degree of disparity between one's self-concept and one's actual experience.

_____   42. The need to fulfill one's potential.

_____   43. People with exceptionally healthy personalities, marked by continued personal growth.

_____   44. The biased interpretation of past events in terms of present information.

_____   45. A theory concerning how people manage the anxiety associated with anticipating their own inevitable deaths.

_____   46. A person's overall assessment of her or his personal adequacy or worth.

	47.	The tendency to focus on positive feedback, exaggerate one's strengths, and see oneself as above average.
	48.	A personality trait marked by an inflated sense of importance and a need for attention and admiration.
	49.	When unconscious, unacceptable impulses are channelled into socially acceptable behaviours.

Answers: 1. personality **2.** personality trait **3.** hierarchy of needs **4.** psychodynamic theories **5.** id **6.** pleasure principle **7.** ego **8.** reality principle **9.** superego **10.** conscious **11.** preconscious **12.** unconscious **13.** defence mechanisms **14.** repression **15.** projection **16.** rationalization **17.** displacement **18.** reaction formation **19.** regression **20.** identification **21.** psychosexual stages **22.** fixation **23.** Oedipal complex **24.** personal unconscious **25.** collective unconscious **26.** archetypes **27.** introverts **28.** extraverts **29.** striving for superiority **30.** compensation **31.** self-report inventories **32.** factor analysis **33.** behaviourism **34.** reciprocal determinism **35.** observational learning **36.** model **37.** self-efficacy **38.** humanism **39.** phenomenological approach **40.** self-concept **41.** incongruence **42.** need for self-actualization **43.** self-actualizing persons **44.** hindsight bias **45.** terror management theory **46.** self-esteem **47.** self-enhancement **48.** narcissism **49.** sublimation.

REVIEW OF KEY PEOPLE

Alfred Adler	Hans Eysenck	Walter Mischel
Albert Bandura	Sigmund Freud	Delroy Paulhus
David Buss	Carl Jung	Carl Rogers
Norman Endler	Abraham Maslow	B.F. Skinner

	1.	The founder of psychoanalysis.
	2.	Developed the theory called analytical psychology; anticipated the humanists' emphasis on personal growth and self-actualization.
	3.	Founder of an approach to personality called individual psychology.
	4.	Modern behaviourism's most prominent theorist, recognized for his theories of operant conditioning.
	5.	A contemporary behavioural theorist who elaborated the concept of observational learning.
	6.	His chief contribution to personality theory has been to focus attention on the extent to which situational factors govern behaviour.
	7.	One of the fathers of the human potential movement, he called his approach a person-centered theory.
	8.	The humanist who developed a theory of self-actualization.
	9.	Proposed that conditionability and introversion-extraversion are largely genetically determined.
	10.	Studied birth order and personality, cultural differences in self-enhancement, and response sets in self-report personality inventories.
	11.	Advocated an interactional (personality traits interacting with situational factors) approach to personality.
	12.	Adopted an evolutionary view toward the existence of the Big Five personality traits.

Answers: 1. Freud **2.** Jung **3.** Adler **4.** Skinner **5.** Bandura **6.** Mischel **7.** Rogers **8.** Maslow **9.** Eysenck **10.** Paulhus **11.** Endler **12.** Buss.

1. What characterizes personality traits?
   a. consistency and distinctiveness
   b. charm and wit
   c. change as a function of the situation
   d. lack of individual differences

2. Someone attributes his thoughts or feelings or conflicts to someone else. For example, although he chronically interrupts people, he thinks that other people interrupt him. What Freudian defence mechanism does this illustrate?
   a. rationalization
   b. reaction formation
   c. regression
   d. projection

3. Which of the following is entirely unconscious, according to Freud?
   a. the id
   b. the ego
   c. the superego
   d. the archetype

4. Although Osmo, at an unconscious level, has great hatred for Cosmo, he believes that he likes Cosmo and, to the outside world, gives all the appearance of liking him. Which defence mechanism is Osmo using?
   a. regression
   b. reaction formation
   c. projection
   d. rationalization

5. When does the Oedipal complex occur?
   a. oral stage
   b. anal stage
   c. phallic stage
   d. genital stage

6. Which of the following concepts did Carl Jung originate?
   a. id
   b. superego
   c. inferiority complex
   d. introversion-extraversion

7. Which of the following concepts did Adler emphasize in his theory of personality?
   a. striving for superiority
   b. castration anxiety
   c. introversion-extraversion
   d. the collective unconscious

8. According to which individual does much of the behaviour that we call personality result from reinforcement and observational learning?
   a. Jung
   b. Skinner
   c. Bandura
   d. Adler

9. What approach tends to emphasize freedom and personal growth in its view of human behaviour?
   a. psychoanalytic approach
   b. biological approach
   c. behavioural approach
   d. humanistic approach

10. According to Rogers, what causes incongruence?
    a. conditioned stimuli
    b. conditional acceptance or affection
    c. unconditional acceptance or affection
    d. unconditioned stimuli

11. Herb had the desire and potential to be a violinist but instead became a trader in hog futures. He decided never to touch the violin again. What is wrong with Herb, according to Maslow?
    a. He suffers from incontinence.
    b. He suffers from castration anxiety.
    c. He has not achieved self-actualization.
    d. He has an inferiority complex.

12. Who views personality in terms of the adaptive significance of the Big Five traits?
    a. Abraham Maslow
    b. William James
    c. Carl Rogers
    d. David Buss

13. Your friend spends money like water. When you learn that he is from a poverty-stricken background, you attribute his spending patterns to his earlier deprivation. According to the critical thinking analysis, why are you likely to do this?
    a. because of the hindsight bias
    b. because of a self-serving attribution
    c. because of the consistency and distinctiveness of personality
    d. because of circular reasoning

14. According to Mischel, what is the major factor that predicts human behaviour?
    a. childhood experience
    b. specifics of the situation
    c. extraversion and introversion
    d. central and peripheral traits

15. You are asked to tell stories about a series of pictures. Which test is being administered to you?
    a. Rorschach
    b. MMPI
    c. TAT
    d. 16PF

16. What did the Featured Study examine about how we view ourselves?
    a. the impact of evaluations of others
    b. the impact of genetics
    c. the impact of person-situation interactions
    d. the impact of the drive for self-actualization

17. What did the Featured Study show that subliminally presented images of a scowling significant other can lead someone to do?
    a. try harder on an exam
    b. avoid that particular person
    c. scowl right back at them
    d. make more negative self-ratings

18. According to Terror Management Theory, what does self-esteem serve as?
   a. a measure of our social acceptability
   b. an anxiety buffer
   c. a measure of one's status
   d. a depression buffer

19. John is feeling depressed. According to Higgins' self-discrepancy theory, he is experiencing a discrepancy between which of the following pairs of "selves"?
   a. the actual self and the ideal self
   b. the actual self and the hidden self
   c. the actual self and the ought self
   d. the actual self and the perceived self

Answers: 1. a **2.** d **3.** a **4.** b **5.** c **6.** d **7.** a **8.** c **9.** d **10.** b **11.** c **12.** d **13.** a **14.** b **15.** c **16.** a **17.** d. **18.** b **19.** a.

Chapter Thirteen

STRESS, COPING, AND HEALTH

REVIEW OF KEY IDEAS

THE NATURE OF STRESS

1. **Define stress, describe the biopsychosocial model, and explain why an understanding of stress is important in Health Psychology.**

   1-1. Stress is defined as any circumstances that _____ or are perceived to threaten one's well-being and that thereby tax one's _____ abilities.

   1-2. The biopsychosocial model holds that _____ illness is caused by a complex interaction of biological, psychological, and _____ factors.

   1-3. Health psychology examines how psychosocial factors relate to health and to the causation, prevention, and treatment of _____. An important psychosocial factor is _____.

   Answers: **1-1.** threaten, coping **1-2.** physical, sociocultural **1-3.** illness, stress.

2. **Discuss the impact of minor stressors.**

   2-1. While some forms of stress arise from unusual, traumatic crises, most stress arises from (infrequent/everyday) problems. These minor hassles appear to be detrimental to mental health because of the _____ nature of stress.

   Answers: **2-1.** everyday, cumulative.

3. **Describe the nature of our appraisals of stress.**

   3-1. The text defines stress as any circumstances that threaten or are perceived to threaten one's well-being, and thereby they tax one's coping abilities. This definition would indicate that the sources of stress are quite (subjective/objective). Or to put it another way, stress lies in the mind of the _____.

   3-2. _____ appraisal involves judging whether an event is irrelevant to you, relevant but not threatening, or stressful. _____ appraisal involves judging your coping resources and options for dealing with stress.

   Answers: **3-1.** subjective, beholder (or individual) **3-2.** Primary, Secondary.

4. Describe frustration as a form of stress.

4-1. Which of the following three situations best illustrates what is meant by frustration?

(a) Your family moves from a large city to a rather small, rural community.

(b) You are late for an appointment and stuck in a traffic jam.

(c) You are forced to choose between two good movies on television.

4-2. If you picked choice (b), then you have caught on that frustration always involves the _____ of the pursuit of some goal.

Answers: 4-1. b **4-2.** thwarting (or blocking).

5. Identify the three basic types of conflict, and discuss which types are most troublesome.

5-1. Many persons do not want to pay their income taxes, but, on the other hand, they don't want to go to jail either. These persons are faced with an _____-_____ conflict.

5-2. Getting married has both positive and negative aspects that make it an excellent example of an_____-_____conflict.

5-3. Consider the problem of the student who has to choose between scholarships for two different universities. Since he cannot accept both, he's faced with an _____-_____ conflict.

5-4. Now that you have correctly identified the three basic types of conflict, list them below in their order of troublesomeness, beginning with the least troublesome.

(a) _____

(b) _____

(c) _____

Answers: 5-1. avoidance-avoidance **5-2.** approach-avoidance **5-3.** approach-approach **5-4.** (a) approach-approach, (b) approach-avoidance, (c) avoidance-avoidance.

6. Summarize evidence on life change and pressure as forms of stress.

6-1. The Social Readjustment Rating Scale (SRRS) measures the stress induced by _____ in daily living routines. The developers of this scale theorized that all kinds of life changes, both pleasant and unpleasant, would induce stress. Early research showed that high scores on the SRRS were correlated with psychological disturbances and many kinds of physical _____.

6-2. Later research began to indicate that high scores on the SRRS were primarily the result of (pleasant/unpleasant) events. At the present time, research seems to indicate that change by itself (is/is not) inevitably stressful.

6-3. There are two kinds of pressure. One is the pressure to get things accomplished, or the pressure to _____. The other is the pressure to abide by rules, or the pressure to

_____.

6-4. Which appears to have the strongest influence on mental health, life changes or pressure?

Answers: **6-1.** changes, illness **6-2.** unpleasant, is not **6-3.** perform, conform **6-4.** pressure.

RESPONDING TO STRESS

7. Identify some common emotional responses to stress, and discuss the effects of emotional arousal.

7-1. The text describes three different dimensions of negative emotions that are particularly likely to be triggered by stress. Identify which of these dimensions is most likely to be present in the following situations.

(a) The emotions in this dimension are likely to be found as a person begins to feel more and more helpless and unable to cope (e.g., you detect signs that your lover is going to leave you).

(b) The emotions in this dimension are likely to be found as a person begins to feel increasingly put upon and treated unfairly (e.g., you are being falsely accused of a deed you didn't commit).

(c) The emotions in this dimension are likely to be found as a person faces increasing degrees of conflict or uncertainty (e.g., you're driving on a highway, and the fog is gradually becoming thicker).

7-2. What did the study of emotional responding in the weeks following 9/11 show?

7-3. According to broaden-and-build theory, positive emotions can promote resilience via three routes. First, positive emotions can broaden people's scope of _____, and increase their creativity and problem-solving. Second, positive emotions can undermine the lingering effects of _____ _____. Third, positive emotions promote rewarding _____ _____.

7-4. There is evidence that positive emotions can protect against _____ disease. And, more broadly, people with higher levels of positive emotions appear to live (longer/shorter) than others.

7-5. What does the inverted U hypothesis say about what happens to the optimal arousal level as tasks become more complex?

Answers: **7-1.** (a) dejection, sadness, and grief, (b) annoyance, anger, and rage, (c) apprehension, anxiety, and fear **7-2.** Although many participants reported negative emotions, positive emotions such as gratitude and love also emerged, and the frequency of positive emotions correlated positively with resilience. **7-3.** attention, negative emotions, social interactions **7-4.** heart, longer **7-5.** The optimal arousal level decreases.

8. Describe the fight-or-flight response and the three stages of the General Adaptation Syndrome.

8-1. What division of the autonomic nervous system mediates the fight-or-flight response?

8-2. Although the body's fight-or-flight response appears to be an evolutionary carry-over from our past, why is it perhaps of more harm than help to modern human beings?

8-3. Indicate which of the three stages of the General Adaptation Syndrome is being described in each of the following.

(a) This is the initial stage, in which the body prepares for the fight-or-flight response.

(b) This is the second stage, in which the body stabilizes its physiological changes as it begins to effectively cope with the stress.

(c) This is the third stage, in which the body's resources are becoming depleted, and the harmful physiological effects of stress can create "disease of adaptation."

Answers: 8-1. sympathetic nervous system **8-2.** Because most stressful situations generally require a more complex response than simple fight or flight. **8-3.** (a) stage of alarm, (b) stage of resistance, (c) stage of exhaustion.

9. **Discuss the two major pathways along which the brain sends signals to the endocrine system in response to stress.**

   9-1.   Fill in the missing parts in the following diagram, detailing the two major pathways along which the brain sends signals to the endocrine system.

CEREBRAL CORTEX

(a) _____

SYMPATHETIC NS   PITUITARY GLAND

                                                                          ACTH

(b) _____ (GLAND)   (c) _____ (GLAND)

CATECHOLAMINES   CORTICOSTEROIDS

Increases heart rate and   Increases energy, inhibits
respiration, etc.   tissue inflammation, etc.

   9-2.   Females' stress responses tend to be (<u>stronger/milder</u>) than men's from puberty through menopause, suggesting a role for _____ in physiological responses to stress.

Answers: 9-1. (a) hypothalamus, (b) adrenal medulla, (c) adrenal cortex **9-2.** milder, estrogen.

10. **Describe some relatively unhealthy coping responses that are common.**

   10-1.   Answer the following questions regarding giving up and blaming oneself as responses to stress.

   (a) What syndrome often results from giving up in response to exposure to unavoidable stressful events?

   (b) What phenomenon often accompanies blaming oneself in response to stress?

   10-2.   Answer the following questions regarding aggression and self-indulgence as responses to stress.

   (a) Which of these responses is illustrated by the saying "When the going gets tough, the tough go shopping"? _____

   (b) Which of these responses is frequently, but not always, triggered by frustration?

   _____

   (c) Which of these responses is linked to gambling? _____

   (d) Which of these responses is linked to Internet addiction? _____

10-3. What is a common fault with both of these behavioural responses to stress?

Answers: 10-1. (a) learned helplessness, (b) catastrophic thinking **10-2.** (a) self-indulgence, (b) aggression, (c) self-indulgence, (d) self-indulgence **10-3.** They divert effort away from solutions to problems.

11. Explain how defence mechanisms work and discuss the value of defensive coping and constructive coping.

11-1. Indicate whether each of the following statements regarding defensive coping is true or false.

_____ (a) Although they are largely unconscious, defence mechanisms can operate at any level of consciousness.

_____ (b) Defence mechanisms are used to shield against emotional discomfort that often occurs with stress, particularly anxiety.

11-2. One shortcoming of defensive coping is that it _____ the real problem.

11-3. What conclusion does the text draw regarding small versus extreme positive illusions?

11-4. In contrast to defensive coping, constructive coping refers to relatively _____ efforts that people make to deal with stressful events. Characteristics of constructive coping include confronting problems _____, making reasonably realistic appraisals of stress and coping resources, learning to recognize and at times inhibit disruptive _____ reactions, and taking steps to ensure that one's body is not especially vulnerable to stress.

Answers: 11-1. (a) true, (b) true **11-2.** avoids **11-3.** Small positive illusions may be beneficial while extreme illusions may be harmful. **11-4.** healthful, directly, emotional.

THE EFFECTS OF STRESS ON PSYCHOLOGICAL FUNCTIONING

12. Discuss the effects of stress on task performance and the burnout syndrome.

12-1. Baumeister's theory as to why stress affects task performance is that pressure to perform makes us self-conscious, and this elevated self-consciousness disrupts our _____. The term we commonly use for this is _____ under pressure. Research shows that this phenomenon is quite (rare/common) among normal persons. Choking under pressure may involve using up one's limited _____ _____ capacity.

12-2. Indicate whether each of the following statements regarding the burnout syndrome is true or false.

_____ (a) Burnout is related to only a few highly stressful occupations.

_____ (b) The onset of burnout is usually sudden.

Answers: 12-1. attention, choking, common, working memory **12-2.** (a) false, (b) false.

13. **Discuss some of the psychological problems and disorders that may result from stress, as well as some positive psychological correlates of stress.**

13-1.　Answer the following questions regarding post-traumatic stress syndrome.

(a)　What is unique about post-traumatic stress disorder?

(b)　What are some of the common causes of this syndrome, besides combat experience?

13-2.　In addition to alcohol abuse and unhappiness, what four other psychological problems appear to be related to chronic stress? (One of them has to do with school, two have to do with sleep, and one involves intimate relationships.)

13-3.　Stress has also been implicated in the onset of serious psychological disorders. In addition to schizophrenia, what three other disorders are mentioned?

13-4.　A positive response to stress can reflect the strength of _____, defined as successful adaptation to significant stress and trauma.

Answers: 13-1. (a) It is caused by a single episode of extreme stress. (b) being exposed to trauma during one's occupation as a police officer or paramedic, or similar position; being exposed to rape, robbery, assault; seeing someone die; serious automobile accidents; major natural disasters **13-2.** poor academic performance, insomnia, nightmares, sexual difficulties **13-3.** anxiety disorders, depression, eating disorders **13-4.** resilience.

THE EFFECTS OF STRESS ON PHYSICAL HEALTH

14. **Describe the evidence linking personality factors to coronary heart disease.**

14-1.　What is the principal cause of coronary heart disorder?

14-2.　Tell whether the following characteristics are found in Type A or Type B persons.

_____ (a) easygoing　　　　　_____ (d) amicable

_____ (b) competitive　　　　_____ (e) hostile

_____ (c) impatient

14-3.　According to McCann's _____-_____ hypothesis, early achievers are at risk for early _____, likely reflecting the Type (A/B) behaviour pattern.

14-4. Which aspect of the Type A behaviour seems to be most highly related to coronary heart disorder?

Answers: 14-1. arteriosclerosis **14-2.** (a) Type B, (b) Type A, (c) Type A, (d) Type B, (e) Type A
14-3. precocity-longevity, death, B **14-4.** hostility (or anger).

15. Summarize the evidence linking emotional reactions and depression to heart disease.

15-1. Research has shown that negative emotions (can/cannot) trigger acute symptoms of heart disease.

15-2. Mental stress can trigger increases in the _____ that is thought to contribute to cardiovascular risk.

15-3. The Featured Study examined whether depression can increase _____ mortality by following participants' health and mortality over a period of four years. Participants were classified as to whether they had cardiac disease at the beginning of the study or not, and whether they developed _____ or not. Results showed that the mortality rate was (increased/decreased) for those who exhibited depression, and that this was true whether or not participants had cardiac disease when the study was initiated. This study suggests that it is most likely that depression (contributed to/was a result of) cardiac disease.

Answers: 15-1. can **15-2.** inflammation **15-3.** cardiac, depression, increased, contributed to.

16. Discuss how stress affects immune functioning.

16-1. Research has found stress to be related to numerous diseases and disorders. What appears to be a common factor that relates stress to so many disorders?

16-2. Chronic inflammation can occur in response to stress, reflecting the overproduction of proteins called _____.

Answers: 16-1. Stress appears to suppress the immune system temporarily. **16-2.** cytokines.

FACTORS MODERATING THE IMPACT OF STRESS

17. Discuss how social support moderates the impact of stress.

17-1. Social support refers to various types of aid and emotional sustenance provided by members of one's social _____. Higher levels of social support are related to physical health. Social support can even increase people's odds of _____.

17-2. Cultures can differ on the type of social support that is preferred. Asians are more likely to prefer _____ social support, whereas Americans prefer _____ social support.

Answers: 17-1. networks, survival **17-2.** implicit, explicit.

18. **Discuss how personality factors are related to stress resistance.**

18-1. What difference was found between optimists and pessimists with respect to good physical health?

18-2. The personality characteristic of _____ was found to be related to longevity in a recent study from a sample of Terman's gifted children, probably because this personality trait fosters better _____ _____.

Answers: 18-1. Optimists were more likely to enjoy good physical health. **18-2.** conscientiousness, health habits.

HEALTH-IMPAIRING BEHAVIOUR

19. **Discuss the negative impact of smoking and lack of exercise on physical health.**

19-1. Answer the following questions regarding the negative impact of smoking on physical health.

(a) How many fewer years can a 25-year-old male smoker expect to live than a 25-year-old nonsmoker?

(b) What are the two most frequent diseases that kill smokers?

(c) What appears to happen with respect to readiness to give up as smokers cycle through periods of abstinence and relapse?

19-2. Answer the following true-false questions.

_____ (a) Regular exercise appears to increase longevity.

_____ (b) Alcohol is the most damaging of all the recreational drugs.

_____ (c) Exercise can reduce chronic inflammation.

Answers: 19-1. (a) 8 years (or 8.3 years), (b) lung cancer and heart disease, (c) Readiness to give up smoking builds gradually. **19-2.** (a) true, (b) true, (c) true.

20. **Discuss the relationship between behavioural styles and AIDS.**

20-1. What two bodily fluids are most likely to transmit AIDS?

20-2. What two general groups have the highest incidence of AIDS in North America?

20-3. In the world as a whole, which form of transmission, gay and bisexual or heterosexual, is most common?

20-4. How can a person virtually guarantee that he or she will not contract AIDS?

Answers: 20-1. blood and semen **20-2.** Gay and bisexual males and intravenous drug users. **20-3.** heterosexual transmission **20-4.** Stay with only one sexual partner (known to prefer this same lifestyle), and don't use intravenous drugs.

21. Explain how health-impairing lifestyles develop.

21-1. The text lists four complementary explanations as to why health-impairing lifestyles develop. Given the hints below, list these four reasons.

(a) slowly

(b) immediate

(c) delayed

(d) "not me"

Answers: 21-1. (a) They develop slowly. (b) The pleasure they provide is immediate. (c) The health-impairing consequences are delayed. (d) The consequences are likely to happen to others (but "not me").

REACTIONS TO ILLNESS

22. Discuss individual differences in willingness to seek medical treatment.

22-1. Indicate whether the following statements regarding individual differences in willingness to seek medical treatment are true or false.

_____ (a) Delay in seeking treatment is perhaps the biggest problem here.

_____ (b) The perception of pain and illness is very subjective.

Answers: 22-1. (a) true, (b) true.

23. Describe some barriers to effective patient–provider communication and ways to overcome these problems.

23-1. Which of the following factors appears to be a barrier to effective patient–provider communication?

(a) economic realities

(d) patient evasiveness

(b) medical jargon

(e) patient passivity

(c) patient forgetfulness

23-2. What does the text recommend as the best way to improve patient–provider communication?

Answers: **23-1.** all of these factors **23-2.** Don't be a passive consumer of medical advice.

24. Discuss the extent to which people tend to adhere to medical advice.

24-1. The text lists three reasons for failure to comply with medical advice. One is that patients often fail to completely _____ treatment instructions. A second is that the treatment may prove to be quite _____. The third reason is not directly related to either instructions or treatment, but rather to the attitude toward the _____. A negative attitude makes compliance (<u>more/less</u>) likely.

Answers: **24-1.** understand, unpleasant (or aversive), physician (or doctor), less.

PUTTING IT IN PERSPECTIVE

25. Explain how this chapter highlighted two of the text's unifying themes.

25-1. The fact that the amount of stress in any given situation primarily lies in the eyes of the beholder nicely illustrates the theme that experience is _____.

25-2. The fact that stress interacts with numerous other factors that affect health illustrates the theme of multifactorial _____.

Answers: **25-1.** subjective **25-2.** causation.

APPLICATION: IMPROVING COPING AND STRESS MANAGEMENT

26. Summarize Albert Ellis's ideas about controlling one's emotions.

26-1. The main idea behind Albert Ellis's rational-emotive therapy is that stress is largely caused by _____ thinking. Therefore, by changing one's catastrophic thinking and taking a more rational approach, one can then reduce the amount of _____ being experienced.

26-2. Ellis illustrates this theory by postulating an A-B-C series of events. Describe below what is going on during each of these events.

(A) activating event:

(B) belief:

(C) consequence:

26-3. Since the emotional turmoil in the A-B-C sequence is caused by the B (Belief) sequence, effort must be directed towards changing irrational beliefs. Ellis proposed two techniques for doing this. One must first learn to _____ instances of irrational beliefs. Then one must learn to actively _____ these irrational beliefs.

Answers: 26-1. catastrophic, stress **26-2.** (A) the activating event that precedes the stress. (B) one's belief about the event. (C) the emotional consequences that result from the belief **26-3.** detect, dispute.

27. Discuss the adaptive value of humour, releasing pent-up emotions, managing hostility, and forgiving others.

27-1. What dual role does humour appear to play in easing stress from difficult situations?

27-2. Why might writing or talking about a problem with a sympathetic friend prove useful when experiencing stress?

27-3. What two common benefits were found among people who learned to manage hostility and people who practised forgiveness?

Answers: 27-1. It allows for both redefining the problem in a less threatening way and releasing tension. **27-2.** It may help to release pent-up tension. **27-3.** Both mental and physical health improved.

28. Discuss the adaptive value of relaxation and exercise.

28-1. Complete the following statements regarding the adaptive value of relaxation and exercise.

(a) A quiet environment, a mental device, a passive attitude, and a comfortable position are conditions that facilitate _____ ____ _____.

(b) Eating a balanced diet, getting adequate sleep and exercise, and staying away from overeating and harmful drugs can help to minimize _____ _____.

Answers: 28-1. (a) learning to relax, (b) physical vulnerability.

CRITICAL THINKING APPLICATION

29. Describe some important considerations in evaluating health statistics and making health decisions.

    29-1. Which kind of faulty statistical reasoning (correlation is no assurance of causation, statistical significance is not equivalent to practical significance, and failure to consider base rates) is illustrated by the following statements?

        (a) Lipitor reduces the risk of stroke by 48%.

        (b) Since heart disease and depression are correlated, heart disease must cause depression.

        (c) In a large sample population it was observed that the prevalence of hypertension was statistically significantly higher in higher sodium intake individuals. Therefore, everyone should reduce their sodium intake.

    29-2. In addition to seeking information to reduce uncertainty, what other two basic principles of quantitative reasoning does the text suggest?

    29-3. What should one do after reaching a decision and initiating action?

Answers: 29-1. (a) failure to consider base rates (i.e., Lipitor reduced stroke from a rate of 2.8% to a rate of 1.5%), (b) correlation is no assurance of causation, (c) statistical significance is not equivalent to practical significance **29-2.** Make risk-benefit assessments and list alternative courses of action. **29-3.** Continue to re-evaluate the decision (in light of treatment progress, new options, etc.).

REVIEW OF KEY TERMS

Acquired Immune Deficiency
Syndrome (AIDS)
Acute stressors

Aggression
Approach-approach conflict
Approach-avoidance conflict
Avoidance-avoidance conflict
Biopsychosocial model
Burnout
Catastrophic thinking
Catharsis
Chronic stressors

Conflict
Constructive coping
Coping

Defence mechanisms
Fight-or-flight response
Frustration
General adaptation syndrome
Health psychology
Immune response
Internet addiction
Learned helplessness

Life changes
Optimism
Post-traumatic stress disorder
(PTSD)
Pressure
Psychosomatic diseases
Rational-emotive therapy
Resilience
Social support
Stress
Type A personality
Type B personality

_____ **1.** Holds that physical illness is caused by a complex interaction of biological, psychological, and sociocultural factors.

_____ **2.** Concerned with how psychosocial forces relate to the promotion and maintenance of health, and the causation, prevention, and treatment of illness.

_____ **3.** Any circumstances that threaten or are perceived to threaten our well-being and thereby tax our coping abilities.

_____ **4.** A passive behaviour produced by exposure to unavoidable aversive events.

_____ **5.** Occurs in any situation in which the pursuit of some goal is thwarted.

_____ **6.** Occurs when two or more incompatible motivations or behavioural impulses compete for expression.

_____ **7.** Occurs when a choice must be made between two attractive goals.

_____ **8.** Occurs when a choice must be made between two unattractive goals.

_____ **9.** Occurs when a choice must be made whether to pursue a single goal that has both attractive and unattractive aspects.

_____ **10.** Any noticeable alterations in one's living circumstances that require readjustment.

_____ **11.** Expectations or demands that one should behave in a certain way.

_____ **12.** A physiological reaction to threat in which the autonomic nervous system mobilizes an organism for either attacking or fleeing an enemy.

_____ **13.** A model of the body's stress response consisting of three stages: alarm, resistance, and exhaustion.

_____ **14.** An active effort to master, reduce, or tolerate the demands created by stress.

_____ **15.** Involves any behaviour that is intended to hurt someone, either physically or verbally.

_____ **16.** Consists of spending an inordinate amount of time on the Internet and the inability to control online use.

_____ **17.** Largely unconscious reactions that protect a person from unpleasant emotions such as anxiety and guilt.

_____ **18.** Relatively healthy efforts to deal with stressful events.

_____ **19.** Involves physical, mental, and emotional exhaustion that is attributable to work-related stress.

_____ **20.** Disturbed behaviour that emerges after a major stressful event is over.

_____ **21.** A behaviour pattern marked by competitive, aggressive, impatient, hostile behaviour.

_____ **22.** A behaviour pattern marked by relaxed, patient, easy-going, amicable behaviour.

_____ **23.** The body's defensive reaction to invasion by bacteria, viral agents, or other foreign substances.

_____ **24.** Various types of aid and succour provided by members of one's social network.

_____ **25.** A general tendency to expect good outcomes.

_____ **26.** An approach to therapy that focuses on altering clients' patterns of irrational thinking to reduce maladaptive emotions and behaviour.

_____ **27.** The release of emotional tension.

_____ **28.** Unrealistic and pessimistic appraisal of stress that exaggerates the magnitude of a problem.

_____ **29.** Physical ailments caused, in part, by psychological factors, especially emotional distress.

_____ **30.** A disorder in which the immune system is gradually weakened and eventually disabled by the human immunodeficiency virus (HIV).

_____ **31.** Threatening events that have a relatively long duration and no readily apparent time limit.

_____ **32.** Threatening events that have a relatively short duration and a clear endpoint.

_____ **33.** Successful adaptation to significant stress and trauma.

Answers: 1. biopsychosocial model **2.** health psychology **3.** stress **4.** learned helplessness **5.** frustration **6.** conflict **7.** approach-approach conflict **8.** avoidance-avoidance conflict **9.** approach-avoidance conflict **10.** life changes **11.** pressure **12.** fight-or-flight response **13.** general adaptation syndrome **14.** coping **15.** aggression **16.** Internet addiction **17.** defence mechanisms **18.** constructive coping **19.** burnout **20.** post-traumatic stress disorder **21.** Type A pattern **22.** Type B pattern **23.** immune response **24.** social support **25.** optimism **26.** rational-emotive therapy **27.** catharsis **28.** catastrophic thinking **29.** psychosomatic diseases **30.** Acquired Immune Deficiency Syndrome (AIDS) **31.** chronic stressors **32.** acute stressors **33.** resilience.

REVIEW OF KEY PEOPLE

Walter Cannon
Robin DiMatteo
Albert Ellis
Meyer Friedman

Thomas Holmes and Richard Rahe
Janice Kiecolt-Glaser
Richard Lazarus
Neal Miller

Hans Selye
Shelley Taylor

_____ 1. Observed that minor hassles were more closely related to mental health than were major stressful events.

_____ 2. Noted for his extensive investigations of the three types of conflict.

_____ 3. These researchers developed the Social Readjustment Rating Scale.

_____ 4. One of the first theorists to describe the "fight-or-flight" response.

_____ 5. Coined the word _stress_ and described the General Adaptation Syndrome.

_____ 6. Found a connection between coronary risk and Type A behaviour.

_____ 7. The developer of Rational-Emotive Therapy.

_____ 8. Researched the notion that "positive illusions" promote well-being.

_____ 9. A leading expert on patient behaviour.

_____ 10. Has conducted research linking stress to temporary suppression of the immune system.

Answers: 1. Lazarus **2.** Miller **3.** Holmes and Rahe **4.** Cannon **5.** Selye **6.** Friedman **7.** Ellis **8.** Taylor **9.** DiMatteo **10.** Kiecolt-Glaser.

SELF-QUIZ

1. Which of the following statements about stress is NOT correct?
   a. Stress is a subjective experience.
   b. The effects of stress are cumulative.
   c. Minor hassles may prove more stressful than major ones.
   d. One should seek to avoid all stress.

2. You are invited to dinner at a nice restaurant on the final night of a TV miniseries that you've been watching. What situation are you confronted with?
   a. pressure
   b. frustration
   c. approach-avoidance conflict
   d. approach-approach conflict

3. What kind of stress do most students experience during the week of final exams?
   a. pressure
   b. change
   c. frustration
   d. conflict

4. What are high scores on the Social Readjustment Rating Scale correlated with?
   a. psychological disturbances and type A behaviour patterns
   b. psychological disturbances and physical illness
   c. psychological disturbances and pessimistic attitudes
   d. psychological disturbances and overeating

5. According to optimal-arousal theories, which of the following situations are least affected by a high optimal-arousal level?
   a. taking a psychology exam
   b. typing a term paper
   c. buttoning a shirt
   d. learning to drive a car

6. What does the General Adaptation Syndrome show?
   a. that the body gradually adapts to a particular stress
   b. that the body gradually adapts to all forms of stress
   c. that the body may gradually weaken and die from continued stress
   d. that the body can react rapidly to all forms of stress

7. Which of the following organs is involved in both of the body's two major stress pathways?
   a. adrenal gland
   b. the master gland
   c. pituitary gland
   d. pineal gland

8. What is aggression frequently triggered by?
   a. helplessness
   b. frustration
   c. loneliness
   d. change

9. What behavioural responses to stress may result in Internet addiction?
   a. defensive coping
   b. self-indulgence
   c. positive illusions
   d. giving up

10. Which of the following situations are mainly caused by rape and seeing someone die?
    a. post-traumatic stress disorder
    b. burnout
    c. learned helplessness
    d. coronary heart disorder

11. Which of the following has the same relationship as smoking to lung cancer?
    a. Type A behaviour to coronary disease
    b. Type A behaviour to AIDS
    c. Type A behaviour to defensive coping
    d. Type A behaviour to mental disorders

12. What may be one of the key links between stress and physical illness?
    a. The body's response to stress increases the optimal-arousal level.
    b. The body's response to stress suppresses the immune system.
    c. The body's response to stress decreases the optimal-arousal level.
    d. The body's response to stress suppresses the adrenal gland.

13. How do health-impairing life styles appear to develop?
    a. rapidly
    b. unconsciously
    c. slowly
    d. as a defence against stress

14. What is a major idea behind Rational-Emotive Therapy?
    a. Stress is caused by conflict.
    b. Stress is caused by frustration.
    c. Stress is caused by pressure.
    d. Stress is caused by catastrophic thinking.

15. When someone analyzes the possible gains and losses before undertaking a health-treatment program, what is exemplified?
    a. seeking information to reduce uncertainty
    b. listing alternative courses of action
    c. making a risk-benefit analysis
    d. analyzing base rates

16. What is the name for threatening events that have a short duration and a clear endpoint?
    a. chronic stressors
    b. acute stressors
    c. brief stressors
    d. hassles

17. Which of the follow correctly matches a particular culture with the type of social support preferred in that culture?
    a. European – illicit social support
    b. Asian – explicit social support
    c. American – explicit social support
    d. Asian – deliberate social support

Answers: 1. d **2.** d **3.** a **4.** b **5.** c **6.** c **7.** a **8.** b **9.** b **10.** a **11.** a **12.** b **13.** c **14.** d **15.** c **16.** b **17.** c.

Chapter Fourteen
PSYCHOLOGICAL DISORDERS

REVIEW OF KEY IDEAS

ABNORMAL BEHAVIOUR: MYTHS, REALITIES, AND CONTROVERSIES

1. Describe the medical model of abnormal behaviour.

1-1. A model is a metaphor or theory that is useful in describing some phenomenon. For example, the computer is frequently used as a model of thinking. The *medical model* uses physical illness as a model of psychological disorders. Under the medical model, maladaptive behaviour is referred to as mental _____.

1-2. The term *mental illness* is so familiar to all of us that we rarely think about the meaning of the concept and whether or not the analogy with disease is a good one. One drawback to the medical model is that medical diagnoses can carry a social _____ that is difficult to shake.

1-3. Among the medical model's critics, Thomas Szasz asserts that words such as *sickness*, *illness*, and *disease* are correctly used only in reference to the _____, and that it is more appropriate to view abnormal behaviour as a deviation from accepted social _____ than as an illness.

1-4. The text takes an intermediate position. While there are problems with the medical model, it may be of value as long as one understands that it is just a(n) _____ and not a true explanation.

1-5. The medical concepts of *diagnosis, etiology,* and *prognosis* have proven valuable in the study of abnormality. For each of the following definitions, identify the appropriate term (diagnosis, etiology, or prognosis):

_____ the apparent causation and developmental history of an illness

_____ a forecast about the probable course of an illness

_____ distinguishing one illness from another

Answers: 1-1. illness (or disease, sickness) **1-2.** stigma **1-3.** body, norms (or behaviour, standards) **1-4.** analogy (or model) **1-5.** etiology, prognosis, diagnosis.

2. Explain the most commonly used criteria of abnormality.

2-1. What does abnormal mean? The three criteria most frequently used are *deviance*, *maladaptive behaviour*, and *personal distress*.

(a) _____ : Does not *conform* to cultural norms or standards.

(b) _____ : Behaviour that *interferes with* the individual's social or occupational functioning.

(c) _____ : Intense *discomfort* produced by depression or anxiety.

2-2. Following are three statements that describe a person with a particular type of disorder. Which criterion of abnormal behaviour is illustrated by each statement? Place the letters from the list above in the appropriate blanks below.

_____ Ralph washes his hands several dozen times a day. His handwashing interferes with his work and prevents him from establishing normal friendships.

_____ Even if Ralph's handwashing compulsion did not interfere with his work and social life, his behaviour still would be considered strange. That is, most people do not do what he does.

_____ It is also the case that Ralph's skin is very raw, and he becomes extremely anxious when he does not have immediate access to a sink.

2-3. In some cultures, hearing voices or speaking with gods may be valued. In our culture, however, such behaviour is likely to be considered abnormal. While the major categories of disorder may transcend culture, our assessments of abnormality are nonetheless value judgments which are strongly influenced by our _____. Thus, one of the problems involved in defining abnormality is that there are no criteria for psychological disorders that are entirely _____-free.

Answers: 2-1. (a) deviance, (b) maladaptive behaviour, (c) personal distress **2-2.** b, a, c **2-3.** culture (or society), value (or culture).

3. List three stereotypes of people with psychological disorders.

3-1. In the space below, list three stereotypes of people with psychological disorders.

(a) The disorders are _____.

(b) People with the disorders are _____ and dangerous.

(c) People with the disorders behave in a bizarre manner and are very _____ from normal people.

Answers: 3-1. (a) incurable, (b) violent, (c) different.

4. Describe Rosenhan's study of mental hospital admissions.

4-1. What type of people did Rosenhan seek to have admitted to mental hospitals?

4-2. Once they were admitted, did the pseudopatients continue to complain of hearing voices, or did they behave normally?

4-3. What proportion of the pseudopatients were admitted to the hospital?

4-4. Indicate *true* of *false* for each of the following statements.

_____ (a) Once the patients no longer claimed to hear voices, the professional staff rapidly recognized that they were not abnormal.

_____ (b) Most of the pseudopatients were dismissed within a couple of days.

_____ (c) The diagnosis for most of the pseudopatients was that they suffered from a relatively mild form of mental disorder.

4-5. What is the major implication to be drawn from Rosenhan's study?

Answers: 4-1. normal individuals **4-2.** behaved normally **4-3.** all of them (Eight people sought admission to mental hospitals in five states, and all of them were admitted.) **4-4.** (a) false, (b) false (The shortest stay was 7 days, the longest 52 days, and the average 19 days.) (c) false (Most were diagnosed with schizophrenia, a severe form of mental illness.) **4-5.** The major implication is that it is difficult, even for mental health professionals, to distinguish normal from abnormal behaviour. (The study may also be interpreted to mean that there is a bias toward seeing abnormality where it may not exist or that abnormality is easily feigned.)

5. List the five diagnostic axes of DSM-IV.

5-1. Below are descriptions of the five axes of the DSM-IV classification system. Label each with the correct axis number (I through V).

_____ Notes concerning the severity of stress experienced by the individual in the past year

_____ Estimates of the individual's current level of adaptive functioning (social and occupational)

_____ Diagnosis of most types of mental disorders

_____ Diagnosis of long-running personality disorders or mental retardation

_____ Listing of physical disorders

Answers: 5-1. IV, V, I, II, III.

6. Discuss estimates of the prevalence of psychological disorders.

6-1. Epidemiological studies assess the _____ of various disorders. Prevalence is the _____ of people who suffer from a disorder across a specific period of time. For our purposes, *lifetime* prevalence is most interesting.

6-2. What percentage of people will exhibit a mental disorder at some point during their lifetime? If drug-related disorders are included, estimates range from one-third to, more recently, _____%. The estimates are complicated by several factors, but recent studies do suggest that there (<u>has been</u>/has not been) a genuine increase in lifetime prevalence.

6-3. Figure 14.5 in the text shows one-year prevalence information for mood, anxiety, and substance disorders in Canada. Women had higher rates _____ and _____ disorders compared to men, whereas men had higher rates of _____ disorders compared to women.

Answers: **6-1.** prevalence, percentage (or proportion) **6-2.** 51, has been **6-3.** mood, anxiety, substance dependence.

ANXIETY DISORDERS

7. List five types of anxiety disorders and describe the symptoms associated with each.

7-1. List the names of the five anxiety syndromes in the space below. As hints, the initial letters of some key words are listed at the left.

GAD: _____

PTSD: _____

PhD: _____

OCD: _____

PDA: _____ and _____

7-2. Match the anxiety disorders with the symptoms that follow by placing the appropriate letters (from the previous question) in the blanks.

(a) _____ Sudden, unexpected, and paralyzing attacks of anxiety

(b) _____ Not tied to a specific object or event

(c) _____ Senseless, repetitive rituals

(d) _____ Brooding over decisions

(e) _____ Fear of specific objects or situations

(f) _____ Persistent intrusion of distressing and unwanted thoughts

(g) _____ Associated with victims of violent crimes or disasters

(h) _____ Frequently includes fear of going out in public

(i) _____ Nightmares, flashbacks, and emotional numbing

(j) _____ Free-floating anxiety

Answers: **7-1.** generalized anxiety disorder, post-traumatic stress disorder, phobic disorder, obsessive-compulsive disorder, panic disorder, agoraphobia **7-2.** (a) PDA (in this example, panic attacks), (b) GAD, (c) OCD, (d) GAD, (e) PhD, (f) OCD, (g) PTSD, (h) PDA (in this case, agoraphobia), (i) PTSD, (j) GAD.

8. Discuss the contribution of biological and cognitive factors, conditioning, and stress to the etiology of anxiety disorders.

8-1. Several types of studies suggest that there are inherited predispositions to anxiety disorders. For example, twin studies find higher concordance rates for anxiety among _____ twins than _____ twins. The _____ temperament may be a risk factor for the development of anxiety disorders.

8-2. Other biological evidence implicates disturbances at synapses using GABA for some types of anxiety disorders and of serotonin for panic attacks and obsessive-compulsive disorder. Thus, the body chemicals known as _____ appear to play an important role in anxiety.

8-3. Conditioning, or learning, clearly plays a role as well. For example, if an individual is bitten by a dog, he or she may develop a fear of dogs through the process of _____ conditioning. The individual may then avoid dogs in the future, a response maintained by _____ conditioning.

8-4. People are more likely to be afraid of snakes than of hot irons. Using Seligman's notion of preparedness, explain why.

8-5. Two types of anecdotal evidence do not support the conditioning point of view. For example, people with phobias (<u>always can/frequently cannot</u>) recall a traumatic incident, and people who have experienced extreme traumas (<u>always/frequently do not</u>) develop phobias.

8-6. As discussed in Chapter 6, the conditioning models are being extended to include a larger role for cognitive factors. For example, children probably acquire fears by _____ the behaviour of anxious parents.

8-7. In addition, cognitive theorists indicate that certain *thinking styles* contribute to anxiety. For example, as indicated in your text, the sentence "The doctor examined little Emma's growth" could refer either to height or to a tumour. People who are high in anxiety will tend to perceive the (<u>tumour/height</u>) interpretation. People's readiness to perceive threat, in other words, appears to be related to their tendency to experience _____ .

8-8. Finally, *stress* is related to anxiety disorders. Studies described in your text indicate that stress is related both to _____ disorder and to the development of social _____.

Answers: **8-1.** identical, fraternal, inhibited **8-2.** neurotransmitters **8-3.** classical, operant
8-4. Preparedness is Seligman's notion that human beings have evolved to be more prepared or more ready to be conditioned to some stimuli than to others. We have evolved to be more afraid of snakes than of hot irons, the latter having appeared only relatively recently in our evolutionary history. (As a whole, research has provided only modest support for the idea of preparedness in acquisition of phobias.) **8-5.** frequently cannot, frequently do not **8-6.** observing **8-7.** tumour, anxiety **8-8.** panic, phobia.

DISSOCIATIVE DISORDERS

9. Describe three dissociative disorders, and discuss their etiology.

9-1. The three dissociative disorders involve memory and identity. Two of the disorders involve fairly massive amounts of forgetting, dissociative _____ and dissociative _____.

9-2. People who have been in a serious accident frequently can't remember the accident or events surrounding the accident. This type of memory loss, which involves specific traumatic events, is known as dissociative _____.

9-3. An even greater memory loss, in which people lose their memories for their entire lives along with their sense of identity, is termed dissociative _____.

9-4. You may have seen media characterizations of individuals who can't remember who they are—what their names are, where they live, who their family is, and so on. While popularly referred to as amnesia, this type of dissociative disorder is more correctly called dissociative _____.

9-5. A few years ago, there was a spate of appearances on talk shows by guests who claimed to have more than one identity or personality. This disorder is still widely known as _____-_____ disorder (MPD), but the formal name in the DSM-IV is _____ _____ disorder (DID). The disorder is also often (<u>correctly/mistakenly</u>) called schizophrenia.

9-6. What causes dissociative disorders? Dissociative amnesia and dissociative fugue are related to excessive _____, but little else is known about why these extreme reactions occur in a tiny minority of people.

9-7. With regard to multiple-personality disorder, the diagnosis is controversial. Although many clinicians believe that the disorder is authentic, Spanos argues that it is the product of media attention and the misguided probings of a small minority of psychotherapists. In other words, Spanos believes that MPD (<u>is/is not</u>) a genuine disorder.

9-8. While the majority of people with multiple-personality disorder report having been emotionally and sexually _____ in childhood, little is known about the causes of this controversial diagnosis. In fact, in a recent survey of American psychiatrists, only _____ of those polled believed that there was enough scientific evidence to warrant including DID as a valid diagnostic category.

Answers: 9-1. amnesia, fugue **9-2.** amnesia **9-3.** fugue **9-4.** fugue **9-5.** multiple-personality, dissociative identity, mistakenly **9-6.** stress **9-7.** is not **9-8.** abused, one-quarter.

MOOD DISORDERS

10. Describe the two major mood disorders.

10-1. While the terms *manic* and *depressive* describe mood, they refer to a number of other characteristics as well, listed below. With one or two words for each characteristic, describe the manic and depressive episodes. (Before you make the lists, review Table 14.1 and the sections on depressive and bipolar mood disorders.)

	Manic	*Depressive*
mood:	_____	_____
sleep:	_____	_____
activity:	_____	_____
speech:	_____	_____
sex drive:	_____	_____

10-2. Be sure to note that mania and depression are not the names of the two affective disorders. What is the name of the disorder accompanied only by depression? _____

By both manic and depressive states? _____

10-3. The DSM refers to persistent but relatively mild symptoms of depressive disorder as _____ disorder, and to persistent but mild symptoms of bipolar disorder as _____ disorder.

10-4. Prevalence data indicate that women are about _____ as likely as men to suffer from depression. According to Moretti, women may be more sensitive to gaps between beliefs about themselves and a(n) _____ view of themselves held by others. According to Nolen-Hoeksema, this gender difference in depression prevalence occurs for several reasons, including women's greater likelihood of experiencing _____ abuse and their tendency to (ignore/ruminate about) setbacks and problems.

Answers: **10-1.** mood: euphoric (elated, extremely happy, etc.) vs. depressed (blue, extremely sad); sleep: goes without or doesn't want to vs. can't (insomnia); activity: very active vs. sluggish, slow, inactive; speech: very fast vs. very slow; sex drive: increased vs. decreased **10-2.** unipolar disorder (major depressive disorder), bipolar disorder **10-3.** dysthymic, cyclothymic **10-4.** twice, idealized, sexual, ruminate about.

11. Describe two additional subcategories of mood disorders.

11-1. _____ disorder (SAD) is a subtype that follows a seasonal pattern. Perhaps ___% of depressed Canadians experience the SAD subtype. Onset of SAD may be related to _____ production and circadian rhythms. A treatment for SAD is _____.

11-2. Another subtype of mood disorder is _____ depression, a type of depression that follows _____. Prevalence estimates suggest that _____ to _____% of women who have given birth may experience postpartum depression. Risk factors include previous episodes of depression, _____, and adjustment problems.

Answers: 11-1. Seasonal affective, 11, melatonin, phototherapy **11-2.** postpartum, childbirth, 10, 20, stress.

12. **Discuss what is known about suicide and mood disorders.**

12-1. Official statistics may underestimate the true rate of suicide, as many are disguised as _____. And attempts outnumber completed suicides by a ratio of as much as _____ to 1. Women attempt suicide (more/less) often than men, but men complete _____ times as many suicides as women.

12-2. About _____% of people who complete suicide have a psychological disorder, most commonly a _____ disorder.

Answers: 12-1. accidents, 20, more, four **12-2.** 90, mood.

13. **Explain how genetic, neurochemical, and hormonal factors may be related to the development of mood disorders.**

13-1. Twin studies implicate genetic factors in the development of mood disorders. In a sentence, summarize the results of these studies.

13-2. While the exact mechanism is not known, correlations have been found between mood disorders and abnormal levels of _____ in the brain, including norepinephrine and serotonin.

13-3. Depression may also involve overactivity of the hypothalamic-_____-adrenocortical (HPA) axis, leading to elevated levels of _____, a key stress hormone.

Answers: 13-1. For mood disorders, the concordance rate for identical twins is much higher than that for fraternal twins (about 65% for the former compared to 15% for the latter). **13-2.** neurotransmitters (or neurochemicals) **13-3.** pituitary, cortisol.

14. **Explain how dispositional factors, cognitive factors, interpersonal factors, and stress may be related to the development of mood disorders.**

14-1. _____, or the setting of excessively high standards, is a dispositional factor associated with depression. According to Beck, two other personality dispositions are related to depression. _____ individuals are highly invested in their interpersonal relationships, whereas _____ individuals are oriented toward their own achievement and independence. Finally, Blatt argues that _____ and self-_____ are two important dispositional variables associated with depression. Both Beck and Blatt argue that a congruency between a type of stressful event experienced and the type of specific personality disposition may promote depression. For example, failure on an exam for a person who is highly _____ may promote depression.

14-2. Beck also emphasized cognitive factors in depression, including the negative _____ _____, reflecting depressed people's tendency to view themselves, their world, and their future in a negative fashion. Beck also argued that _____ schemas may lead depressed people to selectively attend to negative information about the self.

14-3. Seligman's model of depression is referred to as the _____ _____ model. While he originally based his theory of depression on animal research examining exposure to unavoidable aversive stimuli, he has more recently emphasized (cognitive/behavioural) factors. People with a _____ explanatory style are particularly prone to depression. For example, people who attribute obstacles to (situational factors/personal flaws) are more likely to experience depression.

14-4. Building on learned helplessness theory, _____ theory maintains that a pessimistic explanatory style is just one of several factors—stress and low self-esteem are others—that contribute to depression. For example, people who repetitively focus or _____ about their depression are more likely to remain depressed.

14-5. With regard to interpersonal factors, depressed people tend to lack _____ skills. How does this characteristic affect the ability to obtain reinforcers?

14-6. Why do we tend to reject depressed people?

14-7. What is the relationship between stress and the onset of mood disorders?

Answers: 14-1. perfectionism, Sociotropic, autonomous, dependency, criticism, autonomous **14-2.** cognitive triad, depressive **14-3.** learned helplessness, cognitive, pessimistic (or negative), personal flaws **14-4.** hopelessness, ruminate **14-5.** social (or interpersonal). Lack of social skills makes it difficult to obtain certain reinforcers, such as good friends and desirable jobs. **14-6.** Because they are not pleasant to be around. Depressed people complain a lot, are irritable, and tend to pass their mood along to others. **14-7.** There is a moderately strong link between stress and the onset of mood disorders.

15. Describe the association between concussion and depression.

15-1. Depression is a common feature of _____-_____ syndrome. Depression occurs more often among _____ _____ patients than in the general population. This may reflect reduced activation in certain areas of the brain, including prefrontal cortex areas and medial frontal and temporal regions.

Answers: **15-1.** post-concussion, head injury.

16. Describe the general characteristics (symptoms) of schizophrenia.

16-1. Before we review the different types of schizophrenia, consider some general characteristics of the schizophrenic disorders, as follows.

(a) Delusions and irrational thought: Delusions are false (<u>beliefs/perceptions</u>) (e.g., the idea that one is a world-famous political figure who is being pursued by terrorists, when this is not in fact true).

(b) Deterioration of adaptive behaviour: The deterioration usually involves social relationships, work, and neglect of personal _____.

(c) Hallucinations: Hallucinations are _____ that occur in the absence of a real stimulus. The most common hallucinations are (<u>auditory/visual</u>).

(d) Disturbed emotion: Emotional responsiveness may be disturbed in a variety of ways. The person may have little or no responsiveness, referred to as _____ affect, or he or she may show _____ emotional responses, such as laughing at news of a tragic death.

Answers: 16-1. (a) beliefs, (b) hygiene (or cleanliness), (c) sensory perceptions (or perceptions, sensory experiences, perceptual distortions), auditory, (d) flat (or flattened, blunted), inappropriate (or bizarre).

17. Describe two classification systems for schizophrenic subtypes, and discuss the course of schizophrenia.

17-1. Write the names of the four recognized subcategories of schizophrenia next to the descriptions that follow.

(a) _____ type: Particularly severe deterioration, incoherence, complete social withdrawal, aimless babbling and giggling, delusions centering on bodily functions.

(b) _____ type: Muscular rigidity and stupor at one extreme or random motor activity, hyperactivity, and incoherence at the other; now quite rare.

(c) _____ type: Delusions of persecution and grandeur.

(d) _____ type: Clearly schizophrenic but doesn't fit other three categories.

17-2. Several critics have asserted that there are no meaningful differences among the categories listed above and have proposed an alternative classification system. Nancy Andreasen and others have described a classification system consisting of only two categories, one that consists of _____ symptoms and the other of _____ symptoms.

17-3. In Andreasen's system, "positive" and "negative" do not mean pleasant and unpleasant. Positive symptoms *add* something to behaviour (like chaotic speech), and negative symptoms *subtract* something (like social withdrawal). Indicate which of the following are positive and which negative, by placing a P or an N in the appropriate blanks.

_____ flattened emotions

_____ hallucinations

_____ bizarre behaviour

_____ social withdrawal

_____ apathy

_____ nonstop babbling

_____ doesn't speak

17-4. Theorists hoped that classification of schizophrenia into positive and negative symptoms would provide more meaningful categories in terms of etiology and prognosis. Some differentiation between the two types of symptoms has been found; for example, *positive* symptoms seem to be associated with (better/worse) adjustment prior to the onset of schizophrenia and a (better/worse) prognosis. All in all, however, this system (has/has not) produced a classification that can replace the traditional subtypes.

17-5. When does schizophrenia tend to emerge?

17-6. Mark the following T (true) or F (false).

_____ Schizophrenia may have either a sudden or gradual onset.

_____ A person with schizophrenia can never truly recover from the disorder.

_____ With high quality care, about half of people with schizophrenia experience a significant degree of recovery.

_____ Males tend to have an earlier onset of schizophrenia than females.

_____ Males tend to have more hospitalizations and higher relapse rates than females.

Answers: 17-1. (a) disorganized, (b) catatonic, (c) paranoid, (d) undifferentiated **17-2.** positive, negative **17-3.** N, P, P, N, N, P, N **17-4.** better, better, has not **17-5.** generally during adolescence and early adulthood **17-6.** T, F, T, T, T.

18. Explain how genetic vulnerability, neurochemical factors, and structural abnormalities in the brain may contribute to the etiology of schizophrenia.

18-1. As with mood disorders, twin studies implicate genetic factors in the development of schizophrenia. In a sentence, summarize the general results of these studies.

18-2. As with mood disorders, neurotransmitter substances in the brain are implicated in the etiology of schizophrenia. Although the evidence is somewhat clouded, _____ is thought to be involved. Recent research has also examined neural circuits that involve the neurotransmitter _____. And, a link has emerged between _____ use in adolescence and schizophrenia. It is thought that the key ingredient in marijuana (THC) may amplify neurotransmitter activity in _____ circuits.

18-3. In addition to possible neurochemical factors, certain differences in brain structure may be associated with schizophrenia. One of these differences involves enlarged brain _____, which are hollow, fluid-filled cavities in the brain. It is impossible to know at this point whether this brain abnormality is a cause of schizophrenia or a(n) _____.

18-4. Recent brain-imaging studies have also uncovered structural abnormalities, including reductions in both _____ and _____ matter. These findings suggest that disruptions in the brain's neural _____ may be involved in schizophrenia.

Answers: 18-1. For schizophrenia, the concordance rate is higher for identical than for fraternal twins. (The actual concordance rates have been found to be about 48% for identical and 17% for fraternal twins. For comparison, the respective percentages found for mood disorders were about 67% and 15%.) **18-2.** dopamine (thought to be a factor because most drugs useful in treating schizophrenia decrease dopamine activity in the brain), glutamate, marijuana (or cannabis), dopamine **18-3.** ventricles, effect (or result, consequence) **18-4.** grey, white, connectivity.

19. **Summarize evidence on how neurodevelopmental processes, family dynamics, and stress may be related to the development of schizophrenia.**

19-1. The _____ hypothesis of schizophrenia maintains that schizophrenia is caused, in part, by early neurological damage that occurs either prenatally or during the birth process.

19-2. Among the causes of neurological damage are _____ infections; _____, which may occur, for example, during famine; severe levels of maternal _____; and complications that occur during _____.

19-3. Expressed emotion refers to the extent to which a patient's relatives are overly critical or protective or are in other ways overly emotionally involved with the patient. Patients returning to families that are high in expressed emotion have a relapse rate that is much (<u>higher</u>/lower) than that of families low in expressed emotion.

19-4. What role does stress play in the etiology of schizophrenia? Stress is a fact of life, and it is obvious that not everyone who experiences stress develops schizophrenia. Current thinking is that stress may be a precipitating factor for people who are biologically, or for other reasons, already _____ to schizophrenia.

Answers: 19-1. neurodevelopmental **19-2.** viral (or flu), malnutrition (or starvation), stress, delivery (or birth, the birth process) **19-3.** higher **19-4.** vulnerable (or predisposed).

PERSONALITY DISORDERS

20. **Discuss the nature of personality disorders, and describe the three broad clusters of such disorders.**

20-1. The personality disorders, recorded on Axis II, are frequently (<u>less</u>/more) severe versions of disorders on Axis I. These disorders consist of relatively extreme and (<u>flexible/inflexible</u>) sets of personality traits that cause subjective distress or impaired functioning.

20-2. DSM-IV lists ten disorders, classified into three clusters, as follows:

(a) _____-fearful cluster

(b) _____-eccentric cluster

(c) _____-impulsive cluster

20-3. Match the clusters listed in the previous question with the following descriptions by placing the appropriate letters in the blanks.

_____ Distrustful, aloof, unable to connect emotionally with others

_____ Maladaptive efforts to control fear of social rejection

_____ Overly dramatic or impulsive

20-4. A major problem with the classification of personality disorders is that there is an enormous overlap between the ten _____ disorders on Axis II and the disorders listed on Axis I. There is also considerable _____ among the personality disorders themselves.

20-5. For example, one study found that the majority of patients diagnosed with a histrionic personality disorder (<u>also/did not</u>) fit the descriptions of one or more other personality disorders. This blurring of the lines makes diagnosis difficult, and some have questioned the wisdom of separating the two axes.

20-6. In hopes of remedying these problems, some theorists have suggested that rather than using nonoverlapping categories, personality disorders should be described in terms of continuous scores on a set of personality _____. While this approach has many advocates, psychologists are not in agreement about which personality dimensions to use or even whether or not this approach has clinical utility.

Answers: 20-1. less, inflexible **20-2.** anxious, odd, dramatic **20-3.** b, a, c **20-4.** personality, overlap **20-5.** also **20-6.** dimensions (or factors, traits).

21. Describe the antisocial personality disorder, and discuss its etiology.

21-1. The *antisocial* personality disorder is more extensively researched than are the other personality disorders and is described in more detail in your text. Check the concepts from the following list that are likely to correctly describe this disorder.

_____ sexually promiscuous   _____ genuinely affectionate

_____ manipulative   _____ impulsive

_____ feels guilty   _____ lacks an adequate conscience

_____ much more likely to occur in _____ may appear charming
      males than females

_____ may be a con-artist, thug, or unprincipled business executive

21-2. A term often used interchangeably with antisocial personality disorder is _____.
Canadian psychologist Robert Hare devised a measure of psychopathy called the

_____ _____-_____.

21-3. What types of studies support the idea that biological factors are involved in the etiology of
the antisocial personality?

21-4. What environmental factors seem to be related to development of an antisocial personality?

Answers: 21-1. All the terms describe the antisocial personality except for _feels guilty_ and _genuinely affectionate_. **21-2.** psychopathy, Psychopathy Checklist-Revised **21-3.** twin and adoption studies (There also has been mixed support for Eysenck's idea that antisocial personalities are chronically lower in autonomic arousal and therefore less likely to develop conditioned inhibitions.) **21-4.** Studies suggest that erratic or ineffective parental discipline, abuse, or neglect may be involved. Since one or both parents may also exhibit antisocial characteristics, observational learning may also be a factor.

DISORDERS OF CHILDHOOD

22. Describe autism in terms of its symptoms and treatment.

22-1. Autism is classified as a _____ developmental disorder. It has three main
symptoms: impairment in social _____ (e.g., autistic aloneness); impairment in
_____ (e.g., echolalia); and repetitive, _____ behaviour (e.g., rocking,
spinning, or showing keen special interests).

22-2. Treatment options for autism usually include early and extensive interventions to build up
adaptive behaviours, based on early research by _____.

Answers: 22-1. pervasive, interaction, communication, stereotypical **22-2.** Lovaas.

PSYCHOLOGICAL DISORDERS AND THE LAW

23. Explain the legal concept of insanity.

23-1. _____ is an important legal concept because criminal acts must be _____. At times, those with a mental disorder may lack _____.

23-2. Building upon the earlier M'Naghten rule, which stated that insanity exists when a mental disorder makes a person unable to distinguish _____ from _____, Canadian law currently allows a designation of "not _____ _____ on account of mental disorder." Also, an individual unable to participate in his or her own defence because of a psychological disorder may be found "_____ to stand trial." A defence that a defendant is not guilty because he or she was not in control of his or her behaviour for reasons other than mental disorder is referred to as _____. Such reasons could include sleepwalking or a physical blow.

Answers: 23-1. Insanity, intentional, intent **23-2.** right, wrong, criminally responsible, unfit, automatism.

CULTURE AND PATHOLOGY

24. Discuss the evidence on culture and pathology.

24-1. Your text divides viewpoints about culture and pathology into *relativists* and *panculturalists*. The _____ believe that there are basic standards of mental health that are *universal* across cultures. The _____ believe that psychological disorders *vary as a function of culture*.

24-2. Some data support the pancultural view. For example, most investigators agree that the three most serious categories of disorder, listed below, are universal.

_____

_____

_____

24-3. On the other hand, in some cultures, hypochondria, somatization, generalized anxiety disorder, and some of the other (milder/more severe) disturbances are not considered full-fledged disorders.

24-4. In addition, some disorders exist in some cultures and not in others. For example, the obsessive fear about one's penis withdrawing into one's abdomen is found only among Chinese males in Malaya, and, until recently, _____ nervosa was found only in affluent Western societies.

24-5. In summary, are psychological disorders universal, or do they vary across cultures?

a. There are some universal standards of normality and abnormality.

b. There are some disorders that are specific to particular cultures.

c. Both of the above: some aspects of psychopathology are universal; some vary as a function of culture.

PUTTING IT IN PERSPECTIVE

25. **Explain how this chapter highlighted four of the text's organizing themes.**

   25-1.   Below are examples of the highlighted themes. Indicate which theme fits each example by writing the appropriate abbreviations in the blanks: MC for multifactorial causation, HE for the interplay of heredity and environment, SH for sociohistorical context, and C for the influence of culture.

   (a) Mood and schizophrenic disorders will occur if one has a genetic vulnerability to the disorder *and* if one experiences a considerable amount of stress. _____

   (b) Psychological disorders are caused by neurochemical factors, brain abnormalities, styles of child rearing, life stress, and so on. _____

   (c) Anorexia nervosa occurs almost exclusively in affluent Western societies. _____

   (d) Decades ago, homosexuality was classified as a disorder; in recent DSMs it is not. _____ and _____

   Answers: **25-1.** (a) HE, (b) MC, (c) C, (d) SH, C.

PERSONAL APPLICATION * UNDERSTANDING EATING DISORDERS

26. **Describe the symptoms and medical complications of anorexia nervosa, bulimia nervosa, and binge eating disorder.**

   26-1.   What are the names of the two major categories of eating disorder? _____ _____ and _____ _____

   26-2.   The most obvious feature of anorexia nervosa is the drastic weight loss that accompanies the disorder. Other characteristics include an intense _____ of gaining weight, a disturbed _____ _____ (they think they are fat, no matter how emaciated they become), and (struggling/refusal) to maintain normal weight.

   26-3.   There are two major subtypes of anorexia nervosa. The *restricting type* is characterized by _____, or severely limiting, food eaten; the *binge-eating/purging type* is characterized by bingeing and then _____ (by vomiting, using laxatives and diuretics, and excessive exercise).

   26-4.   The weight loss that accompanies anorexia nervosa is substantial, typically 25% to 30% below normal weight. A critical diagnostic criterion for anorexia nervosa in women is amenorrhea, the loss of the _____ cycle.

   26-5.   There are other consequences as well, including serious gastrointestinal difficulties, heart and circulatory problems, and osteoporosis, all of which may lead to death in approximately _____% of cases. Anorexia nervosa patients (usually/rarely) seek treatment on their own.

26-6. Bulimia nervosa shares many of the characteristics of the binge-eating/purging type of anorexia. Its main differentiating feature is the fact that people with bulimia maintain a (relatively normal/drastically decreased) body weight. They are also somewhat more likely to recognize that there is a problem and to cooperate with treatment.

26-7. Binge eating disorder involves _____ but not the purging, fasting, and excessive exercise seen in bulimia. It is (less/more) severe and (less/more) common than bulimia.

Answers: **26-1.** anorexia nervosa, bulimia nervosa **26-2.** fear, body image, refusal **26-3.** restricting, purging **26-4.** menstrual **26-5.** 2–10, rarely **26-6.** relatively normal **26-7.** binging, less, more.

27. Discuss the history, prevalence, and gender distribution of eating disorders.

27-1. Anorexia nervosa was extremely (common/rare) and bulimia nervosa (omnipresent/nonexistent) prior to the middle of the 20th century. Obviously, culture has a great deal to do with this disorder; the combination of abundant food and the desire for thinness seem to have been a major impetus for the problem. Thus, eating disorders are in large part a product of (Western/developing) cultures.

27-2. Probably as a result of the greater pressure on women to fit the current fashion of thinness, about ____% of individuals with eating disorders are female. Studies suggest that about 1% of young women develop _____ nervosa and about 2% to 3% develop _____ nervosa. The typical age of onset of the disorders is (before/after) age 21.

Answers: **27-1.** rare, nonexistent, Western **27-2.** 90–95, anorexia, bulimia, before.

28. Explain how genetic factors, personality, and culture may contribute to eating disorders.

28-1. Data from _____ studies and studies of relatives of people with eating disorders suggest that there is some degree of genetic predisposition for the disorders.

28-2. There are also personality correlates of the disorders that may reflect an underlying vulnerability. For example, people who are impulsive, overly sensitive, and low in self-esteem are more likely to suffer from (bulimia/anorexia) nervosa. People characterized as neurotic, obsessive, and rigid are more likely to have (bulimia/anorexia) nervosa.

28-3. As mentioned previously, cultural values are clearly implicated as well. Over the last half of the 20th century, eating disorders (increased/decreased) in prevalence as the ideal body weight (increased/decreased). Although one cannot make causal conclusions, it seems likely that the cultural milieu is a major factor in eating disorders.

Answers: **28-1.** twin **28-2.** bulimia, anorexia **28-3.** increased, decreased.

29. Explain how family dynamics and disturbed thinking may contribute to eating disorders.

29-1. It is very difficult to sort out cause and effect in case and informal studies, but some theorists contend that parents who are (under-involved/overly involved) in their children's lives unintentionally push their adolescent children to exert autonomy through pathological eating patterns. Other theorists contend that mothers pass along the thinness message by _____ unhealthy dieting practices.

29-2. Disturbed thinking seems to accompany eating disorders, but whether it is a cause or a result of the disorders is hard to say. (For example, studies of food deprivation in volunteer subjects also find disturbed thinking processes.) In any case, the type of thinking may be characterized as _____ thinking (e.g., If I am not thin, I am nothing; if I eat, I am not in control of my life).

Answers: 29-1. overly involved, modelling (or endorsing, agreeing with, passing on) **29-2.** rigid (or all or none, dichotomous).

CRITICAL THINKING APPLICATION * WORKING WITH PROBABILITIES IN THINKING ABOUT MENTAL ILLNESS

30. Discuss how mental heuristics can distort estimates of cumulative and conjunctive probabilities.

30-1. Basing an estimate of probability on the similarity of an event to a prototype (or mental representation) is a distortion in thinking referred to as the _____ heuristic.

30-2. Over a lifetime, what is the probability that someone will be afflicted with mental illness? Higher than most people think, about one chance in three. People underestimate this probability in part because when they think of mental illness, they think of severe disturbances, such as schizophrenia. When a _____ such as this comes to mind, people tend to ignore information about _____. This bias in our thinking is called the _____ _____.

30-3. In fact, the lifetime mental illness referred to could be schizophrenia, or obsessive-compulsive disorder, or phobia, or substance abuse disorder, or any of an enormous number of other disorders. Each "or" in this instance should involve (<u>adding/subtracting</u>) estimates of the appropriate probabilities, an example of (<u>conjunctive/cumulative</u>) probabilities. The representativeness heuristic, however, results in our estimating probabilities based on similarity to a _____.

30-4. Here is another probability question: Which of the following is more likely, a or b?

a. having a phobia

b. having a phobia and being obsessive-compulsive

You don't have to know anything about these disorders or their actual probabilities to know that the answer is ____. In this example, you implicitly know that the likelihood of two events occurring together is less than that of either of these events occurring alone. This example illustrates "and" relationships or _____ probabilities.

30-5. Sometimes the answer is not so apparent. Consider this question: John was reported to have been brain damaged at birth. At age 14, John's IQ was measured as 70. Of the following, which is most likely? ____

a. John wins a Nobel prize at age 40.

b. John is given an experimental treatment for retardation; John wins a Nobel prize at age 40.

c. John was mixed up with another baby; John's IQ test was scored incorrectly; John wins a Nobel prize at age 40.

30-6. The answer to the previous question is another example of _____ probabilities. If you, like most people that I have shown this problem, picked some answer other than "a," you made the error known as the _____ fallacy.

30-7. Why do we make the conjunction fallacy? In part, the mistake results, again, from our tendency to be influenced by prototypes, the _____ heuristic. Even though we know that, logically, the likelihood of two events occurring together is less than the probability of either occurring alone, the additional "explanation" makes the combined result seem more reasonable. In fact, it is just another example of _____ probabilities.

30-8. When you first read about mood disorders, or obsessive-compulsive disorder, or generalized anxiety disorder, or hypochondriasis, did you tend to think that each description might fit you or one of your friends? If so, you were probably influenced by the _____ heuristic.

30-9. The availability heuristic involves the ease with which we can bring something to _____. The more readily we can think of some event, the more likely it is to influence our judgment about its frequency or _____.

30-10. Review. If one estimates probability based on a mental image or prototype, one is using the _____ _____. If we think that it is more likely that two events will occur together than that either will occur alone, we have made the error known as the _____ _____. If we base our estimate of probability on the ease with which something comes to mind, we are using the _____ _____.

Answers: **30-1.** representativeness **30-2.** prototype (or mental representation), probability, representativeness heuristic **30-3.** adding, cumulative, prototype **30-4.** a, conjunctive **30-5.** a **30-6.** conjunctive, conjunction **30-7.** representativeness, conjunctive **30-8.** availability **30-9.** mind, probability **30-10.** representativeness heuristic, conjunction fallacy, availability heuristic.

REVIEW OF KEY TERMS

Agoraphobia
Anorexia nervosa
Antisocial personality disorder
Anxiety disorders
Autism
Availability heuristic
Binge eating disorder
Bipolar disorder
Bulimia nervosa

Diagnosis
Disorganized schizophrenia
Dissociative amnesia
Dissociative disorders
Dissociative fugue
Dissociative identity disorder (DID)
Dysthymic disorder
Eating disorders

Multiple-personality disorder
Negative symptoms
Obsessive-compulsive disorder (OCD)
Panic disorder
Paranoid schizophrenia
Personality disorders
Phobic disorder
Positive symptoms
Postpartum depression

Catatonic schizophrenia   Epidemiology   Prevalence
Comorbidity   Etiology   Prognosis
Concordance rate   Generalized anxiety disorder Representativeness heuristic
Conjunction fallacy   Hallucinations   Schizophrenic disorders
Culture-bound disorders   Major depressive disorder   Seasonal affective disorder
Cyclothymic disorder   Medical model   Undifferentiated schizophrenia
Delusions   Mood disorders

_____ **1.** Proposes that it is useful to think of abnormal behaviour as a disease.

_____ **2.** Involves distinguishing one illness from another.

_____ **3.** Refers to the apparent causation and developmental history of an illness.

_____ **4.** A forecast about the possible course of an illness.

_____ **5.** An eating disorder characterized by fear of gaining weight, disturbed body image, refusal to maintain normal weight, and dangerous measures to lose weight.

_____ **6.** The study of the distribution of mental or physical disorders in a population.

_____ **7.** Refers to the percentage of a population that exhibits a disorder during a specified time period.

_____ **8.** A class of disorders marked by feelings of excessive apprehension and anxiety.

_____ **9.** Disorder marked by a chronic high level of anxiety which is not tied to any specific threat.

_____ **10.** Disorder marked by a persistent and irrational fear of an object or situation that presents no realistic danger.

_____ **11.** Disorder that involves recurrent attacks of overwhelming anxiety that usually occur suddenly and unexpectedly.

_____ **12.** Disorder marked by persistent, uncontrollable intrusions of unwanted thoughts and urges to engage in senseless rituals.

_____ **13.** A fear of going out in public places.

_____ **14.** One part of a two-category classification system of schizophrenia that includes behavioural excesses such as hallucinations, delusions, and bizarre behaviour.

_____ **15.** A class of disorders in which people lose contact with portions of their consciousness or memory, resulting in disruptions in their sense of identity.

_____ **16.** A sudden loss of memory for important personal information that is too extensive to be due to normal forgetting.

_____ **17.** The loss of memory of one's entire life along with one's sense of personal identity.

_____ **18.** Older term, still widely used, that describes the coexistence in one person of two or more personalities.

_____ **19.** The new term that replaced multiple-personality disorder in the DSM-IV.

_____ **20.** A class of disorders marked by depressed or elevated mood disturbances that may spill over to disrupt physical, perceptual, social, and thought processes.

_____ 21. Severe disturbances in eating behaviour, characterized by preoccupation with weight concerns and unhealthy efforts to control weight; includes the syndromes anorexia nervosa and bulimia nervosa.

_____ 22. A disorder marked by persistent feelings of sadness and despair and a loss of interest in previous sources of pleasure.

_____ 23. Disorders marked by the experience of both depressive and manic periods.

_____ 24. Statistic indicating the percentage of twin pairs or other pairs of relatives who exhibit the same disorder.

_____ 25. Estimating the probability of an event based on the ease with which relevant instances come to mind.

_____ 26. A class of disorders marked by disturbances in thought that spill over to affect perceptual, social, and emotional processes.

_____ 27. False beliefs that are maintained even though they clearly are out of touch with reality.

_____ 28. Sensory perceptions that occur in the absence of a real, external stimulus or gross distortions of perceptual input.

_____ 29. Type of schizophrenia dominated by delusions of persecution, along with delusions of grandeur.

_____ 30. Type of schizophrenia marked by striking motor disturbances, ranging from muscular rigidity to random motor activity.

_____ 31. Type of schizophrenia marked by a particularly severe deterioration of adaptive behaviour.

_____ 32. Type of schizophrenia marked by idiosyncratic mixtures of schizophrenic symptoms.

_____ 33. A class of disorders marked by extreme, inflexible personality traits that cause subjective distress or impaired social and occupational functioning.

_____ 34. Disorder marked by impulsive, callous, manipulative, aggressive, and irresponsible behaviour; reflects a failure to accept social norms.

_____ 35. An eating disorder characterized by binges but no purges, laxative use, or excessive exercise.

_____ 36. A part of a two-category classification system of schizophrenia that includes behavioural deficits, such as flattened emotions, social withdrawal, and apathy.

_____ 37. Chronic but relatively mild symptoms of bipolar disturbance.

_____ 38. Abnormal syndromes found only in a few cultural groups.

_____ 39. Chronic depression that is insufficient in severity to merit diagnosis of a major depressive episode.

_____ 40. Estimating the probability of an event based on how similar the event is to a prototype.

_____ 41. An error in thinking that involves estimating that the odds of two uncertain events happening together are greater than the odds of either event happening alone.

_____ 42. An eating disorder that involves binge eating followed by unhealthy compensatory efforts such as vomiting, fasting, abuse of laxatives and diuretics, and excessive exercise.

	43.	The coexistence of two or more disorders in the same individual.
	44.	A type of depression occurring after childbirth.
	45.	A mood disorder involving seasonal variation.
	46.	A childhood pervasive developmental disorder.

Answers: 1. medical model **2.** diagnosis **3.** etiology **4.** prognosis **5.** anorexia nervosa **6.** epidemiology **7.** prevalence **8.** anxiety disorders **9.** generalized anxiety disorder **10.** phobic disorder **11.** panic disorder **12.** obsessive-compulsive disorder **13.** agoraphobia **14.** positive symptoms **15.** dissociative disorders **16.** dissociative amnesia **17.** dissociative fugue **18.** multiple-personality disorder **19.** dissociative identity disorder **20.** mood disorders **21.** eating disorders **22.** major depressive disorder **23.** bipolar disorders **24.** concordance rate **25.** availability heuristic **26.** schizophrenic disorders **27.** delusions **28.** hallucinations **29.** paranoid schizophrenia **30.** catatonic schizophrenia **31.** disorganized schizophrenia **32.** undifferentiated schizophrenia **33.** personality disorders **34.** antisocial personality disorder **35.** binge eating disorder **36.** negative symptoms **37.** cyclothymia **38.** culture-bound disorders **39.** dysthymic disorder **40.** representativeness heuristic **41.** conjunction fallacy **42.** bulimia nervosa **43.** comorbidity **44.** postpartum depression **45.** seasonal affective disorder **46.** autism.

REVIEW OF KEY PEOPLE

Nancy Andreasen   Robert Hare   Regina Schuller
Martin Antony   Susan Nolen-Hoeksema   Thomas Szasz
Aaron Beck   David Rosenhan

	1.	Critic of the medical model; argues that abnormal behaviour usually involves a deviation from social norms rather than an illness.
	2.	Did a study on admission of pseudopatients to a mental hospital; concluded that the mental health system is biased toward seeing pathology where it doesn't exist.
	3.	Studies the interface between psychology and Canadian law.
	4.	Proposed an alternative approach to subtyping that divides schizophrenic disorders into just two categories, based on the presence of negative versus positive symptoms.
	5.	Asserts that dissociative identity disorder (multiple-personality disorder) is not a genuine disorder but the product of media attention and the probings of psychotherapists.
	6.	Conducted research on the association between "rumination" and depression.
	7.	Developed the Psychopathy Checklist—Revised.
	8.	Studied different dimensions, or aspects, of obsessive-compulsive disorder.

Answers: 1. Szasz **2.** Rosenhan **3.** Schuller **4.** Andreasen **5.** Spanos **6.** Nolen-Hoeksema **7.** Hare **8.** Antony.

SELF-QUIZ

1. Which of the following is a major symptom of depression?
   a. alogia
   b. anhedonia
   c. agnosia
   d. aphasia

2. The concordance rate for mood disorders is about 65% among identical twins and 17% among fraternal twins. What does this information suggest about mood disorders?
   a. They are caused primarily by stress.
   b. They have an onset at an early age.
   c. They are due primarily to family environment.
   d. They are caused in part by genetic factors.

3. In Rosenhan's study involving admission of pseudopatients to psychiatric facilities, what occurred for most of these "patients"?
   a. They were diagnosed as seriously disturbed.
   b. They were diagnosed as suffering from a mild neurosis.
   c. They were dismissed within two days.
   d. They were diagnosed correctly by the professional staff but not by the ward attendants.

4. A woman gets sudden, paralyzing attacks of anxiety and also fears going out in public away from her house. What anxiety disorder does this describe?
   a. generalized anxiety disorder
   b. phobic disorder
   c. obsessive-compulsive disorder
   d. panic disorder and agoraphobia

5. Ralph cleans his cupboards seven times a day. What anxiety disorder does this describe?
   a. generalized anxiety disorder
   b. phobic disorder
   c. obsessive-compulsive disorder
   d. panic disorder

6. Human beings may have evolved to be more easily conditioned to fear some stimuli more than others. Which of Seligman's notions corresponds to this statement?
   a. preparedness
   b. anxiety differentiation
   c. somatization
   d. learned helplessness

7. What do delusions and hallucinations likely characterize?
   a. major depressive disorder
   b. hypochondriasis
   c. phobias
   d. schizophrenia

8. Which of the following neurotransmitters has been most implicated in schizophrenia?
   a. serotonin
   b. norepinephrine
   c. dopamine
   d. acetylcholine

9. What syndrome was extremely rare prior to the last half of the 20th century?
   a. manic-depressive disorder
   b. schizophrenia
   c. obsessive-compulsive disorder
   d. anorexia nervosa

10. What term refers to the disorder marked by unusual motor disturbances ranging from rigidity to random motor activity and incoherence?
    a. catatonic schizophrenia
    b. multiple personality
    c. dissociative disorder
    d. paranoid schizophrenia

11. Which of the following disorders occur in all cultures?
    a. generalized anxiety disorder and panic disorder
    b. hypochondriasis, somatization, conversion disorder
    c. schizophrenia, bipolar mood disorder, depression
    d. bulimia and anorexia nervosa

12. What term refers to a syndrome in women that is characterized by amenorrhea (loss of the menstrual cycle)?
    a. generalized anxiety disorder
    b. bipolar mood disorder
    c. anorexia nervosa
    d. bulimia nervosa

13. An individual thinks he is Jesus Christ. He also believes that, because he is Christ, people are trying to kill him. Assume that this individual is not correct—he is not Christ, and people are not trying to kill him. Which of the following would be the most likely diagnosis?
    a. multiple personality
    b. paranoid schizophrenia
    c. obsessive-compulsive disorder
    d. catatonic schizophrenia

14. A Canadian court in 2008 declares that, because of a mental illness, an individual did not know right from wrong. What will likely be determined about this individual?
    a. not criminally responsible on account of mental disorder
    b. psychopathic
    c. psychotic
    d. not guilty by reason of insanity

15. Consider the following options and be careful not to make the conjunction fallacy. Which option is most probable?
    a. Ralph is an alcoholic; Ralph wins a major world tennis tournament.
    b. Ralph is an alcoholic; Ralph enters a treatment program; Ralph wins a major world tennis tournament.
    c. Ralph is an alcoholic; Ralph enters a treatment program; Ralph has been sober for a year; Ralph wins a major world tennis tournament.
    d. Ralph is an alcoholic; Ralph enters a treatment program; Ralph has been sober for a year; Ralph practices tennis 50 hours a week; Ralph wins a major world tennis tournament.

16. Canadian General Romeo Dallaire, winner of the Pearson Peace Medal in 2005, has suffered from which anxiety disorder?
    a. phobic disorder
    b. post-traumatic stress disorder
    c. generalized anxiety disorder
    d. panic disorder

17. What did the Featured Study reveal about the later development of depression?
    a. It can be predicted by earlier measurement of negative thinking
    b. It can be predicted by earlier measurement of traumatic experiences
    c. It can be predicted by earlier measurement of exposure to others who are depressed
    d. It can be predicted by earlier measurement of social isolation

Answers: 1. b **2.** d **3.** a **4.** d **5.** c **6.** a **7.** d **8.** c **9.** d **10.** a **11.** c **12.** c **13.** b **14.** a **15.** a **16.** b **17.** a.

Chapter Fifteen

TREATMENT OF PSYCHOLOGICAL DISORDERS

REVIEW OF KEY IDEAS

THE ELEMENTS OF THE TREATMENT PROCESS

1. **Identify the three major categories of therapy, and discuss how various demographic variables relate to the likelihood of treatment.**

   1-1.   Even though she already owns more than a thousand pairs of shoes, Imelba cannot resist the urge to buy more. She checks the Yellow Pages and calls three different psychotherapists regarding possible treatment for her compulsion.

   (a)   One therapist tells her that treatment will require her to talk with the therapist so as to develop a better understanding of her inner feelings. This therapist probably belongs to the _____ school of psychotherapy.

   (b)   Another therapist suggests that some form of medication may help alleviate her compulsion. This therapist probably pursues the _____ approach to psychotherapy.

   (c)   The third therapist is of the opinion that her urge to buy shoes results from learning, and correcting it requires that she unlearn this compulsion. This therapist probably pursues the _____ approach to psychotherapy.

   1-2.   Indicate whether the following statements about people who seek and choose not to seek psychotherapy are true or false.

   _____ Fewer Canadians are committed to improving their mental health in the future than their physical health.

   _____ The two most common presenting symptoms are excessive anxiety and depression.

   _____ Persons seeking psychotherapy always have identifiable disorders.

   _____ Many people feel that seeking psychotherapy is an admission of personal weakness.

   Answers: 1-1. (a) insight, (b) biomedical, (c) behavioural **1-2.** true, true, false, true.

2. **Describe the various types of mental health professionals involved in the provision of psychotherapy.**

2-1. Identify the following kinds of mental health professionals:

(a) Medically trained persons (physicians) who generally use biomedical and insight approaches to psychotherapy.

(b) Persons with doctoral degrees who emphasize behavioural and insight approaches to psychotherapy in treating a full range of psychological problems (two types).

(c) Nurses who usually work as part of the treatment team in a hospital setting.

(d) These persons often work with both the patient and the family to reintegrate the patient back into society.

(e) Persons who usually specialize in particular types of problems, such as vocational, drug, or marital counselling.

Answers: **2-1.** (a) psychiatrists, (b) clinical and counselling psychologists, (c) psychiatric nurses, (d) clinical social workers, (e) counsellors.

INSIGHT THERAPIES

3. Explain the logic of psychoanalysis, and describe the techniques by which analysts probe the unconscious.

3-1. Freud believed that psychological disturbances originate from unresolved conflicts deep in the unconscious levels of the mind. His theory of personality, which he called _____, would be classified as a(n) _____ approach to psychotherapy. The psychoanalyst plays the role of psychological detective, seeking out problems thought to originate from conflicts left over from early _____.

3-2. The psychoanalyst employs two techniques to probe the unconscious. One technique requires the patient to tell whatever comes to mind, no matter how trivial. This technique is called _____ _____. The other technique requires the patient to learn to remember his or her dreams, which are then probed for their hidden meaning by the psychoanalyst. This technique is called _____ _____.

Answers: **3-1.** psychoanalysis, insight, childhood **3-2.** free association, dream analysis.

4. Discuss resistance and transference in psychoanalysis.

4-1. Freud believed most people (<u>do/do not</u>) want to know the true nature of their inner conflicts and will employ various strategies so as to offer _____ to the progress of therapy. As therapy progresses, the patient often begins to relate to the therapist as though he or she was actually one of the significant persons (mother, father, spouse, etc.) in the patient's life. This phenomenon is called _____.

Answers: 4-1. do not, resistance, transference.

5. Identify the elements of therapeutic climate, and discuss therapeutic process in Rogers's client-centred therapy.

5-1. The emotional bond between the therapist and client, and their agreement on goals and tasks, is called the _____ _____. A positive alliance is related to a positive psychotherapy outcome.

5-2. Client-centred therapy, as developed by Carl Rogers, holds that there are three important aspects necessary for a good therapeutic climate. These are genuineness, unconditional positive regard, and empathy. Match these terms with their correct definitions, as given below.

(a) The ability to truly see the world from the client's point of view and communicate this understanding to the client.

(b) The therapist's openness and honesty with the client.

(c) The complete and nonjudgmental acceptance of the client as a person, without necessarily agreeing with what the client has to say.

5-3. The major emphasis for client-centred therapy is to provide feedback and _____ as the client expresses his or her thoughts and feelings. The idea here is that the client (<u>does/does not</u>) need direct advice. What is needed is help in sorting through personal confusion in order to gain greater _____ into true inner feelings.

5-4. An important extension of client-centred therapy is _____-_____ couples therapy, which addresses _____ issues within a partnership as well as underlying _____.

Answers: 5-1. therapeutic alliance **5-2.** (a) empathy, (b) genuineness, (c) unconditional positive regard **5-3.** clarification, does not, insight (or understanding) **5-4.** emotion-focused, relationship, emotions.

6. Discuss therapies inspired by positive psychology.

6-1. Fava and colleagues developed _____-_____ therapy, which seeks to enhance a client's self-acceptance, purpose in life, autonomy, and personal growth. It has been used in the treatment of _____ and _____ disorders.

6-2. Another approach, developed by Seligman and colleagues, is _____ psychotherapy, which teaches clients to recognize their _____, appreciate their blessings, savour positive experiences, _____ those who have wronged them, and find _____ in their lives. Positive psychotherapy can be an effective treatment for depression. For example, Mongrain's research showed that increasing _____-_____ or _____ both decreased depression.

Answers: 6-1. well-being, mood, anxiety **6-2.** positive, strengths, forgive, meaning, self-compassion, optimism.

7. Describe how group therapy is generally conducted, and identify some advantages of this approach.

7-1. When conducting group therapy, the therapist generally plays a(n) (active/subtle) role, one that is primarily aimed at promoting _____ cohesiveness. Participants essentially function as _____ for each other, providing acceptance and emotional support.

7-2. Besides being less expensive, group therapy also has three other advantages: (1) the realization by the participants that their problems (are/are not) unique, (2) the opportunity to work in a safe environment to build _____ skills, and (3) the fact that group therapy is particularly appropriate for (all/certain) kinds of problems.

Answers: 7-1. subtle, group, therapists **7-2.** are not, social, certain.

8. Describe couples and family therapy and when they are employed.

8-1. Couples therapy has its main focus on _____ issues. Family therapy has its main focus on family dynamics and _____.

8-2. The goals of both couples and family therapy emphasize understanding the entrenched patterns of _____ that produce distress and improving _____ and healthier patterns of interaction.

Answers: 8-1. relationship, communication **8-2.** interaction, communication.

9. Discuss evidence on the efficacy of insight therapies.

9-1. Evaluating the efficacy of therapies is challenging, in part because disorders can improve on their own, a phenomenon called _____ _____.

9-2. A large number of studies have suggested that insight therapies are superior to no treatment or placebo treatment, and are (equal to/better than) drug therapies. Most gains occur (early/late) in the treatment. About _____% of patients show clinically meaningful recovery within about 20 sessions.

Answers: 9-1. spontaneous remission **9-2.** equal to, early, 50.

10. Summarize the general principles underlying behavioural approaches to therapy.

10-1. In contrast to insight therapists, who believe that pathological symptoms are signs of an underlying problem, behaviour therapists believe that the _____ are the problem. Thus, behaviour therapists focus on employing the principles of learning to directly change maladaptive _____. The two general principles underlying this approach are (1) one's behaviour is a product of _____ and (2) what has been learned can be _____.

Answers: 10-1. symptoms, behaviour, learning, unlearned.

11. Describe the goals and procedures of systematic desensitization, exposure therapy, and aversion therapy.

11-1. State whether the following situations would be most applicable to systematic desensitization, exposure therapy, or aversion therapy.

(a) The treatment goal is to lessen the attractiveness of particular stimuli and behaviours that are personally or socially harmful.

(b) The treatment goal is to reduce irrational fears, such as found in phobias and other anxiety disorders.

(c) The three-step treatment involves pairing an imagined anxiety hierarchy with deep muscle relaxation.

(d) This treatment can sometimes be completed in a single session.

(e) Treatment involves presenting an unpleasant stimulus, such as electric shock, while a person is engaged in performing a self-destructive, but personally appealing, act.

(f) This would be the treatment of choice for students who are unduly anxious about public speaking.

(g) Treatment involves direct confrontation with the feared situation.

Answers: 11-1. (a) aversion therapy, (b) systematic desensitization, (c) systematic desensitization, (d) exposure therapy, (e) aversion therapy, (f) systematic desensitization, (g) exposure therapy.

12. Describe the goals and techniques of social skills training.

12-1. As the name implies, social skills training is a behaviour therapy designed to improve a client's social or _____ skills. Three different behavioural techniques are employed. First, the client is required to watch closely the behaviour of socially skilled persons, a technique called _____. Next, the client is expected to imitate and practise the behaviour he or she has just witnessed, a technique called behaviour _____. Finally, the client is expected to perform in social situations requiring increasingly more difficult social skills, a technique called _____.

Answers: 12-1. interpersonal, modelling, rehearsal, shaping.

13. Discuss the logic, goals, and techniques of cognitive therapy.

13-1. Answer the following questions regarding the logic, goals, and techniques of cognitive therapy.

(a) What is the origin of many psychological problems according to cognitive therapy?

(b) What is the primary goal of cognitive therapy?

(c) How do cognitive therapists go about trying to change a client's negative illogical thinking?

(d) What techniques from behaviour therapy do cognitive therapists frequently employ?

(e) What is the aim of mindfulness training?

(f) What skills can be acquired through mindfulness training?

Answers: 13-1. (a) "errors" in thinking, (b) to change the client's negative thoughts and maladaptive beliefs, (c) through identification and challenging the basis in reality of negative thoughts, (d) modelling, systematic monitoring of one's behaviour, and behavioural rehearsal, (e) Training in mindfulness emphasizes attention to, and nonjudgmental acceptance of, present-moment experience. For example, depressed patients might be taught to observe and accept their troubling thoughts or emotions without judging or elaborating on them. (f) increased awareness, adopting a focus on the present moment, self-compassion, and accepting things as they are.

14. Discuss evidence on the effectiveness of behaviour therapies.

14-1. Compared to the evidence in support of insight therapies, the evidence in favour of behaviour therapy is somewhat (<u>weaker/stronger</u>). It is important to remember, however, that behaviour therapies are best suited for treating (<u>specific/general</u>) psychological disorders, and that all of the various behavioural techniques (<u>are/are not</u>) equally effective.

Answers: **14-1.** stronger, specific, are not.

BIOMEDICAL THERAPIES

15. Define biomedical therapy and describe historical uses of surgical treatment of mental disorders.

15-1. Biomedical therapies are _____ interventions intended to reduce symptoms associated with (<u>physical/psychological</u>) disorders. Biomedical therapies include psychosurgery, electroconvulsive shock therapy, and _____ therapies.

15-2. The modern use of psychosurgery dates from the year _____, when a Swiss psychiatrist, Burckhardt, used the procedure to treat hallucinations. The prefrontal leucotomy was developed by Portuguese psychiatrist Moniz in the _____s, and was further developed in the 1940s by Walter _____ in the United States. Performance of lobotomies in Canada declined through the 1970s and the technique has now fallen into disuse. A procedure that is used on occasion is the _____, a treatment reserved for instances of obsessive-compulsive disorder that don't respond to other interventions.

Answers: **15-1.** physiological, psychological, drug **15-2.** 1888, 1930, Freeman, cingulotomy.

16. Describe the principal categories of drugs used in the treatment of psychological disorders.

16-1. Valium and Xanax, popularly called tranquillizers, are used to treat psychological disorders in which anxiety is a major feature. Thus, they are collectively called _____ drugs.

16-2. Another class of drugs is used to treat severe psychotic symptoms, such as hallucinations and confusion. These drugs are collectively called _____ drugs.

16-3. Four classes of drugs (tricyclics, MAO inhibitors, selective serotonin reuptake inhibitors, and serotonin and norepinephrine reuptake inhibitors) have been found to be useful in alleviating depression, but especially for severe depressions. These drugs are collectively called _____ drugs.

16-4. Drugs for bipolar disorder are known as _____ stabilizers. They include lithium and _____.

Answers: **16-1.** antianxiety **16-2.** antipsychotic **16-3.** antidepressant **16-4.** mood, valproate.

17. **Discuss evidence on the effects and problems of drug treatments for psychological disorders.**

   17-1.   Drug therapies have proven useful in the treatment of many psychological disorders. However, they remain controversial for at least three reasons. Use the hints below to describe these three reasons.

   (a) resolve problems

   (b) two areas having to do with excess

   (c) cure is worse than the disease

   17-2.   What problem exists between drug companies and researchers that may influence results regarding the effectiveness and side effects of drugs?

Answers: 17-1. (a) They alleviate rather than solve psychological problems. (b) They are overprescribed and patients are overmedicated. (c) The side effects may be worse than the disease. **17-2.** The researchers are too financially dependent on the drug companies. This may be related to selective publication practices and adoption of research designs that exaggerate positive effects.

18. **Describe the therapeutic effects and risks of ECT and describe newer brain stimulation techniques.**

   18-1.   Answer the following questions about the nature, therapeutic effects, and risks of ECT.

   (a) What is the physical effect of the electric shock on the patient?

   (b) What general class of disorders warrants conservative use of ECT as a treatment technique?

   (c) What are some short-term side effects of ECT?

   18-2.   Answer the following questions about newer brain stimulation techniques.

(a) What is transcranial magnetic stimulation?

(b) What is deep brain stimulation?

Answers: **18-1.** (a) It produces convulsive seizures. (b) severe mood disorders (depression and mania), (c) It can produce intellectual impairment **18-2.** (a) Transcranial magnetic stimulation involves enhancing or depressing activity in specific cortical areas. It has been used to reduce depression. (b) Deep brain stimulation involves implanting an electrode into the brain in order to deliver electrical current. It has been used to treat such movement disorders as Parkinson's disease.

CURRENT TRENDS AND ISSUES IN TREATMENT

19. Discuss the merits of blending or combining different approaches to therapy.

19-1. A significant trend in modern psychotherapy is to blend or combine many different treatment approaches. Psychologists who advocate and use this approach are said to be _____. The chapter's Featured Study suggests there may be merit to this approach. In this study, four different groups of depressed patients were treated by either insight therapy (i.e., interpersonal therapy) with placebo medication, medication alone (the antidepressant nortriptyline), insight therapy along with medication, or placebo medication alone. The greatest improvement was found in patients treated by (drug therapy alone/interpersonal therapy alone/both therapies combined).

Answers: **19-1.** eclectic, both therapies combined.

20. Discuss the barriers that lead to underutilization of mental health services by ethnic minorities and possible solutions to the problem.

20-1. The text lists four general barriers (cultural, language, access, and institutional) to mental health services for ethnic minorities. Indicate which of these barriers is represented in the following statements.

_____ (a) Many of the ethnic minorities are in low-paying jobs and without supplemental health insurance coverage.

_____ (b) Very few mental health facilities are equipped to provide culturally responsive services.

_____ (c) There is a limited number of bilingual therapists.

_____ (d) Psychotherapy was developed by whites in the Western world to treat whites in the Western world.

_____ (e) Asian Canadians are less likely to use and access mental health services.

20-2. Canadian First Nations peoples are at elevated risk of depression, suicide, and substance abuse. Therapy settings that fail to include _____ healing practices for such individuals tend to be ineffective (i.e., those settings create a(n) _____ barrier to treatment).

20-3. Overall, studies show that ethnic minorities are (more/less) likely to go to mental health facilities that are staffed by a higher proportion of people who share their ethnic identity. Individual therapists can also work toward building a strong _____ _____ with their ethnic clients, and interventions can be _____ to be more compatible with specific ethnic groups' values and traditions.

Answers. 20-1. (a) access, (b) institutional, (c) language, (d) cultural, (e) cultural **20-2.** indigenous, institutional **20-3.** more, therapeutic alliance, tailored (or adapted, modified).

INSTITUTIONAL TREATMENT IN TRANSITION

21. Explain why people grew disenchanted with mental hospitals and describe the community mental health movement.

21-1. After more than a century of reliance on government-run mental hospitals, the evidence began to grow that these institutions were not helping the patients; rather, in many instances, they were worsening their condition. What condition, unrelated to funding, was said to be responsible for this state of affairs?

21-2. In order to correct for these shortcomings, the community mental health movement arose as an alternative treatment option. These community-based facilities emphasize (short-term/long-term) therapy and getting patients stabilized and back into the community _____.

Answers: 21-1. The removal of patients from their communities separated them from essential support groups. **21-2.** short-term, swiftly.

22. Describe the deinstitutionalization trend, and evaluate its effects.

22-1. The transferring of mental health care from large government-run institutions to community-based facilities is what is meant by the term _____. As a result of deinstitutionalization, the number of mental patients in large institutional hospitals has _____ remarkably. For example, in Canada, the number of beds per 100 000 people declined from 4 to 1 between 1964 and 1981. The length of stay by patients in mental hospitals has also _____.

22-2. While deinstitutionalization has resulted in a decrease in the number of patients, as well as their length of stay, the number of admissions to psychiatric hospitals has actually _____. This is because of a large number of readmissions for short-term care, which the text calls "the _____ _____ problem." In addition, many end up in _____. Another problem brought about by deinstitutionalization is that a large number of discharged patients who have meagre job skills and no close support groups make up a substantial portion of the nation's _____ persons.

Answers: 22-1. deinstitutionalization, declined, declined **22-2.** increased, revolving door, prison, homeless.

PUTTING IT IN PERSPECTIVE

23. Explain how this chapter highlighted two of the text's unifying themes.

    23-1.   What point does the text make about how theoretical diversity influenced the treatment techniques employed by psychotherapy?

    23-2.   The approaches to psychotherapy discussed in this chapter are not universally accepted or used, and some are actually counterproductive in many cultures. Why is this?

Answers: 23-1. It has resulted in better treatment techniques (because of the many diverse approaches). **23-2.** Cultural factors influence psychological processes.

APPLICATION: LOOKING FOR A THERAPIST

24. Discuss where to seek therapy, and the potential importance of a therapist's sex, professional background, and cost.

    24-1.   Most therapists (are/are not) in private practice. In addition to recommending talking to friends and acquaintances, the text lists many places (Table 15.2) where one might seek psychotherapy. The general idea here is to _____ around when looking for a therapist.

    24-2.   The text concludes that the kind of degree held by the psychotherapist (is/is not) crucial, although a verifiable degree indicating some kind of professional training is important. The sex of the therapist should be chosen according to the feelings of the _____; it is unwise to engage a therapist whose sex makes the client feel uncomfortable.

    24-3.   Answer the following questions regarding the cost of psychotherapy.

        (a) How does the cost of therapists involved in private practice compare with the fees charged by similar professional groups?

        (b) Are the costs of seeing a psychologist covered by provincial health care programs? What about the costs of seeing a psychiatrist?

Answers: **24-1.** are not, shop **24-2.** is not, client **24-3.** (a) The costs are similar. (b) The services of a private practice psychologist are not covered by health care, whereas the services of a psychiatrist are covered.

25. Discuss the importance of a therapist's theoretical approach.

25-1. Studies of the effectiveness of various theoretical approaches to therapy show they are (<u>unequal/equal</u>) in overall success. This equality of results among all theoretical approaches (<u>does/does not</u>) apply to all types of problems. The theoretical approach may make a difference for specific types of problems.

Answers: **25-1.** equal, does not.

26. Summarize what one should look for in a prospective therapist and what one should expect out of therapy.

26-1. The text lists three areas to evaluate when looking for a therapist. Complete the following statements describing these areas.

(a) Can you talk to the therapist _____?

(b) Does the therapist appear to have empathy and _____?

(c) Does the therapist appear to be self-assured and _____?

26-2. What did the Ehrenbergs say about what to expect from psychotherapy?

Answers: **26-1.** (a) openly (or in a candid, nondefensive manner), (b) understanding, (c) confident **26-2.** It takes time, effort, and courage.

CRITICAL THINKING APPLICATION

27. Explain how placebo effects and regression toward the mean can complicate the evaluation of therapy.

27-1. In addition to therapy itself, what other two factors can influence the outcome of a treatment program?

27-2. Which of these two factors is least effected by having only a small sample?

27-3. Which of these factors leads us to predict that persons who score the healthiest on a mental health questionnaire will actually score lower on this questionnaire following a brief therapy intervention?

Answers: 27-1. placebo effects and regression toward the mean **27-2.** placebo effects **27-3.** regression toward the mean.

REVIEW OF KEY TERMS

Antianxiety drugs
Antidepressant drugs
Antipsychotic drugs
Aversion therapy
Behaviour therapies
Biomedical therapies
Client-centred therapy
Cognitive-behavioural treatments
Cognitive therapy
Deep brain stimulation
Deinstitutionalization

Dream analysis
Eclecticism
Electroconvulsive therapy (ECT)
Free association
Group therapy
Insight therapies
Interpretation
Mental hospital
Mood stabilizers
Placebo effects
Psychiatrists

Psychoanalysis
Psychopharmacotherapy
Regression toward the mean
Resistance
Social skills training
Spontaneous remission
Systematic desensitization
Tardive dyskinesia
Transcranial magnetic stimulation
Transference

_____ 1. Delivering electrical current to brain tissue adjacent to an implanted electrode.

_____ 2. Physicians who specialize in the treatment of psychological disorders.

_____ 3. Therapies that involve verbal interactions intended to enhance a client's self-knowledge and thus produce healthful changes in personality and behaviour.

_____ 4. An insight therapy that emphasizes the recovery of unconscious conflicts, motives, and defences through such techniques as free association and transference.

_____ 5. A technique in which clients are urged to spontaneously express their thoughts and feelings with as little personal censorship as possible.

_____ 6. A technique for interpreting the symbolic meaning of dreams.

_____ 7. A therapist's attempts to explain the inner significance of a client's thoughts, feelings, memories, and behaviour.

_____ 8. A client's largely unconscious defensive manoeuvres intended to hinder the progress of therapy.

_____ 9. A process that occurs when clients start relating to their therapist in ways that mimic critical relationships in their lives.

_____ 10. An insight therapy that emphasizes providing a supportive emotional climate for clients who play a major role in determining the pace and direction of their therapy.

_____ 11. A therapy that emphasizes recognizing and changing negative thoughts and maladaptive beliefs.

_____ 12. The simultaneous treatment of several clients.

_____ 13. Therapies that involve the application of learning principles to change a client's maladaptive behaviours.

_____ 14. A behaviour therapy used to reduce anxiety responses through counterconditioning.

_____ 15. A behaviour therapy in which an aversive stimulus is paired with a stimulus that elicits an undesirable response.

_____ 16. Recovery from a disorder that occurs without formal treatment.

_____ 17. A behaviour therapy designed to improve interpersonal skills and which emphasizes shaping, modelling, and behavioural rehearsal.

_____ 18. Therapies that use physiological interventions intended to reduce symptoms associated with psychological disorders.

_____ 19. The treatment of mental disorders with drug therapy.

_____ 20. Drugs that relieve tension, apprehension, and nervousness.

_____ 21. Drugs that gradually reduce psychotic symptoms.

_____ 22. A neurological disorder marked by chronic tremors and involuntary spastic movements.

_____ 23. Drugs that gradually elevate mood and help bring people out of a depression.

_____ 24. A chemical used to control mood swings in patients with bipolar disorder.

_____ 25. A treatment in which electric shock is used to produce cortical seizure accompanied by convulsions.

_____ 26. A medical institution specializing in the provision of inpatient care for psychological disorders.

_____ 27. Involves drawing ideas from two or more systems of therapy, instead of committing to just one system.

_____ 28. Transferring the treatment of mental illness from inpatient institutions to community-based facilities that emphasize outpatient care.

_____ 29. Occur when people's expectations lead them to experience some change, even though they receive a fake treatment.

_____ 30. Occurs when people who score extremely high or low on some trait are measured a second time, and their new scores fall closer to the mean.

_____ 31. Enhancing or depressing brain activity in specific regions of the cortex using a magnetic coil.

_____ 32. The combination of verbal interventions and behaviour modification techniques.

Answers: 1. deep brain stimulation **2.** psychiatrists **3.** insight therapies **4.** psychoanalysis **5.** free association **6.** dream analysis **7.** interpretation **8.** resistance **9.** transference **10.** client-centred therapy **11.** cognitive therapy **12.** group therapy **13.** behaviour therapies **14.** systematic desensitization **15.** aversion therapy **16.** spontaneous remission **17.** social skills training **18.** biomedical therapies **19.** psychopharmacotherapy **20.** antianxiety drugs **21.** antipsychotic drugs **22.** tardive dyskinesia **23.** antidepressant drugs **24.** mood stabilizers **25.** electroconvulsive therapy (ECT) **26.** mental hospitals **27.** eclecticism **28.** deinstitutionalization **29.** placebo effects **30.** regression toward the mean **31.** transcranial magnetic stimulation **32.** cognitive-behavioural techniques.

REVIEW OF KEY PEOPLE

Aaron Beck   Sigmund Freud   Carl Rogers
Dorothea Dix   Les Greenberg   Zindel Segal
Keith Dobson   Donald Meichenbaum   Joseph Wolpe
Hans Eysenck

_____ 1. Developed a systematic treatment procedure, which he called psychoanalysis.

_____ 2. The developer of client-centred therapy.

_____ 3. Noted for his work in the development of cognitive therapy.

_____ 4. His early research showed that insight therapies were ineffective.

_____ 5. The developer of systematic desensitization.

_____ 6. One of the early reformers who helped to establish North American mental hospitals.

_____ 7. Studied the extent to which diversity training was provided in Canadian clinical psychology graduate programs.

_____ 8. University of Waterloo psychologist who made important contributions to cognitive-behavioural therapy, including the use of *self-instructional training*.

_____ 9. Developed emotions-focused couples therapy.

_____ 10. Integrated ideas from cognitive therapy and mindfulness meditation.

Answers: 1. Freud **2.** Rogers **3.** Beck **4.** Eysenck **5.** Wolpe **6.** Dix **7.** Dobson **8.** Meichenbaum **9.** Greenberg **10.** Segal.

SELF-QUIZ

1. Which of the following is NOT a true statement?
   a. People sometimes seek help for everyday problems.
   b. The two most common problems that lead to psychotherapy are sexual problems and depression.
   c. Persons seeking psychotherapy don't always have identifiable problems.
   d. Many people feel that seeking psychotherapy is an admission of personal weakness.

2. Which of the following mental health professionals must have a medical degree?
   a. psychiatric social workers
   b. clinical psychologists
   c. psychiatric nurses
   d. psychiatrists

3. Psychoanalysis is an example of what approach to psychotherapy?
   a. insight
   b. learning
   c. biomedical
   d. humanistic

4. What is exemplified when a client begins relating to his psychoanalyst as though she were his mother?
   a. transference
   b. free association
   c. catharsis
   d. restructuring

5. What is the major emphasis in client-centred therapy?
   a. to provide the client with interpretation of unconscious thinking
   b. to provide the client with cognitive restructuring
   c. to provide the client with feedback and clarification
   d. to provide the client with good advice

6. What approach is likely found in cognitive therapy?
   a. a search for negative, illogical thinking
   b. dream interpretation
   c. free association
   d. an emphasis on childhood conflicts

7. Which therapists are likely to play the least active (most subtle) role in conducting therapy?
   a. behaviour therapists
   b. cognitive therapists
   c. group therapists
   d. psychoanalytic therapists

8. What is the name of the newest category of antidepressants?
   a. monoamine oxidase inhibitors
   b. selective serotonin reuptake inhibitors
   c. serotonin and norepinephrine reuptake inhibitors
   d. tricyclic antidepressants

9. What therapy most likely sees the symptom as the problem?
   a. psychoanalysis
   b. client-centred therapy
   c. cognitive therapy
   d. behaviour therapy

10. What therapy most likely employs aversive conditioning?
    a. psychoanalysis
    b. behaviour therapy
    c. biomedical therapy
    d. client-centred therapy

11. What behaviour therapy techniques are most likely used to treat a fear of flying?
    a. systematic desensitization
    b. aversive conditioning
    c. modelling
    d. biofeedback

12. Electroconvulsive therapy (ECT) is now primarily used to treat what patients?
    a. those suffering from anxiety
    b. those suffering from phobias
    c. those suffering from severe mood disorders
    d. those suffering from psychosis

13. According to the Featured Study on the treatment of depression, which approach was most effective?
    a. drug therapy + exercise therapy
    b. interpersonal therapy + improved sleep
    c. drug therapy + interpersonal therapy
    d. drug therapy + improved sleep

14. Which of the following describes psychotherapists who combine several different approaches in their approach to therapy?
    a. enigmatic
    b. eclectic
    c. unspecific
    d. imaginative

15. Why did the trend toward deinstitutionalization mainly come about?
    a. because large mental institutions were becoming too expensive
    b. because large mental institutions were actually worsening the condition of many patients
    c. because large mental institutions were overstaffed
    d. because large mental institutions were becoming too political

16. Which of the following is NOT a doctoral degree in psychology?
    a. Ph.D.
    b. Psy.D.
    c. Ed.D.
    d. M.D.

17. Which of the following is NOT a biomedical therapy approach?
    a. psychosurgery
    b. drug therapy
    c. ECT
    d. cognitive-behavioural therapy

Answers: 1. b **2.** d **3.** a **4.** a **5.** c **6.** a **7.** c **8.** c **9.** d **10.** b **11.** a **12.** c **13.** c **14.** b **15.** b **16.** d **17.** d.

Chapter Sixteen

SOCIAL BEHAVIOUR

REVIEW OF KEY IDEAS

1. **Define social psychology.**

   1-1. Social psychology is the branch of psychology concerned with the way _____ thoughts, feelings, and behaviours are influenced by _____. The presence of others may be actual, _____, or implied.

   Answers: 1-1. individuals', others, imagined.

PERSON PERCEPTION: FORMING IMPRESSIONS OF OTHERS

2. **Describe how various aspects of physical appearance may influence our impressions of others.**

   2-1. In general, we attribute _____ personality characteristics to good-looking people. For example, we view attractive people as warmer, friendlier, better-adjusted, and more poised. We also believe that attractive people will have better lives, be better spouses, and be more _____ in their careers. Research by Dion reveals that these perceptions are established (<u>early in life/in adulthood</u>). In reality, the correlation between attractiveness and personality traits is (<u>weak/strong</u>).

   2-2. People are good at drawing inferences based on nonverbal expressions. Even judgements of photographs or brief videotapes allow meaningful inferences about _____ and sexual orientation.

   2-3. For the most part, physical attractiveness has relatively little impact on judgments of honesty. However, people do tend to view baby-faced individuals (large eyes, rounded chin) as more _____, helpless, and submissive than others. What about the notorious criminal, Baby-Faced Nelson? Well, recent data indicate that our *perception* of baby-faced people (<u>is/is not</u>) a good match for their actual traits.

   Answers: 2-1. positive (or desirable, favourable), successful, early in life, weak **2-2.** personality **2-3.** honest, is not.

3. **Explain how schemas, stereotypes, and other factors contribute to subjectivity in person perception.**

   3-1. Briefly define the following:

   (a) schemas:

(b) stereotypes:

3-2. Men are competitive, women are sensitive: these are stereotypes. Stereotypes are broad generalizations that tend to ignore the _____ within a group. People who hold stereotypes do not necessarily assume that all members of a particular group have the same characteristics, but merely that there is an increased _____ that they do.

3-3. Stereotypes might also produce a self-_____ prophecy. For example, Word and colleagues showed that, when interviewing a black job applicant, white interviewers adopted a _____ style (i.e., sitting farther away, making more speech errors, looking away). In a follow-up study, white job applicants interviewed with this nonimmediate style performed (<u>less well/better</u>) in the interview.

3-4. Stereotypes we hold can also affect our own behaviour. For example, research by Bargh showed that students primed to think about elderly individuals walked (<u>more quickly/more slowly</u>) thereafter. The influence on behaviour in this case is thought to be (<u>conscious/unconscious</u>).

3-5. Whether probabilistic or absolute, schemas in general and stereotypes in particular direct our perception, so that we tend to see the things we expect to see. Such selective perception results in an overestimation of the degree to which our expectations match actual events, a phenomenon referred to as _____ correlation.

3-6. In one study, discussed in the text, subjects watched a videotape of a woman engaged in various activities (including drinking beer and listening to classical music). For one set of subjects she was described as a librarian and for another as a waitress. What effect did the occupational labels have on subjects' recall of the woman's *activities*? Which of the following is(are) true?

_____ Subjects in the "librarian" condition tended to recall her listening to classical music.

_____ Subjects in the "waitress" condition tended to recall her drinking beer.

3-7. The study just described illustrates subjectivity in person perception. The schemas, in this case the _____ that we have about categories of people, affect how we perceive and what we remember.

Answers: 3-1. (a) clusters of ideas about people and events, (b) a type of schema; widely held beliefs about people based on group membership **3-2.** diversity (or variability), probability **3-3.** fulfilling, nonimmediate, less well **3-4.** more slowly, unconscious **3-5.** illusory **3-6.** both are true **3-7.** stereotypes.

4. **Explain the evolutionary perspective on bias in person perception.**

4-1. How does one explain bias or prejudice in terms of evolution? To explain anything in terms of evolution one assumes that the particular characteristic or trait had _____ value in our evolutionary past. For example, the bias in favour of physical attractiveness might have signalled health, associated with _____ potential in women and the ability to acquire _____ in men. The stereotype of _____-_____ individuals as submissive and honest could simply result from our adaptive reaction to infants.

4-2. Evolutionary theorists also assert that we needed a quick way to categorize people as friend or enemy or, in more technical terms, as members of our _____ or members of the

_____.

4-3. The question still remains: how could prejudice and bias be adaptive? It must be clear that what was adaptive in our evolutionary past (<u>is also/may not be</u>) adaptive now. Nonetheless, from the point of view of evolutionary theory, cognitive mechanisms involving bias have been shaped by natural

_____.

Answers: 4-1. adaptive, reproductive, resources, baby-faced **4-2.** ingroup, outgroup **4-3.** may not be, selection.

ATTRIBUTION PROCESSES: EXPLAINING BEHAVIOUR

5. Explain what attributions are and why we make them.

5-1. Why are you reading this book? The search for causes of events and of our own and others' behaviour is termed _____. For example, you might _____ your reading behaviour to an upcoming test (or to personal interest, lust for knowledge, fear, etc.).

5-2. Attributions are inferences that people make about the _____ of events and their own and others' behaviour.

5-3. Why do we make attributions? We seem to have a strong need to _____ our experiences.

Answers: 5-1. attribution, attribute **5-2.** causes (or origin, source) **5-3.** understand (or explain).

6. Describe the distinction between internal and external attributions.

6-1. Which of the following involve internal and which external attributions? Label each sentence with an I (for internal) or an E (for external).

_____ He flunked because he's lazy.

_____ Our team lost because the officials were biased against us.

_____ The accident was caused by poor road conditions.

_____ He achieved by the sweat of his brow.

_____ Criminal behaviour is caused by poverty.

_____ His success is directly derived from his parents' wealth and influence.

Answers: 6-1. I, E, E, I, E, E.

7. Summarize Weiner's theory of attribution.

7-1. Weiner proposed that attributions are made, not only in terms of an internal-external dimension, but also in terms of a stable-unstable dimension. Suppose that Sally makes a high score on an exam. She could attribute her score to her ability, an (<u>internal/external</u>) factor that is also (<u>stable/unstable</u>). If she attributed her success to her good mood, the attribution would be (<u>internal/external</u>) and (<u>stable/unstable</u>).

7-2. Or, Sally may think she did well because these types of test are always easy, an (<u>internal/external</u>) and (<u>stable/unstable</u>) attribution. If she attributes her score to luck, the attribution would be (<u>internal/external</u>) and (<u>stable/unstable</u>).

Answers: 7-1. internal, stable, internal, unstable **7-2.** external, stable, external, unstable.

8. Describe several types of attributional bias and cultural variations in attributional tendencies.

8-1. Define or describe the following:

(a) fundamental attribution error

(b) actor-observer bias

(c) defensive attribution

8-2. Recent research has indicated that the attributional biases described above may not apply to all cultures. Since collectivist societies emphasize accomplishing the goals of the group over individual achievement, collectivist cultures are (<u>less/more</u>) likely to attribute others' behaviour to personal traits. In other words, people from collectivist cultures tend to be (<u>less/more</u>) prone to the fundamental attribution error.

8-3. Some evidence also indicates that people from collectivist societies would be more likely to attribute their *successes* to (<u>the ease of a task/unusual ability</u>). Similarly, they would be more likely to attribute their *failures* to (<u>bad luck/lack of effort</u>). Thus, in contrast with people from individualistic societies, people from collectivist cultures appear to be (<u>less/more</u>) prone to the self-serving bias.

Answers: 8-1. (a) the tendency for observers to attribute an individual's behaviour to *internal* rather than *external* factors, (b) the tendency for observers to attribute an actor's behaviour to internal rather than external factors, *and the tendency for actors to attribute their own behaviour to external causes* (Yes, there is overlap between these two concepts. The fundamental attribution error is part of the actor-observer bias.), (c) the tendency to attribute other people's misfortunes to internal causes, that is, the tendency to blame the victim **8-2.** less, less **8-3.** the ease of a task, lack of effort, less.

CLOSE RELATIONSHIPS: LIKING AND LOVING

9. Summarize evidence on the role of physical attractiveness and similarity in attraction.

9-1. Physical attractiveness is the key determinant of romantic attraction for

    a. males

    b. females

    c. both males and females

9-2. The *matching hypothesis* asserts that people tend to date and marry others who are

    a. similar to them in attitudes and personality

    b. are approximately equal to them in physical attractiveness

    c. both of the above

9-3. Do opposites really attract, or do we like people who are similar? An overwhelming amount of research supports the idea that we are attracted to people who are (similar to/different from) us on several dimensions, especially in terms of attitudes and personality.

9-4. The similarity-attraction relationship extends to

    a. friendship

    b. romantic relationships

    c. both of the above

Answers: **9-1.** c **9-2.** b **9-3.** similar to **9-4.** c.

10. Describe various distinctions regarding love, described by Berscheid and Hatfield and by Sternberg.

10-1. Hatfield and Berscheid divide love into two types, the intense emotional and sexual feelings of _____ love and the warm and tolerant affection of _____ love.

10-2. Sternberg further divides companionate love into _____, characterized by closeness and sharing, and _____, an intention to maintain a relationship in the face of difficulties.

10-3. Research suggests that (passionate/companionate) love is a powerful motivational force that produces changes in people's thinking, emotion, and behaviour. Sternberg further divides compassionate love into intimacy and _____, both of which increase over time as a relationship progresses.

Answers: **10-1.** passionate, companionate **10-2.** intimacy, commitment **10-3.** passionate, commitment.

11. Summarize the evidence on love as a form of attachment.

11-1. In Chapter 11 we discussed types of attachment styles between infants and their caregivers. What *general* conclusion did Hazen and Shaver reach concerning the association between types of infant attachment and the love relationships of adults?

11-2. Write the names of the three infant attachment styles next to the appropriate letters below.

S: _____

A-A: _____

A: _____

11-3. Using the letters from the previous question, identify the types of romantic relations predicted by the infant attachment styles.

_____ As adults, these individuals tend to use casual sex as a way of getting physically close without the vulnerability of genuine intimacy and commitment.

_____ These people experience more emotional highs and lows in their relationships, find conflict stressful, and have more negative feelings after dealing with conflict.

_____ These individuals easily develop close, committed, well-adjusted, long-lasting relationships.

11-4. Many now believe that adult attachment is best conceptualized with two dimensions: attachment _____ (reflecting concerns about lovability and abandonment) and attachment _____ (reflecting a lack of comfort with closeness and intimacy). Ultimately, _____ types of adult attachment styles are yielded when high and low scores on the two dimensions are combined.

Answers: 11-1. The three types of infant–caretaker attachments (also described in Chapter 11) tend to predict the love relationships that children have as adults. **11-2.** secure, anxious-ambivalent, avoidant **11-3.** A, A-A, S **11-4.** anxiety, avoidance, four.

12. Discuss cross-cultural research on romantic relationships, the role of the Internet and relationships, and evolutionary analyses of mating patterns.

12-1. While there is considerable cross-cultural overlap in what the two sexes want in mates (e.g., kindness, intelligence, dependability), David Buss has found nearly universal differences as well. Buss's data indicate that _____ want mates who can acquire resources that can be invested in children, while _____ want mates who are beautiful, youthful, and in good health. These gender differences in mate preference appear to occur (in virtually all/only in Western) societies.

12-2. There are also differences among cultures in their views on the relationship between romantic love and marriage. The idea that one should be in love in order to marry is in large part an 18th-century invention of (Eastern/Western) culture. Arranged marriages, in which romantic love is less important, tend to be characteristic of (collectivist/ individualist) societies.

12-3. A standard of attractiveness that has been found cross-culturally is facial _____, which from an evolutionary point of view may be an index of health. Another standard of attractiveness that may transcend culture is women's _____-to-_____ ratio, which may be an index of reproductive potential.

12-4. The impact of the Internet on relationships is generally (positive/negative). Virtual relationships tend to be just as intimate as face-to-face relationships, and often evolve into "real" (in-person) relationships. The power of _____ in relationships has been shown by the popularity of _____ websites.

12-5. In terms of mating preferences, men are generally more interested than women in seeking youthfulness and _____ _____ in their mates, while women are more interested than men in seeking such traits as ambition, social _____, and financial potential in their mates.

12-6. Women's _____ _____ can also affect mating preferences. When they are most fertile, women prefer men who exhibit _____ facial and bodily features, attractiveness, and dominance. And men rate masculine males as more _____ when their partners are in the fertile portion of their menstrual cycle.

Answers: 12-1. women, men, in virtually all **12-2.** Western, collectivist **12-3.** symmetry, waist, hip **12-4.** positive, similarity, matching **12-5.** physical attractiveness, status **12-6.** menstrual cycle, masculine, threatening.

ATTITUDES: MAKING SOCIAL JUDGMENTS

13. Describe the components and dimensions of attitudes.

13-1. Do you favour gun control? Do you like expressionist art? Do you hate cottage cheese? Your answers would be *evaluations* and would also express your _____ toward these objects of thought.

13-2. Attitudes are positive or negative _____ of objects of thought. They may include three components: cognition (thought), affect (emotion), and behavioural predispositions. For example, people have attitudes toward cottage cheese. List the three possible components of attitudes next to the examples below.

_____ He likes cottage cheese.

_____ He eats cottage cheese.

_____ He thinks, "Cottage cheese seems kind of lumpy."

13-3. Attitudes also vary along various dimensions, as follows.

_____ The importance, vested interest, or knowledge about the attitude object

_____ How easily the attitude comes to mind

_____ The degree to which the attitude includes both positive and negative aspects

Answers: 13-1. attitudes **13-2.** evaluations, affect, behaviour, cognition (Note that the components may be remembered as the ABCs of attitude.) **13-3.** strength, accessibility, ambivalence.

14. Discuss the relations between attitudes and behaviour.

14-1. As LaPiere found in his travels with a Chinese couple, attitudes (are/are not) consistently good predictors of behaviour. One reason involves a failure to account for attitude _____, the importance of the attitude for the person. In general, the stronger the attitude, the better it will predict _____. Behaviour is also better predicted by attitudes that are highly _____ and that are _____ over time.

14-2. In addition, the actual situation is likely to present new information: possible embarrassment, pressure from others, the unanticipated pleasant or unpleasant aspects of the situation, and so on. In other words, the behavioural component is just a *predisposition* that may change as a function of norms or other constraints of the _____.

Answers: 14-1. are not, strength, behaviour, accessible, stable **14-2.** situation.

15. Differentiate between explicit and implicit attitudes.

15-1. Explicit attitudes are ones that we hold _____ and can describe. Implicit attitudes are _____ attitudes that are expressed in subtle, automatic responses over which we have little conscious control. While we may explicitly condemn negative attitudes, implicit attitudes may reveal _____.

15-2. Implicit attitudes have been assessed with the Implicit _____ Test (IAT), which is based on differences in _____ time to differing pairs of items (e.g., positive words associated with liked or disliked faces). More than ___% of respondents had negative implicit attitudes toward the elderly on the IAT. Higher implicit racism scores among white participants are also associated with decreased smiling, reduced _____ contact, shorter speaking time, and more speech hesitations in interracial interactions.

Answers: 15-1. consciously, covert, prejudice **15-2.** Association, reaction, 80, eye.

16. Summarize evidence on source factors, message factors, and receiver factors that influence the process of persuasion.

16-1. If you are the *source* of a communication, the message giver:

(a) What factors mentioned in your text would you use to make yourself more *credible*? _____ and _____

(b) What else would you hope to emphasize about yourself? _____

16-2. With regard to *message* factors:

(a) Which is generally more effective, a one-sided message or a two-sided message? _____

(b) In presenting your argument, should you use every argument that you can think of or emphasize just the stronger arguments? _____

(c) Is simple repetition a good strategy, or should you say something just once? _____

(d) If you repeat something often enough, people will come to believe it. This may reflect the power of mere _____ (i.e., that repeated exposures promote greater liking).

(e) Do fear appeals tend to work? _____ When? _____

16-3. With regard to *receiver* factors in persuasive communications:

(a) If you know in advance that someone is going to attempt to persuade you on a particular topic, you will be (harder/easier) to persuade. This is the factor referred to as _____.

(b) In addition, in part because they may be anchored in networks of other beliefs that may also require change, _____ attitudes are more resistant to change.

(c) And when people _____ efforts to change attitudes, they often become (more/less) certain of those attitudes.

Answers: 16-1. (a) expertise, trustworthiness, (b) likeability (for example, by increasing your physical attractiveness or emphasizing your similarity with the message receiver) **16-2.** (a) in general, two-sided (That's the kind of speech Mark Antony gave over the body of Caesar in Shakespeare's *Julius Caesar*.), (b) stronger only, (c) repetition (causes people to believe it's true, whether it is or isn't), (d) exposure, (e) yes, *if* they arouse fear (and especially if the audience thinks the consequences are very unpleasant, likely to occur, and avoidable) **16-3.** (a) harder, forewarning, (b) stronger, (c) resist, more.

17. **Discuss how learning processes can contribute to attitudes.**

    17-1.   Following are examples that relate learning theory to attitude change. Indicate which type of learning—classical conditioning, operant conditioning, or observational learning—matches the example.

    _____   Ralph hears a speaker express a particular political attitude that is followed by thunderous applause. Thereafter, Ralph tends to express the same attitude.

    _____   Advertisers pair soft drinks (and just about any other product) with attractive models. The audience likes the models and develops a stronger liking for the product.

    _____   If you express an attitude that I like, I will agree with you, nod, say, "Mm-hmm," and so on. This will tend to strengthen your expression of that attitude.

    Answers: 17-1. observational learning, classical conditioning, operant conditioning.

18. **Explain how cognitive dissonance can account for the effects of counter-attitudinal behaviour and effort justification.**

    18-1.   Dissonance is a truly complicated theory, but the following exercise should help. First read over the text, then see how you do on these questions. Here's a hint: Both problems that follow are contrary to common-sense ideas of reward and punishment; dissonance theory prides itself on making predictions contrary to these common-sense ideas. Item 18-1 indicates that we like behaviours accompanied by less, not more, reward; item 18-2 indicates that we like behaviours accompanied by more, not less, discomfort.

    Ralph bought a used car. However, the car uses a lot of gas, which he doesn't like because he strongly supports conserving energy. He rapidly concludes that conserving fuel isn't so important after all.

    (a) Ralph has engaged in counter-attitudinal behaviour. What were the two contradictory cognitions? (One is a thought about his *behaviour*. The other is a thought about an important *attitude*.)

    (b) Suppose the car was a real beauty, a rare antique worth much more than the price paid. Alternatively, suppose that the car was only marginally worth what was paid for it. In which case would dissonance be stronger? In which case would the attitude about gas guzzling be more likely to change?

    18-2.   Suppose Bruce decides to join a particular club. One possible scenario is that he must travel a great distance to attend, the club is very expensive, and he must give up much of his free time to become a member. Alternatively, suppose that the traveling time is short, the club is inexpensive, and he need not give up any free time. In which case (scenario 1 or 2) will he tend to value his membership more, according to dissonance theory? Briefly explain why.

Answers: 18-1. (a) I know I bought the car. I'm against the purchase of cars that waste gas. (b) The additional reward in the first situation produces less dissonance and will tend to leave Ralph's original attitude about gas consumption intact. Ralph's attitude about gas consumption will change more when there is less justification (in terms of the value of the car) for his action. As described in your text, we tend to have greater dissonance, and greater attitude change, when *less reward* accompanies our counter-attitudinal behaviour. **18-2.** According to dissonance theory, he will value the membership more under scenario 1, even if the benefits of membership are slight, because people attempt to *justify the effort* expended in terms of the benefits received. (While dissonance is a genuine phenomenon with many of the characteristics that Festinger described in 1957, several other variables are operating, so it is difficult to predict when dissonance will occur.)

19. Relate self-perception theory and the elaboration likelihood model to attitude change.

19-1. At a cocktail party, Bruce eats caviar. When asked whether he likes caviar, he responds, "I'm eating it, so I guess I must like it." This example illustrates _____ _____ theory.

19-2. According to self-perception theory, people infer their attitudes by observing their own _____. Thus, if people engage in a behaviour that is not accompanied by high rewards, they are likely to infer that they (enjoy/do not enjoy) the behaviour.

19-3. To illustrate the elaboration likelihood model, suppose that you are to travel in Europe and must decide between two options, renting a car or travelling by train (on a Eurailpass). In the blanks below, indicate which persuasive route, central (C) or peripheral (P), is referred to in these examples.

_____ On the basis of train brochures, showing apparently wealthy and dignified travellers dining in luxury on the train while viewing the Alps, you opt for the train.

_____ Your travel agent is an expert who has advised many of your friends, and she strongly recommends that you take the train. You decide on the train.

_____ A friend urges you to consider details you hadn't previously considered: traffic, waiting in line, additional cab fare, and so on. You seek additional information, and after weighing the relative expenses and conveniences for four travelling together, you decide to rent a car.

19-4. In the elaboration likelihood model, the route that is easier and that involves the least amount of thinking is the _____ route. The route in which relevant information is sought out and carefully pondered is the _____ route. Elaboration, which involves thinking about the various complexities of the situation, is more likely to occur when the _____ route is used.

19-5. Elaboration leads to (more enduring/transient) changes in attitudes. In addition, elaboration (i.e., the more central route) is (more/less) likely to predict behaviour.

Answers: 19-1. self-perception **19-2.** behaviour, enjoy **19-3.** P, P, C **19-4.** peripheral, central, central **19-5.** more enduring, more.

20. Summarize research on the determinants of conformity.

20-1. Briefly summarize the general procedure and results of the Asch line-judging studies.

20-2. Suppose there are six accomplices and one real subject, and that one of the accomplices dissents from the majority. What effect will this "dissenter" have on conformity by the real subject?

20-3. One reason for conforming is fear of negative consequences; this is called _____ influence. Another reason is the need for guidance in ambiguous situations; this is called _____ influence.

Answers: 20-1. Subjects were asked to judge which of three lines matched a standard line, a judgment that was actually quite easy to make. Only one of the subjects was a real subject, however; the others were accomplices of the experimenter, who gave wrong answers on key trials. The result was that a majority of the real subjects tended to conform to the wrong judgments of the majority on at least some trials. **20-2.** Conformity will be dramatically reduced, to about one-fourth the frequency, without a dissenter. **20-3.** normative, informational.

21. Describe the Featured Study on obedience to authority and the ensuing controversy generated by Milgram's research.

21-1. Two individuals at a time participated in Milgram's initial study, but only one was a real subject. The other "subject" was an accomplice of the experimenter, an actor. By a rigged drawing of slips of paper the real subject became the _____, and the accomplice became the _____. There were a total of _____ subjects, or teachers, in the initial study.

21-2. The experimenter strapped the learner into a chair and stationed the teacher at an apparatus from which he could, supposedly, deliver electric shocks to the learner. The teacher was to start at 15 volts, and each time the learner made a mistake, the teacher was supposed to _____ the level of shock by 15 volts—up to a level of 450 volts.

21-3. What percentage of the subjects continued to obey instructions, thereby increasing the shock all the way up to 450 volts? _____

21-4. What is the major conclusion to be drawn from this study? Why are the results of interest?

21-5. As you might imagine, Milgram's studies on obedience were controversial, producing both detractors and defenders. Following are summaries of the objections, involving both *generality* and *ethics*, followed by possible counter-arguments. Complete the counter-arguments by selecting the appropriate alternatives.

(a) "Subjects in an experiment expect to obey an experimenter, so the results don't generalize to the real world."

The flaw in this argument, according to Milgram's defenders, is that in many aspects of the real world, including the military and business worlds, obedience (<u>is not/is also</u>) considered appropriate. So, Milgram's results (<u>do/do not</u>) generalize to the real world.

(b) "Milgram's procedure, by which subjects were allowed to think that they had caved in to commands to harm an innocent victim, was potentially emotionally damaging to the subjects. Milgram's experiment was unethical."

Milgram's defenders assert that the brief distress experienced by the subjects was relatively (<u>slight/great</u>) in comparison with the important insights that emerged.

Answers: 21-1. teacher, learner, 40 **21-2.** increase **21-3.** 65% **21-4.** The major conclusion is that ordinary people will tend to obey an authority, even when their obedience could result in considerable harm (and perhaps even death) to others. The result is of interest because it suggests that such obedience, as occurs in war atrocities (e.g., in World War II, at My Lai in Vietnam, in Cambodia, Rwanda, Yugoslavia, and throughout history), may not be due so much to the evil *character* of the participants as to pressures in the *situation*. (Milgram's results are also of interest because most people would not expect them: even psychiatric experts predicted that fewer than 1% of the subjects would go all the way to 450 volts.) **21-5.** (a) is also, do (b) slight.

22. Discuss cultural variations in conformity and obedience.

22-1. As with other cross-cultural comparisons, replications in other countries yield some similarities and some differences. Indicate true (T) or false (F) for the following statements.

_____ The obedience effect found by Milgram seems to be a uniquely North American phenomenon.

_____ In replications of the Milgram studies in several European countries, obedience levels were even higher than those in North America.

_____ Replications of the Asch line-judging studies have found that cultures that emphasize collectivism are more conforming than are those that emphasize individualism.

Answers: 22-1. F, T, T.

BEHAVIOUR IN GROUPS: JOINING WITH OTHERS

23. Discuss the nature of groups and the bystander effect.

23-1. The word *group* doesn't have the same meaning for social psychologists as it does for everyone else. As I look out across my social psychology class on a Tuesday morning, I might say to myself, "Hmm, quite a large group we have here today." Actually, my class is *not* a group in social psychological terms because it lacks one, and perhaps two, of the essential characteristics of a group. A group consists of two or more individuals who (a) _____ and (b) are _____.

23-2. Which of the following are groups, as defined by social psychologists?

_____ A husband and wife.

_____ The board of directors of a corporation.

_____ A sports team.

_____ Spectators at an athletic event.

_____ Shoppers at a mall.

23-3. What is the bystander effect?

23-4. Why does the bystander effect occur? In part because the presence of onlookers not doing anything produces an _____ situation (no one seems to be upset, so maybe it's not an emergency). In addition, the presence of others causes a _____ of responsibility (we're all responsible, or else someone else will do it).

Answers: 23-1. (a) interact, (b) interdependent **23-2.** The first three are groups, and the last two are not. **23-3.** When people are in groups (or at least in the presence of others), they are less likely to help than when they are alone. Or, the greater the number of onlookers in an emergency, the less likely any one of them is to assist the person in need. **23-4.** ambiguous, diffusion.

24. Summarize evidence on group productivity, including social loafing.

24-1. Individual productivity in large groups is frequently less than it is in small groups. Two factors contribute to this decreased productivity: a loss of _____ among workers in larger groups (e.g., efforts of one person interfere with those of another) and decreased _____ resulting from *social loafing*.

24-2. Social loafing is the reduction in _____ expended by individuals working in groups compared to people working alone.

24-3. Social loafing doesn't always occur. People high in _____ are less likely to engage in loafing, as are those who score high on _____ and _____. In some situations in which members are convinced that individuals' personal contributions to productivity are readily _____ and when group norms encourage _____ and personal involvement, social loafing is (less/more) likely to occur. Social loafing is also less frequent in more cohesive groups. Social loafing is less common in (collectivist/individualistic) societies, for example.

Answers: 24-1. efficiency (or coordination), effort **24-2.** effort **24-3.** achievement motivation, agreeableness, conscientiousness, identifiable, productivity, less, collectivist.

25. Describe group polarization and groupthink.

25-1. This problem should help you understand the concept of group polarization. Suppose that a group of five corporate executives meet to decide whether to *raise* or *lower* the cost of their product, and by how much. Before they meet as a group, the decisions of the five executives (expressed as a percentage) are as follows: +32%, +17%, +13%, +11%, and +2%. After they meet as a group, which of the following is most likely to be the result? Assume that group polarization occurs.

a. +30%, +10%, +3%, +3%, and +2%

b. +32%, +19%, +19%, +15%, and +13%

c. +3%, +1%, 0%, +9%, and +11%

d. -10%, -7%, -3%, 0%, and +2%

25-2. What is group polarization?

25-3. Have you ever been in a group when you thought to yourself, "This is a stupid idea, but my best friends seem to be going along with it, so I won't say anything." If so, you may have been in a group afflicted with groupthink. Groupthink is characterized by, among other things, an intense pressure to _____ to group opinions, accompanied by very low tolerance for dissent.

25-4. Groups afflicted with groupthink tend to ignore important information. Members are under pressure to avoid presenting conflicting views, and they (underestimate/overestimate) the unanimity of the group.

25-5. Recent evidence has also found that group members tend not to pool information. That is, they tend to

a. discuss information that is commonly known among members

b. explore information that is unique to individual members

25-6. According to Janis, the major cause of groupthink is high group _____, the group spirit or attraction that members have for the group. Other factors that may contribute to groupthink include *isolation*, (directive/nondirective) leadership, and *stress* accompanying the decision process.

25-7. Much of the support for groupthink consists of (laboratory studies/retrospective accounts). The theory is difficult to test in formal experiments, but it is a fascinating viewpoint that will undoubtedly inspire continued research.

Answers: 25-1. b **25-2.** Group polarization is the tendency for a group's decision to shift toward a *more extreme position* in the direction that individual members are *already leaning* toward. **25-3.** conform **25-4.** overestimate **25-5.** a **25-6.** cohesiveness, directive **25-7.** retrospective accounts.

SOCIAL NEUROSCIENCE

26. Define social neuroscience and describe how it has been applied to social psychological phenomena.

26-1. Social neuroscience is an approach to research and theory in social psychology that _____ models of neuroscience and social psychology to study the mechanisms of _____ _____.

26-2. One of the major topics within social neuroscience has been _____ relations. For example, Cunningham studied the role of the _____ in people's response to black and white faces. White participants showed greater activation in the amygdala in response to _____ faces, especially under (lengthy/brief) presentation times. And this was particularly true for participants previously judged to be _____ biased.

Answers: 26-1. integrates, social behaviour **26-2.** ethnic, amygdala, black, brief, racially.

PUTTING IT IN PERSPECTIVE

27. Explain how the chapter highlighted three of the text's unifying themes.

27-1. This chapter again illustrates psychology's commitment to empirical research. When people hear the results of psychological studies, they frequently conclude that the research just confirms common sense. Dispute this view by listing and describing *at least one study* with results that are not predictable from common sense assumptions.

27-2. Cross-cultural differences and similarities also reflect one of the unifying themes. People conform, obey, attribute, and love throughout the world, but the manner and extent to which they do so are affected by cultural factors. Important among these factors is the degree to which a culture has an _____ or _____ orientation.

27-3. Finally, the chapter provides several illustrations of the way in which our view of the world is highly subjective. For example, we tend to make ability and personality judgments based on people's physical _____; see what we expect to see as a result of the cognitive structures, termed social _____; distort judgments of physical lines based on pressures to _____; and make foolish decisions when we become enmeshed in the group phenomenon known as _____.

Answers: 27-1. This chapter has described at least three studies that defy the predictions of common sense or of experts. (1) Concerning *Milgram's studies*, psychiatrists incorrectly predicted that fewer than 1% of the subjects would go to 450 volts. (2) Results from *cognitive dissonance* studies are frequently the opposite of common sense. For example, common sense would suggest that the more people are paid, the more they would like the tasks for which they receive payment. Dissonance researchers found that the opposite is true; people paid *more* liked the tasks *less*. (3) Common sense might predict that the larger the number of people who see someone in need of help, the more likely any one is to offer help. Research on the *bystander effect* consistently finds the opposite result. **27-2.** individualistic, collectivistic **27-3.** attractiveness (or appearance), schemas, conform, groupthink.

PERSONAL APPLICATION * UNDERSTANDING PREJUDICE

28. Relate person perception processes and attributional bias to prejudice.

28-1. Prejudice is a negative _____ toward others based on group membership. Like other attitudes, prejudice may include affective, _____, and behavioural components.

28-2. The cognitive component of prejudice may be comprised of schemas about groups. This type of schema is frequently referred to as a _____.

28-3. Stereotypes are part of the *subjectivity* of person perception. People tend to see what they expect to see, and when stereotypes are activated, people see and remember information that (is/is not) congruent with their stereotype.

28-4. Stereotypes are highly accessible and frequently activated automatically, so that even though people reject prejudiced ideas, stereotypes (can not/may still) influence behaviour.

28-5. Our *attributional biases* are also likely to maintain or augment prejudice. For example, observers tend to attribute success in men to (ability/luck) but success in women to (ability/luck).

28-6. People may also attribute other people's behaviour to internal traits, the bias referred to as the _____ attribution error.

Answers: 28-1. attitude, cognitive **28-2.** stereotype **28-3.** is **28-4.** may still **28-5.** ability, luck **28-6.** fundamental.

29. Relate principles of attitude formation and group processes to prejudice.

29-1. Attitudes are to a large extent learned. For example, if someone makes a disparaging remark about an ethnic group that is followed by approval, the approval is likely to function as a _____ that increases that person's tendency to make similar remarks in the future. This is the learning process known as _____. Or, if someone simply *observes* another person making such a remark, the observer may acquire the tendency to make similar remarks through the process known as _____.

29-2. Explicit prejudice involves consciously held negative evaluations of an outgroup, whereas _____ prejudice involves negative associations to an outgroup that are activated _____, without control or intention.

29-3. Realistic group conflict theory asserts that intergroup hostility is a natural outgrowth of _____ between groups. As shown by the Robbers' Cave study, competition between groups breeds _____. Cooperation can reduce prejudicial feelings, as evidenced by Aronson's _____ classroom technique.

29-4. Ingroup members view themselves as different from the outgroup in several ways. First, they tend to see their group as superior to outgroups, a tendency known as _____. In addition, they see themselves as relatively diverse or heterogeneous and outgroup members as relatively _____.

29-5. The tendency for ingroup members to see outgroup members as highly (<u>dissimilar/similar</u>) to one another is known as the illusion of outgroup _____.

29-6. According to the social identity perspective, self-esteem depends on both one's _____ identity and one's _____ identity. Threats to social identity may promote prejudice and discrimination. Two key responses to social identity threat are _____ favouritism and _____ derogation.

Answers: 29-1. reinforcer, operant conditioning, observational learning (or modelling) **29-2.** implicit, automatically **29-3.** competition, hostility, Jigsaw **29-4.** ethnocentrism, homogeneous **29-5.** similar, homogeneity **29-6.** personal, social, ingroup, outgroup.

CRITICAL THINKING APPLICATION * WHOM CAN YOU TRUST? ANALYZING CREDIBILITY AND SOCIAL INFLUENCE TACTICS

30. Discuss some useful criteria for evaluating credibility and some standard social influence strategies.

30-1. We are constantly bombarded with information designed to persuade. Sometimes we are persuaded and happy about it, and sometimes we regret the outcome. How can we resist attempts at manipulation? Two tactics are discussed in this section: evaluating the _____ of the source, and learning about several widely used social _____ strategies.

30-2. To assess credibility, consider these questions: Do they have a _____ interest? If so, information they provide may not be objective. What are the source's _____? Although degrees do not certify competence, they may indicate relevant training.

30-3. Is the information consistent with _____ views on the issue? If not, one should ponder why others haven't arrived at the same conclusion. Finally, what was the _____ of analysis used? One should be particularly sceptical if the source relies on anecdotes or focuses on small inconsistencies in accepted beliefs.

30-4. In addition, learn to recognize social influence strategies. Following are several scenarios. Identify each with one of the four strategies discussed: *foot-in-the-door*, *reciprocity*, *lowball*, and *scarcity*.

_____ Scenario 1: Mail solicitation for a magazine subscription. "Enclosed is a packet of seeds, free of charge, just for you. We hope you enjoy the beautiful flowers they produce! Also, you will benefit from subscribing to Outdoor Beauty magazine. We've enclosed a free copy."

_____ Scenario 2: Newspaper ad. "This weekend only—mammoth blowout car deals!! These beauties will go fast!!!! Don't miss this once-in-a-lifetime opportunity!!"

_____ Scenario 3: A college development office calling alumni. First week: "We don't care about the amount, perhaps $5, just so that we can ensure full participation." You commit to $5. Next week: "Would you become one of our member donors with a contribution of $100?"

_____ Scenario 4: On the phone with a wholesale camera salesman. "Yes, we do have the XXY Camera at $499.00 plus tax. We'll ship that this afternoon. Now, did you want the new lens or the old lens with that? The new lens would be an additional $99. Did you want the carrying case also?" (Your assumption was that the so-called extras were included in the original price.)

_____ Scenario 5: Mail solicitation. First week: "Would you answer this brief survey for us? There are only 12 questions." Next week: "Thanks for responding to our survey! We desperately need money for this worthwhile (candidate, school, charity, etc.)."

_____ Scenario 6: At the car dealer. "We've got a deal, $22 900 plus tax! You'll be very happy with this car! Let me check with my manager to see if that price includes the radio and CD player." (Fifteen minutes pass while the salesman supposedly checks.) "Well, I tried, but the manager won't budge. Fortunately it's not much additional!"

Answers: 30-1. credibility, influence **30-2.** vested, credentials **30-3.** conventional, method
30-4. reciprocity, scarcity, foot-in-the-door, lowball, foot-in-the-door, lowball.

Attitudes
Attributions
Bystander effect
Channel
Cognitive dissonance
Collectivism
Commitment
Companionate love
Conformity
Discrimination
Ethnocentrism
Explicit attitude
External attributions
Foot-in-the-door technique
Fundamental attribution error

Group
Group cohesiveness
Group polarization
Groupthink
Illusory correlation
Implicit attitude
Individualism
Ingroup
Internal attributions
Interpersonal attraction
Intimacy
Lowball technique
Matching hypothesis
Message
Mere exposure effect

Obedience
Outgroup
Passionate love
Person perception
Prejudice
Receiver
Reciprocity norm
Social loafing
Social neuroscience
Social psychology
Social schemas
Source
Stereotypes

_____ 1. The branch of psychology concerned with the way individuals' thoughts, feelings, and behaviours are influenced by others.

_____ 2. The process of forming impressions of others.

_____ 3. Clusters of ideas about categories of social events and people, which we use to organize the world around us.

_____ 4. Widely held beliefs that people have certain characteristics because of their membership in a particular group.

_____ 5. Error that occurs when we estimate that we have encountered more confirmations of an association between social traits than we have actually seen.

_____ 6. Inferences that people draw about the causes of events, others' behaviour, and their own behaviour.

_____ 7. Attributing the causes of behaviour to personal dispositions, traits, abilities, and feelings.

_____ 8. Attributing the causes of behaviour to situational demands and environmental constraints.

_____ 9. The tendency of an observer to favour internal attributions in explaining the behaviour of an actor.

_____ 10. Repeated exposures to a stimulus promotes greater liking.

_____ 11. Covert attitudes over which we have little conscious control.

_____ 12. Liking or positive feelings toward another.

_____ 13. Getting people to agree to a small request to increase the chances that they will agree to a larger request later.

_____ 14. The observation that males and females of approximately equal physical attractiveness are likely to select each other as partners.

_____ 15. Attitudes we hold consciously and can readily describe.

_____ 16. A complete absorption in another person that includes tender sexual feelings and the agony and ecstasy of intense emotion.

_____ 17. A warm, trusting, tolerant affection for another whose life is deeply intertwined with one's own.

_____ 18. Warmth, closeness, and sharing in a relationship.

_____	19.	The intent to maintain a relationship in spite of the difficulties and costs that may arise.
_____	20.	Positive or negative evaluation of objects of thought; may include cognitive, behavioural, and emotional components.
_____	21.	The person who sends a communication.
_____	22.	The person to whom the message is sent.
_____	23.	The information transmitted by the source.
_____	24.	The medium through which the message is sent.
_____	25.	The rule that we should pay back when we receive something from others; may be used in an influence strategy.
_____	26.	A tendency to evaluate people in outgroups less favourably than those in one's ingroup.
_____	27.	Situation that exists when related cognitions are inconsistent.
_____	28.	Yielding to real or imagined social pressure.
_____	29.	Involves getting someone to commit to an attractive deal before its hidden costs are revealed.
_____	30.	A form of compliance that occurs when people follow direct commands, usually from someone in a position of authority.
_____	31.	Involves putting group goals ahead of personal goals and defining one's identity in terms of the group one belongs to.
_____	32.	Involves putting personal goals ahead of group goals and defining one's identity in terms of personal attributes rather than group memberships.
_____	33.	Two or more individuals who interact and are interdependent.
_____	34.	The apparent paradox that people are less likely to provide needed help when they are in groups than when they are alone.
_____	35.	A reduction in effort by individuals when they work together, as compared to when they work by themselves.
_____	36.	Situation that occurs when group discussion strengthens a group's dominant point of view and produces a shift toward a more extreme decision in that direction.
_____	37.	Phenomenon that occurs when members of a cohesive group emphasize concurrence at the expense of critical thinking in arriving at a decision.
_____	38.	The group one belongs to and identifies with.
_____	39.	People who are not a part of the ingroup.
_____	40.	The strength of the liking relationships linking group members to each other and to the group itself.
_____	41.	A negative attitude held toward members of a group.
_____	42.	Behaving differently, usually unfairly, toward the members of a group.
_____	43.	Integrates models of neuroscience and social psychology to study social behaviour.

Answers: 1. social psychology **2.** person perception **3.** social schemas **4.** stereotypes **5.** illusory correlation **6.** attributions **7.** internal attributions **8.** external attributions **9.** fundamental attribution error **10.** mere exposure effect **11.** implicit attitudes **12.** interpersonal attraction **13.** foot-in-the-door technique **14.** matching hypothesis **15.** explicit attitudes **16.** passionate love **17.** companionate love **18.** intimacy **19.** commitment **20.** attitudes **21.** source **22.** receiver **23.** message **24.** channel **25.** reciprocity norm **26.** ethnocentrism **27.** cognitive dissonance **28.** conformity **29.** lowball technique **30.** obedience **31.** collectivism **32.** individualism **33.** group **34.** bystander effect **35.** social loafing **36.** group polarization **37.** groupthink **38.** ingroup **39.** outgroup **40.** group cohesiveness **41.** prejudice **42.** discrimination **43.** social neuroscience.

REVIEW OF KEY PEOPLE

Solomon Asch
Ellen Berscheid
David Buss
John Cacioppo
William Cunningham

Leon Festinger
Elaine Hatfield
Cindy Hazen and Phillip Shaver
Fritz Heider

Irving Janis
Stanley Milgram
Bernard Weiner
Mark Zanna

_____ 1. Was the first to describe the crucial dimension along which we make attributions; developed balance theory.

_____ 2. Did research on infant-caregiver attachment patterns as predictors of adult romantic relationships.

_____ 3. With Hatfield, did research describing two types of romantic love: passionate and companionate.

_____ 4. Originator of the theory of cognitive dissonance.

_____ 5. Devised the "line-judging" procedure in pioneering investigations of conformity.

_____ 6. In a series of "fake shock" experiments, studied the tendency to obey authority figures.

_____ 7. Developed the concept of groupthink.

_____ 8. Under the name of Walster, did early study on dating and physical attractiveness; with Berscheid, described types of romantic love.

_____ 9. Concluded that attribution has not only an internal-external dimension but also a stable-unstable dimension.

_____ 10. Proposed an evolutionary view of attraction; did cross-cultural research on priorities in mate selection.

_____ 11. Studied the "self-fulfilling prophecy."

_____ 12. Helped to create the social neuroscience field.

_____ 13. Studied the neuroscientific basis of prejudice.

Answers: 1. Heider **2.** Hazen and Shaver **3.** Berscheid **4.** Festinger **5.** Asch **6.** Milgram **7.** Janis **8.** Hatfield **9.** Weiner **10.** Buss **11.** Zanna **12.** Cacioppo **13.** Cunningham.

SELF-QUIZ

1. Which of the following characteristics tend to be attributed to physically attractive people?
   a. low intelligence
   b. friendliness
   c. unpleasantness
   d. coldness

2. What term refers to cognitive structures that guide our perceptions of people and events?
   a. attributions
   b. stigmata
   c. schemas
   d. concepts

3. What term refers to inferences that we make about the causes of our own and others' behaviour?
   a. attributions
   b. stigmata
   c. schemas
   d. concepts

4. Bruce's social identity is threatened. Which of the following is he likely to engage in?
   a. outgroup enhancement
   b. outgroup favouritism
   c. outgroup derogation
   d. outgroup attribution

5. According to which of the following views do men emphasize physical attractiveness in mate selection and women emphasize the ability to acquire resources?
   a. evolutionary theory
   b. cognitive dissonance
   c. self-perception theory
   d. attribution theory

6. Which of the following could be an example of the fundamental attribution error?
   a. Ralph described himself as a failure.
   b. Ralph thought that the reason he failed was that he was sick that day.
   c. Jayne said Ralph failed because the test was unfair.
   d. Sue explained Ralph's failure in terms of his incompetence and laziness.

7. Which influence technique involves asking for a small request in order to increase the likelihood of the target complying with a larger request later?
   a. foot-in-the-door
   b. feigned scarcity
   c. reciprocity norm
   d. lowball

8. Which of the following is, in general, likely to reduce the persuasiveness of a message?
   a. The receiver's viewpoint is already fairly close to that of the message.
   b. The receiver has been forewarned about the message.
   c. A two-sided appeal is used.
   d. The source is physically attractive.

9. Subjects in Group A are paid $1 for engaging in a dull task. Subjects in Group B are paid $20 for the same task. Which theory would predict that Group A subjects would enjoy the task more?
   a. social identity theory
   b. cognitive dissonance theory
   c. reinforcement theory
   d. attribution theory

10. In making a decision, you rely on the opinion of experts and the behaviour of your best friends. According to the elaboration likelihood model, which route to persuasion have you used?
   a. central
   b. peripheral
   c. attributional
   d. direct

11. Which of the following best describes the conclusion of Milgram's classic study involving the learner, teacher, and ostensible shock?
    a. Under certain circumstances, people seem to enjoy the opportunity to be cruel to others.
    b. People have a strong tendency to obey an authority even if their actions may harm others.
    c. The more people there are who observe someone in need of help, the less likely anyone is to help.
    d. Aggression seems to be a more potent force in human nature than had previously been suspected.

12. Who are most likely to function as a group?
    a. shoppers at a mall
    b. the audience in a theatre
    c. the board of trustees of a college
    d. passengers in an airplane

13. Someone witnesses a car accident. In which of the following situations would that individual most likely stop and render assistance?
    a. when only she saw the accident
    b. when she and one other person saw the accident
    c. when she and 18 others saw the accident
    d. when the other observers were pedestrians

14. Suppose the original decisions of members of a group are represented by the following numbers in a group polarization study: 3, 3, 4, 4, 6. The range of numbers possible in the study is from 0 to 9. Which of the following possible shifts in decisions would demonstrate polarization?
    a. 2, 3, 3, 4, 5
    b. 7, 7, 6, 5, 5
    c. 5, 4, 0, 2, 3
    d. 9, 9, 7, 7, 5

15. According to Janis, what is the major cause of groupthink?
    a. strong group cohesion
    b. diffusion of responsibility
    c. the tendency of group members to grandstand
    d. group conflict

16. What was demonstrated by the research in which white interviewers interacted with black job candidates in a way that was less personal than how white job candidates were interviewed?
    a. the self-fulfilling prophecy
    b. the fundamental attribution error
    c. diffusion of responsibility
    d. the reciprocity norm

17. What did the Stanford prison experiment demonstrate?
    a. the influence of prejudice
    b. the influence of implicit racism
    c. the influence of attributional biases
    d. the influence of social roles

18. What term refers to prejudice that is hidden or "kept underground"?
    a. explicit
    b. overt
    c. implicit
    d. direct

Answers: 1. b 2. c 3. a 4. c 5. a 6. d 7. a 8. b 9. b 10. b 11. b 12. c 13. a 14. a 15. a 16. a 17. d 18. c.

Appendix B

STATISTICAL METHODS

REVIEW OF KEY IDEAS

1. **Describe several ways to use frequency distributions and graphs to organize numerical data.**

   1-1.   Identify the following methods that are commonly used to present numerical data.

   (a) _____   (b) _____

   1-2.   What data are usually plotted along the

   (a) horizontal axis?

   (b) vertical axis?

Answers: 1-1. (a) histogram, (b) frequency polygon **1-2.** (a) the possible scores, (b) the frequency of each score.

2. Describe the measures of central tendency and variability discussed in the text.

2-1. Tell which measure of central tendency (the mean, median, or mode) would be most useful in the following situations.

(a) Which measure would be best for analyzing the salaries of all workers in a small, low-paying print shop that includes two high-salaried managers? Explain your answer.

(b) Which measure would tell us the most common shoe size for men?

(c) Which measure would be best for pairing players at a bowling match, using their individual past scores, so that equals play against equals?

(d) Where do most of the scores pile up in a positively skewed distribution?

Answers: 2-1. (a) the median, because the high salaries of the two management persons would distort the mean, (b) the mode, (c) the mean, (d) at the bottom end of the distribution.

3. Describe the normal distribution and its use in psychological testing.

3-1. Answer the following questions regarding the normal distribution.

(a) Where do the mean, median, and mode fall in a normal distribution?

(b) What is the unit of measurement in a normal distribution?

(c) Where are most of the scores located in a normal distribution?

(d) Approximately what percentage of scores falls above 2 standard deviations in a normal distribution?

(e) If your percentile ranking on the SAT was 84, what would your SAT score be? (See Fig. B.7 in the text.)

Answers: 3-1. (a) at the centre, (b) the standard deviation, (c) around the mean (plus or minus 1 standard deviation), (d) 2.3%, (e) 600 (approximately).

4. Explain how the magnitude and direction of a correlation is reflected in scatter diagrams and how correlation is related to predictive power.

4-1. Answer the following questions about the magnitude and direction of a correlation, as reflected in scattergrams.

(a) Where do the data points fall in a scattergram that shows a perfect correlation?

(b) What happens to the data points in a scattergram when the magnitude of correlation decreases?

(c) What does a high negative correlation indicate?

4-2. Answer the following questions regarding the predictive power of correlations.

(a) How does one compute the coefficient of determination?

(b) What does the coefficient of determination tell us?

(c) What could we say if the sample study used in the text showed a correlation of -.50 between SAT scores and time watching television?

Answers: 4-1. (a) in a straight line, (b) They scatter away from a straight line. (c) High scores on one variable (X) are accompanied by low scores on the other variable (Y). **4-2.** (a) by squaring the correlation coefficient, (b) It indicates the percentage of variation in one variable that can be predicted based on the other variable. (c) Knowledge of TV viewing allows one to predict 25% of the variation on SAT scores (.50 x .50 = .25).

5. Explain how the null hypothesis is used in hypothesis testing, and relate it to statistical significance.

5-1.   Answer the following questions regarding the null hypothesis and statistical significance.

   (a) In the sample study correlating SAT scores and television viewing, the findings supported the null hypothesis. What does this mean?

   (b) What level of significance do most researchers demand as a minimum before rejecting the null hypothesis?

   (c) What is the probability of making an error when a researcher rejects the null hypothesis at the

Answers: 5-1. (a) We cannot conclude that there is a significant negative correlation between SAT scores and television viewing. (b) the .05 level, (c) 1 in 100.

REVIEW OF KEY TERMS

Coefficient of determination
Correlation coefficient
Descriptive statistics
Frequency distribution
Frequency polygon
Histogram
Inferential statistics

Mean
Median
Mode
Negatively skewed distribution
Normal distribution
Null hypothesis
Percentile score

Positively skewed distribution
Scatter diagram
Standard deviation
Statistics
Statistical significance
Variability

_____ 1. The use of mathematics to organize, summarize, and interpret numerical data.

_____ 2. An orderly arrangement of scores indicating the frequency of each score or group of scores.

_____ 3. A bar graph that presents data from a frequency distribution.

_____ 4. A line figure used to present data from a frequency distribution.

_____ 5. A type of statistics used to organize and summarize data.

_____ 6. The arithmetic average of a group of scores.

_____ 7. The score that falls in the centre of a group of scores.

_____ 8. The score that occurs most frequently in a group of scores.

_____ 9. A distribution in which most scores pile up at the high end of the scale.

_____ 10. A distribution in which most scores pile up at the low end of the scale.

_____ 11. The extent to which the scores in a distribution tend to vary or depart from the mean.

_____ 12. An index of the amount of variability in a set of data.

_____ 13. A bell-shaped curve that represents the pattern in which many human characteristics are dispersed in the population.

_____ 14. Figure representing the percentage of persons who score below (or above) any particular score.

_____ 15. A numerical index of the degree of relationship between two variables.

_____ 16. A graph in which paired X and Y scores for each subject are plotted as single points.

_____ 17. The percentage of variation in one variable that can be predicted based on another variable.

_____ 18. Statistics employed to interpret data and draw conclusions.

_____ 19. The hypothesis that there is no relationship between two variables.

_____ 20. Said to exist when the probability is very low that observed findings can be attributed to chance.

Answers: 1. statistics **2.** frequency distribution **3.** histogram **4.** frequency polygon **5.** descriptive statistics **6.** mean **7.** median **8.** mode **9.** negatively skewed distribution **10.** positively skewed distribution **11.** variability **12.** standard deviation **13.** normal distribution **14.** percentile score **15.** correlation coefficient **16.** scatter diagram **17.** coefficient of determination **18.** inferential statistics **19.** null hypothesis **20.** statistical significance.

Appendix C

INDUSTRIAL/ORGANIZATIONAL PSYCHOLOGY

REVIEW OF KEY IDEAS

1. **Describe the subdivisions of I/O psychology**

   1-1. In a humorous commentary several years ago, psychologist Jerry Burger said he longed to hear, just once, someone in a theatre asking, "Is there a social psychologist in the house?" (Burger, 1986). Burger's comments reflected not only his wish that psychology be recognized outside the halls of academia, but also his desire for application. Industrial/organizational (I/O) psychology is an applied field, and it involves the application of psychological principles to the world of _____.

   1-2. I/O psychology stresses application, but it is also a research area that emphasizes the scientific method. Like clinical psychology, the other major applied area, I/O is committed to the _____-practitioner model.

   1-3. I/O was originally called industrial psychology, a term that now comprises one of the two major subdivisions of the field. Industrial psychology involves mainly (personnel/work environment) issues.

   1-4. The second subdivision is the relatively newer emphasis on the cultural context of the work environment, the norms, values, and ways of interacting that relate to the company's goals. This is the subdivision termed _____ psychology.

   Answers: 1-1. work (or the workplace, industry) **1-2.** scientist **1-3.** personnel **1-4.** organizational.

2. **Discuss recruitment and selection of employees, as well as the issue of employment discrimination.**

   2-1. The bigger the pool of applicants, the more likely it will contain qualified individuals, and to obtain applicants it is necessary to _____ them. So, it is important not only to be able to assess applicants, but also to do those things that cause individuals to _____ for the job in the first place.

2-2. Selection in the recruitment process goes both ways: while the employer is assessing the applicant, the applicant is evaluating the employer. It is important to realize that recruitment is a (mutual/one way) process in which both parties are examining the degree of fit.

2-3. Who is selected for a particular job? Researchers Schmitt and Chan (1998) have identified five major changes that affect hiring in many modern organizations. First, in an age of computers, the speed of technological _____ requires a willingness and ability to continually (learn new/maintain old) job skills.

2-4. Second, there is a growing reliance on (skilled individuals/teams) to accomplish work.

2-5. Third, the advent of fax, email, and cellphones has dramatically changed the way organization members _____ with one another, with potential effects on bonding, morale, and commitment.

2-6. Fourth, most organizations are _____ rather than local, which requires members to be able to work well with people from different cultures.

2-7. Fifth, the Canadian economy is continuing its shift from a *manufacturing* to a *service* orientation, a shift that requires understanding the customers and their needs. For this reason there is also an increased emphasis on applicants' (technical/interpersonal) skills.

2-8. Not all modern companies emphasize the factors outlined above. In a rapidly changing work environment, however, the match tends to be between the person and the (organization/skill requirements) rather than the person and the job.

2-9. _____ _____ legislation in Canada, which prohibits discrimination in the workplace, as well as employment _____ legislation, which promotes the entry and retention of people from designated groups, have had a dramatic impact on the field of industrial psychology.

Answers: **2-1.** recruit, apply **2-2.** mutual **2-3.** change, learn new **2-4.** teams **2-5.** communicate **2-6.** global **2-7.** interpersonal **2-8.** organization **2-9.** Human rights, equity.

3. Discuss the importance of employee training and the ingredients of effective training programs.

3-1. In the modern workplace, many routine tasks have become obsolete, computers have increased in importance, and knowledge requirements are constantly changing. For these reasons, company programs for _____ employees have taken on a special significance. Training programs are needed on a continuous basis in (very few/virtually all) organizations.

3-2. Human Resources and Skills Development Canada (HRSDC) identified essential _____ needed by Canadian workers, including reading text, document use, numeracy, writing, oral communication, working with others, thinking skills, computer use, and continuous learning. HRSDC also provides occupational profiles and skill development and training programs.

3-3. The characteristics of good training programs are as follows: companies must (a) value training, which involves _____ employees to participate; (b) have a clear idea of _____ training is needed and _____ should receive it; (c) match the _____ of training with the type of training task (e.g., lectures may not be best for training widget assembly); and (d) ensure that the training actually works, that training _____ back to the job.

Answers: **3-1.** training, virtually all **3-2.** skills **3-3.** (a) encouraging (or urging), (b) what, who (or which employees), (c) method (or type), (d) generalizes.

4. Summarize how performance appraisals can help organizations.

4-1. If companies are to thrive, they must make rational decisions about their employees. Companies must decide who is to be promoted, receive a pay increase, or be discharged. That is the task of performance appraisals: to help organizations make fair, accurate, and useful _____ about employees.

4-2. Fair and accurate feedback may also be a key factor in motivation, and performance appraisals may help employees develop realistic self-_____.

4-3. A fair, accurate, and rational appraisal system may also help build satisfaction and _____ in company employees.

4-4. Especially in today's litigious environment, decisions about differential pay raises, promotions, or discharge cannot occur without reason. Performance appraisals help provide a _____ defensible basis for decisions.

Answers: **4-1.** decisions (or appraisals, assessments) **4-2.** assessment (or appraisal) **4-3.** morale (or cohesion) **4-4.** legally.

5. Explain the concept of organizational culture and the ASA cycle.

5-1. What has customs, values, and traditions? The answer is: just about any human group, and business organizations are no exception. Companies have traditions, rituals, ways of talking, informal or formalized rules for attire, and so on, which comprise the organization's _____.

5-2. How are these company cultures established? First, the individual who _____ the company may have a strong influence on the values, initial hirings, and vision of the organization.

5-3. Second, the culture evolves as it interacts with the external _____. Some aspects of culture are adaptive in the marketplace, and some are not.

5-4. Third, the values and norms of an organization develop, in part, as a means of maintaining effective working _____ among employees. Different people create different cultures.

5-5. Corporate culture is also communicated through memos, statements of official policy, and corporate philosophy. In other words, culture is communicated not only indirectly through informal contact but _____ as well.

5-6. A basic tenet of social psychology (Chapter 16) is the similarity-attraction relationship, that people are attracted to others who are similar to them in personality and values. In this context, the ASA cycle is not surprising. Organizations are _____ to applicants who fit the company culture, and they _____ those people as employees. Those who don't fit the culture leave, the process of _____.

Answers: **5-1.** culture **5-2.** founded **5-3.** environment (or world, marketplace) **5-4.** relationships **5-5.** directly **5-6.** attracted, select, attrition.

6. **Explain why organizations increasingly depend on work teams.**

6-1. Why has emphasis changed from the individual to work teams? First, there has been an enormous increase in _____ on which business decisions are based, and a pooling of knowledge and skills seems to work better.

6-2. Second, the workforce of today is better _____ than a century ago and more capable of the leadership roles called for in teams.

6-3. Third, teams are thought to be better able to _____ to rapidly changing skills that may be required in the modern workplace. Some research has found, however, that decisions by teams (are always/may not be) superior to those made by individuals.

6-4. Like other social groups, teams vary in size, roles filled by members, and duration. In addition, teams (must/need not) meet face-to-face. That is, some teams may be "virtual" and communicate, for example, through email.

Answers: **6-1.** information **6-2.** educated **6-3.** adapt (or adjust, change), may not be **6-4.** need not.

7. **Describe the nature of the psychological contract between employers and employees and the ramifications of violating the contract.**

7-1. In addition to the written contract that may accompany employment, there exists a _____ contract that involves expectations on the part of employers and employees. For example, employees may believe that they have the obligation to work hard and be loyal and that, in exchange, the company has the _____ to provide job security and promotion.

7-2. While both parties to the contract have beliefs about the obligations of the contract, the two sides (always/may not) share a common understanding about its terms.

7-3. There are differences in power between the two sides. The contract maker is the employer, and the contract taker is the_____. The employee, generally with (less/greater) power, must either accept the terms or leave the relationship.

7-4. As with any contract, violation of the psychological contract weakens trust, and failure of one of the parties to meet its perceived obligations leads to a deterioration of the _____ on which the work is based.

Answers: **7-1.** psychological, obligation **7-2.** may not **7-3.** employee, less **7-4.** relationship.

8. Describe the three dimensions of work motivation.

8-1. Job performance depends on a number of factors, including the employee's ambition or work _____ (related to achievement motivation, discussed in Chapter 10.)

8-2. Work motivation may be described in terms of three dimensions: *direction*, *intensity*, and *persistence*. Label each of the following.

(a) _____: *How much* effort is being shown?

(b) _____: *Toward which* activities is energy expended?

(b) _____: *How long* will the effort endure?

8-3. Each dimension relates both to the organization and to the employee. Organizations want the maximum energy expended, the element of _____; on company tasks, the factor of _____; over a long period of time, the element of _____. To accomplish these aims, employees want jobs that will hold their interest and inspire them.

8-4. Performance in I/O psychology may be thought of as the evaluation of behaviour related to some standard. Job performance is determined by the following three factors: _____, including the intelligence or skill of the employee; _____ constraints, the environment and equipment available; and _____, the willingness to expend effort.

Answers: **8-1.** motivation **8-2.** (a) intensity, (b) direction, (c) persistence **8-3.** intensity, direction, persistence **8-4.** ability, situational, motivation.

9. Summarize prominent themes in research on leadership.

9-1. Research on leadership involves an enormous number of factors, from which three themes seem to emerge: the ability to (1) influence, (2) establish relationships, and (3) make sound decisions. First, leaders must be able to persuade; to change attitudes; to provide an appropriate model; and, in general, to _____ what others do.

9-2. Second, effective leaders have interpersonal skills and inspire the trust and loyalty that permit the development of favourable _____ among subordinates, peers, and superiors.

9-3. Third, effective leaders develop strategies and solve problems. In other words, leaders must make successful _____ that move the company toward its goals.

9-4. What makes a good leader? This is a difficult question to answer because so many factors are involved, but the following three themes emerge: the ability to _____ others, to establish favourable _____, and to make sound _____.

Answers: 9-1. influence **9-2.** relationships **9-3.** decisions **9-4.** influence, relationships, decisions.

Reference: Burger, J. M. (1986) Is there a Ph. D. in the house? *APA Monitor, 17,* 4.

NOTES

NOTES

NOTES

NOTES

NOTES

NOTES

NOTES

NOTES

NOTES

NOTES

NOTES

NOTES

NOTES

NOTES

NOTES

NOTES